Lloyd J. Ogilvie General Editor

# THE
# PREACHER'S
# COMMENTARY

---

1, 2 SAMUEL

---

Kenneth L. Chafin

**THOMAS NELSON PUBLISHERS**
Nashville

THE PREACHER'S COMMENTARY SERIES, Volume 8: *1, 2 Samuel*. Copyright ©
1989 by Word, Inc.

Published in Nashville, Tennessee, by Thomas Nelson, Inc.

The Bible text in this series is from *The Holy Bible, New King James Bible,* copyright ©1979, 1980, 1982, by Thomas Nelson, Inc. Publishers. All rights
reserved. Used by permission. Brief Scripture quotations within the commentary text are also from The *Holy Bible, New King James Version,* unless otherwise identified.

**Library of Congress Cataloging-in-Publication-Data**

The preacher's commentary (formerly The communicator's commentary).

  Includes bibliographical references.
  Contents: v. 8.  1, 2 Samuel/Kennneth L. Chafin
  1. Bible. O.T.—Commentaries. I. Ogilvie, Lloyd John. II. Chafin, Kenneth L.

BS1151.2.C66                 221.7'7                    86–11138
ISBN 0-7852-4781-5


*Printed in the United States of America*

2 3 4 5 6 7 — 08 07 06

*To*
*Barbara Burke Chafin*
*my wife of forty-six years*

# CONTENTS

# EDITOR'S PREFACE

God has called all of His people to be communicators. Everyone who is in Christ is called into ministry. As ministers of "the manifold grace of God," all of us—clergy and laity—are commissioned with the challenge to communicate our faith to individuals and groups, classes and congregations.

The Bible, God's Word, is the objective basis of the truth of His love and power that we seek to communicate. In response to the urgent, expressed needs of pastors, teachers, Bible study leaders, church school teachers, small group enablers, and individual Christians, the Preacher's Commentary is offered as a penetrating search of the Scriptures to enable vital personal and practical communication of the abundant life.

Many current commentaries and Bible study guides provide only some aspects of a communicator's needs. Some offer in-depth scholarship but no application to daily life. Others are so popular in approach that biblical roots are left unexplained. Few offer compelling illustrations that open windows for the reader to see the exciting application for today's struggles. And most of all, seldom have the expositors given the valuable outlines of passages so needed to help the preacher or teacher in his or her busy life to prepare for communicating the Word to congregations or classes.

This Preacher's Commentary series brings all of these elements together. The authors are scholar-preachers and teachers outstanding in their ability to make the Scriptures come alive for individuals and groups. They are noted for bringing together excellence in biblical scholarship, knowledge of the original Hebrew and Greek, sensitivity to people's needs, vivid illustrative material from biblical, classical, and contemporary sources, and lucid communication by the use of clear outlines of thought. Each has been selected to contribute to this series because of his Spirit-empowered ability to help people live in the skins of biblical characters and provide a "you-are-there" intensity to the drama of events of the Bible which have so much to say about our relationships and responsibilities today.

The design for the Preacher's Commentary gives the reader an overall outline of each book of the Bible. Following the introduction, which reveals the author's approach and salient background on the book, each chapter of the commentary provides the Scripture to be exposited. The New King James Bible has been chosen for the Preacher's Commentary because it combines with integrity the beauty of language, underlying Hebrew and Greek textual basis, an thought-flow of the 1611 King James Version, while replacing obsolete verb forms and other archaisms with their everyday contemporary counterparts for greater readability. Reverence for God is preserved in the capitalization of all pronouns referring to the Father, Son, or Holy Spirit. Readers who are more comfortable with another translation can readily find the parallel passage by means of the chapter and verse reference at the end of each passage being exposited. The paragraphs of exposition combine fresh insights to the Scripture, application, rich illustrative material, and innovative ways of utilizing the vibrant truth for his or her own life and for the challenge of communicating it with vigor and vitality.

It has been gratifying to me as editor of this series to receive enthusiastic progress reports from each contributor. As they worked, all were gripped with new truths from the Scripture—God-given insights into passages, previously not written in the literature of biblical explanation. A prime objective of this series is for each user to find the same awareness: that God speaks with newness through the Scriptures when we approach them with a ready mind and a willingness to communicate what He has given; that God delights to give communicators of His Word "I-never-saw-that-in-that-verse-before" intellectual insights so that our listeners and readers can have "I-never-realized-all-that-was-in-that-verse" spiritual experiences.

The thrust of the commentary series unequivocally affirms that God speaks through the Scriptures today to engender faith, enable adventuresome living of the abundant life, and establish the basis of obedient discipleship. The Bible, the unique Word of God, is unlimited as a resource for Christians in communicating our hope to others. It is our weapon in the battle for truth, the guide for ministry, and the irresistible force for introducing others to God.

A biblically rooted communication of the gospel holds in unity and oneness what divergent movements have wrought asunder. This commentary series courageously presents personal faith, caring for individuals, and social responsibility as essential, inseparable dimensions of biblical Christianity. It seeks to present the quadrilateral gospel in its fullness which calls us to unreserved commitment to Christ, unrestricted self-esteem in His grace, unqualified love for others in personal evangelism, and undying efforts to work for justice and righteousness in a sick and suffering world.

A growing renaissance in the church today is being led by clergy and laity who are biblically rooted, Christ-centered, and Holy Spirit-empowered. They have dared to listen to people's most urgent questions and deepest needs and then to God as He speaks through the Bible. Biblical preaching is the secret of growing churches. Bible study classes and small groups are equipping the laity for ministry in the world. Dynamic Christians are finding that daily study of God's Word allows the Spirit to do in them what He wishes to communicate through them to others. These days are the most exciting time since Pentecost. The Preacher's Commentary is offered to be a primary resource of new life for this renaissance.

Once again it is my pleasure to introduce Dr. Kenneth Chafin as an author in the Preacher's Commentary series. His impressive volume on 1, 2 Corinthians was published. From that work thousands of biblical communicators have learned to count upon Dr. Chafin's astute interpretation and application of the New Testament while looking forward eagerly to more of the same in his Old Testament volume.

Kenneth Chafin's vast experience in Christian ministry explains his excellence as an expositor of Scripture. He has pastored two cutting-edge churches, South Main Baptist Church in Houston and Walnut Street Baptist Church in Louisville, Kentucky. Dr. Chafin also taught at the seminary level, most recently at the Southern Baptist Theological Seminary in Louisville. There he trained pastors-to-be in evangelism and preaching. A statesman within the Southern Baptist denomination, Kenneth Chafin was highly respected by persons across a broad spectrum of Christian experience because of his challenging writings and his dynamic leadership of the Schools of Evangelism held in conjunction with the Billy Graham Crusades. Dr. Chafin passed away in 2001. In all facets of his diverse ministry, he evidenced a consistent commitment to evangelism, church renewal, and vital communication of God's Word in today's world.

This commentary reflects a painstaking analysis of the biblical text. Dr. Chafin cared equally about the fine details and the broad scope of each passage in 1, 2 Samuel. He was particularly adept at making the obscurities of ancient Israelite history understandable to the modern reader. Biblical antiquity comes alive in this commentary and speaks to our contemporary situation through compelling illustrations and challenging applications.

As he reminisced in the introduction, Kenneth Chafin fell in love with the books of Samuel as a young lad, fascinated by the heroes of ancient Israel. "Yet," he continues, "it was in the pulpit that I rediscovered as an adult the relevance of these books to my life and to the lives of others." His passion for these chapters of Hebrew history came from the challenge and delight of passing on their eternal truths in our modern world. Thus his work is keenly suited to the needs of the today's biblical communicator.

Kenneth Chafin wished for his readers "the joy and discovery and growth that has come to me in the process of my studying and writing." This exposition of 1, 2 Samuel exudes such vitality and relevance that his wish will assuredly come true. I am indebted to my friend Ken Chafin for authoring another outstanding volume in the Preacher's Commentary series. I commend it to you with confidence and enthusiasm.

—LLOYD J. OGILVIE

# INTRODUCTION

My love for the books of Samuel began when I was nine years old and was introduced to the personalities and events of these two Old Testament books in Sunday school. At that age I was fascinated by the action stories. After I read about his slaying the giant, David became one of my heroes. At that time I had my first close friend, so the friendship between Jonathan and David encouraged me. My favorite story, though, was about the call of Samuel. I can remember thinking that if God were to call me I would want to answer the same way Eli instructed Samuel to answer, "Speak, LORD, for Your servant hears" (1 Sam. 3:9). Studying these stories of how God related to people where they were made it easier for me to make my own profession of faith when God began dealing with me.

An Old Testament survey course during seminary days fixed 1–2 Samuel in my mind as containing a very significant part of Israel's history. Yet it was in the pulpit that I rediscovered as an adult the relevance of these books to my life and to the lives of others. In an effort to bring balance to my preaching I tried to focus my preaching each spring on one book of the Bible, alternating between the testaments. As I was trying to make a decision on an Old Testament book I carefully reread the fifty-five chapters that comprise 1, 2 Samuel. As I began reading, my mind was filled with the kinds of problems being faced by those with whom I ministered, and the stories jumped out at me with a freshness I had not anticipated. After an initial thirteen sermons from the Books of Samuel, I have returned again and again to find contemporary insight into God's working with persons in the context of their lives.

When Lloyd Ogilvie allowed me to choose what books I would do from the Old Testament for the Preacher's Commentary series the decision was easy—I chose 1, 2 Samuel. That decision has forced me into one of the most difficult and most rewarding studies of my life. What has made it both rewarding and difficult is that it has forced me to deal with every character and every event. These two books are crammed with fascinating individuals whose modern counterparts we all know. They also contain elements that are disturbing to Christians who read them against the backdrop of Christian ethics. For instance, there is a great deal of violence in these accounts and often it is done at God's instruction. Dealing with this kind of problem forced me to dig deeper into the context of these events, to study more the needs that these stories met for those who read them first, and then to find their relevance for us today. As I now look back upon the whole process one of the personal rewards for me has come from having gotten closer to the mind of the ones whom God used in bringing to the Scriptures these marvelous books.

### Some Helpful Background to 1, 2 Samuel

The two Books of Samuel are one book in the Hebrew manuscript. The division could have related either to its content or its length and was made either by a translator or a priest. As to content, the first book closes with the death of Saul and the second takes up David's reign. It's possible that two smaller rolls of manuscript were easier to manage than the one large roll.

The Books of Samuel are a part of a larger group of books that trace the history of Israel from the conquest of Palestine to the captivity in Babylon. This history begins with Joshua and Judges and concludes with 1, 2 Kings. The Books of Samuel and Kings were originally grouped together and called the "Book of Reigns." The Books of Samuel cover almost a hundred years of Israel's history and one of its most important centuries. They take Israel from a loose federation of tribes to a settled monarchy under David. The content could be loosely arranged around three personalities: Samuel, Saul, and David.

The title of the book in the Hebrew canon is Samuel, probably because Samuel is the leading character in the early chapters and because he was tied in his ministry to Saul and David, both of whom were more prominent characters. We do not know the authors of any of the historical books. The Hebrew historians were often more compilers than authors. They made use of previously existing documents. Just as John selected and arranged material out of the ministry and teaching of Christ in order that people might come to know Him (John 20:30–31), so the historian edited and arranged the material in the Books of Samuel to show how God had worked through all kinds of people and circumstances to bring David to the throne. The duplications that appear and the different styles that occur are explained by the various sources that the historian used.

Although the historian probably used material preserved by the prophets Samuel, Nathan, and Gad, the books did not take their final shape until the sixth century B.C. as the people were coming back from the captivity. Part of the people were still in Babylon and some were scattered elsewhere. There was no temple, no capital, and no king, although David's family had survived. It was a time when the lessons of Israel's history would be a source of encouragement, comfort, and promise.

It was in my discovering how desperate the people were who first read these books that I gained new insight into God's wisdom in preserving them for us. They spelled out more than history for the children of Israel. They were words of hope—that the God who had been in David's life would continue to be in their lives.

If we look at the Books of Samuel through the eyes of a people desperate for hope, there are several basic ideas about God that emerge and which are illustrated over and over again in the study of the books. First, God overrules in human affairs, great and small, to accomplish His purpose. Second, God always acts in the best interest of His people, whether He blesses, judges, or teaches. Third, God always calls appropriate leaders for His work and uses them to move His plan along. Fourth, God is present with His people and never abandons them. Fifth, God is a righteous God and expects His children to reflect His character. Finally, God is at work in the most minute details of history working out His purpose for His children.

I wish for those of you who will use this book as a guide to studying the Books of Samuel the joy and discovery and growth that has come to me in the process of my studying and writing. These are ancient books reflecting even more ancient sources, but the God whose activity is being reported is the God who works in you today and works out His plan through the details of your life.

# AN OUTLINE OF 1, 2 SAMUEL

*SECTION ONE*

# THE STORY OF SAMUEL
## *1 SAMUEL 1:1—8:22*

# CHAPTER ONE—SAMUEL'S BIRTH AND DEDICATION

## I SAMUEL 1:1—2:11

*Scripture Outline*

Samuel's Roots (1:1–7)

Hannah's Blessing (1:8–18)

Samuel's Birth and Dedication (1:19–28)

Hannah's Song (2:1–11)

From my earliest days these two books have been among my favorite books in the Bible. As a child I was fascinated with the stories of David's exploits. Of course, at that same time I was also an ardent fan of Captain Midnight and Jack Armstrong, the All-American boy. In college, however, I was reminded by my professors of the interest of many great novelists, poets, and sculptors in the characters and themes of the Old Testament books, so I began to read them again. The greatest rewards came when in my mid-forties I began studying them anew and began preaching their stories to people who were trying to find meaning for their lives in an increasingly secular world. While the setting of the prophets is ancient, their prophetic themes are very modern. While the passages must be viewed in the light of the higher revelation we have in Jesus Christ, they are wonderful records of God's relating to people in the midst of their lives—giving them meaning and purpose and hope.

## SAMUEL'S ROOTS

**1:1** Now there was a certain man of Ramathaim Zophim, of the mountains of Ephraim, and his name was

Elkanah the son of Jeroham, the son of Elihu, the son of
Tohu, the son of Zuph, an Ephraimite. ² And he had two
wives: the name of one was Hannah, and the name of the
other Peninnah. Peninnah had children, but Hannah had
no children. ³ This man went up from his city yearly to worship and sacrifice to the LORD of hosts in Shiloh. Also the
two sons of Eli, Hophni and Phinehas, the priests of the
LORD, were there. ⁴ And whenever the time came for Elkanah
to make an offering, he would give portions to Peninnah his
wife and to all her sons and daughters. ⁵ But to Hannah he
would give a double portion, for he loved Hannah, although
the LORD had closed her womb. ⁶ And her rival also provoked her severely, to make her miserable, because the LORD
had closed her womb. ⁷ So it was, year by year, when she
went up to the house of the LORD, that she provoked her;
therefore she wept and did not eat.

*—1 Samuel 1:1–7*

It's interesting that the book which tells the story of the
establishing of the monarchy begins with the story of a very
unhappy woman. While the text begins with "there was a certain
man," the story is about Hannah, his wife.

The listing here of the lengthy genealogy of Elkanah is probably due to the importance of his son, Samuel. Even today parents
have been known to gain stature as a result of the accomplishments of their children.

The mentioning that Elkanah had two wives relates to Hannah's
story. His having two wives would suggest that polygamy was permitted and practiced to some extent among the Israelites. It served
several purposes; chiefly polygamy gave greater assurance that a
man would have a son to keep his name alive. Often, when the
first wife did not produce a male offspring, a second wife would
be taken. This may have been the case in this story. The problems
of this practice are illustrated in the rivalrous relationship of
Hannah and Peninnah and the unhappiness that resulted. While
our society does not sanction polygamy, many of the same kinds
of problems are created by serial marriages.

Modern women may find it hard to grasp the burden of the
phrase, "Hannah had no children." We live in a society in which
many young couples have decided not to have children. In a
male-centered society, however, where the focus was on producing an heir to continue the family name, to be barren was to fail

the family. Barrenness was also considered to be a punishment from God. Hannah's sense of failure was heightened by Peninnah's constant taunting her about her condition. In a world worrying about overpopulation and in which both birth control and abortion are widely promoted and often sponsored by the government, it is hard for people to identify with the sense of failure and lack of fulfillment that haunted Hannah. Her story is a reminder that the world is full of people who feel inadequate or incomplete for one reason or another.

One of the worst aspects of Hannah's plight was that she tended to feel worse when she went to church. While we normally think of the comfort of taking our troubles to the house of God, it was when the family made its annual pilgrimage to Shiloh to worship and sacrifice to God that Hannah would feel the worst. Shiloh was an important worship center some fifteen miles from their home. It wasn't the only place of worship, but it was an important place probably because the ark of the covenant was there. The ritual they observed must have been the peace offering because a part of the offering was the practice of giving a portion of meat to each member of the family. To sit and watch each of Peninnah's sons and daughters receive a portion was a painful reminder to Hannah that she had no children. Even if Elkanah favored her with a "double portion" or a choice piece from the offering, it did not comfort her.

It is easy to see how Hannah must have dreaded everything associated with getting ready for the annual trip to Shiloh for the festival. While everyone else was eating and drinking and enjoying the time of fellowship, she was having her sense of failure heightened. Today there are people for whom worship is not a time of forgiveness and renewal but a time of heightened guilt. Once in an interim pastorate I preached a sermon on "Is There Life after Divorce?" The main point of the message was to believe that people who had experienced the failure of a marriage were not outside God's love and forgiveness. The following Sunday an elderly member of the church came to me and with great feeling said, "Today is the first time I've felt good in church in forty years." Then she poured out the story of a teenage marriage, a divorce, the anger of her parents for "embarrassing them in the community," and the feeling that every time she came to church she was a spiritual leper. Although I was thankful that she had finally heard the word of God's grace, I wondered how many people, like her and like Hannah, come to places of worship and have their pain increased over past failures, unfulfilled dreams, and senses of inadequacy.

## HANNAH'S BLESSING

8 Then Elkanah her husband said to her, "Hannah, why do you weep? Why do you not eat? And why is your heart grieved? Am I not better to you than ten sons?"

9 So Hannah arose after they had finished eating and drinking in Shiloh. Now Eli the priest was sitting on the seat by the doorpost of the tabernacle of the LORD. 10 And she was in bitterness of soul, and prayed to the LORD and wept in anguish.
11 Then she made a vow and said, "O LORD of hosts, if You will indeed look on the affliction of Your maidservant and remember me, and not forget Your maidservant, but will give Your maidservant a male child, then I will give him to the LORD all the days of his life, and no razor shall come upon his head."

12 And it happened, as she continued praying before the LORD, that Eli watched her mouth. 13 Now Hannah spoke in her heart; only her lips moved, but her voice was not heard. Therefore Eli thought she was drunk. 14 So Eli said to her, "How long will you be drunk? Put your wine away from you!"

15 But Hannah answered and said, "No, my lord, I am a woman of sorrowful spirit. I have drunk neither wine nor intoxicating drink, but have poured out my soul before the LORD. 16 Do not consider your maidservant a wicked woman, for out of the abundance of my complaint and grief I have spoken until now."

17 Then Eli answered and said, "Go in peace, and the God of Israel grant your petition which you have asked of Him."

18 And she said, "Let your maidservant find favor in your sight." So the woman went her way and ate, and her face was no longer sad.

—*1 Samuel 1:8–18*

There are conditions that show no signs of relief, and Hannah's seemed to be one of them. She appears trapped in the words, "So it was, year by year." These verses, however, tell the story of a day in the temple that changed her life completely. There is a sense of mystery in the way a cycle of failure can be broken in a moment. The woman who spoke with Jesus at the well of Sychar considered her situation hopeless, but something happened to her as she talked with Jesus, and that changed everything. Many people can look back to what had started as an ordinary day, with no promise of relief, which then became "the day" that they will never forget. This was the kind of day Hannah had.

This day began with her husband's efforts to comfort her. From the conversation it seems that Elkanah had married Hannah for love and Peninnah for children. The more he tried to show his love for Hannah, the more Peninnah tormented her. Most likely, Peninnah's accusation would have been, "You're barren because God is punishing you for some sin." Hannah heard it so often that, like an abused child, she came to feel that maybe she did deserve it. Her husband showed a certain insensitivity with his question, "Am I not better to you than ten sons?" Her answer was to go to the temple in "bitterness of soul" where she prayed and "wept in anguish."

The focus of this passage is Hannah's vow in verse 11. The text does not record the statement of her distress which probably preceded it, but it's fairly easy to reconstruct it from our reading of the preceding verses. Today a barren woman would visit her gynecologist or a fertility clinic. Hannah's day lacked our scientific knowledge of the reproductive system. She felt that "the LORD had closed her womb," so the most natural thing for her to do was to ask God for help. The nature of her vow was clear. If God would do something for her, she would do something for God. On the surface of it, the idea of "making a deal with God" seems a bit offensive, but it is one of our basic instincts, even today. There is something in us that makes us believe we can negotiate with God.

To ask for a male child reflected the normal desire of a woman of her time. To be willing to forego the pleasure of rearing the child and enjoy watching him grow up was, however, the ultimate sacrifice, and this was what Hannah promised. Besides being willing to "give him to the LORD," she seemed also to commit him to be a Nazirite with the promise that no razor would come upon his head, although there is no other mention in the Bible of Samuel's not cutting his hair.

The text suggests that Hannah did not speak words which could be heard but that her lips moved as she spoke the words "in her heart." This may be the clue to the success of her prayer. The indication in the Bible is that God hears those who cry out to Him in their distress. The Book of Exodus tells of the Israelites crying out to God in their slavery, and "He heard their groaning" (Ex. 2:23–24). It is a breakthrough in our relationship with God when we recognize that God can handle our anger and frustration. This brings a new dimension of honesty to prayer and worship and fellowship with God.

In reading a story like Hannah's we need to be very careful not to conclude that we can manipulate God by making promises to

Him. In what has been labeled a health-and-wealth theology, there are those who leave the impression that we can force God to bless us physically and materially by the things we do or promise to do. This violates our best understanding of God's sovereignty. In Hannah's instance, the answer she received was closer to God's eternal purpose than to her promise.

Woven into these first three chapters of 1 Samuel which tell of Samuel's birth and calling is the story of the fall of Eli's house. Eli and his sons' being at Shiloh is mentioned in verse 3. In those verses we see Eli's role in pronouncing God's blessing upon Hannah. His first impression of Hannah, however, was that she was drunk. He was an old man and could see her lips move, but he heard nothing. He was accustomed to people attending the festivals and drinking too much or arriving intoxicated. Yet he was moved by Hannah's seriousness and convinced by her explanation, thus he pronounced God's blessing upon her with "Go in peace, and the God of Israel grant your petition which you have asked of Him." These were the words that changed her life.

There is a sense in which nothing had changed and yet everything had changed. Her past misery had taken her appetite, but now she went and ate. The woman who only moments before had described herself to Eli as a woman of "a sorrowful spirit" is now described with the phrase "her face was no longer sad." The word of Eli had created in her a hope that affected how she looked and felt. She experienced at a deep level what the author of the Book of Hebrews called "evidence of things not seen." During the years of my ministry I have often seen people experience the transformation which hope brings, and I have experienced it myself.

## SAMUEL'S BIRTH AND DEDICATION

19 Then they rose early in the morning and worshiped before the LORD, and returned and came to their house at Ramah. And Elkanah knew Hannah his wife, and the LORD remembered her. 20 So it came to pass in the process of time that Hannah conceived and bore a son, and called his name Samuel, saying, "Because I have asked for him from the LORD."

21 Now the man Elkanah and all his house went up to offer to the LORD the yearly sacrifice and his vow. 22 But Hannah did not go up, for she said to her husband, "Not until the child is weaned; then I will take him, that he may appear before the LORD and remain there forever."

23 So Elkanah her husband said to her, "Do what seems best to you; wait until you have weaned him. Only let the LORD establish His word." Then the woman stayed and nursed her son until she had weaned him.

24 Now when she had weaned him, she took him up with her, with three bulls, one ephah of flour, and a skin of wine, and brought him to the house of the LORD in Shiloh. And the child *was* young. 25 Then they slaughtered a bull, and brought the child to Eli. 26 And she said, "O my lord! As your soul lives, my lord, I *am* the woman who stood by you here, praying to the LORD. 27 For this child I prayed, and the LORD has granted me my petition which I asked of Him. 28 Therefore I also have lent him to the LORD; as long as he lives he shall be lent to the LORD." So they worshiped the LORD there.

*—1 Samuel 1:19–28*

The New King James Version uses two beautiful phrases to announce Hannah's good news. The first was held over from the King James Version which speaks of sexual intimacy as "knowing." It involves not just the sharing of bodies but of all of life. The other phrase is "the LORD remembered her." This does not suggest that God was not aware of her existence but that He acted upon her request. So Hannah conceived and bore a male child and named him Samuel. Hannah's explanation for the name was that she had "asked for him from the LORD."

The phrase telling of Elkanah's going up to Shiloh to redeem "his vow" gives us insight into a time when women were treated as if they were the property either of their fathers or of their husbands. The way a woman's vows were redeemed by her male protector is fully discussed in Numbers 30. According to these regulations, if Elkanah had felt that his wife's vow was rash or unwise, he could have repudiated it and "even the LORD will absolve her." While the Israelites had a much higher view of women than many of the surrounding nations, this view of a woman's needing her husband's consent to keep a vow that she had made to God leaves room for growth in our understanding of the worth, work, and worship of women. The text suggests that Elkanah, who loved Hannah, was not only willing to redeem her vow but was supportive of his wife and of her promises to God. This common allegiance to the covenant with God gives additional insight into the home in which Samuel would spend his first years. While Elkanah went to Shiloh with the rest of the family, Hannah stayed home to nurse her son until the time of his weaning, possibly as long as three years.

When she did go up to the temple, Hannah took with her all the offerings appropriate to her worship and her sacrifices: a bullock, meal, wine, and her son. While the bullock was a very expensive offering, it was as nothing compared to her willingness to leave her only child at the temple to serve God for the rest of his life. A cynic might suggest that after delivering Samuel to Eli, Hannah was back where she had been before when she was so unhappy—without a child. That perspective misses the point of her circumstances. Before Samuel's birth, she was "as nothing" in the eyes of her rival and in her own eyes as well. Now she had self-respect because she had borne a male child. She had the blessing of God and the respect of both her husband and of Eli. Later she was to be given three sons and two daughters, but they were not necessary to her joy. In the gift of her son, God had given her a larger reason for living and much happiness.

As a parent of three children I've tried to imagine the emotions that Hannah experienced as she delivered her son to the temple. I recall from one of Andrew Greeley's novels the story of a daughter of wealthy parents who decided to become a nun to the great displeasure of her parents. They had "other plans" for her life. Yet I have also witnessed firsthand Hannah's kind of selflessness in parents. Once, in a student pastorate, I invited a missionary couple to speak to our congregation. They were scheduled to return to Japan the day following. That night a large number of the couple's relatives were among our visitors: their parents, brothers, sisters, aunts, uncles, and others. During that service it began to dawn upon me the sacrifices being made by every relative there in order for this one couple to serve God in Japan. At the same time I sensed that they all had a feeling of deep pride in what this missionary couple was doing. This must have been something like what Hannah felt as she contemplated her son's life in God's service.

When I was younger I wondered why so many ministers used the story of Hannah for Mother's Day sermons or for sermons on parenting. The most common text seemed to be *I also have lent him to the LORD; as long as he lives* (v. 28). Yet as ancient as this story is, there are wonderful insights that can be applied to parents today.

1. Hannah prayed for a child.
2. She treated the child as a gift from God.
3. She dedicated her child to God for his whole life.

4. She continued to be concerned for her child when he was no longer at home.

The first six chapters of 1 Samuel focus on Samuel's becoming a prophet, a judge, and a leader of his people. This first chapter gives us many clues to his character, and we find them rooted in the piety of his parents and especially in the faith and commitment of his mother, Hannah. Since the family is the people-making "unit" of society, it's a good place to begin when we want to know why our leaders are like they are.

## HANNAH'S SONG

2:1 And Hannah prayed and said:
"My heart rejoices in the LORD;
My horn is exalted in the LORD.
I smile at my enemies,
Because I rejoice in Your salvation.
2 "No one is holy like the LORD,
For there is none besides You,
Nor is there any rock like our God.
3 "Talk no more so very proudly;
Let no arrogance come from your mouth,
For the LORD is the God of knowledge;
And by Him actions are weighed.
4 "The bows of the mighty men are broken,
And those who stumbled are girded with strength.
5 Those who were full have hired themselves out for bread,
And the hungry have ceased to hunger.
Even the barren has borne seven,
And she who has many children has become feeble.
6 "The LORD kills and makes alive;
He brings down to the grave and brings up.
7 The LORD makes poor and makes rich;
He brings low and lifts up.
8 He raises the poor from the dust
And lifts the beggar from the ash heap,
To set them among princes
And make them inherit the throne of glory.
"For the pillars of the earth are the LORD's,
And He has set the world upon them.
9 He will guard the feet of His saints,

But the wicked shall be silent in darkness.
"For by strength no man shall prevail.
10 The adversaries of the LORD shall be broken in
pieces;
From heaven He will thunder against them.
The LORD will judge the ends of the earth.
"He will give strength to His king,
And exalt the horn of His anointed."
11 Then Elkanah went to his house at Ramah. But the
child ministered to the LORD before Eli the priest.

*—1 Samuel 2:1–11*

The student of the Bible soon learns that chapter and verse
designations were inserted to make reference to certain passages
easier and were not a part of the original text. This is illustrated by
verse 1, which begins, "And Hannah prayed and said." Her prayer
is the climax of their worship upon the occasion of the dedication
of Samuel to God which is recorded in the first chapter.

What is here called a prayer is actually a song or psalm. Most
translations set passages like these in verse, as a poem would be
printed. If it is spoken aloud it needs a tune because it brings together thoughts and feelings about God. Cliff Barrows once told
me that when he is reading a psalm devotionally he will make up
a tune, as a cantor would, and sing it. As a result, the psalms have
come to mean more to him.

The form of the psalm in this text reflects a later time. Verse 10
makes it clear that this is a royal psalm belonging to that later
period when Israel had a king. Nevertheless, it matches the mood
and circumstances of Hannah on this occasion. It isn't difficult to
imagine her singing with great feeling:

Even the barren has borne seven
And she who has many children
has become feeble (v. 5).

There is a great similarity between Hannah's song and Mary's song
recorded by Luke (Luke 1:46–55). Both share many of the same
themes.

I have always been impressed at the way in which Israel put
her theology in her psalms. Everything the people believed about
or experienced of God they sang in their worship. Many church
historians feel that Methodism got its theology more from Charles

Wesley's hymns than from John Wesley's sermons and books of theology. Hannah's psalm highlights most of Israel's basic themes of worship. She celebrates the fact that God is powerful and holy (vv. 1–2), God silences His people's critics (v. 3), God reverses fortunes (vv. 4–8), God provides for His people (v. 9), and God deals with His adversaries and exalts the king (v. 10).

Hannah's song is a reminder of the believer's need to come into God's presence with praise and to celebrate how God deals with people and situations. All who feel weak and helpless in a world where it seems that the strong get stronger can find hope in the truth that God has a history of reversing circumstances that appear irreversible. It is in moments of worship that we are lifted high enough to see the final triumph of the people of God even in the midst of difficult and discouraging circumstances.

# CHAPTER TWO—FROM ONE PROPHET TO ANOTHER

I SAMUEL 2:12—4:1a

*Scripture Outline*
Contrasts in Ministry (2:12–21)
God's Judgment on Eli's House (2:22–36)
The Call of Samuel (3:1–10)
Samuel's First Message (3:11–18)
The Establishment of the Leader (3:19—4:1a)

Following Hannah's psalm of praise, the remainder of chapter 2 is essentially the story of the prophecy against Eli's house. The stories of Samuel's growth and development, however, are woven into the accounts of the deterioration of the household of Eli. The conditions at the temple in Shiloh stand in stark contrast to the piety and devotion of Elkanah and Hannah. The material is arranged so that the reasons for establishing a monarchy are obvious. Also the foundation is laid for Samuel's rise to leadership.

## CONTRASTS IN MINISTRY

12 Now the sons of Eli were corrupt; they did not know the LORD. 13 And the priests' custom with the people was that when any man offered a sacrifice, the priest's servant would come with a three-pronged fleshhook in his hand while the meat was boiling. 14 Then he would thrust it into the pan, or kettle, or caldron, or pot; and the priest would take for himself all that the fleshhook brought up. So they did in Shiloh to all the Israelites who came there. 15 Also, before they burned the fat, the priest's servant would come and say to the man who

33

sacrificed, "Give meat for roasting to the priest, for he will not take boiled meat from you, but raw."

16 And if the man said to him, "They should really burn the fat first; then you may take as much as your heart desires," he would then answer him, "No, but you must give it now; and if not, I will take it by force."

17 Therefore the sin of the young men was very great before the LORD, for men abhorred the offering of the LORD.

18 But Samuel ministered before the LORD, even as a child, wearing a linen ephod. 19 Moreover his mother used to make him a little robe, and bring it to him year by year when she came up with her husband to offer the yearly sacrifice. 20 And Eli would bless Elkanah and his wife, and say, "The LORD give you descendants from this woman for the loan that was given to the LORD." Then they would go to their own home.

21 And the LORD visited Hannah, so that she conceived and bore three sons and two daughters. Meanwhile the child Samuel grew before the LORD.

*—1 Samuel 2:12–21*

This passage details the vices of Eli's sons and probably lays the foundation for our understanding the move toward a national monarchy, but it also is a frightening passage for those of us who are parents and those who assume places of leadership in the church. Yet the closing verses (vv. 18–21) tell of the earliest days of Samuel's service in the temple. By moving from one to the other, the editor of the Books of Samuel paints for us a very convincing picture of why God sent judgment upon Eli's house and why Samuel assumed leadership in Israel.

Eli's sons, Hophni and Phinehas, were also priests in the temple of God. The phrase *they did not know God* (v. 12) more likely meant they did not have regard for Him or that they "never gave Him a thought." The text then details the contempt they seemed to have for their responsibility and for God. According to the law of Moses, the fat portions of the offerings were to be burnt as a sacrifice to God. The breast and right thigh were given to the priest, and the rest of the animal was cooked and eaten by the offerer and his family. So Hophni and Phinehas sinned against the people by taking their share and they sinned against God by demanding for themselves what had been reserved for God alone. Their action was summarized as abhorring *the offering of God* (v. 17) and is translated by others as bringing the Lord's sacrifice "into general contempt" (NEB).

34

Many people read this story and are reminded of others who seemed to have unlimited opportunity because of their background and calling and then turned out like Eli's sons. They wonder how it could happen. People who live in a secular world and are daily exposed to so many temptations are tempted to look at the children of ministers as being under a special protection. What they fail to realize is that every circumstance has its special temptation. Familiarity has a tendency to breed contempt. Thus it's easy to learn the words and rituals of religion without coming to love or understand God. Leaders and worshipers alike live with the danger of settling for religious ceremony and forgetting the moral and ethical dimensions of authentic religion.

To me, the tragic character in this story is Eli. He must have observed the contrast in the spirit of Samuel and that of his sons. He must have wondered, "What did I do wrong? What did I leave undone? What could I have done differently?" The "second thoughts" of parents are often painful.

Years ago I wrote a book entitled *Is There a Family in the House?* The publisher sent me on a short media tour throughout the Southwest, visiting television and radio stations and doing interviews with the religion editors of several newspapers. In Albuquerque, my host for the day was a longtime friend, Calvin Horn, who was a lay leader in his church and a successful businessman, author, and legislator. After an interview at a Christian radio station where the questions had all dealt with the perils of parenting in today's world, Calvin asked me a very direct question: "Kenneth, if you could start over with your children, what's one thing you would do differently?" While I was still mulling over the question in my mind, he gave me his answer. He said, "If I could start over, the one thing I would do differently would be to read the Bible aloud at the table at mealtimes." Then he told me that after his father's death, he and his younger brother had to help their mother make ends meet by taking on any available jobs. He recalled that "although we didn't always have a lot to eat, when we sat down at the table the one thing we always had was a passage from the Bible. I think that's where many of the values which have made my life different came from."

All of us have thoughts like these, and I imagine Eli also had them. Being able to pass our values on to our children is not easy. Even Samuel learned in his old age that he had the same problem with his sons that Eli did with his.

The verses which tell that Samuel *"ministered before the LORD even as a child"* (vv. 18–21) contrasts the unspoiled innocence of

Hannah's child with the calloused, greedy, spiritual indifference of Eli's sons. His linen ephod was probably a short skirt or an apron worn as a part of a priest's vestments. The *"little robe"* which his mother brought to him each year was probably an ordinary garment for him to wear and was a continuing expression of his mother's love and concern for him. The blessing of Eli upon Elkanah and Hannah (which resulted in the birth of three sons and two daughters) is a reminder that the Lord is not to be outdone in generosity. The description of Samuel's growth and development (vv. 21, 26) is very similar to the description of Jesus' growth in Luke 2:52.

## GOD'S JUDGMENT ON ELI'S HOUSE

22 Now Eli was very old; and he heard everything his sons did to all Israel, and how they lay with the women who assembled at the door of the tabernacle of meeting. 23 So he said to them, "Why do you do such things? For I hear of your evil dealings from all the people. 24 No, my sons! For it is not a good report that I hear. You make the LORD's people transgress. 25 If one man sins against another, God will judge him. But if a man sins against the LORD, who will intercede for him?" Nevertheless they did not heed the voice of their father, because the LORD desired to kill them.

26 And the child Samuel grew in stature, and in favor both with the LORD and men.

27 Then a man of God came to Eli and said to him, "Thus says the LORD: 'Did I not clearly reveal Myself to the house of your father when they were in Egypt in Pharaoh's house? 28 Did I not choose him out of all the tribes of Israel to be My priest, to offer upon My altar, to burn incense, and to wear an ephod before Me? And did I not give to the house of your father all the offerings of the children of Israel made by fire? 29 Why do you kick at My sacrifice and My offering which I have commanded in My dwelling place, and honor your sons more than Me, to make yourselves fat with the best of all the offerings of Israel My people?' 30 Therefore the LORD God of Israel says: 'I said indeed that your house and the house of your father would walk before Me forever.' But now the LORD says: 'Far be it from Me; for those who honor Me I will honor, and those who despise Me shall be lightly esteemed. 31 Behold, the days are coming that I will cut off your arm and the arm of your father's house, so that there will not be an old man in

your house. [32] And you will see an enemy in My dwelling place, despite all the good which God does for Israel. And there shall not be an old man in your house forever. [33] But any of your men whom I do not cut off from My altar shall consume your eyes and grieve your heart. And all the descendants of your house shall die in the flower of their age. [34] Now this shall be a sign to you that will come upon your two sons, on Hophni and Phinehas: in one day they shall die, both of them. [35] Then I will raise up for Myself a faithful priest who shall do according to what is in My heart and in My mind. I will build him a sure house, and he shall walk before My anointed forever. [36] And it shall come to pass that everyone who is left in your house will come and bow down to him for a piece of silver and a morsel of bread, and say, "Please, put me in one of the priestly positions, that I may eat a piece of bread."'"

—*1 Samuel 2:22–36*

This passage tells of God's judgment upon Eli's house and is introduced by Eli's unsuccessful effort to get his sons to change their ways (vv. 22–25). The phrase *"Eli was very old"* (v. 22) suggests a kind of helplessness to control his sons at this point in their lives. There may have been a time when his words might have changed things, but that time is long past. His speech is but a reminder of the depths to which his sons had gone in their abuse of position. By tolerating the abuses of his sons, Eli was judged guilty of honoring his sons above God (v. 29).

Exactly who the women were "at *the door of the tabernacle"* (v. 22) is not known. If, as some suggest, they were there to sweep the entrance of the temple and keep it clean, then the sin of sexual immorality would appear even more reprehensible. Eli's reasoning with his sons about having no one to intercede for them because they have sinned *"against the LORD"* (v. 25) is similar to Job 9:2, where Job raises the question about who the umpire would be if a person had a quarrel with God.

Taken literally, the phrase that ties the unwillingness of the sons to listen to their father with the Lord's desire *"to kill them"* (v. 25) can create all kinds of problems. It could leave the false impression that the sons were not free to obey and that they were merely pawns being used to play out some larger game. The Old Testament, however, often ties together the idea of disobedience and God's desire to bring judgment, as in the case of Pharaoh where the Scriptures leave the impression that God hardened his heart in order to punish him (Ex. 7:3). People today would be more inclined to tie God's punishment of Eli's sons to their continued unwillingness to obey God. The sense of the passages is very close to the verses in Paul's letter to the Romans where the Scripture says "God gave them up" to their various evil desires (Rom. 1:24, 26, 28). This passage in 1 Samuel seems to teach that when people continue to disregard the truth of God long enough, God may give them up. When God no longer struggles with us and leaves us to our own devices, we are doomed.

The word of God's judgment came from a person whose name we do not know. He is described only as *a man of God.* He could have been one of the many unnamed prophets. Whoever he was, his message was characteristically organized like those of the prophets. He began by announcing the divine word, *"This is the word of the LORD"* (v. 27). Then he traced God's goodness in dealing with Eli and his house, beginning in Egypt with deliverance and a calling to the priesthood (vv. 27–28). This is followed by God's complaint against Eli (v. 29) for the abuse of the prophetic office. The man of God plowed no new ground up to this point in the judgment announcement. All of it was familiar to Eli and may have been similar to what he had said to his sons on many occasions.

Here, however, the prophetic messenger finishes the "whereas" and is ready for the *"Therefore the LORD God of Israel says"* (v. 30). Then he begins a series of devastating pronouncements against Eli and his family. The first is the decision to reverse God's previous promise of a perpetual priesthood because of Eli's failure (v. 30). It is a reminder to all who enjoy the privileges bestowed by God: Blessings cannot go on forever in the face of disobedience. In verses 31–33, the prophet lets the hammer of God's judgment fall in a series of frightening pronouncements. In a society where length of life was considered a symbol of God's blessing, the prophet announced that *"there will not be an old man in your house"* (v. 31). Even those who live will have no place of honor (v. 33).

The sign that God gave the prophet to confirm that he was speaking for God was that Eli's sons would die on the same day (v. 34). Thus the evidence that the man of God spoke the truth would be the carrying out of God's promise that *"the descendants of your house shall die in the flower of their age"* (v. 33).

We live in a day that does not like to hear words of judgment. Some of it may be a reaction to the history of the church, when all that was heard from Christian pulpits were too many words of judgment and not enough of love and of forgiveness and of grace.

I suspect, however, that we are not too different today from the people of Eli's day. We enjoy celebrating the blessings and privileges of God, but we do not want to be held accountable for our lives. There has crept into the churches and the denominations a sense of carelessness about our responsibilities and a feeling that we are immune to God's judgments. This sense of exemption has even found its way into our national attitudes with the feeling that we are "safe" regardless of how we operate in the world. The lesson of the house of Eli ought to be a reminder that God still holds us accountable for the kind of people we are and for what we do. Thus we should pray that He will never give up on us and "give us up."

The bleakness of the judgment is given just a ray of hope with the promise: *"I will raise up for Myself a faithful priest who shall do according to what is in My heart and in My mind"* (v. 35). It is the promise that while Eli's house is falling, a priestly dynasty will endure. While one might think first of Samuel as the "faithful priest" who is to come, this is probably a reference added later about the house of Zadok, which served during the monarchy. This word of hope is characteristic of the messages of the prophets and of God's dealing with us. Even in the midst of God's sternest judgment, there is the promise of hope.

This passage puts aside the present temple leadership, for they are essentially "lame duck" participants, and prepares us for the call of Samuel. He is to be the new leader, and he will play a most pivotal role in the establishment of the monarchy and in the lives of the first two kings.

## THE CALL OF SAMUEL

**3:1** Now the boy Samuel ministered to the LORD before Eli. And the word of the LORD was rare in those days; there was no widespread revelation. ² And it came to pass at that time, while Eli was lying down in his place, and when his eyes had begun to grow so dim that he could not see, ³ and before the lamp of God went out in the tabernacle of the LORD where the ark of God was, and while Samuel was lying down, ⁴ that the LORD called Samuel. And he answered, "Here I am!" ⁵ So he ran to Eli and said, "Here I am, for you called me."

And he said, "I did not call; lie down again." And he went and lay down.

⁶ Then the LORD called yet again, "Samuel!"

So Samuel arose and went to Eli, and said, "Here I am, for you called me." He answered, "I did not call, my son; lie down again." [7] (Now Samuel did not yet know the LORD, nor was the word of the LORD yet revealed to him.) [8] And the LORD called Samuel again the third time. So he arose and went to Eli, and said, "Here I am, for you did call me." Then Eli perceived that the LORD had called the boy. [9] Therefore Eli said to Samuel, "Go, lie down; and it shall be, if He calls you, that you must say, 'Speak, LORD, for Your servant hears.'" So Samuel went and lay down in his place.

[10] Now the LORD came and stood and called as at other times, "Samuel! Samuel!" And Samuel answered, "Speak, for Your servant hears."

*—1 Samuel 3:1–10*

Each semester I used to have my students prepare a sermon from either 1 or 2 Samuel. Although they had all fifty-five chapters to choose from, with all of their interesting characters and exciting experiences, each semester at least one-third of the sermons were from these verses that describe the call of Samuel. This happened so consistently that I stopped and gave some thought to what made this text so popular. One reason was that they were familiar with it. It's rather sad, but many young adults today have not been exposed regularly to the great stories of the Old Testament. This was a story they knew, but when I talked with them, I discovered that the larger reason for their choice was that as men and women who had experienced the call of God in their own lives, this was the kind of call with which they could identify. They had stood before no burning bush, as did Moses, nor had a vision in the temple, as did Isaiah, but they had heard the voice of God when they were young and often had help from wise friends in understanding that voice.

Chapter 3 begins with an interesting statement: *"The word of the LORD was rare in those days."* The statement is made as a backdrop to the story of the word of the Lord coming to Samuel, but it also bears witness to the low religious ebb of the day. The Scripture did not say that "there was no religious activity in those days" because the people went on with the business of their religion whatever. Many people today are confused by the fact that there is a religious revival in the land and also some of the worst moral and ethical problems at the same time. Could it be that while there is no shortage of religious words experienced, nonetheless the "Word of the Lord is rare." The lack of the word was not so much connected with God's reluctance to communicate with the people as with the lack of a human instrument to receive and speak the word of the Lord.

There's more to the words *"the LORD called Samuel"* (v. 4) than is obvious at first reading. His mother had lent him to God for his entire life, but only the Lord could call him to prophesy. Most people don't think of Samuel as a prophet because they associate the word "prophet" with predicting future events. While there is that aspect, the main business of the prophets was to speak God's word to their contemporary situation. My Old Testament professor reminded us that we are so fascinated with the "fore-telling" aspect that we forget the importance of the "telling-forth." When we read the accounts of the calls of the different prophets it helps us to understand their lives and ministries. The clues to the rest of Samuel's life are found in this text.

Several years ago a national religious magazine ran an article by a former pastor entitled, "Why I Left the Ministry." Over lunch one day with a senior pastor, we discussed the article, which had made quite a ripple among the clergy. My friend confessed that he had read the man's reasons for leaving the ministry and at some time or another he had experienced every one of them himself. Then he noted with some sadness, "The one thing I kept looking for in the article was why he had entered the ministry in the first place." We both agreed that there were probably aspects of the situation which might alter our opinion if they were known. But our feeling from just reading the article was that if he had entered the ministry for a more compelling reason, then none of the reasons for which be left would have really mattered.

Often when I am a guest lecturer at a seminary, I will use one session to discuss the importance of the call. It's what gets men and women into the ministry. It's what keeps them in the ministry. And the call is what tends to define the nature of their ministry. It begins with the feeling that God has initiated it and that somehow it relates to God's larger purpose for our lives.

When the call came to Samuel, he thought it was his master, Eli, calling. How easy it still is not to be able to discern God's voice from other voices. It would be so much easier if all of God's messages to us came with a clearly printed label: "From God." But, as my colleague, Frank Tupper, says, "God speaks to us through familiar voices." While there is a tendency to think of the more dramatic revelations of God as normative, most people experience God's guidance in quite ordinary ways: through experiences good and bad, while reading the Scripture, through the counsel of another, or out of a growing interest. My sense of God's special call for my life came while I was an invalid youth in bed with a juvenile form of rheumatoid arthritis, and the people who put me in the place where God could speak to me were some young people who literally carried me to church.

A marvelous aspect of Samuel's call was the provision of Eli to help him interpret the call. There is an interesting set of contrasts involved. First, Eli is much more tuned into Samuel's spiritual experience than he was to Samuel's mother whom he thought at first was drunk. But the most interesting contrast is between Eli's physical and spiritual vision. Verse 2 says that his eyes *"had begun to grow so dim that he could not see."* Fortunately his spiritual vision was better than his eyesight because he *"perceived that the LORD had called the boy"* (v. 8). And it was Eli who worded for Samuel the response, *"Speak, LORD, for Your servant hears"* (v. 9). Servants listen to the master differently than others. Eli's wise counsel is a good reminder that God can often use us to give better counsel to the children of others than we have been able to give to our own.

Most people, if they reflect a while, will realize that God is always supplying people like Eli at different times when we are finding it difficult to discern God's direction for our lives at some critical juncture. Questions like what to do about a relationship, which job to take, how to deal with a problem, or what to do with our lives are often made clearer by someone with spiritual wisdom who helps us to hear God's voice in the familiar and encourages obedience as the best way. These people have come to me in the form of professors, pastors, aunts and uncles, parents, classmates, my wife, and even my children. And in recent years I've begun to find a way of paying back all those who played the role of "Eli" to me. I've done it by trying to give wise counsel to others who needed a little help in interpreting the voices they heard.

## SAMUEL'S FIRST MESSAGE

11 Then the LORD said to Samuel: "Behold, I will do something in Israel at which both ears of everyone who hears it will tingle. 12 In that day I will perform against Eli all that I have spoken concerning his house, from beginning to end. 13 For I have told him that I will judge his house forever for the iniquity which he knows, because his sons made themselves vile, and he did not restrain them. 14 And therefore I have sworn to the house of Eli that the iniquity of

Eli's house shall not be atoned for by sacrifice or offering forever."

¹⁵ So Samuel lay down until morning, and opened the doors of the house of the LORD. And Samuel was afraid to tell Eli the vision. ¹⁶ Then Eli called Samuel and said, "Samuel, my son!"

He answered, "Here I am."

¹⁷ And he said, "What is the word that the Lord spoke to you? Please do not hide it from me. God do so to you, and more also, if you hide anything from me of all the things that He said to you." ¹⁸ Then Samuel told him everything, and hid nothing from him. And he said, "It is the LORD. Let Him do what seems good to Him."

*—1 Samuel 3:11–18*

The first word that Samuel received from God was against the house of the one who had blessed his parents, taught him to minister in the temple, and helped him to discern the voice of God. While the content of the message was a reiteration of the one brought by the man of God to Eli (2:27–36), this one came for Samuel to deliver to Eli. If Samuel's love for Eli had shielded him from accepting the full implication of the other prophecy against the house of Eli, this word from the Lord forced him to recognize the truth. Because it was such a hard word, rather than go immediately to Eli with it, as Samuel had when he thought Eli was calling, he went to bed and arose the next morning to perform his usual temple duties. The Scripture merely says, *"Samuel was afraid to tell Eli the vision"* (v. 15). In addition to his love for Eli, Samuel may have been restrained by the fact that in those days the messenger who brought bad news was often held responsible for the news.

Most people studying this chapter are so moved by the wise counsel to Samuel concerning his call that they completely miss this magnificent passage where Eli teaches him what to do with the message once he has received it. Even if Eli had forgotten the conversations during the night, he must have noticed a difference in Samuel's manner. When he insisted that Samuel tell him the message, he warned him of the dire consequences of withholding anything (v. 17). This may have been Eli's greatest gift. It was a plea to be open and honest about God's word, not to try to please people with the message, to resist the temptation to edit or moderate the word, or even to try to be a mediator between God and the one to whom the word was sent.

43

All this was not merely done for Samuel's sake; Eli wanted to hear every word because he wanted to know the truth. In one of the textbooks that I used in my classes in preaching, there was a statement that the preacher in preparing a message should always assume that the people who will hear the message really want to know the truth about the subject being preached. Over the years I've had people tell me that they disagree with that particular statement more than any other in the book. Our discussion usually takes the direction that all people really want when they come to church is to have their particular prides and prejudices reinforced by the sermon, then they close their argument with some illustration of a member who got upset because a prized belief or practice was questioned. I think that there is a level at which we are always seeking affirmation, and it ruffles our feathers when we do not receive it. But at a much deeper level, there is a noble desire to know what the real situation is, whether from the doctor who conducted the tests or the preacher who has interpreted the text. This desire needs to be nourished by the people and honored by the preacher.

Once the whole message had been delivered, there is a wonderful new surrender to the will of God by Eli, as reflected in his, *"It is the LORD. Let Him do what seems good to Him"* (v. 18). At this place in Eli's life, it was in accepting the whole implication of God's judgment that he was to find mercy and peace. Eli not only surrendered himself to God's judgment but recognized Samuel as Israel's new leader. He is a tragic figure who will play no further role in Israel's future except to experience the death of his sons and to witness the capture of the ark from Shiloh.

## THE ESTABLISHMENT OF THE LEADER

[19] So Samuel grew, and the Lord was with him and let none of his words fall to the ground. [20] And all Israel from Dan to Beersheba knew that Samuel had been established as a prophet of the Lord. [21] Then the Lord appeared again in Shiloh. For the Lord revealed Himself to Samuel in Shiloh by the word of the Lord.

**4:1a** And the word of Samuel came to all Israel.

*—1 Samuel 3:19—4:1a*

These verses bring to a close the story of Samuel's birth and call, and they serve as a link for his reappearance in chapter 7. They simply describe what it was about him that caused his reputation to grow until it covered the whole land. This is what the expression *"from Dan to Beersheba"* (v. 20) really meant. It was like saying, "From California to New York and from the Gulf of Mexico to Canada."

The clues to Samuel's growing influence are found in verse 19: *"Samuel grew, and the LORD was with him and let none of his words fall to the ground."* It was a time of maturing. There were things to learn about people and life and God and self, and there were experiences from which to learn. There was the sense of God's presence in his life and thoughts and actions. This is why the word spread that the *"LORD appeared again in Shiloh"* (v. 21). God had a sensitive receptor for His word, and there was a reliable word being spoken. For years I've been fascinated with the phrase "let none of his words fall to the ground." It meant that the things which he said would happen did happen. They were God's words, and Samuel stood by them, and people knew it and were glad.

As I come to the end of this beautiful chapter, I find myself thinking, not about the temple at Shiloh, but of the church where I worship. And I think not so much of Samuel but of all those young men and women in my classes. And I am reminded what a precious thing it is to hear a word from God and to share that word with love and integrity.

# CHAPTER THREE—LOSING THE ARK OF THE COVENANT

## I SAMUEL 4:1b—7:1

*Scripture Outline*

Chapters 4—6 have no mention of Samuel even though he dominates the first three chapters. While the deaths of Eli and his sons are recorded, in keeping with the judgment of God which had been announced both by the man of God (2:27) and by Samuel (3:18), the focus of these chapters is really on the ark of the covenant. Exodus 25:10–22 gives an elaborate description of the ark. These three chapters tell of its capture by the Philistines (ch. 4), its power over the Philistine's gods (ch. 5), and its return to the Israelites (ch. 6).

## WHEN OUR SYMBOLS FAIL US

**4:1b** Now Israel went out to battle against the Philistines, and encamped beside Ebenezer; and the Philistines encamped in Aphek. ² Then the Philistines put themselves in battle array against Israel. And when they joined battle, Israel was defeated by the Philistines, who killed about four thousand men of the army in the field. ³ And when the people had come into the camp, the elders of Israel said, "Why has the LORD defeated us today before the Philistines? Let us bring the ark of the covenant of the LORD from Shiloh to us, that when it comes among us it may save us from the hand of our enemies." 4 So the people sent to Shiloh, that they might bring from there the ark of the covenant of the LORD of hosts, who dwells between the cherubim. And the two sons of Eli, Hophni and Phinehas, were there with the ark of the covenant of God.

5 And when the ark of the covenant of the LORD came into the camp, all Israel shouted so loudly that the earth shook. 6 Now when the Philistines heard the noise of the shout, they said, "What does the sound of this great shout in the camp of the Hebrews mean?" Then they understood that the ark of the LORD had come into the camp. 7 So the Philistines were afraid, for they said, "God has come into the camp!" And they said, "Woe to us! For such a thing has never happened before. 8 Woe to us! Who will deliver us from the hand of these mighty gods? These are the gods who struck the Egyptians with all the plagues in the wilderness. 9 Be strong and conduct yourselves like men, you Philistines, that you do not become servants of the Hebrews, as they have been to you. Conduct yourselves like men, and fight!"

10 So the Philistines fought, and Israel was defeated, and every man fled to his tent. There was a very great slaughter, and there fell of Israel thirty thousand foot soldiers. 11 Also the ark of God was captured; and the two sons of Eli, Hophni and Phinehas, died.

*—1 Samuel 4:1b–11*

The story of this ancient battle between the Israelites and the Philistines seems so far removed from our methods of warfare or our understanding of God that at first we wonder what its study will bring us except for some historical data that might be useful in a game of religious trivia. But once we get into the story, we discover some frightening similarities between their situation and ours and some probing questions about our own understanding of God's nature and relationship with His people.

The first three chapters give no hint of the political situation or of Israel's relationship with her neighbors. Without any explanation, we are told that the *"Philistines put themselves in battle array against Israel"* (v. 2). The Philistines were a non-Semitic people who lived mainly along the coastal plain. First Samuel 6:17 lists their five main settlements as Ashdod, Ashkelon, Ekron, Gath, and Gaza. It was usually from these areas that the Philistines came up the valleys into the hill country to attack the Israelites. The two armies took positions over against each other at Aphek and Ebenezer (v. 1).

Israel lost the first engagement. No reason is given for the defeat, but back in the camp the elders of Israel raised the question, *"Why has the LORD defeated us today before the Philistines?"* (v. 3). This is merely an analysis of a military disaster and not an effort to find an offender or to fix blame. To them, all that happened was of God, whether victory or defeat, so this could just as easily be understood as "What went wrong?" There seemed no inclination to take the loss as a judgment sent from God.

The conclusion of the elders, with which the people seemed to agree, was that they should bring the ark from the temple at Shiloh to the battlefield *"that when it comes among us it may save us from the hand of our enemies"* (v. 3). From their perspective the strategy was quite logical. They believed that God was present in the ark, therefore the only thing necessary in order to involve God on their side in the battle was to bring the ark into the camp. This is what they did, and the text tells us that this is how Phinehas and Hophni came to be at the battlefront. The presence of the ark in the camp encouraged the Israelites and created great fear among the Philistines. Both the rejoicing and the anxiety were based upon the false assumption that the presence of the ark assured the presence of the God who had delivered Israel out of slavery from Egypt.

This story reminds us that the temptation to exploit the paraphernalia of worship is very old. No mistake is older and more attractive than the desire to control or manipulate God into doing our bidding. While we are far too sophisticated in this day to think that we can capture God in a magic box, we still make the same efforts to create a God whose presence we can control and use for our own interests. Some find it difficult to distinguish between the Bible, which is the written Word, and the eternal God, who is the living Word. They think that they have captured God in the Scriptures, and they try to control God and manipulate people with their interpretations.

It is so easy to try to capture God in the rituals of the church. Baptism celebrates forgiveness, new life, and the presence of God in the life of the believer. The Lord's Supper celebrates the acting out of God's love on the Cross on our behalf. Yet it is so easy to drop the reality and keep the symbol and somehow have the mistaken notion that with these ordinances (or sacraments) we control God.

We make the same mistake Israel did with our formulas for answered prayer or for revival or renewal. In each of these the clue is to be found when you discover "the way" to get what you want from God. I have been frightened as I have heard prayer leaders share their formula for "success in prayer." And I have been embarrassed as I have heard people conclude a discussion of revival based on 2 Chronicles 7:14 by saying, "When you've done what God has asked you to do, then He has to honor your request." In all of these there is the idea that we have control of God for our purposes.

We eventually all learn what Israel discovered in battle against the Philistines. Having the paraphernalia of God and having God are not the same. The army was defeated, the sons of Eli were slain, the ark of the covenant was captured, and Israel was devastated. It was a dark moment.

## WHEN THE GLORY IS GONE

12 Then a man of Benjamin ran from the battle line the same day, and came to Shiloh with his clothes torn and dirt on his head. 13 Now when he came, there was Eli, sitting on a seat by the wayside watching, for his heart trembled for the ark of God. And when the man came into the city and told it, all the city cried out. 14 When Eli heard the noise of the outcry, he said, "What does the sound of this tumult mean?" And the man came quickly and told Eli. 15 Eli was ninety-eight years old, and his eyes were so dim that he could not see.

16 Then the man said to Eli, "I am he who came from the battle. And I fled today from the battle line."

And he said, "What happened, my son?"

17 So the messenger answered and said, "Israel has fled before the Philistines, and there has been a great slaughter among the people. Also your two sons, Hophni and Phinehas, are dead; and the ark of God has been captured."

18 Then it happened, when he made mention of the ark of God, that Eli fell off the seat backward by the side of the gate; and his neck was broken and he died, for the man was old and heavy. And he had judged Israel forty years.

19 Now his daughter-in-law, Phinehas' wife, was with child, due to be delivered; and when she heard the news

that the ark of God was captured, and that her father-in-law and her husband were dead, she bowed herself and gave birth, for her labor pains came upon her. [20] And about the time of her death the women who stood by her said to her, "Do not fear, for you have borne a son." But she did not answer, nor did she regard it. [21] Then she named the child Ichabod, saying, "The glory has departed from Israel!" because the ark of God had been captured and because of her father-in-law and her husband. [22] And she said, "The glory has departed from Israel, for the ark of God has been captured."

*—1 Samuel 4:12–22*

This section of the chapter details the disorder which was generated by the defeat of the army and the capture of the ark. The report was brought by a man from the tribe of Benjamin who ran directly from the battlefield, some twenty miles away from Shiloh. He wore the signs of mourning, *"with his clothes torn and dirt on his head"* (v. 12). While this might have been the garb for personal grief, in this case it was an occasion for national mourning. The entire city awaited the news, but no person was more anxious than Eli, who had stationed himself on a seat outside the temple. But the populace heard the message first and were so stunned that *"all the city cried out"* (v. 13).

There were many dimensions to their grief. Many homes had suffered the loss of sons, husbands, or fathers. There was a crisis of leadership. There was a possibility of domination and exploitation by the victorious Philistines. But the loss that outweighed all the others was the loss of the ark. This loss raised disturbing religious questions. Did this defeat mean that God had lost His power to deliver His people? Did the capture of the ark mean that the Philistines now controlled Israel's God? Did this mean that God was no longer present with Israel? What had Israel done to merit this disaster? How could this happen to a chosen people? This was the agenda of much of the discussion among the elders and the common people.

Nothing equips me at an experiential level to identify with the feelings of the people as a nation. I've watched the desperate panic of people, those who have lived with the illusion that the United States has a special relationship with God, when they see the country slipping from the ranks of leader nations. I've watched great denominations experience unheralded growth and grow arrogant, believing that their growth was somehow connected to a monopoly on truth, and then I've watched their efforts at rationalizing the growth's stopping and atrophy beginning. I've watched it as sincere people complained, "We all prayed, believing, but she still died. What's wrong?" But all of these combined could not equal the impact of the Benjaminite's message to the city.

When Eli finally heard the news, the shock killed him. His heart had *"trembled for the ark of God"* (v. 13) from the moment his two sons had accompanied it into battle. The messenger arranged the report so the worst news was last. It was as though Eli did not hear the news of the army's fleeing, the slaughter of the people, or of the death of his two sons. It was the mention of the ark's being captured that caused him to fall from his seat and break his neck (v. 18).

When the news came to Phinehas's wife, the shock of it sent her into premature labor. Seeing that she was dying, the women who had attended the birth tried to cheer her with the news that she had given birth to a son. With her dying breath she named the child Ichabod, meaning, literally, "No glory." Since the word "glory" was often used to express the presence of God, and since her statement seems to have been related to the capture of the ark, the meaning of the child's name meant *"The glory has departed from Israel"* (v. 21).

Of course, the readers of 1 Samuel do not sense the great crisis of leadership described in these verses because they know that God has already chosen Samuel to step into the vacuum left by the deaths of Eli and his sons. The next chapter is going to reassure everyone that while God is not willing to be kept in a box and used by His people, He is still a powerful God. More than anything else, God will help the people understand that when an inadequate understanding of His nature of mission falls by the wayside, what seems like the end of God is but the beginning of a larger and better understanding.

This has been true for Christians throughout the centuries. When Galileo first announced that our world was not the center of the universe, the church fought the idea as dangerous to the true faith. Yet when the truths about the size and age of the universe were finally accepted, rather than diminishing faith, the church discovered a larger understanding of the greatness of God.

## WHEN GODS FALL

5:1 Then the Philistines took the ark of God and brought it from Ebenezer to Ashdod. 2 When the Philistines took the ark of God, they brought it into the house of Dagon and set it by Dagon. 3 And when the people of Ashdod arose early in the morning, there was Dagon, fallen on its face to the earth before the ark of the LORD. So they took Dagon and set it in its place again. 4 And when they arose early the next morning, there was Dagon, fallen on its face to the ground before the ark of the LORD. The head of Dagon and both the palms of its hands were broken off on the threshold; only Dagon's torso was left of it. 5 Therefore neither the priests of Dagon nor any who come into Dagon's house tread on the threshold of Dagon in Ashdod to this day.

6 But the hand of the LORD was heavy on the people of Ashdod, and He ravaged them and struck them with tumors, both Ashdod and its territory. 7 And when the men of Ashdod saw how it was, they said, "The ark of the God of Israel must not remain with us, for His hand is harsh toward us and Dagon our god." 8 Therefore they sent and gathered to themselves all the lords of the Philistines, and said, "What shall we do with the ark of the God of Israel?"

And they answered, "Let the ark of the God of Israel be carried away to Gath." So they carried the ark of the God of Israel away. 9 So it was, after they had carried it away, that the hand of the LORD was against the city with a very great destruction; and He struck the men of the city, both small and great, and tumors broke out on them.

10 Therefore they sent the ark of God to Ekron. So it was, as the ark of God came to Ekron, that the Ekronites cried out, saying, "They have brought the ark of the God of Israel to us, to kill us and our people!" 11 So they sent and gathered together all the lords of the Philistines, and said, "Send away the ark of the God of Israel, and let it go back to its own place, so that it does not kill us and our people." For there was a deadly destruction throughout all the city; the hand of God was very heavy there. 12 And the men who did not die were stricken with the tumors, and the cry of the city went up to heaven.

*—1 Samuel 5:1–12*

These brief twelve verses tell the story of the ark in exile. While the Israelites in Shiloh may have been wondering whether or not the ark had lost its power, the residents of the cities of the

Philistines were discovering that the power of God was alive and functioning in their midst. When these incidents were told over and over by the Jewish storytellers, they must have provoked laughter because they tell of the humiliation of the Philistine's god and of the destruction of the dignity of the Philistine men.

When the Philistines captured the ark, they took it to Ashdod, one of their main cities, and into their temple and sat it by their god Dagon. Dagon was the god of the harvest and was considered to be the father of Baal. When they had settled in the area, the Philistines had adopted the religion of the land, probably combining what they found with their own beliefs and practices. This is still going on today. Missionaries tell how people have responded to the gospel but have continued to hold on to primitive superstitions and practices. As a college student, I saw this when I asked a very devout man why all the window sills were painted blue and was told in a matter-of-fact manner, "to keep out the demons." In countries where people tend to doubt the existence of demons, many people try to combine the worship of the living God with the gods of materialism and hedonism, in much the same fashion as did the Philistines.

Placing the ark in their temple may have involved several motives. The ark was a trophy of war and could stand there as a reminder of the defeat of the Israelites. They may have thought that, by putting the ark in their temple, they could accumulate for themselves whatever power it might have. It could be that they planned to use it as a religious symbol representing the subjected people. It was common for conquerors to combine deities and then have the vanquished people make "courtesy calls" at the temple of the conqueror. This may seem crude and primitive, but the practice continues in different forms in all cultures. It was a way of consolidating one's gains. Whatever the motive, no one anticipated the results.

If the ark seemed powerless to assist the Israelite soldiers on the battlefield, things were altogether different all alone in the temple of Dagon. When the Philistines came to their temple the day after the ark had been installed, they found their god Dagon prostrate before the ark of the Lord, showing deference (v. 3). Rather than joining their god in worship, they set him in place again. In the days to come, the prophet Isaiah analyzed the impotence of idols and the inconsistency of the idol makers (Is. 44:14–20). It must have disturbed a conquering people to discover their god bowing down before the ark of a vanquished people. Their instinct to prop their god back up is a natural one. It is not easy to relinquish an inadequate understanding of God. Even today when our little gods fall, our first instinct is not to abandon them but to prop them up again. The prophets constantly reminded Israel (and us) that the gods we make are always impotent when they face the living God.

On the second morning, the people found the torso of Dagon prostrate before the ark with its head and hands broken off (v. 4). This time they abandoned the temple. It's interesting that they did not consider falling down before the ark in worship.

The story of the Lord's affliction upon the people is both humorous and tragic (vv. 6–10). The Septuagint, which is the ancient Greek translation of the Old Testament, adds in verse 6: "And in the midst of their land rats sprang up, and there was a great death panic in the city." This may mean that an outbreak of bubonic plague, which is spread by rats, was interpreted by the people to have been caused by the God of Israel. The phrase that the New King James Version translates "tumors" (v. 6) was probably hemorrhoids resulting from dysentery, which had prostrated the men of the city. First, Dagon was humbled, and now the men all lost their dignity.

When they gathered the leaders to decide what should be done, the suggestion was made that the ark be sent to Gath, which was another of the five major cities of the Philistines. If the men of that city suffered no ill health, then it would mean that what happened in Ashdod was merely a coincidence. But when the ark was moved to Gath, the same thing happened (v. 9). So when the ark was brought to Ekron the people protested that *"They have brought the ark of the God of Israel to us, to kill us and our people"* (v. 10). When the destruction began, they gathered the leaders and pled with them to send the ark back to *"its own place"* (v. 11).

This is the middle chapter of the three that deal with the ark of the Lord. Chapter 4 dealt with its capture. Chapter 5 dramatizes that the God of Israel is not powerless. Chapter 6 will tell the story of the ark's return. The story for Israel and for us is that while God may not come through for His people in just the way they want Him to, God still has great power and will ultimately triumph.

## HOW TO GET RID OF THE ARK OF GOD

6:1 Now the ark of the LORD was in the country of the Philistines seven months. 2 And the Philistines called for the priests and the diviners, saying, "What shall we do with the ark of the LORD? Tell us how we should send it to its place."

3 So they said, "If you send away the ark of the God of Israel, do not send it empty; but by all means return it to Him with a trespass offering. Then you will be healed, and it will be known to you why His hand is not removed from you."

4 Then they said, "What is the trespass offering which we shall return to Him?"

They answered, "Five golden tumors and five golden rats, according to the number of the lords of the Philistines. For the same plague was on all of you and on your lords. 5 Therefore you shall make images of your tumors and images of your rats that ravage the land, and you shall give glory to the God of Israel; perhaps He will lighten His hand from you, from your gods, and from your land. 6 Why then do you harden your hearts as the Egyptians and Pharaoh hardened their hearts? When He did mighty things among them, did they not let the people go, that they might depart? 7 Now therefore, make a new cart, take two milk cows which have never been yoked, and hitch the cows to the cart; and take their calves home, away from them. 8 Then take the ark of the LORD and set it on the cart; and put the articles of gold which you are returning to Him as a trespass offering in a chest by its side. Then send it away, and let it go. 9 And watch: if it goes up the road to its own territory, to Beth Shemesh, then He has done us this great evil. But if not, then we shall know that it is not His hand that struck us—it happened to us by chance."

10 Then the men did so; they took two milk cows and hitched them to the cart, and shut up their calves at home. 11 And they set the ark of the LORD on the cart, and the chest with the gold rats and the images of their tumors. 12 Then the cows headed straight for the road to Beth Shemesh, and went along the highway, lowing as they went, and did not turn aside to the right hand or the left. And the lords of the Philistines went after them to the border of Beth Shemesh.

*—1 Samuel 6:1–12*

After seven months of distress, the Philistines decided that they had to do something, so they called for their priests and diviners. The text has them asking two questions (v. 2), but the first one was really rhetorical. The answer assumed by everyone who asked "What shall we do with the ark of the Lord?" was to send it back. After what they had suffered, this was agreed upon. The question that they wanted answered was "How?" It is often easier to know what needs to be done rather than how to accomplish it. What had happened to their god Dagon, to themselves, and to their land had created a certain fear of making things worse by not observing the proper protocol.

The Philistine theologians made two suggestions. First they warned against sending the ark of the God of Israel back "empty" (v. 2). It should not go back as it had come. They needed to make some kind of trespass offering. This was to be a confession of sin and a plea for forgiveness and relief. This offering needed to be costly—made of gold. It had to be related to their punishment—in the shape of the tumors and rats. This was the ancient principle of "like cures like." They were to be representative—five of each representing the major cities of the Philistines. The Philistine priests evoked the memory of Israel's deliverance from Egypt to warn that if the Philistines were to harden their hearts, worse things could happen (v. 6). This offering was an attempt to remove the anger of Israel's God.

The procedure suggested for returning the ark was very interesting. After the trespass offering had been placed inside it, the ark was to be placed on a new cart (v. 7). There was the feeling that objects which were new had greater sanctity and, therefore, greater effectiveness in discerning divine action. The cart was to be pulled by two milk cows that had never been yoked to a cart. This alone would have probably assured chaos, but the priests evoked a second restriction that seemed to assure that the ark would not go anywhere. They suggested that the cow's calves, which were still nursing, be penned up away from the mothers. On the farm, there are few more inseparable things than a cow and its nursing calf.

Although the suggestion of a trespass offering seemed to assume that all their problems had occurred because Israel's God was angry with them, there is in this second suggestion a continuing exploration of the possibility that there was no connection between what had happened and the ark's presence. It's interesting that the method which they used put the burden of proof upon God. There was no way for the ark to be taken back to Israel by these two cows separated from their calves unless the God of Israel helped them to transcend their very nature.

This kind of test is found at other places in the Old Testament. The example that has the most similar aspects is the story of

Gideon and his fleece (Judg. 6). In both, the focus was on asking God to do the unlikely. This stands in contrast to the tendency to ask for God's guidance in such a way that we identify our desire with what is "most likely" to happen. Some of our prayers suggest, "Lord, if you want me to do this, let the sun come up in the east." The Philistine priests wanted to be absolutely sure that they were dealing with God's action, and they designed the best test they were capable of with their limited knowledge of God's nature.

When the ark was loaded and the cows yoked to the cart, the Scripture says that they *"headed straight for the road to Beth Shemesh"* (v. 12), which was the nearest Israelite village. That this was not the natural thing for them to do is revealed in the little phrase *"lowing as they went"* (v. 12). It was as if something larger and more powerful than their desire to stay with their calves had taken charge, nevertheless they called to their calves as they went. What happened was interpreted by the Philistines as Israel's God accepting their trespass offering and, along with it, His promising relief. In order to be sure of what happened and to be able to report to the people, the lords of the Philistines followed the cart to the edge of Beth Shemesh and stayed to watch what would happen.

## HOW TO RECEIVE THE ARK OF GOD

13 Now the people of Beth Shemesh were reaping their wheat harvest in the valley; and they lifted their eyes and saw the ark, and rejoiced to see it. 14 Then the cart came into the field of Joshua of Beth Shemesh, and stood there; a large stone was there. So they split the wood of the cart and offered the cows as a burnt offering to the LORD. 15 The Levites took down the ark of the Lord and the chest that was with it, in which were the articles of gold, and put them on the large stone. Then the men of Beth Shemesh offered burnt offerings and made sacrifices the same day to the LORD. 16 So when the five lords of the Philistines had seen it, they returned to Ekron the same day.

17 These are the golden tumors which the Philistines returned as a trespass offering to the LORD: one for Ashdod, one for Gaza, one for Ashkelon, one for Gath, one for Ekron; 18 and the golden rats, according to the number of all the cities of the Philistines belonging to the five lords, both fortified cities and country villages, even as far as the large stone of Abel on which they set the ark of the LORD, which stone remains to this day in the field of Joshua of Beth Shemesh.

<sup>19</sup> Then He struck the men of Beth Shemesh, because they had looked into the ark of the LORD. He struck fifty thousand and seventy men of the people, and the people lamented because the LORD had struck the people with a great slaughter.

<sup>20</sup> And the men of Beth Shemesh said, "Who is able to stand before this holy LORD God? And to whom shall it go up from us?" <sup>21</sup> So they sent messengers to the inhabitants of Kirjath Jearim, saying, "The Philistines have brought back the ark of the LORD; come down and take it up with you."

**7:1** Then the men of Kirjath Jearim came and took the ark of the LORD, and brought it into the house of Abinadab on the hill, and consecrated Eleazar his son to keep the ark of the LORD.

*—1 Samuel 6:13—7:1*

This brief passage tells of the return of the ark to Israel. It begins with the people harvesting in the fields *"rejoicing to see it"* (v. 13) and ends with a request of the people to Kirjath Jearim to *"come down and take it up with you"* (v. 21). The cows stopped, as though directed, at a great stone in the field of a man named Joshua. In their great joy at the return of the ark, they used the cart for the fire and the cows for a sacrifice and worshiped God in the place. The Levites, who alone could handle the ark, were the ones who took the ark down from the cart. When the five lords of the Philistines saw this, they assumed that the ark was back where it belonged, and they returned to Ekron (v. 16).

There is some confusion among biblical scholars about the exact statement and meaning of verse 19. It's not known exactly what happened and why. There seemed to be great contrast between the original disrespectful treatment by the Philistines and the reverent reception by the Israelites. There is even mystery as to how many were affected, since the figures 50,000 and 70 appear side by side in different manuscripts. The one idea which is clear is that God's holiness is not to be taken lightly—it is not something to play with. In the end, the people of Beth Shemesh voiced the same cry as the Philistines, a cry for someone to come and take the ark away, which the people of Kirjath Jearim did (7:1).

This ends the story of the ark and little is heard about it until much later when David makes provision to bring it to a more permanent dwelling place. After this brief interlude about the ark the following chapters pick up the story of Samuel, who hasn't been mentioned since his call in chapter 3, and then moves on to the story of Saul and the establishment of the monarchy.

# CHAPTER FOUR—THE LAST JUDGE OF ISRAEL
## I SAMUEL 7:2—8:22

*Scripture Outline*

Samuel reappears in this chapter, not as a child at the temple in Shiloh, but as the judge over Israel. The details of his life for the past twenty years are left unanswered. While the focus of this chapter is to picture Samuel's role as a judge of Israel, it also prepares the reader to understand the large role he played in the establishment and guidance of the monarchy.

When reading various commentaries about this section, one is apt to find statements which suggest that many of these stories are more "theological than historical." All the phrase means is that as the author collected and arranged these stories, the focus was more on making sure that the spiritual truth of the event was understood than on giving a detailed chronological history of the period. This is a common practice in both the Old and New Testaments, and if we are to properly interpret a particular Scripture, we need to remember the perspective from which it was written.

The first two verses complete the story of the ark. At the request of the people of Beth Shemesh, the people of Kirjath Jearim took it to the house of Abinadab, whose son, Eleazar, was set aside to keep it (v. 1). Evidently the return of the ark, while it may have relieved the Philistines of the plague and the tumors, did not change anything in their domination of the Israelites.

The theme of this story is very familiar in the Bible: the turning of Israel to God and the renewing of their relationship. This repeats a cycle observed often in the Book of Judges: a period of faithfulness and blessings, a drift into unfaithfulness that results in all sorts of problems, and after a long time the people despair of their circumstances and cry to God for help.

When I was first exposed to this cycle, I wondered why Israel never seemed to learn from her experiences. Then, as I studied the history of the church, I observed that Christians have also shared Israel's pattern of behavior. Only as I observed the ups and downs of my own spiritual life did I realize how difficult it is for growth to be uninterrupted and how easy it is to take our lives into our own hands and attempt to live without God's guidance or help. Yet in the process of failure and turning to God, there is new insight about ourselves and new knowledge of God's nature and purpose and sometimes there is growth.

*Review*

## THE RENEWING OF A COVENANT

2 So it was that the ark remained in Kirjath Jearim a long time; it was there twenty years. And all the house of Israel lamented after the LORD.

3 Then Samuel spoke to all the house of Israel, saying, "If you return to the LORD with all your hearts, then put away the foreign gods and the Ashtoreths from among you, and prepare your hearts for the LORD, and serve Him only; and He will deliver you from the hand of the Philistines." 4 So the children of Israel put away the Baals and the Ashtoreths, and served the LORD only.

5 And Samuel said, "Gather all Israel to Mizpah, and I will pray to the LORD for you." 6 So they gathered together at Mizpah, drew water, and poured it out before the LORD. And they fasted that day, and said there, "We have sinned against the LORD." And Samuel judged the children of Israel at Mizpah.

*—1 Samuel 7:2–6*

These verses tell the story of Israel's turning back to God under Samuel's guidance. When they were urged to put away their idols and return to their God, they were ready. The text says, *"all the house of Israel lamented after the LORD"* (v. 2). No mention is made as to what created the "longing" for God, but it most likely had to do with the oppression that they experienced under the Philistines.

Ever since the Garden of Eden, disobedience has had a way of seeming attractive and full of promise. But when we turn away from God, things never work out the way we anticipate they will.

It may be that the message concerning what to do in order to *"return to the LORD"* (v. 3) had been preached by Samuel in all the cities where he traveled. The message makes it clear that there's more to renewing a covenant than desire. There are things to do. First, those things which had replaced God in their affections were to be put away. In their case, it was the male and female deities worshiped by the Canaanites. Samuel pleaded that they *"put away the Baals and the Ashtoreths"* (v. 4). These gods were connected with the fertility cults and with all sorts of sexual immorality. The strong armies of the Philistines had established political control, but it was the gods of the Philistines that captured the soul of Israel.

Often the greatest dangers Christians face are not from external coercion but from our attraction to "other gods." We spend billions in our country each year for what we call "national defense" to keep our nation free. Yet we have used that precious freedom to fall down and worship the gods of materialism and hedonism, the prizing of things and the exalting of pleasure. What dialectical materialism as a political philosophy could not do to us, we have done to ourselves by following "other gods."

In order to formally acknowledge Israel's turning back to God, Samuel gathered the people at Mizpah, where he had promised that he would pray to the Lord on their behalf (v. 5). When the people had gathered, Samuel poured out water as a ceremony of confession (v. 6), and the people, after fasting throughout the day, verbally confessed their sins to God. The longing of our hearts to be right with God needs tangible, external expression. To read the Scripture aloud in private devotion, to pray aloud, or even to write one's feelings in a journal all help externalize and focus our feelings about God. As was true with Israel, our turning needs to be done in the context of the community of believers. This is why public worship on a regular basis helps us to confess our sins and find closure on the past and free us for the days ahead.

## Rely DEPENDING ON GOD

7 Now when the Philistines heard that the children of Israel had gathered together at Mizpah, the lords of the Philistines went up against Israel. And when the children of Israel heard of it, they were afraid of the Philistines. 8 So the children of Israel said to Samuel, "Do not cease to cry out to

the LORD our God for us, that He may save us from the hand of the Philistines."

9 And Samuel took a suckling lamb and offered it as a whole burnt offering to the LORD. Then Samuel cried out to the LORD for Israel, and the LORD answered him. 10 Now as Samuel was offering up the burnt offering, the Philistines drew near to battle against Israel. But the LORD thundered with a loud thunder upon the Philistines that day, and so confused them that they were overcome before Israel. 11 And the men of Israel went out of Mizpah and pursued the Philistines, and drove them back as far as below Beth Car.

*—1 Samuel 7:7–11*

That all Israel was gathering at Mizpah did not escape the attention of the Philistines. While it is possible that they saw the gathering for worship as an ideal time to attack, more likely they were frightened that a renewed and united nation would soon try to deliver itself from bondage. Whatever their understanding, they gathered for battle and *"went up against Israel"* (v. 7). The Israelites were frightened and urged Samuel not to *"cease to cry out to the LORD"* (v. 8) in their behalf. Samuel made an offering to God and cried out, and *"the LORD answered him"* (v. 9). The answer involved loud thunder which confused the Philistines and sent them in retreat so that all the Israelites had to do was pursue a fleeing army (vv. 10–11). The defeat was so complete that the Philistines did not continue to come into the land as they had done before.

This account is a good example of what the commentaries mean by giving a theological perspective. Here we have a theological view of the battle. It does not do away with the role of the Israelites in the battle. The text states that they *"drove them back as far as below Beth Car"* (v. 11). This was a battle with hard combat in which the Philistines were soundly defeated. But the story is told in such a way that it is clear that the real hero of the battle wasn't the soldiers but the Lord. The incident is not intended to idealize war or slaughter but to express confidence that it is God who gives the victory.

Often in the telling of our stories, we leave out the role that God has had in our lives. It's a mistake to do so, because the role that God plays in our lives transforms circumstances and gives our lives perspective. There is a wonderful example of the difference that a theological perspective can make in comparing what Jacob told Pharaoh about his life and the report that he gave to his sons.

To Pharaoh, Jacob lamented "The years of my earthly sojourn are one hundred and thirty; hard years they have been and few, not equal to the years my fathers lived in their time" (Gen. 47:9). But when Jacob spoke to Joseph about his life, he spoke of God's appearing to him and of the promises that had been made (Gen. 48:3–4). The details of his life were the same, but the different perspective changed what had sounded like a dirge when it was told to Pharaoh into a cause of celebration when told to his sons.

If the average Christian were to tell the story of his or her life and leave out the perspective God brings, it would change the story. This is because the thing that distinguishes a Christian from someone who isn't is seldom the circumstances. The same things happen to all people. The difference is the different view one's life has when God is involved in it. Just as these verses give a theological description of the battle, we need to learn to give theological interpretations to our work, our marriages, our problems, our successes, and our plans.

## BUILDING REMEMBERING PLACES

*Remember*

12 Then Samuel took a stone and set it up between Mizpah and Shen, and called its name Ebenezer, saying, "Thus far the Lord has helped us."

13 So the Philistines were subdued, and they did not come anymore into the territory of Israel. And the hand of the Lord was against the Philistines all the days of Samuel. 14 Then the cities which the Philistines had taken from Israel were restored to Israel, from Ekron to Gath; and Israel recovered its territory from the hands of the Philistines. Also there was peace between Israel and the Amorites.

15 And Samuel judged Israel all the days of his life. 16 He went from year to year on a circuit to Bethel, Gilgal, and Mizpah, and judged Israel in all those places. 17 But he always returned to Ramah, for his home was there. There he judged Israel, and there he built an altar to the Lord.

*—1 Samuel 7:12–17*

The high moments of our lives need to be remembered and often we need something to force us to remember. When they first came into the land, Joshua had led in the erection of a monument made from stones taken from the bed of the Jordan River. When asked the purpose of the monument he told the people that when their children asked, "what mean these stones?" (Josh. 4:6), that it would give them an opportunity to tell the story of the hand of the Lord in the crossing of the Jordan. After the rout of the Philistines, Samuel set up a stone and called it "Ebenezer," meaning literally "the stone of help." Whether it was the identical spot or not, it was a reminder of that other Ebenezer when Israel had been defeated and the ark of the Lord captured (1 Sam. 4:11). At the first Ebenezer, the people had acted on their own, but this time the Lord had been their strength.

Creating occasions for remembering is important in life. Often we receive stability in our present and hope for our future as we are reminded how God has dealt with us in the past. This is why one aspect of worship should always be remembering what God has done for us. This creates praise that fortifies us against temptation. Often an individual can work out of a time of discouragement simply by stopping to remember all the blessings God has brought into his or her life. People may stand in worship and sing the words of the hymn:

> Here I raise mine Ebenezer;
> Hither by thy help I'm come;
> And I hope, by thy good pleasure,
> Safely to arrive at home.

And although they may not know what an "Ebenezer" is, they do need to build places for remembering. The psalms are filled with the reciting of the acts of God in the life of Israel, and this habit was cultivated by experiences like the one that undergirds this text.

The concluding verses of the chapter serve to establish the role of Samuel as a judge in Israel. The rather idealistic picture of peace with the Philistines and the Amorites may describe a condition that was fulfilled only in later years. This incident probably was preserved in the account to lay the foundation for why Samuel played such a key role in the selection of the first kings of the monarchy.

The chapter closes with a poignant insight into one thing that Samuel did. *"He always returned to Ramah, for his home was there"* (v. 17). This is where the Book of Samuel begins, with the story of his mother, Hannah. Now, as the established leader of Israel, Samuel comes there to judge the people and to worship God. We are not told whether his parents were still living. We only learn in the next chapter that Samuel is married and has sons. But it doesn't take much imagination to understand the very special place Ramah must have had for Samuel. People must never forget where they come from.

## WHEN LEADERS FAIL

8:1 Now it came to pass when Samuel was old that he made his sons judges over Israel. 2 The name of his firstborn was Joel, and the name of his second, Abijah; they were judges in Beersheba. 3 But his sons did not walk in his ways; they turned aside after dishonest gain, took bribes, and perverted justice.

4 Then all the elders of Israel gathered together and came to Samuel at Ramah, 5 and said to him, "Look, you are old, and your sons do not walk in your ways. Now make us a king to judge us like all the nations."

*—1 Samuel 8:1–5*

This passage has particular significance because it tells the story of the transition from the time of the judges to the time of the kings. This is the time of Samuel's old age. Yet when many would have been spending their time reminiscing, Samuel was about to begin the most significant part of his life.

Even a casual reader of 1 Samuel will notice that the establishment of the monarchy in Israel is frequently pictured as an act of rebellion against God, but at times the monarchy seems to be a divinely ordained institution. This passage seems to favor what has been called the theocratic form of rule, which heretofore has been represented by the divinely appointed charismatic judge or ruler such as Samuel. In chapter 9, however, God tells Samuel that He is sending "a man from the land of Benjamin, and you shall anoint him commander over My people Israel" (1 Sam. 9:16). That these views are both recorded indicate that there was never unanimity about having a king.

These specific verses tell the unhappy story of what happened when Samuel attempted to pass the mantle of leadership along to his sons. It's like a rerun of Eli's experience with his children. Samuel's two sons were Joel and Abijah, meaning "Yahweh is God" and "Yahweh is father," respectively. Their father had made them judges in Beersheba, at the southern edge of the country. The phrase often used in the Bible to indicate that children were different from their parents is *"his sons did not walk in his ways"*

(v. 3). This exposes at least one of the problems of hereditary positions of responsibility. Often the heir of a great king would rather be a playboy, or the son of a great administrator would rather study marine life. And often leaders of sterling character have children who lack integrity. This problem is not limited to leaders of nations. It is one that haunts every parent who seeks to pass on to children moral and spiritual values.

The accusations against Samuel's sons were serious. They *"turned aside after dishonest gain, took bribes, and perverted justice"* (v. 3). The power that the sons had as judges brought with it pressures to compromise and temptations to sell favors. Their father had the same opportunities and temptations that they had, but he had resisted them. Their personal greed caused their sense of justice to erode, and after a while it was known by everyone, with the possible exception of Samuel, that Israel was being ruled by judges who were for sale, and there was contempt for the law. Where people do not receive justice, whether caused by prejudices or payoffs, it is hard to respect the law. The sin of the perversion of justice was a central theme in the preaching of the prophets. Listen to Amos's cry, "You . . . turn justice to wormwood, / And lay righteousness to rest in the earth" (Amos 5:7).

While these verses were put here to explain why the people of Israel wanted a king, they probe the minds of people who love their children and want them to share their love for God and the moral and spiritual values which grow out of that relationship. I first became aware of this when a pastor friend discussed with me a sermon he had preached on "Third Generation Religion." In the sermon he pointed out how unusual it was when religion was passed on to succeeding generations to find it with the same vigor that it had in previous generations. His example was Timothy who seemed to possess the same commitment and love that had been possessed by his mother and his grandmother (2 Tim. 1:5). The sermon's Old Testament examples of religion that moved from vitality to form to farce were the children of Eli and Samuel. Parents are not without hope. They can model for their children and surround them with good influence. But children have minds and choices of their own, and parents cannot make those choices for them. Samuel's children walked a different path, and it changed Israel's history.

Given the circumstance, the request of the elders of Israel seemed reasonable, but it met stiff resistance from Samuel. The petition to *"make us a king"* (v. 5) probably dealt more with the urgent political situation than with the inadequacy of his sons. After all, their work was confined to Beersheba. Israel was feeling the effect of being a people surrounded by hostile forces, and the people wanted stability and security. Up to now Israel's life had been characterized by disunity, with each tribe going its own way. There seemed to be no pattern for the emergence of the judges. Therefore the request for a king made good sense, except that it left God entirely out. This omission, coupled with Israel's tendency toward idolatry, flawed the plan.

## WHAT IT MEANS TO HAVE A KING

6 But the thing displeased Samuel when they said, "Give us a king to judge us." So Samuel prayed to the LORD. 7 And the LORD said to Samuel, "Heed the voice of the people in all that they say to you; for they have not rejected you, but they have rejected Me, that I should not reign over them. 8 According to all the works which they have done since the day that I brought them up out of Egypt, even to this day—with which they have forsaken Me and served other gods—so they are doing to you also. 9 Now therefore, heed their voice. However, you shall solemnly forewarn them, and show them the behavior of the king who will reign over them."

10 So Samuel told all the words of the LORD to the people who asked him for a king. 11 And he said, "This will be the behavior of the king who will reign over you: He will take your sons and appoint them for his own chariots and to be his horsemen, and some will run before his chariots. 12 He will appoint captains over his thousands and captains over his fifties, will set some to plow his ground and reap his harvest, and some to make his weapons of war and equipment for his chariots. 13 He will take your daughters to be perfumers, cooks, and bakers. 14 And he will take the best of your fields, your vineyards, and your olive groves, and give them to his servants. 15 He will take a tenth of your grain and your vintage, and give it to his officers and servants. 16 And he will take your male servants, your female servants, your finest young men, and your donkeys, and put them to his work. 17 He will take a tenth of your sheep. And you will be his servants. 18 And you will cry out in that day because of your king whom you have chosen for yourselves, and the LORD will not hear you in that day."

19 Nevertheless the people refused to obey the voice of Samuel; and they said, "No, but we will have a king over us, 20 that we also may be like all the nations, and that our king may judge us and go out before us and fight our battles."

21 And Samuel heard all the words of the people, and he repeated them in the hearing of the LORD. 22 So the LORD said to Samuel, "Heed their voice, and make them a king."

And Samuel said to the men of Israel, "Every man go to his city."

*—1 Samuel 8:6–22*

Samuel was very upset with the request of the people, and there could have been a number of reasons why he was so upset. He could have taken offense that the people were linking his age with the need for a king. Many people find it difficult to admit that there may come a time when they are no longer able to do what they once did. He could have been surprised concerning the attitude toward his sons. Often those of us who have 20/20 vision in evaluating the children of others can be blind to the faults of our own. The desire to find immortality through our children is very strong and might cause a parent to minimize flaws of character or give a too kind interpretation to their actions. The larger objection, which isn't mentioned but would be natural, would be to the possible diminished role in a monarchy for the judges. Human beings are territorial and resent any reordering of the structure that lessens their power or authority. Mixed in with all of the other feelings, Samuel could have been personally threatened by the request of the elders.

Instead of arguing with the people, Samuel *"prayed to the LORD"* (v. 6) and received from the Lord both personal affirmation, which made him feel good, and instructions to honor the people's request, which frustrated him. The encouraging words were *"they have not rejected you, but they have rejected Me, that I should not reign over them"* (v. 7). This word is intended to comfort Samuel who was feeling rejected after a lifetime of faithful service to Israel. But it also introduces the idea that there are implications in the request that have grave consequences for Israel's future. Israel's request is seen as much more than the desire for an earthly king, they are rejecting the Kingship of God in their lives. At an earlier time the people had tried to make Gideon their king. In his refusal, he replied, "I will not rule over you, nor shall my son rule over you; the LORD shall rule over you" (Judg. 8:23).

A word of warning needs to be given about the possible abuse of God's word to Samuel in verse 7. We need to remember that these are God's words and not Samuel's. When religious leaders meet opposition, there is a natural tendency to feel that people who disagree with them are at odds with God, and this is often not the case. Religious leaders are human, are conditioned by their background, can lack experience or information, can get their personal ambitions confused with God's purposes, and do not always speak for God. There will probably be times when the rejection of the minister's leadership is also the rejection of God for their lives, but it would be the height of arrogance for a minister to quote this verse to all who don't agree with his or her leadership. That is a judgment which needs to be left to God.

While God reminded him that Israel had a long history of turning away from God (v. 8), Samuel was told to *"heed their voice"* (v. 9). God had called them out of slavery to be sons, and, unlike a tyrant who might compel obedience, God would seek to win them. One of the threads that is woven throughout the Bible is how God works with people in the midst of their compromises to accomplish His purpose. Israel's motives were confused. They wanted to be "like all the nations" (v. 5). When we live in the world, we are influenced by the political and cultural environment more than we realize, and we often lose the ability to distinguish between what comes out of our environment and what comes out of our relationship with God. Yet God does not reject us or give up on us. He works with us to bring good out of less than ideal situations. This is what God did with Israel's request.

Samuel was instructed to warn the people about the ways of kings, and verses 11–18 are a litany of the known behaviors of kings. While the descriptions given are the natural consequence of establishing a centralized government, none of the advantages and all of the negatives are given, making it a very slanted report. God wants them to know exactly what it is that they are choosing and what the cost will be. The tendency to view political decisions exclusively in terms of benefits and to ignore the real cost is not a new problem. In that day when taxes were oppressive, when sons were being drafted for the armed forces, daughters added to the king's household, and the people cried out to God for relief, God wanted them to remember that they had been warned. It is a loving act, though there may be pain involved, to help people see the long-term implications of their decision.

The chapter concludes with the people's continued request for a king and God's instruction to Samuel to *"make them a king"* (v. 22).

Unlike the foreign kings who often ruled over Israel, this would be a king whom God permitted and who would be anointed and advised by Samuel, God's prophet. The next chapter introduces Israel's first king. While Samuel did not favor a monarch, he came really to love Saul to the extent that he was able to rejoice in the good that he did and grieve at his mistakes.

## SECTION TWO

# THE STORY OF SAUL
### 1 SAMUEL 9:1—14:52

# CHAPTER FIVE—THE FIRST KING OF ISRAEL
## I SAMUEL 9:1—12:25

*Scripture Outline*
> A King Is Chosen (9:1–27)
> The Anointing and Assuring of a King (10:1–16)
> Israel Meets Her King (10:17–27)
> The Kingship Ratified (11:1–15)
> Samuel's Sermon at Saul's Coronation (12:1–25)

Chapter 9 contains the beautiful story of the choosing of Saul to be the first king of Israel. It begins without any connection with what precedes.

### A KING IS CHOSEN

**9:1** There was a man of Benjamin whose name was Kish the son of Abiel, the son of Zeror, the son of Bechorath, the son of Aphiah, a Benjamite, a mighty man of power. **2** And he had a choice and handsome son whose name was Saul. There was not a more handsome person than he among the children of Israel. From his shoulders upward he was taller than any of the people. **3** Now the donkeys of Kish, Saul's father, were lost. And Kish said to his son Saul, "Please take one of the servants with you, and arise, go and look for the donkeys." **4** So he passed through the mountains of Ephraim and through the land of Shalisha, but they did not find them. Then they passed through the land of Shaalim, and they were not there. Then he passed through the land of the Benjamites, but they did not find them.

5 When they had come to the land of Zuph, Saul said to his servant who was with him, "Come, let us return, lest my father cease caring about the donkeys and become worried about us."

6 And he said to him, "Look now, there is in this city a man of God, and he is an honorable man; all that he says surely comes to pass. So let us go there; perhaps he can show us the way that we should go."

7 Then Saul said to his servant, "But look, if we go, what shall we bring the man? For the bread in our vessels is all gone, and there is no present to bring to the man of God. What do we have?"

8 And the servant answered Saul again and said, "Look, I have here at hand one-fourth of a shekel of silver. I will give that to the man of God, to tell us our way." 9 (Formerly in Israel, when a man went to inquire of God, he spoke thus: "Come, let us go to the seer"; for he who is now called a prophet was formerly called a seer.)

10 Then Saul said to his servant, "Well said; come, let us go." So they went to the city where the man of God was.

11 As they went up the hill to the city, they met some young women going out to draw water, and said to them, "Is the seer here?"

12 And they answered them and said, "Yes, there he is, just ahead of you. Hurry now; for today he came to this city, because there is a sacrifice of the people today on the high place. 13 As soon as you come into the city, you will surely find him before he goes up to the high place to eat. For the people will not eat until he comes, because he must bless the sacrifice; afterward those who are invited will eat. Now therefore, go up, for about this time you will find him."

14 So they went up to the city. As they were coming into the city, there was Samuel, coming out toward them on his way up to the high place.

15 Now the LORD had told Samuel in his ear the day before Saul came, saying, 16 "Tomorrow about this time I will send you a man from the land of Benjamin, and you shall anoint him commander over My people Israel, that he may save My people from the hand of the Philistines; for I have looked upon My people, because their cry has come to Me."

17 So when Samuel saw Saul, the LORD said to him, "There he is, the man of whom I spoke to you. This one

shall reign over My people." [18] Then Saul drew near to Samuel in the gate, and said, "Please tell me, where is the seer's house?"

[19] Samuel answered Saul and said, "I am the seer. Go up before me to the high place, for you shall eat with me today; and tomorrow I will let you go and will tell you all that is in your heart. [20] But as for your donkeys that were lost three days ago, do not be anxious about them, for they have been found. And on whom is all the desire of Israel? Is it not on you and on all your father's house?"

[21] And Saul answered and said, "Am I not a Benjamite, of the smallest of the tribes of Israel, and my family the least of all the families of the tribe of Benjamin? Why then do you speak like this to me?"

[22] Now Samuel took Saul and his servant and brought them into the hall, and had them sit in the place of honor among those who were invited; there were about thirty persons. [23] And Samuel said to the cook, "Bring the portion which I gave you, of which I said to you, 'Set it apart.'"

[24] So the cook took up the thigh with its upper part and set it before Saul. And Samuel said, "Here it is, what was kept back. It was set apart for you. Eat; for until this time it has been kept for you, since I said I invited the people." So Saul ate with Samuel that day.

[25] When they had come down from the high place into the city, Samuel spoke with Saul on the top of the house. [26] They arose early; and it was about the dawning of the day that Samuel called to Saul on the top of the house, saying, "Get up, that I may send you on your way." And Saul arose, and both of them went outside, he and Samuel.

[27] As they were going down to the outskirts of the city, Samuel said to Saul, "Tell the servant to go on ahead of us." And he went on. "But you stand here awhile, that I may announce to you the word of God."

*—1 Samuel 9:1–27*

The first two verses give his background and a physical description. He was from the tribe of Benjamin, the smallest in Israel. While it may have been an unlikely source for leadership, the fact that the tribe had shown no pretensions to leadership meant that the choice of Saul wouldn't split the tribes into competing factions. His father, Kish, was a man of substance. The phrase that describes him means "warrior" and suggests that he had been valiant in battle as well as a man of wealth. Saul himself was described as handsome and tall. His name meant "that which had been asked for."

The story of the young man and his servant looking for the lost asses seems rather ordinary on the surface, but it introduces the reader to God's involvement in the process of choosing a king for Israel. In those days fields were marked by boundary stones but had no fences, so when there was a shortage of grass the animals could easily wander. To recover the animals, Saul and a servant made a sweep of the territory going into three different areas (v. 4) without success and arrived ready to quit in the *"land of Zuph"* (v. 5). Saul, realizing that by now his father would be more worried about his son than his donkeys, suggested that the search be abandoned. But the servant, knowing of a man of God who lived in the city suggested that they might get help from him in their search (v. 6). They were not a great distance from their home, but the storyteller does not say how it was that the servant knew of the seer and Saul didn't. Neither of them seem to know his name. The story details what seems to be a series of chance events in which the larger purpose of God is at work in the lives of His people.

Every Christian can look back over his or her life and see how God was at work in a series of incidents that at the time seemed to have no relationship. As an older teenager I had a crippling case of rheumatoid arthritis. When I didn't seem to be able to handle the stress of my freshman year of college in Oklahoma, my doctor suggested that if I lived in either Arizona or New Mexico the drier Southwest might give me some relief. I had an aunt who lived in Albuquerque who was happy for me to live with her. She had a daughter who was a nurse at the Lovelace Clinic, which she recommended to me. When the experiments to test the use of cortisone on people was funded, it was my doctor who was selected to choose the patients and supervise the experiment. I was one who was chosen, and my positive response to the medicine is what made my ministry possible. At the time these events were taking place they didn't seem related, nor did I have a sense of God's being involved in them. But looking back, it seems more than a coincidence that I happened to be in that city as a patient of that doctor at that precise time.

Saul's story is full of surprises. As he and the family servant entered the city they learned from some young women, who had come to the well for water, that a religious sacrifice was about to be observed and that the prophet Samuel had just arrived to bless the sacrifice (vv. 12–13). Neither Saul nor his servant knew that on the previous day the Lord appeared to Samuel and told him that *"Tomorrow about this time I will send you a man from the land of Benjamin, and you shall anoint him commander over My people Israel"* (v. 16). So Samuel keeps an appointment to bless a sacrifice and ends up anointing a king. Saul goes out seeking his father's livestock and finds a crown. Often in the midst of striving for lesser goals, God comes with a more significant plan for our lives.

The story shows Samuel to have all the credentials of the prophet. The meeting with Saul had been predicted to him (v. 16). He knew both what Saul's mission was and that the donkeys had been found (v. 20). He also was able to announce to Saul *"the word of God"* (v. 27). And, as Saul and his servant approached, the Lord revealed to Samuel that *"This one shall reign over My people"* (v. 17). The story of Saul's selection and anointing begins a relationship that will serve the monarch well—the prophet of God and the chosen king working together. It created some checks and balances to protect the people from an autocratic king. And it reminded Israel that their true king was not Saul but the Lord. The role of the prophet was a reminder to the people not to place all their trust in armies or in treaties but in God. The world in which we live today places too much trust in the stockpiling of arms and in the treaties that we negotiate with our enemies. There is seldom an accompanying concern for moral and spiritual weapons.

Samuel's invitation for Saul to be his guest at the blessing of the sacrifice and for the meal that followed caught Saul by surprise. His plea of unworthiness (v. 21) has the same ring of humility as Gideon, who cried, "Indeed my clan is the weakest in Manasseh, and I am the least in my father's house" (Judg. 6:15). There is no agreement as to what is meant when Samuel says, *"I . . . will tell you all that is in your heart"* (v. 19). The first thought would be that he is promising that on the next day he would tell him where his father's donkeys are. But he tells him that immediately, leading to all sorts of speculation as to the meaning of the words. Since, at this point in the story, both Samuel and the readers know that Saul is God's choice as king it may be a veiled reference to the larger implications of the visit.

If Saul was surprised by the invitation to eat with Samuel, he must certainly have been mystified that the place of honor had been reserved for him and the choice serving of meat given to him (vv. 22–24). At this ceremonial meal Samuel is beginning the process of welding a relationship between Saul and the people. After the meal Saul spent the night with Samuel, sleeping on the flat roof, which was customary. Early the next morning, Samuel awoke Saul and went with him to the edge of the city, where, after sending the servant on by himself, Samuel anointed Saul and spoke to him "the word of God" (v. 27). Unlike David's anointing, which was done before the house of Jesse (1 Sam. 16:13), the anointing of Saul was done without witnesses. The act of setting Saul aside to be king merely symbolized what God had already done. Apart from the action of God it would have been an empty act.

Does God still set people aside for special service as he did Saul? Are the stories of people who begin ordinary tasks and discover royal responsibilities nothing but antiques preserved in the Old Testament? Are there still people like Samuel through whom God can give guidance to our lives? In societies where political power is shared by more people, is it possible for God to guide in the choice of a leader? Can congregations of Christians or an individual seek to know God's will for a given situation? The answer to all these questions is a resounding yes. First Samuel 9 is the story of God at work in the life of Samuel and Saul. In a relationship with God the story of our lives takes on new meaning and significance.

## THE ANOINTING AND ASSURING OF A KING

**10:1** Then Samuel took a flask of oil and poured it on his head, and kissed him and said: "Is it not because the LORD has anointed you commander over His inheritance? **2** When you have departed from me today, you will find two men by Rachel's tomb in the territory of Benjamin at Zelzah; and they will say to you, 'The donkeys which you went to look for have been found. And now your father has ceased caring about the donkeys and is worrying about you, saying, "What shall I do about my son?"' **3** Then you shall go on forward from there and come to the terebinth tree of Tabor. There three men going up to God at Bethel will meet you, one carrying three young goats, another carrying three loaves of bread, and another carrying a skin of wine. **4** And they will greet you and give you two loaves of bread, which you shall receive from their hands. **5** After that you shall come to the hill of God where the Philistine garrison is. And it will happen, when you have come there to the city, that you will meet a group of prophets coming down from the high place with a stringed instrument, a tambourine, a flute, and a harp before them; and they will be prophesying. **6** Then the Spirit of the LORD will come upon you, and you will prophesy with them and be turned into another man. [7] And let it be, when these signs come to you, that you do as the occasion demands; for God is with you. [8] You shall go down before me to Gilgal; and surely I will come down to you to offer burnt offerings and make sacrifices of peace offerings. Seven days you shall wait, till I come to you and show you what you should do."

[9] So it was, when he had turned his back to go from Samuel, that God gave him another heart; and all those signs came to pass that day. [10] When they came there to the hill, there was a group of prophets to meet him; then the Spirit of God came upon him, and he prophesied among them. [11] And it happened, when all who knew him formerly saw that he indeed prophesied among the prophets, that the people said to one another, "What is this that has come upon the son of Kish? Is Saul also among the prophets?" [12] Then a man from there answered and said, "But who is their father?" Therefore it became a proverb: "Is Saul also among the prophets?" [13] And when he had finished prophesying, he went to the high place.

[14] Then Saul's uncle said to him and his servant, "Where did you go?"

So he said, "To look for the donkeys. When we saw that they were nowhere to be found, we went to Samuel."

[15] And Saul's uncle said, "Tell me, please, what Samuel said to you."

[16] So Saul said to his uncle, "He told us plainly that the donkeys had been found." But about the matter of the kingdom, he did not tell him what Samuel had said.

*—1 Samuel 10:1–16*

This chapter continues the story begun in chapter 8 with Israel's request for a king and continued in chapter 9 with the choosing of Saul. Chapter 10 divides clearly into two parts: Saul is anointed and given signs of his calling in verses 1–16; Saul is proclaimed to be the king before the people in verses 17–27. The later section seems almost like an extension of chapter 8, with Samuel expressing again his feelings about a monarchy.

The setting for verse 1 reaches back into chapter 9 for its context. Saul had spent the night with Samuel after having been the guest of honor at the sacrificial feast. Early in the morning Samuel woke Saul and walked to the edge of the city with him. Then, after sending the servant ahead, Samuel *"took a flask of oil and poured it on his head, and kissed him"* (v. 1). Kings and prophets were anointed with olive oil. The kiss was a sign of homage. It was felt that this action stamped upon the person a special character. The specialness derives from the one who anoints, in this case Samuel acting as the Lord's representative. Later, after Saul had been rejected, David refused to take advantage of the opportunity to kill him because Saul was "God's anointed."

Nothing is recorded in the story about Saul's response. I've never known a king, but during my entire ministry I've been associated with men and women who felt that they had been "set aside" by God for some special task. The most often expressed emotions of these are a sense of unworthiness, a wanting to be sure, and a sense of inadequacy to do what they feel called to do. If Saul had felt unworthy of the place of honor at the feast, imagine how he must have felt when he heard *"the Lord has anointed you commander over His inheritance"* (v. 1). Either he questioned Samuel's actions or expressed doubt as to his own ability, or Samuel may have sensed Saul's need for reassurance. Saul needed to be sure that Samuel had really spoken for God and he needed assurance that he would have God's help in the task.

Samuel gave Saul three signs to authenticate the anointing. First, he told Saul that he would find two men by Rachel's tomb who would report to him that the donkeys have been found and that his father was worried about him (v. 2). Second, Saul would meet three men by the *"terebinth tree of Tabor"* who will be carrying gifts of goats, bread, and wine to the temple at Bethel, and he was to accept the gift of bread that they would offer to him (vv. 3–4). Finally, Saul would meet a band of prophets, and God's Spirit would come upon him and change and empower him (vv. 5–7). The text tells us that all three signs came to pass on the same day and that the effect upon Saul was that it *"gave him another heart"* (v. 9). It would probably be a mistake to interpret this in a New Testament sense as a "new birth" (John 3:3) but more as a sense of encouragement. It was God's way of saying to Saul, "I have anointed you for a task, and I am able to give you the strength that you will need." This kind of encouragement is needed by God's people on a continuing basis. While we may not need the kinds of signs that Saul was given, we need the constant affirmation of our calling in Christ.

The only sign whose fulfillment was detailed in the biblical text was the third, probably because it played a more significant role for Saul. The first sign merely authenticated Samuel's earlier statement about the lost donkeys (1 Sam. 9:20). There may have been special significance connected with the second sign that gifts which were being taken "up to God" would be shared with Saul. But that the encounter with the band of prophets is important is clear.

The ecstatic prophets did not communicate a divine message as an Amos or a Hosea would later do. Their "prophesying" consisted of an excited ecstatic behavior or possession trance. The verb is also translated "rave" (1 Kin. 18:29). The situation was stimulated by the use of music, rhythmic dancing, and sometimes the cutting of their bodies. It was held that all this was a sign of divine energy invading the personalities of the prophets. There is evidence, even in this chapter, that they were not highly regarded by the people, and the practice ceased to be prominent in the religious life of Israel.

But the experience with the band of prophets gave Saul the assurance that the power of God was going to be evident in his reign. The most important sign was an inward one for Saul. The experience inspired him, confirmed him, and gave him a vision for the task. This is another example of the way in which God often uses those who are at hand to encourage His children in the work. In the first stages of sensing God's call in my life, I was filled with an almost insurmountable feeling that I would not be able to do what I had been called to do. While I had no Samuel to give me three signs as a source of encouragement, looking back I can still recall people and experiences through which God did for me what was done for Saul. It seems that with the hand of God on our lives there comes the assurance of His help.

After the experience with the prophets, Saul went home and did not discuss his having been anointed king, even with his close relatives (vv. 14–16). Samuel had instructed him to wait *"till I come to you and show you what you should do"* (v. 8). It was a time for sorting out all the things that had happened to him since leaving home to look for his father's animals.

### ISRAEL MEETS HER KING

[17] Then Samuel called the people together to the LORD at Mizpah, [18] and said to the children of Israel, "Thus says the LORD God of Israel: 'I brought up Israel out of Egypt, and delivered you from the hand of the Egyptians and from the hand of all kingdoms and from those who oppressed you.' [19] But you have today rejected your God, who Himself saved you from all your adversities and your tribulations; and you have said to Him, 'No, set a king over us!' Now therefore,

present yourselves before the LORD by your tribes and by your clans."

20 And when Samuel had caused all the tribes of Israel to come near, the tribe of Benjamin was chosen. 21 When he had caused the tribe of Benjamin to come near by their families, the family of Matri was chosen. And Saul the son of Kish was chosen. But when they sought him, he could not be found. 22 Therefore they inquired of the LORD further, "Has the man come here yet?"

And the LORD answered, "There he is, hidden among the equipment."

23 So they ran and brought him from there; and when he stood among the people, he was taller than any of the people from his shoulders upward. 24 And Samuel said to all the people, "Do you see him whom the LORD has chosen, that there is no one like him among all the people?"

So all the people shouted and said, "Long live the king!"

25 Then Samuel explained to the people the behavior of royalty, and wrote it in a book and laid it up before the LORD. And Samuel sent all the people away, every man to his house. 26 And Saul also went home to Gibeah; and valiant men went with him, whose hearts God had touched. 27 But some rebels said, "How can this man save us?" So they despised him, and brought him no presents. But he held his peace.

*—1 Samuel 10:17–27*

Up to now in the story only Samuel and Saul are aware that God has chosen a king for Israel. These verses are a sequel to chapter 8. Samuel called a national assembly in Mizpah and reviewed God's relationship to them (vv. 17–18) and their rejection of God in requesting a king (v. 19). Saul was kept completely in the background as Samuel led Israel in the casting of lots with sacred objects in order to see whom God had chosen. It was a process of elimination from the nation, to the tribe, to the family, to the person.

This process led to the discovery of Saul. To a generation that is familiar with professional "head-hunters" and search committees, this random method seems unlikely to discover the best person to be king. Cynics would suggest that the chances of the one whom Samuel had already anointed being chosen were too slim to be believable. Since the reader already knows who has been chosen, the casting of the lots seems almost ceremonial. What we need to remember is that those who engaged in the procedure had absolute confidence that God would work through the system to pick a leader. This system was still in use when the early church chose a successor to Judas after discussing qualifications, naming nominees, and praying to God for guidance. When they drew lots "the lot fell to Matthias" (Acts 1:26). Those who look critically upon what seems to them an inadequate method of discerning God's will need only study how most religious decisions are made to realize how little progress has been made.

What most surprised everyone was not the process for discerning whom God had chosen as king, but that the one who was chosen wasn't there. After a search, he was discovered *"hidden among the equipment"* (v. 22). This action may have been taken as a sign of Saul's humility. When he was brought in, everyone was struck by his physical appearance for *"he was taller than any of the people from his shoulders upward"* (v. 23). Samuel then presented him as the one whom God had chosen and the people responded with *"Long live the king!"* (v. 24).

Israel now had a king, but before Samuel adjourned the assembly he explained to the people the behavior of royalty and wrote what he had said in a book and deposited it in the temple (v. 25). While some of this is a restatement of what had been said in chapter 8 concerning the actions of kings, others feel that it may have been a listing of rights and responsibilities for a king who would rule under God. Whether kings, deacons, or ministers, it is always good to remember that the process of exercising leadership has both rights and responsibilities.

The chapter ends on a slightly sour note. Samuel had sent the people away (v. 25) and Saul had gone home to Gibeah (v. 26). And from the meeting some *"valiant men . . . whose hearts God had touched"* (v. 26) accompanied Saul. But the text goes on to reveal that there were some who gave no credence to the choice of Saul and had no confidence in his ability to save Israel from her enemies (v. 27). They showed their contempt for Saul by bringing him no presents. While this is an entirely normal situation, Saul's response wasn't. In the midst of the praise of the multitudes, it is easy to become preoccupied with the criticism of one or two. The Scripture says, *"He held his peace"* (v. 27). The more likely action for his day would have been to slay the critics and begin the reign with total approval. Saul's action gave evidence that God really had given him "another heart" (v. 9) for that day.

## THE KINGSHIP RATIFIED

**11:1** Then Nahash the Ammonite came up and encamped against Jabesh Gilead; and all the men of Jabesh said to Nahash, "Make a covenant with us, and we will serve you."

² And Nahash the Ammonite answered them, "On this condition I will make a covenant with you, that I may put out all your right eyes, and bring reproach on all Israel."

³ Then the elders of Jabesh said to him, "Hold off for seven days, that we may send messengers to all the territory of Israel. And then, if there is no one to save us, we will come out to you."

⁴ So the messengers came to Gibeah of Saul and told the news in the hearing of the people. And all the people lifted up their voices and wept. ⁵ Now there was Saul, coming behind the herd from the field; and Saul said, "What troubles the people, that they weep?" And they told him the words of the men of Jabesh. ⁶ Then the Spirit of God came upon Saul when he heard this news, and his anger was greatly aroused. ⁷ So he took a yoke of oxen and cut them in pieces, and sent them throughout all the territory of Israel by the hands of messengers, saying, "Whoever does not go out with Saul and Samuel to battle, so it shall be done to his oxen."

And the fear of the Lord fell on the people, and they came out with one consent. ⁸ When he numbered them in Bezek, the children of Israel were three hundred thousand, and the men of Judah thirty thousand. ⁹ And they said to the messengers who came, "Thus you shall say to the men of Jabesh Gilead: 'Tomorrow, by the time the sun is hot, you shall have help.' " Then the messengers came and reported it to the men of Jabesh, and they were glad. ¹⁰ Therefore the men of Jabesh said, "Tomorrow we will come out to you, and you may do with us whatever seems good to you."

¹¹ So it was, on the next day, that Saul put the people in three companies; and they came into the midst of the camp in the morning watch, and killed Ammonites until the heat of the day. And it happened that those who survived were scattered, so that no two of them were left together.

¹² Then the people said to Samuel, "Who is he who said, 'Shall Saul reign over us?' Bring the men, that we may put them to death."

13 But Saul said, "Not a man shall be put to death this day, for today the LORD has accomplished salvation in Israel."

14 Then Samuel said to the people, "Come, let us go to Gilgal and renew the kingdom there." 15 So all the people went to Gilgal, and there they made Saul king before the LORD in Gilgal. There they made sacrifices of peace offerings before the LORD, and there Saul and all the men of Israel rejoiced greatly.

—*1 Samuel 11:1–15*

Chapter 11 gives us our first view of the new king in action. It is one thing to be anointed king by Samuel and to hear the people shout "Long live the king." It is another thing altogether to lead a nation against her enemies. But the relationship between a king and the people is nurtured as they solved common problems together.

Chapter 10 closed with the question being asked about Saul "How can this man save us?" (v. 27). The story of this chapter answers that question convincingly. The story is similar to other accounts of heroic deliverances recorded in the Book of Judges, but the real significance of this story is its role in uniting the people behind Saul as their king.

The story of the siege of Jabesh Gilead in verses 1–4 illustrates how fragmented Israel was as a people and how vulnerable they were to their enemies. Their major threat came from the Philistines, but there were others such as the Ammonites who had to be dealt with as well. Also, because Jabesh Gilead was located on the east side of the Jordan River and bordered with Ammon, it was a logical target for attack. Realizing their inferior position, the leaders of Jabesh Gilead tried to get Nahash to *"make a covenant with us"* (v. 1). The word they used described an agreement reached between unequals in which the stronger party set the terms of the covenant. Nahash's terms, that the right eye of each citizen be put out (v. 2), revealed that his motive was to humiliate them and to ridicule Israel. That he would give them seven days in which to try to find help suggests that Nahash considered the possibility of outside help unlikely. The text only gives a report of the messengers who came to Gibeah, Saul's hometown. It would be interesting to know how the messengers were received in the other cities. Many people find it hard to be concerned for the troubles of others.

After his anointing by Samuel (1 Sam. 10:1) and his being chosen by lot at Mizpah (1 Sam. 10:21), Saul had gone home and continued his work on the family farm. There were probably times as he went about his work that Saul himself doubted the significance of what had happened to him. As he struggled to get two of his father's oxen to pull in the same direction he may have personalized the question of his critics, "How could a person like me save Israel from her enemies?" The answer came in the reaction Saul had to the plea for help from the people of Jabesh Gilead. The Scripture says, *"the Spirit of God came upon Saul when he heard this news, and his anger was greatly aroused"* (v. 6). It could have been written "the Spirit leaped upon him," for his reaction to the news had an element of divine anger to it and it equipped him to take bold and dramatic action. The capacity to share God's anger at great injustice is a gift that more people should seek.

Inspired and empowered by the Spirit, Saul *"took a yoke of oxen and cut them in pieces"* (v. 7). They were not hacked up in a fit of anger but cut like pieces to be offered as sacrifice to God. The pieces were given to the messengers with instructions to deliver them throughout all the territory with the message that those who did not go forth to battle the Ammonites would have the same thing done to their oxen. The call was to join *"Saul and Samuel,"* both the prophet and the king, and made the venture a holy war. The call was for obedience to the king and for unified action against the enemy. Evidently the Spirit that led Saul to such action prepared the people, for one sentence summarizes the amazing response— *"the fear of the LORD fell on the people, and they came out with one consent"* (v. 7). The combination of a common enemy and a charismatic leader had done a new thing for Israel— it had united her.

The Israelites gathered at Bezek, some fifteen miles west of the besieged city. Word was sent to the leaders of Jabesh Gilead that on the next day they would have help (v. 9). Knowing when help was coming, the leaders sent word to Nahash saying, *"'Tomorrow we will come out to you, and you may do with us whatever seems good to you'"* (v. 10). They sent the message in a form that could have meant that they were coming out to surrender or to do battle, knowing that the assumption of the Ammonites was that they were going to submit themselves to having their right eyes gouged out. As this story was told and retold over the centuries, the cleverness of the people of Jabesh Gilead must have generated laughter and admiration. On the next day, Saul divided the army into three groups, as had Gideon (Judg. 7:16), and attacked early in the morning and waged battle until *"the heat of the day"* (v. 11) and defeated the Ammonites. The one telling the story illustrates the completeness of the defeat by saying that the Ammonites were so scattered that *"no two of them were left together"* (v. 11).

The story is wrapped up with four verses that help us to see the larger significance of what happened. A suggestion was made to Samuel that those who had questioned Saul's leadership should be found and put to death (v. 12). But it is Saul, not Samuel, who answers that such an action would be inappropriate *"for today the LORD has accomplished salvation in Israel"* (v. 13). (It would have been good had Saul been able to retain the sense of security which allowed him to deal graciously with his critics.) Now Samuel joins in with a countersuggestion, that they gather at Gilgal to *"renew the kingdom"* (v. 14)—which they did in a great act of worship.

Two significant things happened at Gilgal. First, the people were able to acclaim Saul as their king after seeing his charismatic leadership in unifying the country and leading them to defeat their enemy. There is a sense in which leadership, whether of a nation or a business or a church, has to be earned. But the second thing was just as important. At Gilgal, the idea of a king over Israel "like the other nations" began to be modified. At least at this point, everyone knew that what had happened had been God's work and not done in human strength. At Gilgal, there was rejoicing that God was the real king.

## SAMUEL'S SERMON AT SAUL'S CORONATION

**12:1** Now Samuel said to all Israel: "Indeed I have heeded your voice in all that you said to me, and have made a king over you. <sup>2</sup> And now here is the king, walking before you; and I am old and grayheaded, and look, my sons are with you. I have walked before you from my childhood to this day. <sup>3</sup> Here I am. Witness against me before the LORD and before His anointed: Whose ox have I taken, or whose donkey have I taken, or whom have I cheated? Whom have I oppressed, or from whose hand have I received any bribe with which to blind my eyes? I will restore it to you."

<sup>4</sup> And they said, "You have not cheated us or oppressed us, nor have you taken anything from any man's hand."

<sup>5</sup> Then he said to them, "The LORD is witness against you, and His anointed is witness this day, that you have not found anything in my hand."

And they answered, "He is witness."

⁶ Then Samuel said to the people, "It is the Lord who raised up Moses and Aaron, and who brought your fathers up from the land of Egypt. ⁷ Now therefore, stand still, that I may reason with you before the Lord concerning all the righteous acts of the Lord which He did to you and your fathers: ⁸ When Jacob had gone into Egypt, and your fathers cried out to the Lord, then the Lord sent Moses and Aaron, who brought your fathers out of Egypt and made them dwell in this place. ⁹ And when they forgot the Lord their God, He sold them into the hand of Sisera, commander of the army of Hazor, into the hand of the Philistines, and into the hand of the king of Moab; and they fought against them. ¹⁰ Then they cried out to the Lord, and said, 'We have sinned, because we have forsaken the Lord and served the Baals and Ashtoreths; but now deliver us from the hand of our enemies, and we will serve You.' ¹¹ And the Lord sent Jerubbaal, Bedan, Jephthah, and Samuel, and delivered you out of the hand of your enemies on every side; and you dwelt in safety. ¹² And when you saw that Nahash king of the Ammonites came against you, you said to me, 'No, but a king shall reign over us,' when the Lord your God was your king.

¹³ "Now therefore, here is the king whom you have chosen and whom you have desired. And take note, the Lord has set a king over you. ¹⁴ If you fear the Lord and serve Him and obey His voice, and do not rebel against the commandment of the Lord, then both you and the king who reigns over you will continue following the Lord your God. ¹⁵ However, if you do not obey the voice of the Lord, but rebel against the commandment of the Lord, then the hand of the Lord will be against you, as it was against your fathers.

¹⁶ "Now therefore, stand and see this great thing which the Lord will do before your eyes: ¹⁷ Is today not the wheat harvest? I will call to the Lord, and He will send thunder and rain, that you may perceive and see that your wickedness is great, which you have done in the sight of the Lord, in asking a king for yourselves."

¹⁸ So Samuel called to the Lord, and the Lord sent thunder and rain that day; and all the people greatly feared the Lord and Samuel.

¹⁹ And all the people said to Samuel, "Pray for your servants to the LORD your God, that we may not die; for we have added to all our sins the evil of asking a king for ourselves."

²⁰ Then Samuel said to the people, "Do not fear. You have done all this wickedness; yet do not turn aside from following the LORD, but serve the LORD with all your heart. ²¹ And do not turn aside; for then you would go after empty things which cannot profit or deliver, for they are nothing. ²² For the LORD will not forsake His people, for His great name's sake, because it has pleased the LORD to make you His people. ²³ Moreover, as for me, far be it from me that I should sin against the LORD in ceasing to pray for you; but I will teach you the good and the right way. ²⁴ Only fear the LORD, and serve Him in truth with all your heart; for consider what great things He has done for you. ²⁵ But if you still do wickedly, you shall be swept away, both you and your king."

*—1 Samuel 12:1–25*

Chapter 12 is a sermon. The preacher is Samuel. The audience are the people of Israel and their new king. The setting is probably Gilgal, where they had gathered after the defeat of the Ammonites in order to "renew the kingdom." While Samuel mentions the threat of Nahash, the king of the Ammonites, it is not to celebrate the victory but to suggest that it was this threat which caused Israel to demand a king. Even the casual reader will sense that the mood of chapter 12 fits more with the content and spirit of chapters 7 and 8. As chapter 11 closes, all Israel is rejoicing at the blessings of God on the new king. Now this chapter dwells once more on the sin of asking for a king.

The most reverent of biblical scholars feels that the establishing of an exact chronology for these events is not possible since that did not seem to be the goal of those who preserved the accounts for us in their present form. They were much more interested in theology than in history as we think of it. This was true of the Gospel writers as well. John did not write his Gospel that we might be able to memorize an exact history of Christ's life and work but that we might "believe that Jesus is the Christ, the Son of God, and that believing you may have life in His name" (John 20:31). Samuel's sermon is about a people's relationship with the living God.

This chapter is often called "Samuel's farewell address," but there is nothing in it that suggests he is bowing out of the picture. He closes the chapter with the promise that he will continue to pray for his people and teach them the way (v. 23). But the acknowledgment of the existence of the monarchy becomes the occasion for summarizing Samuel's ministry. The phrase *"here is the king, walking before you"* is followed immediately by *"and I am old and grayheaded"* (v. 2). In those days the picture of the king was less apt to be in military terms and more likely to be a pastoral analogy—a shepherd going before his sheep. At this point Samuel could not resist reminding the people that *"I have walked before you from my childhood to this day"* (v. 2). Change is never easy and turning loose is harder. When I said goodbye to a people I had come to love and stepped down from a significant pulpit that I had occupied for only a dozen years, I suffered a genuine grief experience. I cannot imagine the range of emotions that must have been Samuel's at this juncture in his life.

Samuel began his sermon with a focus upon himself and the kind of judge he had been (vv. 3–5). The manner was direct and remarkable. At this point the focus was less on the length of his leadership than on the quality. Samuel opened the way for anyone who knew of any corruption during his tenure to bear witness to the wrongdoing before *"the LORD and his anointed"* (v. 3) with the promise of restitution for the wronged. The areas mentioned were those that the prophets most often accused those in power of abusing. The people answered in chorus, *"You have not cheated us or oppressed us, nor have you taken anything from any man's hand"* (v. 4). He had been incorruptible and had not favored private interests. Samuel was not on an ego trip, for his character and his conduct were crucial to his office as a man of God.

The integrity of Samuel stands as a model for us today. I can still remember the shock that many registered when they learned that bribes are a standard part of doing business in many countries. There was almost a patronizing tone in the voices of those who insisted that "though we do not believe in these practices, we have no other option if we hope to be involved in world trade." But in recent years we have had stockbrokers imprisoned for insider trading, defense contractors fined for cheating the public out of hundreds of millions of dollars, enthusiastic alumni exposed for paying money under the table to college athletes, and countless public officials convicted for betraying the public trust. While we live in a high-tech society with amazing potential for improving the lot of people, improvement isn't happening because there are too many people in too many high places whose lives and work lack integrity. To be able to come to the end of a career of any sort with Samuel's "clean hands" would be a noble goal for anyone.

The sermon continues with a short summary of Israel's historic experience (vv. 6–11). It takes the form of a lawsuit with God as the protagonist and the people as the accused. Since the Exodus from Egypt was the decisive historic event with Israel, he began there (v. 8) and then moved to the period of the judges, which included himself (v. 11). The pattern was the same: forgetting the Lord, getting into trouble, crying to God, and being provided a deliverer by God.

One of the phrases in Samuel's sermons that is often used of God's people in trouble is *"they cried out to the LORD"* (v. 10). Psalm 107 has long been a favorite of mine. It has a series of stanzas that tell of people in different kinds of trouble: those who had lost their way, those in darkness, those trapped in rebellious ways, and even those lost at sea. Each stanza ends with this phrase that Samuel used to describe Israel's action— "Then they cried out to the LORD in their trouble" (vv. 6, 13, 19, 28). The verses that precede the call of Moses tell how God "heard their groaning" (Ex. 2:24) down in Egypt. The message is clear. No person is so oppressed or so powerless but that when he cries out to God he is heard. This truth ought to be a source of comfort to those who suffer and a warning to those who perpetuate injustice and who exploit the poor and the powerless.

While the issue of the sin of requesting a king was reintroduced in the sermon (vv. 12–13), Samuel accepts the fact of the monarchy and urges obedience to God on the part of the king and the people (v. 14) and warns of calamities to come if they rebel against God's commandment (v. 15). To assure everyone that he is still speaking for God, Samuel calls upon God to *"send thunder and rain"* (v. 18) at that season when it never rained. The people were so struck with fear that they confessed their sins and asked Samuel to pray for them so they would not die (v. 19). Samuel reassured the people that though they had sinned, God would forgive them.

Then he gave to them two great assurances: first, that God would not forsake His people (v. 22). There is always comfort that our security rests in the knowledge that God wants to make of us His people and that He will not abandon us. During the years of my ministry I have been confronted with every conceivable situation, many of which defied explanation. When I was a younger minister I would try to explain to people why things happened. Eventually I came to realize that often things happen and no one understands why. Then I came to realize that the one thing I could say to the people in difficult times was that "God is not going to abandon you." Israel took great comfort in Samuel's assurance of God's persistent love and grace.

But the other word of assurance concerned Samuel's continuing relationship to the people. He began the sermon with "I have walked before you from my childhood" (v. 2), and he concludes with the assurance that he would continue to represent them to God and teach them what was right (v. 23). His commitment was so strong that he suggested that it would be a sin for him to cease to pray for them. While the role is different, this is not the sermon of a man who is "stepping down." Samuel's commitment is that he will continue to counsel both people and the king as to God's word. It will be up to them to obey.

# CHAPTER SIX—THE WARS OF LIBERATION
## 1 SAMUEL 13:1—14:52

*Scripture Outline*
>  Fighting Against Odds (13:1–7)
>  Learning to Trust God (13:8–15)
>  When Things Seem Hopeless (13:16–23)
>  If God Is in It (14:1–23)
>  Conflict Within Victory (14:24–46)
>  The Summary of Saul's Wars (14:47–52)

This chapter has all sorts of challenges to scholarship, such as figuring how old Saul was when his reign began and how long he reigned. Most of the best manuscripts don't even contain the first verse. But the larger challenge of this passage is to understand the encounter between Saul and Samuel. This chapter introduces a tragic quality to their relationship and inaugurates Saul's reign under a cloud. It leaves the impression that before the very first battle, immediately after his coronation, Saul was rejected as the king.

One scholar, in discussing the problems created by our not always being given precise chronologies, offered this helpful suggestion. It's like looking at a photograph that was taken from a very great distance through a telephoto lens. All the details are there, but things that are actually miles apart are seen together. The application of this analogy to 1 Samuel is that incidents which actually happened at different times show up in the same story, creating a challenge for the interpreter. But the crisis of this chapter is not Saul's age but his relationship with Samuel.

### FIGHTING AGAINST ODDS

**13:1** Saul reigned one year; and when he had reigned two years over Israel, **2** Saul chose for himself three thousand

95

men of Israel. Two thousand were with Saul in Michmash and in the mountains of Bethel, and a thousand were with Jonathan in Gibeah of Benjamin. The rest of the people he sent away, every man to his tent.

3 And Jonathan attacked the garrison of the Philistines that was in Geba, and the Philistines heard of it. Then Saul blew the trumpet throughout all the land, saying, "Let the Hebrews hear!" 4 Now all Israel heard it said that Saul had attacked a garrison of the Philistines, and that Israel had also become an abomination to the Philistines. And the people were called together to Saul at Gilgal.

5 Then the Philistines gathered together to fight with Israel, thirty thousand chariots and six thousand horsemen, and people as the sand which is on the seashore in multitude. And they came up and encamped in Michmash, to the east of Beth Aven. 6 When the men of Israel saw that they were in danger (for the people were distressed), then the people hid in caves, in thickets, in rocks, in holes, and in pits. 7 And some of the Hebrews crossed over the Jordan to the land of Gad and Gilead.

As for Saul, he was still in Gilgal, and all the people followed him trembling.

*—1 Samuel 13:1–7*

Whatever the length of his reign, Saul was a warrior king and this chapter begins the stories of his battles. He chose three thousand men of Israel as a standing army. Samuel had warned that "he will take your sons" (1 Sam. 8:11), and Saul did. A later description tells us that "when Saul saw any strong man or any valiant man, he took him for himself" (1 Sam. 14:52). Saul commanded two thousand men at Michmash and in the hills of Bethel, and Jonathan, his son, commanded the other thousand in Gibeah of Benjamin.

Up to this point the Philistines, who totally dominated the area, seemed to pay little attention to the happenings in Israel. They seemed to attach no significance to the new leadership and the new spirit.

The Philistines controlled the Israelites from strategically placed garrisons. When Jonathan attacked the garrison at Geba (v. 3), it was such a novelty that all the Philistines heard immediately and were furious. Saul spread the word to his people knowing that what the attack symbolized would encourage them (v. 3). But the Philistines soon grasped that something was happening in Israel and decided to put a stop to it. They gathered an awesome military force with the plan of nipping in the bud any dream Israel had of freeing themselves from the Philistine domination. Even if the *"thirty thousand chariots"* (v. 5) were only three thousand, as the footnote in the New King James suggests, the chariots established an absolute superiority for the Philistines. In addition, they had horsemen and foot soldiers, whom the text calls merely *"people as the sand which is on the seashore in multitude"* (v. 5).

Whatever hope had been created in the people's minds and hearts by Jonathan's attack on the garrison was short-lived. When they saw the large, well-equipped, well-trained military machine that was about to attack, they were terrorized and responded accordingly. While no report is given of Saul's army, the people who had gathered to him at Gilgal (v. 4) did everything they could to hide from the enemy. They *"hid in caves, in thickets, in rocks, in holes, and in pits"* (v. 6). Some even crossed the Jordan *"to the land of Gad and Gilead"* (v. 7). Those who stayed with Saul, presumably soldiers, *"followed him trembling"* (v. 7).

When we read of Saul's precipitous action (vv. 8–15), we need to at least remember the odds Israel faced as a nation and the stresses that Saul faced as a new king. While most of us cannot project ourselves into their political and military situation, in recent years I have begun to understand the overwhelming odds that are faced by Christians in an increasingly secular world. We find a certain amount of comfort and affirmation as we gather to worship and we take delight when one of "Satan's garrisons" is attacked by the church, without stopping to realize that the victory was largely symbolic. But we are so outnumbered by the forces of evil that they are as oblivious to most of our doings as the Philistines were to the anointing of Saul or the preaching of Samuel.

The secular press usually limits its coverage of Christianity to when a highly visible Christian does something immoral or a denomination does something utterly stupid. During the rest of the time they patronize us with trivial articles in the Saturday papers when the circulation is lowest. But if we are honest about the situation in the world, when the forces of evil line up against us, we seem so outnumbered and so powerless to face them that we wish that we had pits and rocks and thickets to hide in, as the Israelites did. And like Saul, we fail to resist the temptation to take things into our own hands.

## LEARNING TO TRUST GOD

[8] Then he waited seven days, according to the time set by Samuel. But Samuel did not come to Gilgal; and the people

were scattered from him. [9] So Saul said, "Bring a burnt offering and peace offerings here to me." And he offered the burnt offering. [10] Now it happened, as soon as he had finished presenting the burnt offering, that Samuel came; and Saul went out to meet him, that he might greet him.

[11] And Samuel said, "What have you done?"

Saul said, "When I saw that the people were scattered from me, and that you did not come within the days appointed, and that the Philistines gathered together at Michmash, [12] then I said, 'The Philistines will now come down on me at Gilgal, and I have not made supplication to the LORD.' Therefore I felt compelled, and offered a burnt offering."

[13] And Samuel said to Saul, "You have done foolishly. You have not kept the commandment of the LORD your God, which He commanded you. For now the LORD would have established your kingdom over Israel forever. [14] But now your kingdom shall not continue. The LORD has sought for Himself a man after His own heart, and the LORD has commanded him to be commander over His people, because you have not kept what the LORD commanded you."

[15] Then Samuel arose and went up from Gilgal to Gibeah of Benjamin. And Saul numbered the people present with him, about six hundred men.

*—1 Samuel 13:8–15*

I never read this passage of Scripture without a certain amount of sadness. It pictures the first open conflict between Saul and Samuel, two men who needed to work together in leading Israel. What happened here laid the foundation for Saul's rejection and for David's becoming king. Most people have so identified the phrase "a man after God's own heart" with David that they are surprised to find it here in Samuel's speech to Saul (v. 14). In this story we learn that, as a result of Saul's sin, his son Jonathan will not succeed him as king (v. 14). And in addition to all this, until a person really studies the story in depth, it seems that Saul did the reasonable thing and that Samuel is wrong. This confrontation lacks the drama and the final rejection of the story in 1 Samuel 15, but it lays the foundation for what is to follow and gives us early clues into the flaws that finally brought Saul down.

The account opens with Saul waiting a week for Samuel to show up, while the Philistines continued to intimidate them and his soldiers continued to drift away (v. 8). In the minds of the people, for Samuel not to show up was the same as God's not being present, and they dared not go into battle against such odds unless the Lord's servant joined their king in leading them into battle. At this stage in Israel's history they felt that each war was waged with God's guidance and protection and also that it was to accomplish His purpose. It is easier to understand their blending of political and theological goals in those days than when secular nations in the twenty-first century quote the Bible as their guide for conquests that are more economically than spiritually motivated. Saul, fearing that any further delay would mean the total dissipation of his fighting force, decided to make the sacrifice to God himself since it didn't seem that Samuel was coming. In retrospect, this was the beginning of the end for Saul, but it seemed so logical at the time. One of the problems of the Christian life is that often actions that are so easy to rationalize seem so wrong when we look back at them.

Saul had just finished the offering to God when Samuel arrived and asked for an explanation (v. 11). As soon as Saul had explained his actions, Samuel announced that it was a foolish thing to do and that he had *"not kept the commandment of the LORD"* (v. 13). If we had nothing but this story, we would tend to feel that it was Samuel who was wrong. But the whole history of Saul gives support to Samuel's reading of the situation.

Saul was a great soldier but a lesser king. And in this story, the panic that he experienced as he saw his already outmanned army dwindling revealed a failure to trust God, who had always been Israel's only hope for freedom or victory. This incident suggests that Saul's reign was flawed from the beginning. There is a kind of funeral sadness to the parting of the two as Samuel *"went up . . . to Gibeah"* and Saul *"numbered the people present with him"* (v. 15), about six hundred men. Because Samuel's love for Saul was real, what had happened created grief. Saul's mood was more likely confusion and desperation.

Before we leave this passage we need to admit how often we play Saul's role in this drama. Sometimes it is hard to know the difference between when we are acting wisely and when we are acting out of lack of trust in God. Most people don't feel comfortable with people who use the phrase "we just need to trust God" as a way to hide from reality or responsibility. And most Christians don't identify with those people who have made a doctrine out of "God helps those who help themselves." But in spite of this, the church has not been able to resist the temptation to adopt the corporation's definition of success and Madison Avenue's method of selling its products and the twenty-first century's confidence in itself. The temptation to trust organization, structure, plans, and programs is always strong. Learning to think vigorously, plan wisely, and work hard are good, but they are not substitutes for placing our ultimate confidence in God. The church has plenty of Sauls. What it's lacking are a few Samuels who can see through all the well-reasoned action and remind us that to fail to place our ultimate trust in God is a sin against God.

## WHEN THINGS SEEM HOPELESS

[16] Saul, Jonathan his son, and the people present with them remained in Gibeah of Benjamin. But the Philistines encamped in Michmash. [17] Then raiders came out of the camp of the Philistines in three companies. One company turned onto the road to Ophrah, to the land of Shual, [18] another company turned to the road to Beth Horon, and another company turned to the road of the border that overlooks the Valley of Zeboim toward the wilderness.

[19] Now there was no blacksmith to be found throughout all the land of Israel, for the Philistines said, "Lest the Hebrews make swords or spears." [20] But all the Israelites would go down to the Philistines to sharpen each man's plowshare, his mattock, his ax, and his sickle; [21] and the charge for a sharpening was a pim for the plowshares, the mattocks, the forks, and the axes, and to set the points of the goads. [22] So it came about, on the day of battle, that there was neither sword nor spear found in the hand of any of the people who were with Saul and Jonathan. But they were found with Saul and Jonathan his son.

[23] And the garrison of the Philistines went out to the pass of Michmash.

*—1 Samuel 13:16–23*

These verses merely illustrate that from a purely human point of view there was little hope of Israel's continued existence. The Philistine raiding parties operated at will (vv. 17–18). But the greatest handicap that Saul's men suffered was a lack of arms. The Philistines, who were fairly advanced, controlled all the blacksmiths in the area. They had confiscated all the weapons and made it illegal for the Israelites to own swords or spears. Saul's men were farmers who, before joining his army, were subjected to going to the Philistine blacksmiths when they wanted their axes or plowshares or other tools sharpened. The record states that of all the people, only Saul and Jonathan had weapons for battle. As though this were not enough, the chapter closes with the word that the Philistines moved out to the *"pass of Michmash"* (v. 23), which would have put them over against Saul and his men.

The tables seem to turn in chapter 13 for everyone, except the Philistines. It opens with a heroic exploit by Jonathan which both destroyed the confidence of the Philistines and rekindled the courage of the Israelites (vv. 1–15). It closes with a summary of the wars of Saul and the stabilizing effect that his reign had on the land (vv. 47–52). The central part of the chapter climbs the heights of victory with the rout of the Philistines (vv. 16–23) and plumbs the depths of frustration with Saul's rash command that almost caused the death of his potential heir (vv. 24–46). This chapter makes no mention of Samuel. Instead the priest from Shiloh, who accompanies Saul is Eli's great-grandson (v. 3). And the whole account is told so that there can be little doubt in the reader's mind that it was the Lord who was responsible for the remarkable victory over the previously unstoppable enemy.

## IF GOD IS IN IT

**14:1** Now it happened one day that Jonathan the son of Saul said to the young man who bore his armor, "Come, let us go over to the Philistines' garrison that is on the other side." But he did not tell his father. **2** And Saul was sitting in the outskirts of Gibeah under a pomegranate tree which is in Migron. The people who were with him were about six hundred men. **3** Ahijah the son of Ahitub, Ichabod's brother, the son of Phinehas, the son of Eli, the LORD's priest in Shiloh, was wearing an ephod. But the people did not know that Jonathan had gone.

**4** Between the passes, by which Jonathan sought to go over to the Philistines' garrison, there was a sharp rock on one side and a sharp rock on the other side. And the name of one was Bozez, and the name of the other Seneh. **5** The front of one faced northward opposite Michmash, and the other southward opposite Gibeah.

**6** Then Jonathan said to the young man who bore his armor, "Come, let us go over to the garrison of these uncircumcised; it may be that the LORD will work for us. For nothing restrains the LORD from saving by many or by few."

⁷ So his armorbearer said to him, "Do all that is in your heart. Go then; here I am with you, according to your heart."

⁸ Then Jonathan said, "Very well, let us cross over to these men, and we will show ourselves to them. ⁹ If they say thus to us, 'Wait until we come to you,' then we will stand still in our place and not go up to them. ¹⁰ But if they say thus, 'Come up to us,' then we will go up. For the LORD has delivered them into our hand, and this will be a sign to us."

¹¹ So both of them showed themselves to the garrison of the Philistines. And the Philistines said, "Look, the Hebrews are coming out of the holes where they have hidden." ¹² Then the men of the garrison called to Jonathan and his armorbearer, and said, "Come up to us, and we will show you something."

Jonathan said to his armorbearer, "Come up after me, for the LORD has delivered them into the hand of Israel." ¹³ And Jonathan climbed up on his hands and knees with his armorbearer after him; and they fell before Jonathan. And as he came after him, his armorbearer killed them. ¹⁴ That first slaughter which Jonathan and his armorbearer made was about twenty men within about half an acre of land.

¹⁵ And there was trembling in the camp, in the field, and among all the people. The garrison and the raiders also trembled; and the earth quaked, so that it was a very great trembling. ¹⁶ Now the watchmen of Saul in Gibeah of Benjamin looked, and there was the multitude, melting away; and they went here and there. ¹⁷ Then Saul said to the people who were with him, "Now call the roll and see who has gone from us." And when they had called the roll, surprisingly, Jonathan and his armorbearer were not there.

¹⁸ And Saul said to Ahijah, "Bring the ark of God here" (for at that time the ark of God was with the children of Israel). ¹⁹ Now it happened, while Saul talked to the priest, that the noise which was in the camp of the Philistines continued to increase; so Saul said to the priest, "Withdraw your hand." ²⁰ Then Saul and all the people who were with him assembled, and they went to the battle; and indeed every man's sword was against his neighbor, and there was very great confusion. ²¹ Moreover the Hebrews who were with the Philistines before that time, who went up with them into the camp from the surrounding country, they also joined

the Israelites who were with Saul and Jonathan. [22] Likewise all the men of Israel who had hidden in the mountains of Ephraim, when they heard that the Philistines fled, they also followed hard after them in the battle. [23] So the LORD saved Israel that day, and the battle shifted to Beth Aven.

—*1 Samuel 14:1–23*

During my student days someone placed in my hand the biography of a respected scholar of the Southwest entitled *J. B. Tidwell plus God*. The thesis of the biographer was that many remarkable things can be accomplished when the resources of God are joined with the commitment of one faithful follower. That is a theme which many Christians assent to intellectually but which few are able to act upon. If the biographer had been seeking an Old Testament model for his thesis, Jonathan would have been a good one, and this incident would have been the best example.

The account gives an excellent description of the setting. The two armies occupied high positions facing each other, separated by a rocky valley. Saul was at the outskirts of Gibeah with his tiny band of six hundred, accompanied by Ahitub, the Lord's priest from Shiloh, whose father was brother to Ichabod (1 Sam. 4:21). The priest was wearing an "ephod," a sacred object associated with the priestly status and used for discerning the Lord's will. In general, however, nothing seemed to be happening at Saul's command center located in a tent under a giant pomegranate tree, which seems to have been a well-known landmark.

Without the knowledge or permission of his father, Jonathan decided to go over to the Philistine garrison across the valley which lay between the two armies, taking with him only his armorbearer (v. 1). The act seemed more spontaneous than something that had been mulled over for a long time. It had much of the idealism of youth, to whom the impossible often seems more attainable. The optimistic spirit of Jonathan is very much like that of young David when he looked across a valley at a giant Philistine (1 Sam. 17:45–46).

But there was much more to this action than youthful impetuousness. This is our first good look at Jonathan, and it is easy to see how he would later inspire such confidence as a warrior and why his armorbearer would follow him gladly on such a dangerous mission. Several things stand out. First, he felt that the only way for him to be victorious was for God to be involved in it. He discussed this with his servant when he said *"it may be that the LORD will work for us"* (v. 6). While Jonathan seems to be taking the initiative, he is not counting on his own superior swordsmanship, nor the element of surprise, but the fact that God was in the cause. There are people who clothe themselves in "holy talk" even when they are filled with personal ambition, and they are repulsive to all who see through them. But Jonathan intended for it to be a victory not for himself but for God, and he was sincere in this conviction.

The first time I introduced Billy Graham to a group of ministers I made a terrible mistake and learned something wonderful about the man as a result. Out of a genuine appreciation for Dr. Graham I went into great detail to remind the people of all the things he had done to strengthen God's work through his ministry. When he rose to speak he seemed agitated about my introduction, and before he read his text and brought the message he took time to tell all of us that it would be wrong for him to take credit for the things that God had done. As he talked I sensed he felt that if the time ever came that he began to see what was happening as "his accomplishments," then they would stop. Maybe that's why one of the songs always heard at a Billy Graham crusade is "To God Be the Glory."

A second interesting aspect of Jonathan's insight was the idea of God's overcoming the many through the few. This theme permeates the Old Testament, and our minds go immediately to Gideon who had to keep making his army smaller so that people would know that the victory was the Lord's (Judg. 6—7). Jonathan's *"nothing restrains the LORD from saving by many or by few"* (v. 6) doesn't limit God to the minority but is a reminder that to be victorious in life does not require either consensus or a majority. So many people stand before situations in life where they are inadequate within themselves and they need to be constantly reminded what God can do with one, or a few. A good friend of mine loves to sing the words from a very old gospel song: "Little is much when God is in it." It is a truth that Jonathan knew long ago.

The most interesting aspect of this account was the way in which Jonathan sought a sign that God was in it. He concluded that the sign from God would be in how the Philistines greeted them, and he seems to have chosen the least likely response     (vv. 9–10). When they moved into view below the garrison, they were met at first with words of contempt: *"Look, the Hebrews are coming out of the holes where they have hidden"* (v. 11). But then, to his delight, Jonathan heard the words that signaled victory to him: *"Come up to us"* (v. 12). He still had to climb the precipice and engage in fierce battle, but the climb was made with a faith in God that allowed him to experience in the present what God would do in the future (Heb. 11:1).

Almost every time this passage is discussed in a group, someone will ask the question, "What do you think about asking God for a sign today?" The answers vary with the size and variety of the group, but very few of the groups ever discuss the profound difference in Jonathan's day and ours. His father took a priest who cast lots to answer yes-or-no questions to discern the will of God. Christians today have two thousand years of insights into the Bible; we have the church which is the body of Christ from which we can seek help; and we have the Holy Spirit which is God working within us. In the light of this wealth of resources, to make major decisions in our lives on the basis of our interpretation of some "sign" might be reverting to a lesser method than we have available as a result of Jesus Christ.

The story of the battle was given in far less detail than the account of the preparation, because to the storyteller that Jonathan was relying upon God and had been directed by God into this battle was of much greater importance than the nature of the swordplay. Once they had climbed up the steep embankment, in an area no larger than a man could plow in half a day, Jonathan and his armorbearer killed twenty soldiers (vv. 13–14). The immediate effect was the spread of fear, probably fed by the awareness that more was involved in Jonathan's victory than the surprise of his attack or the unusual circumstances of that particular garrison. The biblical text repeats the phrase "trembled," for both the Philistine soldiers trembled and the earth trembled (v. 15). It was the enemy's response to Jonathan's feat under God which laid the foundation for the great victory that day. It was a classic example of God bringing victory "by few."

Saul's watchmen noticed the confusion and the *"melting away"* in the Philistine camp (v. 16). But Saul's camp knew of no action and only discovered after a roll call that Jonathan and his armorbearer were missing (v. 17). At first, Saul called the priest to inquire of the Lord what was happening, but when it became obvious that the Philistines were in retreat he told the priest to withdraw his hand (v. 19), and Saul himself and all the people joined in battle. Israelites who were with the Palestinians as slaves revolted and joined the battle (v. 21). People who had hidden in caves and thickets came out from hiding and participated in the victory (v. 22). What began as the adventure of a young man, soon became the cause of the whole nation. And it was a victory for which God was given the credit (v. 23).

## CONFLICT WITHIN VICTORY

24 And the men of Israel were distressed that day, for Saul had placed the people under oath, saying, "Cursed is the man who eats any food until evening, before I have taken vengeance on my enemies." So none of the people tasted food. 25 Now all the people of the land came to a forest; and there was honey on the ground. 26 And when the people had come into the woods, there was the honey, dripping; but no one put his hand to his mouth, for the people feared the oath. 27 But Jonathan had not heard his father charge the people with the oath; therefore he stretched out the end of the rod that was in his hand and dipped it in a honeycomb, and put his hand to his mouth; and his countenance brightened. 28 Then one of the people said, "Your father strictly charged the people with an oath, saying, 'Cursed is the man who eats food this day.'" And the people were faint.

29 But Jonathan said, "My father has troubled the land. Look now, how my countenance has brightened because I tasted a little of this honey. 30 How much better if the people had eaten freely today of the spoil of their enemies which they found! For now would there not have been a much greater slaughter among the Philistines?"

31 Now they had driven back the Philistines that day from Michmash to Aijalon. So the people were very faint. 32 And the people rushed on the spoil, and took sheep, oxen, and calves, and slaughtered them on the ground; and the people ate them with the blood. 33 Then they told Saul, saying, "Look, the people are sinning against the LORD by eating with the blood!"

So he said, "You have dealt treacherously; roll a large stone to me this day." 34 Then Saul said, "Disperse yourselves among the people, and say to them, 'Bring me here every man's ox and every man's sheep, slaughter them here, and eat; and do not sin against the LORD by eating with the blood.'" So every one of the people brought his ox with him that night, and slaughtered it there. 35 Then Saul built an altar to the LORD. This was the first altar that he built to the LORD.

36 Now Saul said, "Let us go down after the Philistines by night, and plunder them until the morning light; and let us not leave a man of them."

And they said, "Do whatever seems good to you."

Then the priest said, "Let us draw near to God here."

37 So Saul asked counsel of God, "Shall I go down after the Philistines? Will You deliver them into the hand of Israel?" But He did not answer him that day. 38 And Saul said, "Come over here, all you chiefs of the people, and know and see what this sin was today. 39 For as the LORD lives, who saves Israel, though it be in Jonathan my son, he shall surely die." But not a man among all the people answered him. 40 Then he said to all Israel, "You be on one side, and my son Jonathan and I will be on the other side."

And the people said to Saul, "Do what seems good to you."

41 Therefore Saul said to the LORD God of Israel, "Give a perfect lot." So Saul and Jonathan were taken, but the people escaped. 42 And Saul said, "Cast lots between my son Jonathan and me." So Jonathan was taken. 43 Then Saul said to Jonathan, "Tell me what you have done."

And Jonathan told him, and said, "I only tasted a little honey with the end of the rod that was in my hand. So now I must die!"

44 Saul answered, "God do so and more also; for you shall surely die, Jonathan."

45 But the people said to Saul, "Shall Jonathan die, who has accomplished this great deliverance in Israel? Certainly not! As the LORD lives, not one hair of his head shall fall to the ground, for he has worked with God this day." So the people rescued Jonathan, and he did not die.

46 Then Saul returned from pursuing the Philistines, and the Philistines went to their own place.

*—1 Samuel 14:24–46*

Nowhere in the accounts of his reign does Saul come through with a more obvious desire to please God than in this chapter. Yet even his efforts to serve God continued to have a way of backfiring. A classic example is found in these verses. The first inkling that all was not well on this day of victory came in the shift in mood between verse 23, which tells how *"the LORD saved Israel that day,"* and the next verse which states, *"And the men of Israel were distressed that day"* (v. 24). The cause of the concern was tied to an oath that Saul had given the entire army—to fast the entire day. Saul's motives were good and his actions were appropriate for such a desperate situation. The tragedy of Saul's oath was that instead of making the men so wholly dedicated to God that they were invigorated, they were so exhausted and famished that they grew faint. Consequently, Saul's act had the opposite effect. There were two situations that developed as a result which lessened the extent of the victory and also undermined Saul's leadership with the people. In retrospect his decision seemed rash. The existence of this account, and others like it in the Scriptures, ought to remind all of us that even the most sincere people can make promises to God which stand in God's way for our lives.

One problem created by the oath was that when evening came and the fast was over, the people were so hungry that they slew and ate the flesh of the animals without observing the proper ritual (v. 32). Blood was the symbol of life, and they were forbidden to consume it. They were to pour it out as an offering to God. It was the latter that they were failing to do. Saul, who is pictured in this chapter as having great concern for God's law, quickly created an altar to God and had the people bring their animals there for slaughter before they prepared them for food (vv. 33–35). Even as they prepared their food, it was important for them to stop and acknowledge that the source of all life is God.

With that problem solved Saul discovered a much larger one. After the soldiers had eaten, Saul wanted to lead them on a nighttime raid of the Philistine camps to *"plunder them until the morning light"* (v. 36), but first he inquired of the priest. When he asked whether or not God would deliver the Philistines into their hands there was no answer (v. 37). The assumption was that the reason God did not answer was due to someone's sin against a divine command (v. 38). Saul, who has already made one rash oath in the call for the fast, makes another by saying *"though it be Jonathan my son, he shall surely die"* (v. 39). By the use of the casting of the lots, first eliminating the people and then Saul, it was determined that the guilty person was Jonathan (vv. 40–42).

Before this time the reader already knows that Jonathan was the one who violated the oath, though unwittingly (v. 27), and that he had been critical of the negative effect the oath had on the people and had called attention to how eating the honey had helped him (v. 29). When the lot fell to Jonathan, he first answered his father's question as to what he had done and then he submitted himself to the punishment without question. As in the story of Achan, where the sin of one person brought defeat to the whole nation (Josh. 7), so Jonathan's violating of the oath created a gulf between God and Israel.

We have breathed so much of the air of "individualism" that some may tend to find the whole story unfair. "Why should all suffer because of the sin of one?" we ask. What we have forgotten is that there is still a corporateness to life and the things which one person does, for good or evil, is still felt in the whole of society. I can still recall going to country revivals when I was a teenager where, if things were not going well, the evangelist would preach a sermon on a text such as this. The inference was that "someone in this church has sinned and it is preventing God from doing what He wants to do in this church." The church may turn away from the preacher who makes every occasion of worship a guilt trip, but it needs to recover the biblical concept of corporate responsibility among the people of God.

Saul would have sacrificed his son (v. 44), but the people intervened. They reasoned that God had shown divine favor on Jonathan in using him to accomplish *"this great deliverance"* (v. 45). This brought into conflict God's divine use of Jonathan in battle and the divine displeasure for the infringement of Saul's oath. We are not told how the people *"rescued Jonathan"* (v. 45), only that he did not die. But the whole experience left the impression that Saul was much better equipped to be a soldier than to be a king.

## THE SUMMARY OF SAUL'S WARS

[47] So Saul established his sovereignty over Israel, and fought against all his enemies on every side, against Moab, against the people of Ammon, against Edom, against the kings of Zobah, and against the Philistines. Wherever he turned, he harassed them. [48] And he gathered an army and attacked the Amalekites, and delivered Israel from the hands of those who plundered them.

[49] The sons of Saul were Jonathan, Jishui, and Malchishua. And the names of his two daughters were these: the name of the firstborn Merab, and the name of the younger Michal. [50] The name of Saul's wife was Ahinoam the daughter of Ahimaaz. And the name of the commander

of his army was Abner the son of Ner, Saul's uncle. [51] Kish was the father of Saul, and Ner the father of Abner was the son of Abiel.

[52] Now there was fierce war with the Philistines all the days of Saul. And when Saul saw any strong man or any valiant man, he took him for himself.

*—1 Samuel 14:47–52*

These verses at the end of the chapter detail the way in which Saul *"established his sovereignty over Israel"* (v. 47), and it lists all the foes he did battle with: the Moabites, Ammonites, Edomites, Zobarites, Philistines, and Amalekites. My mother was taught American geography in a small one-room school by "bounding the state." The teacher would call the name of a state and the pupil would have to name all the states that touched its borders. The list of those with whom Saul went to war is a list of those who touch Israel's borders.

The other verses give details about Saul's family (vv. 49–51). Of those listed, his daughter Michal would later become David's wife; his son Jonathan would become David's best friend; and his commander Abner would be in conflict with David by trying to place Saul's son upon the throne. But the message that the listing in these verses communicated was that Saul was consolidating Israel into a nation through his wars and through his enlarging family.

The chapter closes with a reminder that *"there was fierce war with the Philistines all the days of Saul"* (v. 52). His life was defined by fighting, but in the establishing of the monarchy he served an important purpose. It is in the next chapter that the tension that began with Samuel at Gilgal comes to a head and results in a tragic break between the two leaders and Saul's rejection as king.

# THE STORY OF SAUL AND DAVID

## *1 SAMUEL 15:1—31:1*

# Chapter Seven—The Beginning of the Decline of Saul's Dynasty

## 1 Samuel 15:1—17:58

*Scripture Outline*

The Superiority of Obedience (15:1–23)

When Repentance Is Too Late (15:24–35)

God's Unlikely Choices (16:1–13)

The Future King as a Servant (16:14–23)

The Giants That Intimidate (17:1–11)

Faith in the Family (17:12–29)

The Source of Confidence (17:30–40)

Claiming God's Victory (17:41–53)

Meeting the King (17:54–58)

Chapter 15 is one of the most dramatic chapters in 1 Samuel. It begins with a story that has troubled thoughtful Christians for years: God's instructing Saul to destroy the people of Amalek completely (vv. 2–3). On the surface the story seems to make God like those who created the Holocaust in Europe during World War II or the more recent "killing fields" of Southeast Asia or Kosovo. The way in which Saul carried out God's order becomes the basis of Saul's rejection as king (v. 11ff.), and a small theological problem is created for the reader with the idea of "God repenting" (v. 11). Samuel's prophetic statement on the priority of obeying God over religious observances (vv. 22–23) still stands as our best understanding of what pleases God. Saul's pleading with Samuel for forgiveness and reinstatement in God's favor is full of pathos and tragedy, climaxing with the final parting of the two, full of sadness for them personally and also for the nation as it will suffer while Saul functions without Samuel's counsel. As remote as the setting is from us, when this chapter is studied, it forces us to rethink our understanding of God, our approach to interpreting Scripture, and the ways in which we try to please God without obeying Him.

## THE SUPERIORITY OF OBEDIENCE

**15:1** Samuel also said to Saul, "The LORD sent me to anoint you king over His people, over Israel. Now therefore, heed the voice of the words of the LORD. [2] Thus says the LORD of hosts: 'I will punish Amalek for what he did to Israel, how he ambushed him on the way when he came up from Egypt. [3] Now go and attack Amalek, and utterly destroy all that they have, and do not spare them. But kill both man and woman, infant and nursing child, ox and sheep, camel and donkey.'"

[4] So Saul gathered the people together and numbered them in Telaim, two hundred thousand foot soldiers and ten thousand men of Judah. [5] And Saul came to a city of Amalek, and lay in wait in the valley.

[6] Then Saul said to the Kenites, "Go, depart, get down from among the Amalekites, lest I destroy you with them. For you showed kindness to all the children of Israel when they came up out of Egypt." So the Kenites departed from among the Amalekites. [7] And Saul attacked the Amalekites, from Havilah all the way to Shur, which is east of Egypt. [8] He also took Agag king of the Amalekites alive, and utterly destroyed all the people with the edge of the sword. [9] But Saul and the people spared Agag and the best of the sheep, the oxen, the fatlings, the lambs, and all that was good, and were unwilling to utterly destroy them. But everything despised and worthless, that they utterly destroyed.

[10] Now the word of the LORD came to Samuel, saying, [11] "I greatly regret that I have set up Saul as king, for he has turned back from following Me, and has not performed My commandments." And it grieved Samuel, and he cried out to the LORD all night. [12] So when Samuel rose early in the morning to meet Saul, it was told Samuel, saying, "Saul went to Carmel, and indeed, he set up a monument for himself; and he has gone on around, passed by, and gone down to Gilgal." [13] Then Samuel went to Saul, and Saul said to him, "Blessed are you of the LORD! I have performed the commandment of the LORD."

14 But Samuel said, "What then is this bleating of the sheep in my ears, and the lowing of the oxen which I hear?"

15 And Saul said, "They have brought them from the Amalekites; for the people spared the best of the sheep and the oxen, to sacrifice to the LORD your God; and the rest we have utterly destroyed."

16 Then Samuel said to Saul, "Be quiet! And I will tell you what the LORD said to me last night."

And he said to him, "Speak on."

17 So Samuel said, "When you were little in your own eyes, were you not head of the tribes of Israel? And did not the LORD anoint you king over Israel? 18 Now the LORD sent you on a mission, and said, 'Go, and utterly destroy the sinners, the Amalekites, and fight against them until they are consumed.' 19 Why then did you not obey the voice of the LORD? Why did you swoop down on the spoil, and do evil in the sight of the LORD?"

20 And Saul said to Samuel, "But I have obeyed the voice of the LORD, and gone on the mission on which the LORD sent me, and brought back Agag king of Amalek; I have utterly destroyed the Amalekites. 21 But the people took of the plunder, sheep and oxen, the best of the things which should have been utterly destroyed, to sacrifice to the LORD your God in Gilgal."

22 So Samuel said:

"Has the LORD as great delight in burnt offerings and sacrifices,
As in obeying the voice of the LORD?
Behold, to obey is better than sacrifice,
And to heed than the fat of rams.
23 For rebellion is as the sin of witchcraft,
And stubbornness is as iniquity and idolatry.
Because you have rejected the word of the LORD,
He also has rejected you from being king."

*—1 Samuel 15:1–23*

While Saul was a warrior king, the battle described in this chapter was initiated by God and not Saul, thus making it what the Old Testament called a holy war. The object of the war was to punish a Bedouin tribe for what it had done to Israel as it made its way from Egypt to the Promised Land (v. 2). After they had attacked Israel during the Exodus period, God had promised

Moses that He was resolved to "blot out the remembrance of Amalek from under heaven," and an altar was built and an oath taken that the Lord would be at war with Amalek "generation to generation" (Ex. 17:14–16). When Moses delivered God's laws to the people, he reminded them that once they had peace on every side from their enemies then they were to "blot out the remembrance of the Amalek from under heaven" (Deut. 25:17–19).

God's instruction to Saul through Samuel was to *"utterly destroy all that they have, and do not spare them"* (v. 3). No person or animal was to be left alive, and it was to be done as an act of obedience to God. This war of extermination has been referred to as "putting under the ban." This made the war a sacred act, so Saul and his warriors did not think of themselves as slaughtering the Amalekites but as delivering them up to God. This idea of the holy war was prevalent among the nations at the time and there exist copies of dedications of such battles to the nation's gods.

To many Christians today, this whole story is barbaric and seems to stand in such contrast to the ethics of Jesus Christ who commanded that his followers "Love your enemies, do good to those who hate you" (Luke 6:27). The contrast between this picture of God and the one who is revealed in Jesus Christ led some early Christian scholars to wonder if they were really the same God. That conclusion was rejected by the church, but later scholars tried to help our understanding of certain Old Testament concepts with the idea of "progressive revelation," that God's self-revelation was a gradual process.

In more recent years scholars have helped us by developing principles for interpreting the Scriptures. Two very basic principles would apply here. First, always study a passage in its historical and cultural context. When this is done with this passage, the event teaches us about Israel's early history and of her development of her understanding of God's mission in the world. For an Iran or a United States or any nation to believe that it was an instrument of God in an armed conflict could never find its justification by reference to this Scripture. The second principle is that when applying any teaching of the Bible to life, the teaching must be taken at its highest point of revelation. This makes what God has revealed in Jesus Christ the ultimate basis of interpreting the rest of the Bible.

After first warning the Kenites (v. 6), who had been friendly to Israel during her Exodus and were related to Moses' father-in-law, Saul attacked the enemy and *"utterly destroyed all the people with the edge of the sword"* (v. 8). But in spite of very specific instruction from God through Samuel, he spared Agag, the king, and some of the prize animals (v. 9). No reason is given for sparing the king. Saul was certainly not driven by humanitarian motives. The later explanation for the animals was that they were to be kept as a special offering to God. Under the conditions of the ban, everything that was destroyed was holy unto God, so this is not consistent. It seems that they dedicated to God the worthless and kept for themselves that which was good.

Samuel received word of Saul's disobedience from God, telling him, *"I greatly regret that I have set up Saul as king"* (vv. 10–11). What the New King James translates as "I greatly regret" is elsewhere translated "I repent." For us this phrase means that we have done wrong, are admitting it, and are prepared to turn from it. The picture isn't of God's suggesting that He had made a mistake in choosing Saul. Saul was chosen, but in the exercise of his freedom he had failed to measure up to the demands of the office. Now God found it necessary to seek someone else to carry out His purpose through Israel. The call of God is always related to His purpose and is never separated from the responsibility of our obedience to God.

Early in my Christian life I thought of God's will for my life as a builder might think of a set of specifications which an architect had drawn for a house. But as I came to know God better and became more honest about myself, I realized that this was a more dynamic relationship than that. There is a sense in which God is always having to design new contingencies for us as we fail to measure up in some area or another. There might be things that God wants done and plans to get done through me, but if for any reason I'm unwilling to live, believe, or do what God wants, then He might repent that He had chosen me and choose someone else to do what must be done. He would not quit loving me, but He couldn't continue to use me. This may have been the dynamic with Saul.

At this point in the story Samuel is the only one who knows that Saul has been rejected as king, and he is angry. The basic meaning of the word translated "grieved" is "to be hot" and is often translated "was angry." It's not certain whether he was angry with Saul for his disobedience or with God for His judgment on Saul, but *"he cried out to the LORD all night"* (v. 11). Because the prophet was often seen confronting Saul with the word of the Lord, we are apt to miss those times when the prophet cried unto God on behalf of Israel. This is a beautiful picture of Samuel as an intercessor. In the midst of his anger and frustration, he pleaded Saul's case before God, but to no avail.

While Samuel was agonizing in prayer, Saul was building a monument to himself at Carmel—probably memorializing the victory over the Amalekites (v. 12). When the two met, if Saul had any inkling that he was in trouble with God, it didn't show. His greeting was *"Blessed are you of the LORD! 1 have performed the commandment of the LORD"* (v. 13). Saul didn't seem to realize that Samuel's question about the *"bleating of the sheep"* was a reminder of God's strict instruction. There is a believable piety as Saul begins to tell Samuel about the religious purpose for which the animals had been saved (v. 15). Finally, Samuel can take no more and he shouts, *"Be quiet! And I will tell you what the LORD said to me last night"* (v. 16). Samuel's probe of his action took the form of a reminder of God's anointing and of his mission and concluded with *"Why then did you not obey the voice of the LORD?"* (v. 19)

In his defense of his actions, Saul continued to insist that he had obeyed God but blamed the people for the plunder. He still insisted that his only motive was to *"sacrifice to the LORD your God in Gilgal"* (v. 21). Saul seemed oblivious to the fact that in this single act of disobedience he had built a wall between himself and God, had estranged himself from Samuel, and had wasted his opportunity as king.

Samuel finally broke through Saul's effort to rationalize his disobedience with his famous speech that we have often reduced to six words: *"To obey is better than sacrifice"* (v. 22) In verses 22–23 Samuel contrasts the inner reality of authentic religion with its external trappings. Long after Israel had ceased to have a problem with idolatry, she still had a tendency to prize the external in religion, whether that be sacrificing in the temple or keeping the external demands of the law.

There are aspects of chapter 15 that have little contemporary relevance, but Samuel's word to Saul concerning what delights God is a word for today, probing our inadequate views of religion. Like Saul we are still more interested in "sacrifice" than "obedience." This inversion of religious priorities has created a nation that has experienced a religious revival at the same time it has experienced an eroding of personal and corporate morality and ethical living. There are cities where there is great poverty, unemployment, hunger, and oppression. Often in the midst of such need are found religious institutions with multimillion dollar budgets, expensive television ministries, country-club type accommodations for its members, and a pulpit pumping out a gospel of health and wealth. But the more common sin for us all is simply to equate going to church with pleasing God. We forget that God has always been more interested in our character than our liturgy and more impressed by our compassion than our doctrine.

To a Saul who found it difficult to believe that he had done anything wrong, Samuel connected his act of rebellion with both witchcraft and idolatry. Samuel concludes his magnificent statement with *"Because you have rejected the word of the* LORD, / *He also has rejected you from being king"* (v. 23). It was only at this time that Saul began to fathom the depths of his troubles. His response was predictable but too late.

## WHEN REPENTANCE IS TOO LATE

24 Then Saul said to Samuel, "I have sinned, for I have transgressed the commandment of the LORD and your words, because I feared the people and obeyed their voice.
25 Now therefore, please pardon my sin, and return with me, that I may worship the LORD."
26 But Samuel said to Saul, "I will not return with you, for you have rejected the word of the LORD, and the LORD has rejected you from being king over Israel."
27 And as Samuel turned around to go away, Saul seized the edge of his robe, and it tore. 28 So Samuel said to him, "The LORD has torn the kingdom of Israel from you today, and has given it to a neighbor of yours, who is better than you. 29 And also the Strength of Israel will not lie nor relent. For He is not a man, that He should relent."
30 Then he said, "I have sinned; yet honor me now, please, before the elders of my people and before Israel, and return with me, that I may worship the LORD your God." 31 So Samuel turned back after Saul, and Saul worshiped the LORD.
32 Then Samuel said, "Bring Agag king of the Amalekites here to me." So Agag came to him cautiously.
And Agag said, "Surely the bitterness of death is past."
33 But Samuel said, "As your sword has made women childless, so shall your mother be childless among women." And Samuel hacked Agag in pieces before the LORD in Gilgal.
34 Then Samuel went to Ramah, and Saul went up to his house at Gibeah of Saul. 35 And Samuel went no more to see Saul until the day of his death. Nevertheless Samuel

mourned for Saul, and the LORD regretted that He had made Saul king over Israel.

*—1 Samuel 15:24–35*

The title that I have given the last verses of this chapter may make some readers slightly uncomfortable and I can understand why. Most of us like to think that however serious our disobedience, once we repent of that sin, we are forgiven and experience no real loss. The Scripture teaches that genuine repentance always meets forgiveness, but it does not teach that there are no losses. Actually, every reflective Christian knows of permanent losses that are the result of our failure to live up to God's ideals for our lives.

Even after Saul realized that he had sinned, he tended to minimize its seriousness. He used as his excuse his fear of the people (v. 24). In describing his sin, he used a word that clearly means a failing which could be forgiven in the usual manner (v. 25). It is a common human frailty that we try to blame others for our sins, and when this isn't possible, we try to minimize the importance of our transgression. He could not believe Samuel's refusal to return with him and was told again *"for you have rejected the word of the LORD, and the LORD has rejected you from being king over Israel"* (v. 26).

When Samuel moved to leave, Saul grabbed his robe and it tore. Samuel used it as a symbol of what had happened to the kingdom— *"The LORD has torn the kingdom of Israel from you today"* (v. 28). When Saul pled with Samuel to return with him, Samuel relented and went, but it changed nothing. At the close of the sacrifice Samuel finished the task that Saul had been given by slaying Agag, the king. Afterward the two men went to their separate homes.

One of the saddest verses in the Bible is the last verse in this chapter. Saul continued to be king of Israel for the rest of his life, but Samuel never saw him again. While Samuel was the prophet through whom the word of judgment came, he suffered under the punishment. One of the characteristics of the true prophet is that he finds no joy in the word of judgment. The Scripture pictured Samuel as mourning for Saul.

## GOD'S UNLIKELY CHOICES

**16:1** Now the LORD said to Samuel, "How long will you mourn for Saul, seeing I have rejected him from reigning over Israel? Fill your horn with oil, and go; I am sending you to Jesse the Bethlehemite. For I have provided Myself a king among his sons."

² And Samuel said, "How can I go? If Saul hears it, he will kill me."

But the LORD said, "Take a heifer with you, and say, 'I have come to sacrifice to the LORD.' ³ Then invite Jesse to the sacrifice, and I will show you what you shall do; you shall anoint for Me the one I name to you."

⁴ So Samuel did what the LORD said, and went to Bethlehem. And the elders of the town trembled at his coming, and said, "Do you come peaceably?"

⁵ And he said, "Peaceably; I have come to sacrifice to the LORD. Sanctify yourselves, and come with me to the sacrifice." Then he consecrated Jesse and his sons, and invited them to the sacrifice.

⁶ So it was, when they came, that he looked at Eliab and said, "Surely the LORD's anointed is before Him!"

⁷ But the LORD said to Samuel, "Do not look at his appearance or at his physical stature, because I have refused him. For the LORD does not see as man sees; for man looks at the outward appearance, but the LORD looks at the heart."

⁸ So Jesse called Abinadab, and made him pass before Samuel. And he said, "Neither has the LORD chosen this one." ⁹ Then Jesse made Shammah pass by. And he said, "Neither has the LORD chosen this one." ¹⁰ Thus Jesse made seven of his sons pass before Samuel. And Samuel said to Jesse, "The LORD has not chosen these." ¹¹ And Samuel said to Jesse, "Are all the young men here?" Then he said, "There remains yet the youngest, and there he is, keeping the sheep."

And Samuel said to Jesse, "Send and bring him. For we will not sit down till he comes here." ¹² So he sent and brought him in. Now he was ruddy, with bright eyes, and good-looking. And the LORD said, "Arise, anoint him; for this is the one!" ¹³ Then Samuel took the horn of oil and anointed him in the midst of his brothers; and the Spirit of the LORD came upon David from that day forward. So Samuel arose and went to Ramah.

*—1 Samuel 16:1–13*

Chapter 16 begins that part of 1 Samuel which tells of both Saul and David. It covers the rest of 1 Samuel and the first chapter of 2 Samuel (1 Sam. 16:1—2 Sam. 1:27). These chapters chronicle the deterioration of Saul who, though he has been rejected by God, still reigns. They also tell the story of the development of David from the shepherd lad in his father's house to his place as the shepherd king of Israel. While the events take place in a more primitive setting than ours, there is insight to be gained as we watch God relating to nations and to individuals in order to work out His eternal purpose for creation.

This particular chapter follows God's rejection of Saul (1 Sam. 15:23, 26) with the choosing and anointing of the one who will eventually be his successor (vv. 1–13) and also tells of David's first contact with Saul and his household (vv. 14–23). Chapter 16 contains, as a part of God's guidance of Samuel to a new king, one of the most familiar verses in the Old Testament, *"for man looks at the outward appearance, but the LORD looks at the heart"* (v. 7).

The first verse ties the account to the previous chapter, for in both of them Samuel is mourning for Saul (1 Sam. 15:35; 16:1). Part of his grief was caused by his love for Saul and his family and some of it must have been tied to his anxiety about what would happen to the country, so recently united. Like most people, Samuel tried to hold on to the past. He had a hard time abandoning the era of the judges in order to establish the monarchy. Now with Saul's kingship having been rejected by God, he mourns Saul. God did two things for Samuel. He reminded Samuel that he needed to accept God's judgment of Saul. Then God pointed Samuel to the days ahead by involving him in the anointing of a king to succeed Saul.

Through the centuries, Christians have often been trapped by their inability to turn loose of those things which no longer seem to serve God's purpose. We grow accustomed to institutions, organizations, programs, ways of thinking, and ways of doing things. We develop such an emotional attachment to them that long after their usefulness to God is past we hold tenaciously to them. Sometimes the hardest thing to get rid of is something that no longer meets a need. We often need help from God to turn loose of what is past and to face the future that God has planned for us.

This second king was not to come at the insistence of the people but at God's own initiative, for even before giving His instructions to Samuel God had chosen the tribe, the family, and the particular member of the family (v. 1). Unlike Saul, who was a Benjaminite, the new king would be from the tribe of Judah, and his lineage would be connected with the coming of Jesus Christ, God's eternal King.

Samuel's fear was natural. Bethlehem was not a part of his regular territory. And traveling from Ramah he would have to travel though Gibeah, which was Saul's home. A man of Samuel's power and influence could not make such a trip without someone reading into it political implications. So Samuel was given a cover story. He was to take a heifer with him and make a sacrifice to Jehovah in Bethlehem (v. 2). This would allow the anointing of a new king to be done without creating unnecessary anxiety. It also proved to be a helpful move in relieving the anxiety of the elders of the city who *"trembled at his coming"* (v. 4), either not wanting to be caught up in a conflict between the king and the prophet or fearing that Samuel may have come with some word of judgment against them.

It's not known whether the call to *"Sanctify yourselves"* (v. 5) was issued to all the elders of the city or just to the family of Jesse. Because the main focus of the account is on the anointing of a new king, we are not told. We are told that Samuel *"consecrated Jesse and his sons, and invited them to the sacrifice"* (v. 5). But before they made their procession round the altar, Samuel wanted to take care of the business for which he had come. He thought that he had before him all the sons of Jesse, so as he viewed them he imagined that in one of them he was looking upon Israel's next king.

The eldest, Eliab, was a striking looking person who may have reminded Samuel of Saul. When Samuel saw Eliab he felt sure that he must be *"the LORD's anointed"* (v. 6) but was told by God that Eliab had been rejected. The reminder that God looks at people and situations and circumstances differently than human beings do (v. 7) gives an insight into the nature of God that we need to remember more often. Like Samuel, we are too impressed by the things that can be seen with the physical eyes. Consequently we live in a world where physical beauty outranks spiritual depth, where success in business and in church tends to be defined in materialistic terms, and where charisma is prized above character. As a result we are often moved to pick leaders more by the images their managers can create on television than by the character of the person or a candidate's stand on the issues that really matter. We need, with God's help, to learn to look upon the inward qualities.

Samuel worked his way through all seven sons of Jesse, getting the same message from God each time, *Neither has the LORD chosen this one"* (vv. 8, 9, 10). It was only after inquiring directly of Jesse that Samuel learned that the youngest son, David, was tending the sheep. So, like Saul who at the time of his choice was not present but with the baggage, David has to be called from his task of tending his father's sheep to be anointed the new shepherd of Israel.

The choice of the least likely person, from a human perspective, is a theme found throughout the Bible. The apostle Paul, in discussing the gospel of Christ, contends that God has always made choices that have surprised the world (1 Cor. 1:26–28). The study of church history or the study of the history of any congregation will usually reveal that God has often worked His purpose through some very unlikely choices.

When David was brought in, while God's interest lay in his heart, he is described as *"good-looking."* Samuel was instructed to anoint him and he did (v. 13). It was probably a secret anointing, marking the person who was to be king eventually. In the final verse of this section, we find the clue to David's success in the statement that *"the Spirit of the LORD came upon David from that day forward"* (v. 13).

In the Old Testament, the Spirit of the Lord came mainly on prophets and kings. In the New Testament, the apostles preached that those who repented and were baptized were not only forgiven of their sins but would receive the "gift of the Holy Spirit" (Acts 2:38). In the letter to the Corinthians Paul wrote to believers that "the manifestation of the Spirit is given to each one for the profit of all" (1 Cor. 12:7). Just as the Spirit of the Lord came to empower David to reign over Israel, the Spirit of God dwells in those who believe to create in us joy, love, and peace, which are the fruits of the Spirit (Gal. 5:22–23).

It's a long way from Bethlehem, where David was anointed, to Hebron, where he finally ascended the throne. As the story unfolds in the next seventeen chapters there are intrigues, battles, and alliances. But this short account is placed at the beginning of David's relationship with Saul as a reminder that more important than anything else is the fact that David was chosen of God. It's always as God touches our lives that our lives become truly significant.

## THE FUTURE KING AS A SERVANT

14 But the Spirit of the LORD departed from Saul, and a distressing spirit from the LORD troubled him. 15 And Saul's servants said to him, "Surely, a distressing spirit from God is troubling you. 16 Let our master now command your servants, who are before you, to seek out a man who is a skillful player on the harp. And it shall be that he will play it with his hand when the distressing spirit from God is upon you, and you shall be well."

17 So Saul said to his servants, "Provide me now a man who can play well, and bring him to me."

18 Then one of the servants answered and said, "Look, I have seen a son of Jesse the Bethlehemite, who is skillful in playing, a mighty man of valor, a man of war, prudent in speech, and a handsome person; and the LORD is with him."

19 Therefore Saul sent messengers to Jesse, and said, "Send me your son David, who is with the sheep." 20 And Jesse took a donkey loaded with bread, a skin of wine, and a young goat, and sent them by his son David to Saul. 21 So David came to Saul and stood before him. And he loved him greatly, and he became his armorbearer. 22 Then Saul sent to Jesse, saying, "Please let David stand before me, for he has found favor in my sight." 23 And so it was, whenever the spirit from God was upon Saul, that David would take a harp and play it with his hand. Then Saul would become refreshed and well, and the distressing spirit would depart from him.

*—1 Samuel 16:14–23*

These verses begin with the story of a devastating loss on Saul's part, the *"Spirit of the LORD departed from Saul"* (v. 14). The divine presence had been given to guide and empower him as the king, and now that God had rejected Saul, the Spirit was removed. He remained king for the rest of his life, but he no longer knew the power and presence of God in his life nor did he receive words from God through the prophet. We do not know how conscious he was of his condition. He could have been like Samson after his hair was cut, unaware that the strength had gone from him. There is no emptiness that compares to the life from whom God has withdrawn.

Into the void of Saul's life *"a distressing spirit from the LORD troubled him"* (v. 14). At the time, it was commonly believed that all physical and mental illness was caused by evil spirits. The Israelites were so frightened of dualism (the idea that good and evil have different sources) that whatever happened was attributed to God. This is why the cause given for Pharaoh's changing his mind about freeing the people was that God had hardened his heart (Ex. 7:3). It was their way of insisting that God was sovereign in all things. In this verse, Saul's mental illness is given as a sign that the Spirit of the Lord had left him.

His servants were concerned for Saul and suggested that having someone to play the harp when he was ill might be good therapy for him (vv. 15–16). Music was believed, even then, to have power to soothe and to heal. The suggestion seemed good to Saul who instructed the servants to *"Provide me now a man who can play well, and bring him to me"* (v. 17). At that point, another servant remembers someone whom he thinks might be ideal. David is described as *"skillful in playing, a mighty man of valor, a man of war, prudent in speech, and a handsome person; and the LORD is with him"* (v. 18).

The David whom Samuel met at the house of Jesse and the David who confronted Goliath in the next chapter are pictured differently. That he was more than a musician would have interested Saul since he was constantly on the lookout for "any valiant man" (1 Sam. 14:52). The most telling phrase in the description of David was "and the LORD is with him."

Saul immediately sent messengers to Jesse, asking for David to be sent (v. 19). The request was honored and, with his son, Jesse sent an offering of bread, wine, and a young goat for the king (v. 20). Saul was so impressed with David that he made him his armorbearer and asked permission from Jesse for David to stay with him. The chapter closes with a beautiful picture of David comforting Saul in his times of illness by playing the harp, a small handheld lyre. There seems to be no knowledge on Saul's part that Samuel has anointed David and, as yet, there is no resentment of his new friend.

The chapter closes with the king who has been rejected bringing to minister to him in times of mental distress the very person whom God has chosen to succeed him.

## THE GIANTS THAT INTIMIDATE

**17:1** Now the Philistines gathered their armies together to battle, and were gathered at Sochoh, which belongs to Judah; they encamped between Sochoh and Azekah, in Ephes Dammim. ² And Saul and the men of Israel were gathered together, and they encamped in the Valley of Elah, and drew up in battle array against the Philistines. ³ The Philistines stood on a mountain on one side, and Israel stood on a mountain on the other side, with a valley between them.
⁴ And a champion went out from the camp of the Philistines, named Goliath, from Gath, whose height was six cubits and a span. ⁵ He had a bronze helmet on his head, and he was armed with a coat of mail, and the weight of the coat was five thousand shekels of bronze. ⁶ And he had bronze

armor on his legs and a bronze javelin between his shoulders. [7] Now the staff of his spear was like a weaver's beam, and his iron spearhead weighed six hundred shekels; and a shield-bearer went before him. [8] Then he stood and cried out to the armies of Israel, and said to them, "Why have you come out to line up for battle? Am I not a Philistine, and you the servants of Saul? Choose a man for yourselves, and let him come down to me. [9] If he is able to fight with me and kill me, then we will be your servants. But if I prevail against him and kill him, then you shall be our servants and serve us." [10] And the Philistine said, "I defy the armies of Israel this day; give me a man, that we may fight together." [11] When Saul and all Israel heard these words of the Philistine, they were dismayed and greatly afraid.

*—1 Samuel 17:1–11*

This chapter contains one of best-known and most loved stories in the entire Bible—the story of young David's defeat of the Philistine giant Goliath. The story has embedded itself in the culture and language of the nations of the world. It is so well known that it has become the way of describing any conflict in which there is a marked disparity between the combatants, whether describing athletes, companies, or nations. The phrase, "It was a David-and-Goliath situation" creates a certain image, and this story is the source of that picture.

The story has a special appeal for Christians. Part of the attraction is the natural support of the underdog. But a larger reason for its popularity is that so many identify with the whole situation. They are constantly challenged in their lives by the giants of the world, and they find courage and inspiration in David's unspoiled idealism and in his faith in God. Unfortunately most people, even though they have a general knowledge of the story, have never really studied it carefully. As a result they aren't able to see the role this incident played in the rise of David and of his relationship with Saul.

While these verses are given to set the scene for the combat between David and Goliath, they tell much more. First, they give a vivid illustration of the change after the "Spirit of the LORD departed from Saul" (1 Sam. 16:14). This passage tells the story of a time when the Philistines and Israel had gathered to do battle. It was probably a localized incident of a war that heated up from time to time between Israel and the Philistines. The two groups faced each other across a valley for forty days. But instead of both forces engaging in combat, each morning one of the Philistines had walked into the valley and challenged the Israelites to send forth someone who would fight him on behalf of the entire army. The concept of a single combat replacing combat between armies was known in those times. While it was part of a different age, it still fascinates people.

It wasn't the idea of settling the fate of the many in a battle between two representatives that frightened the Israelites. It was the representative whom the Philistines sent—Goliath. He was nine feet tall. I have stood next to a seven-foot basketball player and felt dwarfed by his presence. The weight of the giant's armor exceeded a hundred pounds and the spear he carried had a head which weighed sixteen pounds. His very presence struck fear into the hearts of the Israelites. The storyteller took more words to describe his armor than to describe the battle (vv. 4–7). To this very day, people continue to be interested in weapons. Ours are more expensive and more dangerous, but our trust in them is the same as in these more primitive times described in these verses.

If his presence created fear, Goliath's words added shame to the fear. The speech that he gave each day for forty days, morning and evening, is recorded in verses 8–10 and it represented a challenge not just to the army of Israel but to the God of Israel. To either ignore the challenge or to decline it was a humiliation both to Israel and to her God. Yet the Scripture records, *"When Saul and all Israel heard these words of the Philistine, they were dismayed and greatly afraid"* (v. 11).

This is the difference that not having the Spirit of the Lord made. When Saul had been anointed, everyone had been struck by his size. When the spirit of God came upon him, he became a fearless warrior. But now, where there had previously been courage and daring, there was only caution and fear. Those challenges that seemed so possible in God's strength now appeared as impossible missions. And all Israel felt the way their leader did. This is also an example of what happens to a people when their leadership is frightened. There is no place where fear is more contagious than in a leader. It is sad to observe this in a nation and even sadder when it happens in the church.

The setting has now been set for the classic confrontation. The next verses bring David to the place where the armies are camped and introduces him to the situation.

## FAITH IN THE FAMILY

12 Now David was the son of that Ephrathite of Bethlehem Judah, whose name was Jesse, and who had eight sons. And the man was old, advanced in years, in the days of Saul. 13 The three oldest sons of Jesse had gone to follow Saul to the battle. The names of his three sons who went to the battle were Eliab the firstborn, next to him Abinadab, and the third Shammah. 14 David was the youngest. And the three oldest followed Saul. 15 But David occasionally went and returned from Saul to feed his father's sheep at Bethlehem.

16 And the Philistine drew near and presented himself forty days, morning and evening.

17 Then Jesse said to his son David, "Take now for your brothers an ephah of this dried grain and these ten loaves, and run to your brothers at the camp. 18 And carry these ten cheeses to the captain of their thousand, and see how your brothers fare, and bring back news of them." 19 Now Saul and they and all the men of Israel were in the Valley of Elah, fighting with the Philistines.

20 So David rose early in the morning, left the sheep with a keeper, and took the things and went as Jesse had commanded him. And he came to the camp as the army was going out to the fight and shouting for the battle. 21 For Israel and the Philistines had drawn up in battle array, army against army. 22 And David left his supplies in the hand of the supply keeper, ran to the army, and came and greeted his brothers. 23 Then as he talked with them, there was the champion, the Philistine of Gath, Goliath by name, coming up from the armies of the Philistines; and he spoke according to the same words. So David heard them. 24 And all the men of Israel, when they saw the man, fled from him and were dreadfully afraid. 25 So the men of Israel said, "Have you seen this man who has come up? Surely he has come up to defy Israel; and it shall be that the man who kills him the king will enrich with great riches, will give him his daughter, and give his father's house exemption from taxes in Israel."

26 Then David spoke to the men who stood by him, saying, "What shall be done for the man who kills this Philistine and takes away the reproach from Israel? For who is this uncircumcised Philistine, that he should defy the armies of the living God?"

27 And the people answered him in this manner, saying, "So shall it be done for the man who kills him."

28 Now Eliab his oldest brother heard when he spoke to the men; and Eliab's anger was aroused against David, and he said, "Why did you come down here? And with whom have you left those few sheep in the wilderness? I know your pride and the insolence of your heart, for you have come down to see the battle."

29 And David said, "What have I done now? Is there not a cause?"

*—1 Samuel 17:12–29*

The scene now moves from the encampment of the two armies to David's home in Bethlehem. Jesse, his father, was old enough to be exempt from the army, but he was interested in a word about his three sons who were with Saul. Since the battle was stationary and there was no loot from which to provision the army, the soldiers made provisions for themselves, usually through their families. The occasion for David's hearing Goliath's challenge was when he brought food from home for his brothers. His father had sent parched grain and bread for his brothers and a token gift of cheese for the brothers' commanding officer (vv. 17–18). More than anything, Jesse wanted word about his sons and his parting word to David was to *"bring back news of them"* (v. 18). In a day of nuclear-powered submarines, satellite communications, and computer-guided missiles it's hard to realize that there were times, not long ago, when this was what war was like.

David left home very early and arrived at the camp just as the rival armies took their places on the opposite ridges and shouted at each other. Not wanting to miss anything, he left the food for his brothers with the quartermaster and ran to where his brothers were (vv. 20–22). He arrived in time to hear Goliath's speech and to observe the reaction of his brothers and the other Israelites (vv. 23–24). But when he is told by some of the men that Saul has promised a reward for the one who defeats the Philistine, David seemed less interested in the reward and more amazed that a heathen who worshiped Dagon should *"defy the armies of the living God"* (vv. 25–27).

Up to now everyone had been dealing with what they felt was a military problem. It was the shepherd lad, David, who raised the larger theological issue. And David's question irritated his brothers, who criticized the fact that he was there, that he had left the sheep, and his motives for coming (v. 28). The spirit of the brothers is similar to that of Joseph's brothers who held "the dreamer" in such contempt.

Even after considering the normal rivalry between older and younger brothers, their reaction may have been caused by their sense of shame at being afraid and embarrassed because their baby brother had witnessed it. They probably pictured themselves as "realists" and David as "hopelessly naive," but there was something in his spirit that convicted them. There is a sense in which people who see things clearly are never liked by those who are blind to what is going on. Had Samuel listened to Eliab talk to David, he would have known why God had said of Eliab, "I have refused him" (1 Sam. 16:7).

## THE SOURCE OF CONFIDENCE

30 Then he turned from him toward another and said the same thing; and these people answered him as the first ones did.

31 Now when the words which David spoke were heard, they reported them to Saul; and he sent for him.
32 Then David said to Saul, "Let no man's heart fail because of him; your servant will go and fight with this Philistine."

33 And Saul said to David, "You are not able to go against this Philistine to fight with him; for you are a youth, and he a man of war from his youth."

34 But David said to Saul, "Your servant used to keep his father's sheep, and when a lion or a bear came and took a lamb out of the flock, 35 I went out after it and struck it, and delivered the lamb from its mouth; and when it arose against me, I caught it by its beard, and struck and killed it. 36 Your servant has killed both lion and bear; and this uncircumcised Philistine will be like one of them, seeing he has defied the armies of the living God." 37 Moreover David said, "The LORD, who delivered me from the paw of the lion and from the paw of the bear, He will deliver me from the hand of this Philistine."

And Saul said to David, "Go, and the LORD be with you!"

38 So Saul clothed David with his armor, and he put a bronze helmet on his head; he also clothed him with a coat of mail. 39 David fastened his sword to his armor and tried to walk, for he had not tested them. And David said to Saul, "I cannot walk with these, for I have not tested them." So David took them off.

⁴⁰ Then he took his staff in his hand; and he chose for himself five smooth stones from the brook, and put them in a shepherd's bag, in a pouch which he had, and his sling was in his hand. And he drew near to the Philistine.

*—1 Samuel 17:30–40*

Turning from his brothers who were unequipped to understand, David began to raise the same question with others, getting the same answer from everyone (v. 30). His spirit created enough interest that the word of his presence came to Saul who sent for him (v. 31). It was to Saul that David announced his offer to fight the giant (v. 32), and the king tried to discourage him. His reasoning made sense: Saul contrasted David's youth with Goliath's professionalism (v. 33). David dealt with this obstacle by telling how he had killed both a lion and a bear as he protected his father's sheep.

The clue to David's confidence was shown in his interpretation of those battles when applied to the one he was about to enter. The reason David felt that the Philistine would meet the same fate at his hands as had the lion and the bear was that *"The LORD, who delivered me from the paw of the lion and from the paw of the bear, He will deliver me from the hand of this Philistine"* (v. 37). David's great confidence did not come from his ability, or even from past experiences, but from the feeling that the battle was one in which God would be with him. The speech David made was similar to the one Saul's son, Jonathan, had made to his armor-bearer earlier (1 Sam. 14:6). I wonder if David's impassioned speech to the king stirred memories in Saul of himself at another time. Memories of days when we were more in fellowship with God can be haunting memories.

Whether it was not having had any other volunteer or that something in David's spirit impressed Saul, he gave him permission to represent Israel and meet the giant with the prayer *"the LORD be with you"* (v. 37). Then he made a gesture that was very moving, even though it was not helpful. He offered David his own armor. Since only the king and his son possessed full battle dress, this was a most generous offer. David dressed himself in it and tried walking around in it, but found it difficult. It was probably much too large for him, but its main drawback was that he had no experience using such weapons. He wisely refused them saying, *"I have not tested them"* (v. 39).

Saul's effort to help David has been copied by many since then. Nothing comes more naturally to people than trying to get someone to fight our battles the way we would were we fighting them. Through the centuries that Christians have been reading this story they have been moved by the wisdom of David for not trying to do battle with someone else's armor. People need to have confidence in their own gifts, experiences, and abilities if they are to face the giants in their lives.

David went into battle equipped just as he had come into the camp that morning, with the staff of a shepherd and his sling. The only additions were five smooth stones that he picked up from the bed of the stream as he went out to face Goliath (v. 40). His hidden weapon was the confidence that God was going to deliver the Philistine into his hands. It was this weapon that kept him from being frightened and gave to him a holy boldness.

## CLAIMING GOD'S VICTORY

41 So the Philistine came, and began drawing near to David, and the man who bore the shield went before him. 42 And when the Philistine looked about and saw David, he disdained him; for he was only a youth, ruddy and good-looking. 43 So the Philistine said to David, "Am I a dog, that you come to me with sticks?" And the Philistine cursed David by his gods. 44 And the Philistine said to David, "Come to me, and I will give your flesh to the birds of the air and the beasts of the field!"

45 Then David said to the Philistine, "You come to me with a sword, with a spear, and with a javelin. But I come to you in the name of the LORD of hosts, the God of the armies of Israel, whom you have defied. 46 This day the LORD will deliver you into my hand, and I will strike you and take your head from you. And this day I will give the carcasses of the camp of the Philistines to the birds of the air and the wild beasts of the earth, that all the earth may know that there is a God in Israel. 47 Then all this assembly shall know that the LORD does not save with sword and spear; for the battle is the LORD's, and He will give you into our hands."

48 So it was, when the Philistine arose and came and drew near to meet David, that David hurried and ran toward the army to meet the Philistine. 49 Then David put his hand in his bag and took out a stone; and he slung it and struck the Philistine in his forehead, so that the stone sank into his forehead, and he fell on his face to the earth. 50 So David prevailed over the Philistine with a sling and a stone, and

struck the Philistine and killed him. But there was no sword in the hand of David. [51] Therefore David ran and stood over the Philistine, took his sword and drew it out of its sheath and killed him, and cut off his head with it.

And when the Philistines saw that their champion was dead, they fled. [52] Now the men of Israel and Judah arose and shouted, and pursued the Philistines as far as the entrance of the valley and to the gates of Ekron. And the wounded of the Philistines fell along the road to Shaaraim, even as far as Gath and Ekron. [53] Then the children of Israel returned from chasing the Philistines, and they plundered their tents.

*—1 Samuel 17:41–53*

More space is given to the verbal combat than the actual physical battle. Goliath saw the shepherd's staff and mocked David, saying, *"Am I a dog, that you come to me with sticks?"* and he pronounced a curse on David *"by his gods"* (v. 43). He threatened not only to kill David but to leave his body unburied, so the buzzards and jackals could devour it (v. 44). The awesome presence and verbal threats that had spread fear through the camp of the Israelites didn't make the slightest dent in David's intentions.

David's speech to Goliath (vv. 45–47) was more of an announcement than a threat. First, he announced that their armor was different. David came, not with sword, spear, or javelin, but *"in the name of the LORD of hosts, the God of the armies of Israel, whom you have defied"* (v. 45). Second, he announced that God was about to deliver Goliath into his hand and promised that what Goliath had threatened to do to David's body would happen to all the Philistines (v. 46). Finally, he announced that the result would be that everyone would know that there *"is a God in Israel"* (v. 46) and that the battle was God's.

With the speeches over, they approached each other. The battle was over almost before it started. David took one of the smooth stones from his pouch and, with his sling, embedded the stone in the forehead of Goliath. The blow rendered him unconscious so David was able to step forth and use Goliath's own sword to sever his head (vv. 49–51). The shepherd lad had slain the warrior, with the help of his God. And he had done it with the ordinary tools of his trade.

## MEETING THE KING

[54] And David took the head of the Philistine and brought it to Jerusalem, but he put his armor in his tent.

<sup>55</sup> When Saul saw David going out against the Philistine, he said to Abner, the commander of the army, "Abner, whose son is this youth?"

And Abner said, "As your soul lives, O king, I do not know."

<sup>56</sup> So the king said, "Inquire whose son this young man is."

<sup>57</sup> Then, as David returned from the slaughter of the Philistine, Abner took him and brought him before Saul with the head of the Philistine in his hand. <sup>58</sup> And Saul said to him, "Whose son are you, young man?"

So David answered, "I am the son of your servant Jesse the Bethlehemite."

*—1 Samuel 17:54–58*

The theological point of the story of David and Goliath is so evident that a child can read the story and get the message. But some of the details of this chapter are so difficult to figure out that they baffle the most serious student of the Bible. David is said to have taken Goliath's head to Jerusalem and to have put the giant's armor in his tent (v. 54). At the time of this battle, the Israelites did not occupy Jerusalem, and if David had come from home to bring food to his brothers, he didn't have a tent. Also, the fact that neither Saul nor Abner seemed to know who David was (vv. 55–56) seems to contradict the previous chapter where David was brought to the king's court to play the harp for him (1 Sam. 16:21). Earlier in this chapter there seems to be an attempt to suggest some chronology to David's relationship with Saul by suggesting that David was spending time with Saul but returned home to "feed his father's sheep" (v. 15).

None of these are important to the main teaching of the account, and they illustrate what happens when the historian whom God used to compile all the different accounts blends different accounts in order to have the full story without being interested in sequence or in overlapping stories. It may be that we are more at fault for frequently having more interest in chronology than in theology and more interest in the vessel than in the treasure that it contains.

The next chapter gives the beginnings of one of the most noble friendships in the Bible, that of David and Jonathan. And the chapter starts graphing the deterioration of the relationship between David and Saul.

# CHAPTER EIGHT—THE WAR BETWEEN THE ANOINTEDS

## 1 SAMUEL 18:1—20:42

*Scripture Outline*
> When Success Breeds Envy (18:1–16)
> Openness and Trust Meet Deceit (18:17–30)
> Friends Who Intercede (19:1–7)
> When Family Intervenes (19:8–17)
> When the Spirit Distracts (19:18–24)
> When Friendships Are Tested (20:1–23)
> When Friends Are Loyal (20:24–42)

This is a section filled with wild contrasts. It tells of the beginning of the lifelong friendship of Saul's son with David, of the love of Saul's daughter for David, and of Saul's first attempt to kill David. Chapter 18 charts the early days of David's meteoric rise to fame in Israel and describes the beginnings of Saul's total deterioration. These verses describe the activities of a young man for whom everything brings success and a king who doesn't seem to be able to do anything right. The whole range of emotions is experienced in this chapter: friendship, love, celebration, envy, deceit, violence, and fear.

The casual reader of these chapters might wonder how it could be that Saul would on one day love and honor David and bring him into his house to live and then on the next day hate him and seek to kill him. If Saul were that unstable, it would be hard to understand how he could command sufficient respect of the people to lead the nation. The impression of things happening so quickly was created by having incidents which took place over a long period of time tied together as though one followed the other immediately. To make things even more confusing for the person who is trying to get a sense of lapsed time, often events which happened at different times are woven together into the same story. The reader needs to remember that the one whom God used to arrange these stories in the form in which we have them was mainly interested in telling the theological history of the founding of the monarchy. The eroding of Saul's relationship with David and his subsequent efforts to take his life should be seen as encompassing years and not months.

## WHEN SUCCESS BREEDS ENVY

**18:1** Now when he had finished speaking to Saul, the soul of Jonathan was knit to the soul of David, and Jonathan loved him as his own soul. <sup>2</sup> Saul took him that day, and would not let him go home to his father's house anymore. <sup>3</sup> Then Jonathan and David made a covenant, because he loved him as his own soul. <sup>4</sup> And Jonathan took off the robe that was on him and gave it to David, with his armor, even to his sword and his bow and his belt.

<sup>5</sup> So David went out wherever Saul sent him, and behaved wisely. And Saul set him over the men of war, and he was accepted in the sight of all the people and also in the sight of Saul's servants. <sup>6</sup> Now it had happened as they were coming home, when David was returning from the slaughter of the Philistine, that the women had come out of all the cities of Israel, singing and dancing, to meet King Saul, with tambourines, with joy, and with musical instruments. <sup>7</sup> So the women sang as they danced, and said:

"Saul has slain his thousands,
And David his ten thousands."

<sup>8</sup> Then Saul was very angry, and the saying displeased him; and he said, "They have ascribed to David ten thousands, and to me they have ascribed only thousands. Now what more can he have but the kingdom?" <sup>9</sup> So Saul eyed David from that day forward.

<sup>10</sup> And it happened on the next day that the distressing spirit from God came upon Saul, and he prophesied inside the house. So David played music with his hand, as at other times; but there was a spear in Saul's hand. <sup>11</sup> And Saul cast

the spear, for he said, "I will pin David to the wall!" But David escaped his presence twice.

12 Now Saul was afraid of David, because the LORD was with him, but had departed from Saul. 13 Therefore Saul removed him from his presence, and made him his captain over a thousand; and he went out and came in before the people. 14 And David behaved wisely in all his ways, and the LORD was with him. 15 Therefore, when Saul saw that he behaved very wisely, he was afraid of him. 16 But all Israel and Judah loved David, because he went out and came in before them.

—*1 Samuel 18:1–16*

The friendship between Jonathan and David is one of the most noble relationships in the Bible. Its beginnings are described here and it lasts their whole lives. The lament of David after the death of Jonathan reveals the bond between them (2 Sam. 1:17–27). Later David will remember his covenant with Jonathan by showing great kindness to Jonathan's crippled son, Mephibosheth (2 Sam. 9). During their lifetimes, this friendship will face trials and temptations, but it will grow and mature and be a source of comfort and strength to both Jonathan and David. And there are ways in which their relationship could serve as a model for building and nurturing significant friendships.

Friendships are often more a "gift" than a development. They are not necessarily formed along conventional lines of background, age, or social standing. The Scripture states that when David had finished speaking to Saul, *"the soul of Jonathan was knit to the soul of David"* (v. 1). In ways they were alike and in ways they were different. Jonathan was the prince of Israel, heir to the throne, and David was the son of Jesse, a keeper of sheep. But both were full of courage and idealism and faith. Yet this friendship, like all such relationships, was not the result of a great deal of thought or analysis. There was something in the chemistry of how they saw each other, the way they related to each other, the ease with which they communicated that created the soil in which their friendship could grow and develop.

But friendships cannot survive on just the right chemistry, they require commitments. The Bible pictures David and Jonathan as making a conscious commitment to each other, a solemn compact, *"a covenant"* (v. 3). The concept of friendship needs to be rescued from a too casual use and there need to be rights and duties.

Jonathan's gift was the seal of the covenant the two had made, and it had profound significance both in their relationship and as it pointed to David's future (v. 4). In a way, the gift anticipates the time when Jonathan will give up his right to the throne to his friend.

The gift prepared David for court and for battle. The friendship prepared him for a better life. Apart from God's love and forgiveness, Jonathan's friendship was the most precious gift David was ever given, because the gift was followed by faithfulness, unselfishness, and sacrifice. There is in each of us the need to have friends and the need to be a friend. And like most things that are valuable, these don't just happen. They have to be worked at. And when we do, our lives are enriched immeasurably.

But Saul was as captured by the charm of David as was his son and he *would not let him go home to his father's house anymore* (v. 2). He immediately put David in charge of a unit of soldiers, and he began to participate in the wars with the Philistines (vv. 5–6). At this point there is no indication that Saul knows that Samuel has already anointed David to be his successor nor is there any sign of jealousy. Saul is delighted to have an aide who is able to lead others, to win battles, and to be a friend to his son.

David was naturally popular with the army after the slaying of Goliath, and his popularity increased as he joined them in battle after battle. But he also came to be loved by *"Saul's servants,"* the people at court. Then and now, those people who find significance in their lives by serving the great are often very protective of the reputation of the one they serve and look with suspicion at anyone whose success might diminish their master. Their natural defensiveness has earned them the title of "the palace guard." Yet even this group loved David.

Eventually David was *"accepted in the sight of all the people"* (v. 5). The most natural reaction to a person who rises so far so fast is often negative, with the suggestion that the person is too ambitious or opportunistic. But this did not seem to be true of David, who was perceived to have *"behaved wisely"* (v. 5). The word that some translate "successful" is connected in Hebrew with the idea of success, wisdom, and prudence. Far from being a climber, David showed discretion and practical ability. While on the surface he was a lovable person who stole everyone's heart, underneath there was a keen awareness of God's loving purpose for Israel. He brought to the court the gifts of a born leader and a profound trust in the God who gave him the gifts.

It was the almost unanimous love of the people for David that drove a wedge between him and Saul. At a time when the soldiers came back from a victory over the Philistines, the women came out of *"all the cities of Israel, singing and dancing, to meet King Saul"* (v. 6). It was an occasion of joy and celebration and as they danced they chanted a verse:

> *"Saul has slain his thousands,*
> *And David his ten thousands."*
> (1 Sam. 18:7)

The song was not designed to disparage Saul but to celebrate the victories of their king and his aide. But the words went to Saul's heart like an arrow and he was very angry and was heard to say *"Now what more can he have but the kingdom?"* (v. 8).

The Scripture says that from that moment on Saul kept his eye on him (v. 9). For the first time, Saul begins to think of David, not as a faithful aide, but as a rival for the throne. The next day Saul made his first attempt on David's life, without success. Saul had one of the attacks to which he was so susceptible. While the translation says he "prophesied," the word literally means "to rave." As David played for him, Saul decided to use the spear in his hand to pin David to the wall and tried twice to kill David (vv. 10–11). The root of Saul's fear was *"because the LORD was with him* [David], *but had departed from Saul"* (v. 12).

What Saul could not do directly, he decided to try indirectly. He promoted David to be captain over a thousand soldiers, hoping that the Philistines would help him get rid of his rival. (It was a method David later used on Uriah the Hittite.) But throwing him out of the palace and into the danger of battle merely increased David's popularity with the army and with the people, and *"all Israel and Judah loved David"* (v. 16). The constant theme that connects each of David's exploits and victories is the phrase: *"David behaved wisely in all his ways, and the LORD was with him"* (v. 14). While there is yet much to come, the first half of this chapter gives us a glimpse at David's potential as a future leader of Israel.

## OPENNESS AND TRUST MEET DECEIT

17 Then Saul said to David, "Here is my older daughter Merab; I will give her to you as a wife. Only be valiant for me, and fight the LORD's battles." For Saul thought, "Let my

hand not be against him, but let the hand of the Philistines be against him."

18 So David said to Saul, "Who am I, and what is my life or my father's family in Israel, that I should be son-in-law to the king?" 19 But it happened at the time when Merab, Saul's daughter, should have been given to David, that she was given to Adriel the Meholathite as a wife.

20 Now Michal, Saul's daughter, loved David. And they told Saul, and the thing pleased him. 21 So Saul said, "I will give her to him, that she may be a snare to him, and that the hand of the Philistines may be against him." Therefore Saul said to David a second time, "You shall be my son-in-law today."

22 And Saul commanded his servants, "Communicate with David secretly, and say, 'Look, the king has delight in you, and all his servants love you. Now therefore, become the king's son-in-law.'"

23 So Saul's servants spoke those words in the hearing of David. And David said, "Does it seem to you a light thing to be a king's son-in-law, seeing I am a poor and lightly esteemed man?" 24 And the servants of Saul told him, saying, "In this manner David spoke."

25 Then Saul said, "Thus you shall say to David: 'The king does not desire any dowry but one hundred foreskins of the Philistines, to take vengeance on the king's enemies.'" But Saul thought to make David fall by the hand of the Philistines. 26 So when his servants told David these words, it pleased David well to become the king's son-in-law. Now the days had not expired; 27 therefore David arose and went, he and his men, and killed two hundred men of the Philistines. And David brought their foreskins, and they gave them in full count to the king, that he might become the king's son-in-law. Then Saul gave him Michal his daughter as a wife.

28 Thus Saul saw and knew that the LORD was with David, and that Michal, Saul's daughter, loved him; 29 and Saul was still more afraid of David. So Saul became David's enemy continually. 30 Then the princes of the Philistines went out to war. And so it was, whenever they went out, that David behaved more wisely than all the servants of Saul, so that his name became highly esteemed.

*—1 Samuel 18:17–30*

Once Saul's fear of David took control, almost all his dealings with David were designed to destroy him. There were no lengths to which Saul would not go. These verses begin with the offer of his daughter Merab to be David's wife (v. 17). This is probably done to honor the promise he had made to whomever killed Goliath (1 Sam. 17:25). It was a commitment the people all knew about and one that had to be kept. But Saul continued to hope that the Philistines would kill him in battle so that he wouldn't have to have him for a son-in-law (v. 17). When this failed to materialize, Saul withdrew his offer, and married Merab to another (v. 19).

Then Saul discovered that his daughter Michal loved David and decided that he could use that love against David (v. 21). Saul communicated the desire to have David as his son-in-law through servants, and David expressed reluctance since he was from a poor family. It was a custom for a groom to make a gift to the father of the bride to offset his loss in giving a daughter in marriage. The gift for the daughter of a king was totally beyond David's ability as the youngest son of a poor farmer. Instead of waiving the gift, as he could have easily done, Saul decided to use David's situation to create another chance to kill him. He sent word that he would accept as an adequate gift the foreskins of a hundred Philistines. The repugnant demand was designed to assure David's death. But David gathered some warriors around him and met double the king's demand (v. 27). Saul had no recourse but give Michal to be David's wife (v. 28).

The chapter closes on the same note that permeates it, that *"the LORD was with David"* (v. 28), and as a subtheme that *"Saul was still more afraid of David"* (v. 29). But as Saul tries harder to undermine, David rises higher and higher in the minds and hearts of the people (v. 30). The next chapter picks up Saul's open persecution of David and its effect on his own family and upon David. On the surface, there is the feeling that it would have been so much better had David been able to ascend to the throne without all the problems. But there is a sense in which the kind of people we are is determined not just by the friendships which we make, but by how we deal with the enemies we are given. David has enjoyed God's presence with him in all his victories. Now he must find that same God in persecution and eventually in exile.

## FRIENDS WHO INTERCEDE

**19:1** Now Saul spoke to Jonathan his son and to all his servants, that they should kill David; but Jonathan, Saul's son, delighted greatly in David. <sup>2</sup> So Jonathan told David, saying, "My father Saul seeks to kill you. Therefore please be on your guard until morning, and stay in a secret place and hide. <sup>3</sup> And I will go out and stand beside my father in the field where you are, and I will speak with my father about you. Then what I observe, I will tell you."

<sup>4</sup> Thus Jonathan spoke well of David to Saul his father, and said to him, "Let not the king sin against his servant, against David, because he has not sinned against you, and because his works have been very good toward you. <sup>5</sup> For he took his life in his hands and killed the Philistine, and the LORD brought about a great deliverance for all Israel. You saw it and rejoiced. Why then will you sin against innocent blood, to kill David without a cause?"

<sup>6</sup> So Saul heeded the voice of Jonathan, and Saul swore, "As the LORD lives, he shall not be killed." <sup>7</sup> Then Jonathan called David, and Jonathan told him all these things. So Jonathan brought David to Saul, and he was in his presence as in times past.

*—1 Samuel 19:1–7*

The theme continues of Saul attempting to destroy David while God continues to protect him. But in these three incidents, the human instruments through whom David is protected are two of Saul's children, Jonathan and Michal, and Samuel the prophet. Saul's obsession not only endangered David but divided his household.

While those close to Saul must have observed the gradual change that took place in his feelings about David, this is the first record of his openly saying that he wanted David killed. Prior to this, Saul had manipulated the circumstances of David's life in an effort to make him vulnerable to the Philistines. Even those who were aware of his previous effort to pin David to the wall with a spear might have blamed that on his mental illness and told themselves that the violent action did not represent Saul's true feelings. From hoping the Philistines would kill him, to trying to kill David himself, Saul has now come to the place that he tries to involve his son and his servants in the murder.

Jonathan's action was wise and loving and courageous. He first warned his friend (vv. 2–3). There is some confusion as to where they met or what the instruction was to David, but it is clear that Jonathan was willing to risk a great deal to protect his friend. The king had absolute power over his subjects, and to help one whom the king considered to be his enemy was a treasonable act. Had there been even a shred of jealousy or envy toward David in Jonathan's heart, it would have been such an easy thing to rationalize not taking the risk involved in saving his friend. To will for another what is best for them, whatever the cost to self, is what true love is.

The second thing that Jonathan did was to plead with his father on David's behalf (vv. 4–5). This took courage because those in power seldom like to be challenged in their judgment and those who question their decisions are apt to be accused of disloyalty. In this case, Jonathan could have been accused of treason. The approach was direct and honest. Jonathan insisted that to do David harm would be a *"sin against his servant"* (v. 4), and he gave two simple reasons. First, David had done Saul no harm. Second, David had done Saul much good. He illustrated the second argument by recounting the risk that David had taken when he killed Goliath (v. 5). As a result, Saul *"heeded the voice of Jonathan"* and swore never to kill David (v. 6), after which David was restored to the court and the relationship seemed to be *"as in times past"* (v. 7).

Most people are never called to do this kind of high-level interceding for another. But almost daily we find ourselves in situations where people whom we know and love are being threatened. While the threat might not be their life, often their reputation or happiness is involved. When we are more worried about ourselves than about others or the truth, we are often tempted to sit quietly and listen to someone being maligned without raising a question. We are more worried that our raising questions will keep people from liking us than we are about the potential damage to a friend. Friends who will not risk for another are not friends.

## WHEN FAMILY INTERVENES

8 And there was war again; and David went out and fought with the Philistines, and struck them with a mighty blow, and they fled from him.

9 Now the distressing spirit from the LORD came upon Saul as he sat in his house with his spear in his hand. And David was playing music with his hand. 10 Then Saul sought to pin David to the wall with the spear, but he slipped away from Saul's presence; and he drove the spear into the wall. So David fled and escaped that night.

¹¹ Saul also sent messengers to David's house to watch him and to kill him in the morning. And Michal, David's wife, told him, saying, "If you do not save your life tonight, tomorrow you will be killed." ¹² So Michal let David down through a window. And he went and fled and escaped. ¹³ And Michal took an image and laid it in the bed, put a cover of goats' hair for his head, and covered it with clothes. ¹⁴ So when Saul sent messengers to take David, she said, "He is sick."

¹⁵ Then Saul sent the messengers back to see David, saying, "Bring him up to me in the bed, that I may kill him." ¹⁶ And when the messengers had come in, there was the image in the bed, with a cover of goats' hair for his head. ¹⁷ Then Saul said to Michal, "Why have you deceived me like this, and sent my enemy away, so that he has escaped?"

And Michal answered Saul, "He said to me, 'Let me go! Why should I kill you?'"

*—1 Samuel 19:8–17*

The verse telling about the continuing war with the Philistines seems out of place in this chapter which tells of several attempts on David's life. But it has been put there as a reminder to the reader of what was behind Saul's irrational fear of David. Every time David fought the Philistines, they *"fled from him"* (v. 8), and each victory made David more popular with the people and increased Saul's fear of him.

While the second attempt to kill David with a spear seems just like the first (1 Sam. 18:10–11), the fact that Saul has now talked to others about killing David makes it different. It would be easier at this point to believe that Saul was using his mental condition as an excuse for violence. Nothing is more common than for persons to try to find ways to implement their heart's desire without accepting the responsibility for their action. It's made more repugnant when it's done in the name or under the guise of religious experience. Saul was unsuccessful and David escaped, as before (v. 10).

When David fled Saul, he went to his own house. Evidently he thought that the effort against his life was due solely to Saul's "distressing spirit" and that there was no longer any danger. The things that had previously happened had not damaged David's capacity to forgive and to trust. But his wife, Michal, discovered that her father had sent *"messengers"* to kill David when he left the following morning (v. 11). That she helped her husband escape by letting him *"down through a window"* (v. 12) probably means that the house joined the wall of the city, allowing him to be lowered without being detected by those who watched the house.

The love and loyalty that David was able to inspire, even among the king's children, makes David's innocence of Saul's accusations more believable. Though he was her husband, Michal risked a lot by saving David from her father, who considered that his daughter's first responsibility was to him. No reason is given for her elaborate scheme to make the servants think her husband was sick in bed (vv. 13–16). She may have been trying to buy time for David to make good his escape. When her father asked why she had deceived him, she told her father that her husband had threatened to kill her if she didn't help him (v. 17). It was a lie, and Saul probably knew it and understood.

In reading these two stories, we are apt to think of Michal and Jonathan only in their roles in rescuing David. But we need to remember that they were acting in their father's best interest also, although he was not able to understand their actions. There are times when the kindest thing that can be done for someone who is deeply loved, is to make it more difficult for them to implement plans which would be destructive to others and to themselves.

## WHEN THE SPIRIT DISTRACTS

<sup>18</sup> So David fled and escaped, and went to Samuel at Ramah, and told him all that Saul had done to him. And he and Samuel went and stayed in Naioth. <sup>19</sup> Now it was told Saul, saying, "Take note, David is at Naioth in Ramah!" <sup>20</sup> Then Saul sent messengers to take David. And when they saw the group of prophets prophesying, and Samuel standing as leader over them, the Spirit of God came upon the messengers of Saul, and they also prophesied. <sup>21</sup> And when Saul was told, he sent other messengers, and they prophesied likewise. Then Saul sent messengers again the third time, and they prophesied also. <sup>22</sup> Then he also went to Ramah, and came to the great well that is at Sechu. So he asked, and said, "Where are Samuel and David?"

And someone said, "Indeed they are at Naioth in Ramah." <sup>23</sup> So he went there to Naioth in Ramah. Then the Spirit of God was upon him also, and he went on and prophesied until he came to Naioth in Ramah. <sup>24</sup> And he also stripped off his clothes and prophesied before Samuel in like manner, and lay down naked all that day and all that night. Therefore they say, "Is Saul also among the prophets?"

*—1 Samuel 19:18–24*

While his wife was delaying her father, David fled to Ramah and to the prophet Samuel (v. 18). By now David must have been thoroughly confused as to the dynamics of what was happening. His most obvious choice of a person to counsel with was Samuel. We do not know the exact location of *"Naioth"* where the two of them stayed. It may have been a section of Ramah or a community close to where the prophets lived. We do know their agenda. They discussed all the things that *"Saul had done to him"* (v. 18). What a help it must have been to David at that critical time in his life to have a significant person like Samuel as mentor. No matter how ordinary our lives, everyone has times when they need to talk about the load they are carrying to someone who knows and loves them.

The focus of the story, however, isn't David's visit with Samuel but rather the result of Saul's effort to capture him there. When Saul heard where David was, he immediately made plans to arrest him. He sent three different sets of messengers, each of which met the same fate. As they came to Samuel, he was surrounded by a group of prophets who were prophesying, which meant they were singing and dancing and speaking in a very frenzied way. The ecstasy was stimulated by circular dances which increased in intensity to such an extent that those who watched it would often be caught up in it. The Scripture says, *"the Spirit of God came upon the messengers of Saul, and they also prophesied"* (v. 20). They became so caught up in a spiritual frenzy that they were unable to perform the mission for which they had come.

After no success with three sets of messengers, Saul came and had the same experience as the others, with one exception. The Scripture says that in his frenzied activity, Saul tore all his clothing off and lay naked before Samuel *"all that day and all that night"* (v. 24). That this incident occurs after the Scripture which said that "Samuel went no more to see Saul until the day of his death" (1 Sam. 15:35) has added weight to the idea that the stories are not arranged in an exact chronology. While it was held that such prophesying was of the Lord, the picture of the king of Israel rolling on the ground naked and incoherent certainly lessened him in the eyes of those who looked on. He had come to capture David and had himself been captured.

The point of all the accounts in this chapter is the same. Saul continues to try to destroy the one whom he considers to be his rival, and God continues to protect him. Even though the efforts are not successful, changes are taking place in the lives of all who are involved. In the next chapter we will see the friendship of David and Jonathan strained almost to the breaking point and will discover the high price Jonathan is paying for his loyalty to David.

## WHEN FRIENDSHIPS ARE TESTED

**20:1** Then David fled from Naioth in Ramah, and went and said to Jonathan, "What have I done? What is my iniquity, and what is my sin before your father, that he seeks my life?"

2 So Jonathan said to him, "By no means! You shall not die! Indeed, my father will do nothing either great or small without first telling me. And why should my father hide this thing from me? It is not so!"

3 Then David took an oath again, and said, "Your father certainly knows that I have found favor in your eyes, and he has said, 'Do not let Jonathan know this, lest he be grieved.' But truly, as the LORD lives and as your soul lives, there is but a step between me and death."

4 So Jonathan said to David, "Whatever you yourself desire, I will do it for you."

5 And David said to Jonathan, "Indeed tomorrow is the New Moon, and I should not fail to sit with the king to eat. But let me go, that I may hide in the field until the third day at evening. 6 If your father misses me at all, then say, 'David earnestly asked permission of me that he might run over to Bethlehem, his city, for there is a yearly sacrifice there for all the family.' 7 If he says thus: 'It is well,' your servant will be safe. But if he is very angry, be sure that evil is determined by him. 8 Therefore you shall deal kindly with your servant, for you have brought your servant into a covenant of the LORD with you. Nevertheless, if there is iniquity in me, kill me yourself, for why should you bring me to your father?"

9 But Jonathan said, "Far be it from you! For if I knew certainly that evil was determined by my father to come upon you, then would I not tell you?"

10 Then David said to Jonathan, "Who will tell me, or what if your father answers you roughly?"

11 And Jonathan said to David, "Come, let us go out into the field." So both of them went out into the field. 12 Then Jonathan said to David: "The LORD God of Israel is witness! When I have sounded out my father sometime tomorrow, or the third day, and indeed there is good toward David, and I do not send to you and tell you, 13 may the LORD do so and much more to Jonathan. But if it pleases my father to do you evil, then I will report it to you and send you away, that you may go in safety. And the LORD be with you as He has been with my father. 14 And you shall not only show me the kindness of the LORD while I still live, that I may not die; 15 but you shall not cut off your kindness from my house forever, no, not when the LORD has cut off every one of the enemies of David from the face of the earth." 16 So Jonathan made a covenant with the house of David, saying, "Let the LORD require it at the hand of David's enemies."

17 Now Jonathan again caused David to vow, because he loved him; for he loved him as he loved his own soul. 18 Then Jonathan said to David, "Tomorrow is the New Moon; and you will be missed, because your seat will be empty. 19 And when you have stayed three days, go down quickly and come to the place where you hid on the day of the deed; and remain by the stone Ezel. 20 Then I will shoot three arrows to the side, as though I shot at a target; 21 and there I will send a lad, saying, 'Go, find the arrows.' If I expressly say to the lad, 'Look, the arrows are on this side of you; get them and come'—then, as the LORD lives, there is safety for you and no harm. 22 But if I say thus to the young man, 'Look, the arrows are beyond you'—go your way, for the LORD has sent you away. 23 And as for the matter which you and I have spoken of, indeed the LORD be between you and me forever."

*—1 Samuel 20:1–23*

The student of the monarchy will find this chapter interesting because of the details it gives of David's reasoning for leaving the court. There was great interest in demonstrating that David was not driven out because of wrongdoing on his own part, that he was not guilty of seeking to become king by his own cunning. His innocence is attested to earlier by Saul's daughter Michal, then by the prophet Samuel, and in this chapter by Saul's heir, Jonathan.

In addition to establishing the ultimate legitimacy of David's throne, this chapter adds further dimensions to our understanding of the inspiring friendship between David and Jonathan. Under the most extreme conditions they established, nourished, and maintained a personal relationship that is a model for people to this day.

The impression is left that the incidents in this chapter followed closely the events in the previous chapter. But the course of the conversation between David and Jonathan suggests that, as has been true of other accounts, the sequence of the narratives is controlled more by theological considerations than by historical recitation. In chapter 19 Saul tried to spear David (v. 10), tried to have him captured at his house (vv. 11–17), and made several efforts to capture him at Naioth (vv. 19–24). It would strain the imagination to believe that these things happened without Jonathan's being aware of them. Nor would it seem natural for David to be expected to be at the king's table after what had happened at Naioth.

The initial exchange between David and Jonathan is as spirited and direct as can be imagined. With great excitement David insists upon his own innocence of any wrongdoing that would explain Saul's effort to take his life (v. 1). Jonathan disagrees with David, not about his innocence, but about his father's intentions. He insisted that David would not die and based his feelings on his confidence in his own relationship with his father. Jonathan felt that his father would *do nothing either great or small* without first telling him (v. 2). He could not imagine his father's hiding anything from him.

There is a sense in which Jonathan was trapped between his love for his father and his love for his friend. Also, because of the dynamic of parental relationships, it is often easier to be objective about someone else's parent than one's own. There is a natural tendency either to idealize them or to caricature them. But there was also in Jonathan that rare and prized ability to trust people and to believe the best about their motives and intentions. David's life was ennobled by Jonathan's attitude toward him, and all who have such a friend find their lives enriched. The same spirit that made it easy for Jonathan to believe in his friend's innocence made it difficult for him to believe his father's guilt. It is encouraging to know that in a home where the father was suspicious of everyone there could grow up a son who trusted everyone.

But David was not reassured by Jonathan and insisted that there was *but a step between me and death* (v. 3). Then David gave Jonathan a believable reason for his father's hiding his intentions from his son—their friendship. Whether this was information that David had picked up from contacts in the palace, or an attitude that he had observed when he was with Saul and Jonathan, or just good insight into human nature is not known. But Jonathan sensed his friend was right and offered to do whatever was necessary to help him (v. 4).

The exchange recorded here reminds us that real friendships face tests. At the beginning neither David nor Jonathan could have imagined either the source or the intensity of them. But honesty about fears and anxieties doesn't have to destroy a relationship. Actually it is necessary for the health and well-being of the friendship. Relationships that will not survive differences are not healthy, and friends who can't be honest with each other about things of great importance will always have a superficial relationship.

David took the initiative with a plan to discover Saul's true intent. If this incident took place soon after one of Saul's attempts to harm David during one of his fits of illness, it could mean that David wasn't completely sure that Saul intended to kill him. Or the plan could have been mainly to help Jonathan see the situation as it really was. The plan involved David's missing a feast that he was expected to attend. Jonathan was to offer a somewhat reasonable excuse for his absence, and Saul's response was to be the clue to his real attitude toward David (vv. 5–7).

In the verses that follow there is some confusion about how the information gathered at the dinner is to be communicated. Parts of more than one account seem to be mixed together. But there is no confusion about the strong passions at work and about the deepening of the relationship between David and Jonathan. David pleads with his friend to kill him rather than let him fall into Saul's hands (v. 8). Jonathan swore to David that if he discerned any evil intent on his father's part, he would disclose it to David so that he could escape, although this would be a treasonable act (vv. 9, 13). He would not turn his back on his friend.

But the most important exchange seemed to look into the far future and involved both a renewal of their friendship covenant and an expansion of its significance (vv. 14–17). In this strengthened relationship there were two ingredients. First, they were to show each other kindness while they lived. Second, kindness to Jonathan's house should extend beyond his own life. In this passage Jonathan seems to acknowledge that the kingship will eventually come to David. This is one of the most moving scenes in the Scripture's coverage of their friendship.

## WHEN FRIENDS ARE LOYAL

24 Then David hid in the field. And when the New Moon had come, the king sat down to eat the feast. 25 Now the king sat on his seat, as at other times, on a seat by the wall. And Jonathan arose, and Abner sat by Saul's side, but David's place was empty. 26 Nevertheless Saul did not say anything that day, for he thought, "Something has happened to him; he is unclean, surely he is unclean." 27 And it happened the next day, the second day of the month, that David's place was empty. And Saul said to Jonathan his son, "Why has the son of Jesse not come to eat, either yesterday or today?"

28 So Jonathan answered Saul, "David earnestly asked permission of me to go to Bethlehem. 29 And he said, 'Please let me go, for our family has a sacrifice in the city, and my brother has commanded me to be there. And now, if I have found favor in your eyes, please let me get away and see my brothers.' Therefore he has not come to the king's table."

30 Then Saul's anger was aroused against Jonathan, and he said to him, "You son of a perverse, rebellious woman! Do I not know that you have chosen the son of Jesse to your own shame and to the shame of your mother's nakedness? 31 For as long as the son of Jesse lives on the earth, you shall not be established, nor your kingdom. Now therefore, send and bring him to me, for he shall surely die."

32 And Jonathan answered Saul his father, and said to him, "Why should he be killed? What has he done?" 33 Then Saul cast a spear at him to kill him, by which Jonathan knew that it was determined by his father to kill David.

34 So Jonathan arose from the table in fierce anger, and ate no food the second day of the month, for he was grieved for David, because his father had treated him shamefully.

35 And so it was, in the morning, that Jonathan went out into the field at the time appointed with David, and a little lad was with him. 36 Then he said to his lad, "Now run, find the arrows which I shoot." As the lad ran, he shot an arrow beyond him. 37 When the lad had come to the place where the arrow was which Jonathan had shot, Jonathan cried out after the lad and said, "Is not the arrow beyond you?" 38 And Jonathan cried out after the lad, "Make haste, hurry, do not delay!" So Jonathan's lad gathered up the

arrows and came back to his master. <sup>39</sup> But the lad did not know anything. Only Jonathan and David knew of the matter. <sup>40</sup> Then Jonathan gave his weapons to his lad, and said to him, "Go, carry them to the city."

<sup>41</sup> As soon as the lad had gone, David arose from a place toward the south, fell on his face to the ground, and bowed down three times. And they kissed one another; and they wept together, but David more so. <sup>42</sup> Then Jonathan said to David, "Go in peace, since we have both sworn in the name of the LORD, saying, 'May the LORD be between you and me, and between your descendants and my descendants, forever.'" So he arose and departed, and Jonathan went into the city.

*—1 Samuel 20:24–42*

The concluding verses in this chapter tell how the plan that David devised (vv. 5–7) was implemented and its result. Since the reader already has a clear picture of Saul's intentions toward David, there are no real surprises. But no matter how many times I read this passage, I never fail to get caught up in the dynamic of the relationship between Saul and Jonathan. It is a tragic story told vividly. It's a story of contrasts, with Saul reaching his lowest ebb and Jonathan in one of his best moments.

When they met for the New Moon feast on the first night, David was absent, but Saul made an excuse for him (vv. 25–26). When David was absent the second day, Saul asked where he was, and Jonathan told the story that they had agreed upon as the test of Saul's intentions (vv. 28–29). A clue to Saul's mood might be read into Saul's not calling David's name, referring to him as *"the son of Jesse"* (v. 27). Likewise, Jonathan gives a clue to his relationship by calling him by his name (v. 28).

While the test was to determine Saul's real attitude toward David, the king exploded in anger toward his son. Saul accused Jonathan of being disloyal to his own family, of betraying the king, and of acting against his own self-interest. He orders Jonathan to send for David in order that he may be killed (vv. 30–31). It was a moving speech and from Saul's perspective a very rational one. It was both a father-to-son and a king-to-his-heir speech. Knowing his sensitive nature, it must have touched Jonathan.

But even after the emotional outburst and the irrational accusations pointed at Jonathan by Saul, rather than defending himself to his father, Jonathan tries to reason with his father about David. He asked what David had done to deserve death (v. 32). Because Saul was operating more from his own insecurity than from facts, he answered his son's reason with violence. He attempted to kill his son with the spear by his side in the same manner in which he had attempted to kill David (v. 33). Completely apart from his own physical danger, it was a painful moment for Jonathan. Whatever illusions he may have maintained about his father's intentions were now shattered. His friend was in mortal danger from his father and he was caught in the middle.

Jonathan's response was a mixture of anger and grief (v. 34). His leaving the table disassociated him from his father's conclusions about his friend, but he still grieved because of the shameful way his father had treated David. There is a sense in which Jonathan was faithful to his father at a much higher level than Saul could appreciate. Jonathan bore his father's anger and hostility without denouncing him. He never turned against him, never left him, and died beside him in battle. Though he did warn David of his father's intentions, there was a sense in which he was true to both his father and to his friend. But he grieved for circumstances he didn't create and couldn't change.

The following morning, Jonathan got word to David by the prearranged signal (vv. 35–40). Then after the lad who carried the bow and arrows was gone, David and Jonathan met briefly to say goodbye and to reassure each other of their love and their covenant with each other before they parted (vv. 41–42). David had years ahead of him as a fugitive fleeing from Saul and as a refugee living with the Philistines. Jonathan faced a father who no longer trusted him and whose obsession was the destruction of his friend. This is why they *"wept together"* (v. 41). The next chapter tells of the beginning of David's life as a fugitive. It begins on a high level with his visit to the temple at Nob and ends on a disgusting note when David has to fain madness to escape betrayal by the king of Gath. But we will learn that it was during these down years of his life that God was preparing David to be the king whom He wanted.

# CHAPTER NINE—DAVID BECOMES A FUGITIVE

## 1 SAMUEL 21:1—26:25

*Scripture Outline*

Chapter 21 introduces that period of David's life when he was a fugitive and in exile. Though later he would draw around him a band of followers, at this point he was completely alone, without food or weapon. He was no rebel leading a rebellion. The two stories in this chapter picture both the extremity of his plight and the way in which God was protecting David.

When most people think of the life of King David, they forget this long "down" period of his life. It would be nice if we could go from his anointing by Samuel (1 Sam. 16:13) to his being anointed king by the people (2 Sam. 2:4) with nothing in between. David's meteoric rise to fame would then make a nice fairy tale—rags to riches without pain. We harbor these same fantasies about our own lives—that we can build marriages, rear children, or succeed in careers without any reversals or any "down" periods. There are even "health-and-wealth" preachers who attempt to define the Christian life as immune from trouble. What we fail to realize is that times of trouble are inevitable and the test of faith is not whether we have troubles but what we do with our troubles. When we look closely at the life of David during this difficult period of his life, we discover that God used this time to prepare him to be the king of Israel.

## FINDING RESOURCES FOR TROUBLED TIMES

**21:1** Now David came to Nob, to Ahimelech the priest. And Ahimelech was afraid when he met David, and said to him, "Why are you alone, and no one is with you?"

² So David said to Ahimelech the priest, "The king has ordered me on some business, and said to me, 'Do not let anyone know anything about the business on which I send you, or what I have commanded you.' And I have directed my young men to such and such a place. ³ Now therefore, what have you on hand? Give me five loaves of bread in my hand, or whatever can be found."

⁴ And the priest answered David and said, "There is no common bread on hand; but there is holy bread, if the young men have at least kept themselves from women."

⁵ Then David answered the priest, and said to him, "Truly, women have been kept from us about three days since I came out. And the vessels of the young men are holy, and the bread is in effect common, even though it was con-secrated in the vessel this day."

⁶ So the priest gave him holy bread; for there was no bread there but the showbread which had been taken from before the LORD, in order to put hot bread in its place on the day when it was taken away.

⁷ Now a certain man of the servants of Saul was there that day, detained before the LORD. And his name was Doeg, an Edomite, the chief of the herdsmen who belonged to Saul.

⁸ And David said to Ahimelech, "Is there not here on hand a spear or a sword? For I have brought neither my sword nor my weapons with me, because the king's business required haste."

⁹ So the priest said, "The sword of Goliath the Philistine, whom you killed in the Valley of Elah, there it is, wrapped in a cloth behind the ephod. If you will take that, take it. For there is no other except that one here."

And David said, "There is none like it; give it to me."

—1 Samuel 21:1–9

David's flight from Saul was so hasty that he was alone. At an earlier time he had fled to Samuel the prophet. On this occasion he fled to Ahimelech the priest. The reader of the accounts in 1 Samuel who has any doubt about David's role in coming to the throne need only remember that he was supported by Michal, Jonathan, Samuel, and, here, Ahimelech.

On the surface this is a well-told story of the fugitive David using deceit to get food and weapon from an innocent priest. But at a deeper level, there seems to be an awareness on Ahimelech's part of God's plan for David in Israel's future. Though it is not recorded in this brief account, in addition to seeking provisions and weapons, David also asked the priest to inquire of the Lord for him (1 Sam. 22:10).

There is a sense in which times of trouble can cause us to seek God's point of view in a situation. When things are going well there is a natural tendency to depend upon ourselves and to even take credit for our well-being. But when turns of events make us helpless, we are more aware of our own mortality and of the need for a larger perspective than our circumstances reveal. It's at these times that we often find help by turning to those "significant" others who bring a spiritual perspective to our lives. The story of David's life pictures him putting himself under the influence of those who knew God. There was a never-dying desire to understand how God related to what was happening in his life. Even in his failures he sought ultimately the perspective of God.

Nob was close to Jerusalem and en route to David's home. It was called the "city of priests" and may have been successor to

Shiloh after its destruction. Ahimelech, who was Eli's grandson, would have known David by sight. We do not know whether it was having a person of David's importance appear at the temple which made the priest afraid or that Ahimelech sensed something amiss from David's being alone which made him wonder. It was unusual for a captain in Saul's army to appear without weapon or accompanying soldiers. It could also have been a sense of awe in the presence of the one whom he sensed would be the king.

David did not reveal to Ahimelech the fact that he was a fugitive, but rather told him that he was on a secret mission for the king and was planning a later rendezvous with his men (v. 2). David's request for bread, the discussion of the *"holy bread,"* and the eventual giving of the bread is full of symbolism. God gave Israel specific instructions for building the table on which the *"showbread"* was to be placed (Ex. 25:23–30). The Scripture even includes the recipe for the bread and instruction for its use (Lev. 24:5–9).

While Ahimelech had no *"ordinary bread,"* he had the twelve loaves that were placed in the shrine before God and removed to be replenished with fresh loaves at intervals. This was the bread David asked for. After satisfying himself that David and his men were ritually clean, Ahimelech gave David the bread. Those who preserved the story must have made the association of the holy bread being food for a king.

Jesus referred to the story to illustrate how important it is not to become captive to the letter of the law and to miss the spirit of it. When the Pharisees were critical of Jesus' disciples for reaping seeds and eating them as they walked through the fields on the Sabbath, Jesus silenced them by reminding them how David ate the holy bread (Mark 2:25).

Having received the bread, David inquired about the possibility of a spear or sword, and seemed to feel that his lack of a weapon required an explanation (*"because the king's business required haste,"* v. 8). When the priest explained that the only weapon on hand was Goliath's sword, David took it. Whether it was a weapon that he would continue to use was of little significance, the weapon had great symbolic value. Even the fact that he had gotten it at the temple of God was important. David had come alone, without food or weapon, and left with bread and a sword. They were symbols of God's provision and protection.

The sinister character in this passage is Doeg, the Edomite, who had been *"detained before the LORD"* (v. 7) and who witnessed David's transactions with the priest. The telling phrase in his description was that he was *"of the servants of Saul"* (v. 7). His knowledge of Ahimelech's help of David would soon find its way to Saul with horrifying results.

## FINDING SAFETY IN HELPLESSNESS

[10] Then David arose and fled that day from before Saul, and went to Achish the king of Gath. [11] And the servants of Achish said to him, "Is this not David the king of the land? Did they not sing of him to one another in dances, saying:
'Saul has slain his thousands,
And David his ten thousands'?"
[12] Now David took these words to heart, and was very much afraid of Achish the king of Gath. [13] So he changed his behavior before them, pretended madness in their hands, scratched on the doors of the gate, and let his saliva fall down on his beard. [14] Then Achish said to his servants, "Look, you see the man is insane. Why have you brought him to me? [15] Have I need of madmen, that you have brought this fellow to play the madman in my presence? Shall this fellow come into my house?"

*—1 Samuel 21:10–15*

The second story in this chapter tells of David's first venture outside Palestine, to Gath. He later returned to Gath with his soldiers (1 Sam. 27, 29). But at this time he has no soldiers and is alone, hoping to remain incognito. This proved impossible because his reputation had preceded him. They even knew the little song that had been sung by the Israelite women and which had made Saul jealous (v. 11). Whether their referring to him as *"the king"* meant that he was considered a chief over an area or that they recognized him as the king, David sensed immediately that their knowledge of his identity endangered his life (v. 12).

In those days, and in many places today, insanity was looked upon as an affliction of "the gods," and they were treated as holy people and were not harmed. Knowing this, David *"changed his behavior"* (v. 13) and convinced them that he was truly mad. The contrast between the man who inspired the singing in the streets as he came home from a victorious battle and the David who scratched the doors of the gate like a madman and let the spit drool over his beard was so great that King Achish concluded that he was really insane.

In studying any story in the Bible one of the interesting questions to ask oneself is "What is the purpose behind including this story in the Scripture?" There are at least two apparent reasons. One was to remind the readers of how God was able to protect David, even when he was with those who were Israel's enemies. Another was to illustrate how resourceful and how quick of mind David was in the direst of circumstances. It was a quality he would often need later when he served as king.

## THE GATHERING OF A PEOPLE

**22:1** David therefore departed from there and escaped to the cave of Adullam. So when his brothers and all his father's house heard it, they went down there to him. ² And everyone who was in distress, everyone who was in debt, and everyone who was discontented gathered to him. So he became captain over them. And there were about four hundred men with him.

³ Then David went from there to Mizpah of Moab; and he said to the king of Moab, "Please let my father and mother come here with you, till I know what God will do for me." ⁴ So he brought them before the king of Moab, and they dwelt with him all the time that David was in the stronghold.

⁵ Now the prophet Gad said to David, "Do not stay in the stronghold; depart, and go to the land of Judah." So David departed and went into the forest of Hereth.

*1 Samuel 22:1–5*

Chapter 22 introduces the polarization of Israel over the conflict between Saul and David, necessitating the moving of David's family out of the country for their protection and precipitating the gathering of a small band of supporters around David. For the first time the conflict reaches out and brings suffering and destruction to a whole city of innocent people. The chapter records yet another step in the decline of Saul's ability to lead Israel and another step in David's preparation to be king.

Until now David had been alone, but at this juncture in his life he gathered people around him. The first to come were *"his brothers and all his father's house"* (v. 1). There was a unity to the clan or family that made this a natural move, but they were also now in danger from Saul who might be expected to attack them merely because they were David's family. As society has moved from a pastoral to an urban culture, and from a sense of corporateness to the prizing of the individual, there have been losses as well as gains. One loss is the strong support system that families are capable of providing for their members.

The second group that was drawn to David did not seem as attractive, for they were people who were drawn to him because of common troubles. They had been made into a family not by blood ties but by suffering similar problems. While the one-sentence description in the text is not exhaustive, it paints a clear picture of David's four hundred men as *"everyone who was in distress, everyone who was in debt, and everyone who was discontented"* (v. 2). The establishing of the monarchy had not solved all their problems and had probably created new ones, and these were the people caught in the social upheaval. It's easy to see why they accepted David as their captain.

While the group bore no resemblance to the elite unit that David had commanded for Saul, they made a contribution to his preparation for being king. First, they taught him the problems of the common people. Had he stayed in the palace, eating with the king and enjoying the company of the prince, he would have never been able to understand the people who came to him. When people suffer they discover others who are suffering and are able to communicate with them at a deeper level than is ever possible for those who have not shared the experience.

Some time ago a friend of mine underwent radical surgery for cancer. During the years since I've watched with fascination how people who learn they have cancer are drawn to him. Although he was always a caring person, living with cancer has developed in him a dimension of concern and compassion for other cancer patients that would have been otherwise impossible. Like David, he salvaged good from a bad experience.

A second contribution the four hundred made was that they forced him to develop leadership skills that would serve him well during the years he was to be king. If David could mold these men into a disciplined fighting unit, he could lead anyone. There was a small church in a town I often visited that seemed to gather every person in town who was unhappy with their previous church. My preacher uncle once said, "That is an ideal church for a pastor who wants to develop leadership skills because the pastor who can lead that church can lead any church." David's preparation to lead the nation began with the four hundred.

Sensing the danger to his parents and their inability to be a part of a roving band of warriors, David asked the king of Moab for permission to leave them with him. Moab was on the other side of the Dead Sea, to the east of Palestine. The Moabites were distantly related through Ruth, who was David's great-grandmother. Making arrangements for his parents' safety was David's first effort at political negotiation with another country, and it was the beginning of the development of diplomatic skills that would later help him to secure Israel's borders by making treaties with her neighbors. If we will allow them to be our teachers, very few of life's experiences will be wasted.

No information is given to the reader about the identity or history of *"the prophet Gad"* (v. 5), although he appears again as a prophetic adviser (2 Sam. 24). He counseled David not to stay in his *"stronghold,"* but no reason was given. It could have been that he was in danger of being trapped there or it might have been important for David to return to Judah. The incident was probably preserved in the Bible as a reminder that even though David was being treated as an outlaw, God was still sending messengers to him. It was a reminder that those who have political power don't always have access to spiritual insight. That God's leadership continued to be important to David was reflected in the wording of David's request of the king of Moab, *"till I know what God will do for me"* (v. 3). At the center of his being David seemed to believe that his life was ultimately not in Saul's hands but in God's care.

## THE BREAKDOWN OF LEADERSHIP

6 When Saul heard that David and the men who were with him had been discovered—now Saul was staying in Gibeah under a tamarisk tree in Ramah, with his spear in his hand, and all his servants standing about him— 7 then Saul said to his servants who stood about him, "Hear now, you Benjamites! Will the son of Jesse give every one of you fields and vineyards, and make you all captains of thousands and captains of hundreds? 8 All of you have conspired against me, and there is no one who reveals to me that my son has made a covenant with the son of Jesse; and there is not one of you who is sorry for me or reveals to me that my son has stirred up my servant against me, to lie in wait, as it is this day."

9 Then answered Doeg the Edomite, who was set over the servants of Saul, and said, "I saw the son of Jesse going to Nob, to Ahimelech the son of Ahitub. 10 And he inquired of the LORD for him, gave him provisions, and gave him the sword of Goliath the Philistine."

<sup>11</sup> So the king sent to call Ahimelech the priest, the son of Ahitub, and all his father's house, the priests who were in Nob. And they all came to the king. <sup>12</sup> And Saul said, "Hear now, son of Ahitub!"

He answered, "Here I am, my lord."

<sup>13</sup> Then Saul said to him, "Why have you conspired against me, you and the son of Jesse, in that you have given him bread and a sword, and have inquired of God for him, that he should rise against me, to lie in wait, as it is this day?"

<sup>14</sup> So Ahimelech answered the king and said, "And who among all your servants is as faithful as David, who is the king's son-in-law, who goes at your bidding, and is honorable in your house? <sup>15</sup> Did I then begin to inquire of God for him? Far be it from me! Let not the king impute anything to his servant, or to any in the house of my father. For your servant knew nothing of all this, little or much."

<sup>16</sup> And the king said, "You shall surely die, Ahimelech, you and all your father's house!" <sup>17</sup> Then the king said to the guards who stood about him, "Turn and kill the priests of the LORD, because their hand also is with David, and because they knew when he fled and did not tell it to me." But the servants of the king would not lift their hands to strike the priests of the LORD. <sup>18</sup> And the king said to Doeg, "You turn and kill the priests!" So Doeg the Edomite turned and struck the priests, and killed on that day eighty-five men who wore a linen ephod. <sup>19</sup> Also Nob, the city of the priests, he struck with the edge of the sword, both men and women, children and nursing infants, oxen and donkeys and sheep—with the edge of the sword.

<sup>20</sup> Now one of the sons of Ahimelech the son of Ahitub, named Abiathar, escaped and fled after David. <sup>21</sup> And Abiathar told David that Saul had killed the LORD's priests. <sup>22</sup> So David said to Abiathar, "I knew that day, when Doeg the Edomite was there, that he would surely tell Saul. I have caused the death of all the persons of your father's house. <sup>23</sup> Stay with me; do not fear. For he who seeks my life seeks your life, but with me you shall be safe."

*—1 Samuel 22:6–23*

These verses shift the scene from David, who with his men were in the "forest of Hereth" (v. 5), to Saul who was at his headquarters at Gibeah. He was so obsessed with David that he seemed unable to speak his name, referring to him as *"the son of Jesse"* (v. 7). His question of those in his army from the tribe of Benjamin was probably an assertion that there would be more material rewards from following him than David could offer. The effort to buy loyalty with material rewards rather than integrity of leadership is not a new technique.

Next, Saul accused his son of being the one who incited David to rebel and his soldiers of being guilty by being silent about what was going on (v. 8). In this scene Saul modeled the kind of paranoia that captures people and makes them think that everyone is plotting against them. Saul was the king and had absolute control over the lives of those around him, but as a person he was totally controlled by his own fears.

One of the people listening to Saul's ranting was Doeg the Edomite, who was at the temple at Nob when David received the bread and the sword (1 Sam. 21:7). Doeg was not a patriot but an opportunist, and he decided to use the information he had to advance his own standing with Saul. The account which Doeg gave (vv. 9–10) was the truth, but he knew that Saul would hear it and jump to conclusions which were lies. Doeg did have one bit of information not included in the account in 1 Samuel 21, that Ahimelech "*inquired of the LORD for him.*" While Doeg's words were accurate, the impression that he left was not, namely, that David was indeed leading a rebellion and that Ahimelech was siding with him by giving him spiritual advice and provisions. Opportunists are artists at telling people what they want to hear, and insecure leaders surround themselves with this type of person.

Upon hearing Doeg's testimony, Ahimelech and his relatives and all the priests from Nob were brought to Gibeah to answer for their actions. The trial of Ahimelech was a mockery because Saul was no longer capable of either discovering the truth or believing it. When he was confronted with what he had done, Ahimelech did not deny his actions but denied the motives that Saul attached to them. There was real courage in questioning the king's interpretation of his actions. He could rightly have contended that he had been deceived by David and as a result was innocent of any wrongdoing. Rather, like Jonathan had done before, he tried to reason with Saul concerning David's loyalty to the king. The king was closed to reasoning and seemed not to hear. To Saul any assistance to David was an act of treason, and he pronounced the death sentence upon Ahimelech and his family (v. 16). The sentence was then extended to every living thing in the city of Nob (v. 19).

When the king's select guards refused to carry out Saul's command to slay all the priests, the task was given to Doeg the Edomite and none were spared the slaughter (vv. 17–19). While the incident was more an act of anger than policy, putting Nob under the ban sent a clear message to all other communities in Judea as to what happened to those who helped David. It also creates an interesting contrast between the Saul who refused to kill Israel's enemy (1 Sam. 15) and the Saul who refused to spare Israel's own priests in this account.

Years ago I was leading a study of this chapter as a part of a Wednesday night Bible series. The study took place around the tables after dinner and there was always a discussion time when individuals reacted to various parts of the passage studied. On this chapter everyone was angry at the senseless slaughter of Ahimelech, but they were especially incensed at the slaying of the women and children and even the animals. After several had spoken of their repulsion by Saul's violence, one of the adult Bible teachers said to the group, "I identify with everything that has been said about this passage. But as bad as it is, we can see that the source of the suffering is a king whom even God has rejected. But this story is easier for me to understand than the story in 1 Samuel 15 where it is the God who rejected Saul who is ordering the killing." Her comment reminded us all that it is very important to draw our final picture of God from His revelation in Jesus Christ, and not from some of the narratives of the Old Testament.

The chapter closes with the story of one person who escaped the slaughter at Nob, Abiathar, one of Ahimelech's sons (v. 20). The fact that he fled to David would indicate that he blamed Saul for what happened rather than David. Abiathar was the last surviving descendant of Eli, and his coming to David's side symbolized that there would be continued access to God.

While Abiathar did not blame David for what happened, David blamed himself (v. 22). The most costly lesson David learned from this experience was that the things which he did affected the lives of others, often tragically. Every time he looked at Abiathar, he must have thought of that day at the temple at Nob and wondered "what if . . ." It was a painful lesson for David, but it is one that everyone must learn. Our actions set into motion events we are helpless to change, for good or for bad, and the lives of others are affected.

The next chapter tells of David's efforts on behalf of the town of Keilah, which the Philistines were attacking. Out of the experience David learned a valuable lesson about the fickleness of human nature.

## PUTTING OTHERS AHEAD OF SELF

**23:1** Then they told David, saying, "Look, the Philistines are fighting against Keilah, and they are robbing the threshing floors."

2 Therefore David inquired of the LORD, saying, "Shall I go and attack these Philistines?"

And the LORD said to David, "Go and attack the Philistines, and save Keilah."

3 But David's men said to him, "Look, we are afraid here in Judah. How much more then if we go to Keilah against the armies of the Philistines?" 4 Then David inquired of the LORD once again.

And the LORD answered him and said, "Arise, go down to Keilah. For I will deliver the Philistines into your hand." 5 And David and his men went to Keilah and fought with the Philistines, struck them with a mighty blow, and took away their livestock. So David saved the inhabitants of Keilah.

6 Now it happened, when Abiathar the son of Ahimelech fled to David at Keilah, that he went down with an ephod in his hand.

7 And Saul was told that David had gone to Keilah. So Saul said, "God has delivered him into my hand, for he has shut himself in by entering a town that has gates and bars." 8 Then Saul called all the people together for war, to go down to Keilah to besiege David and his men.

9 When David knew that Saul plotted evil against him, he said to Abiathar the priest, "Bring the ephod here." 10 Then David said, "O LORD God of Israel, Your servant has certainly heard that Saul seeks to come to Keilah to destroy the city for my sake. 11 Will the men of Keilah deliver me into his hand? Will Saul come down, as Your servant has heard? O LORD God of Israel, I pray, tell Your servant."

And the LORD said, "He will come down."

12 Then David said, "Will the men of Keilah deliver me and my men into the hand of Saul?"

And the LORD said, "They will deliver you."

13 So David and his men, about six hundred, arose and departed from Keilah and went wherever they could go. Then it was told Saul that David had escaped from Keilah; so he halted the expedition.

*—1 Samuel 23:1–13*

The events of this chapter illustrate that Saul is still very much in charge of the situation and able to create such fear that a city which David has just delivered from the Philistines would have been willing to surrender their deliverer to him. Yet the chapter also reminds the reader that David is in God's hands as he receives direction from God through the priest, encouragement from his friend Jonathan, and even help from Israel's enemies, the Philistines, when he is about to be captured.

The story of David's deliverance of the city of Keilah from a raiding party of Philistines demonstrates his ability to put the interests of his fellow citizens ahead of his own. The city was in the hill country, not far from Adullam. In the rich valleys they grew grain and during harvest they both threshed and stored the grain outdoors. The Philistine raiding parties made a habit of raiding those places and taking the already harvested grain, which was all that stood between the people and famine and starvation. Word came to David that the people of the city were being robbed (v. 1).

When Abiathar came over to David's side after Saul murdered his father and all the other priests at Nob (1 Sam. 22:16–19), he brought with him the *"ephod in his hand"* (v. 6). This was either the garment or the box by which lots were used to discern the will of God. David would put a question to the priest that could be answered by a yes or a no, and the priest would use the ephod and give David an answer from God.

Those who live in the time since Christ, with the Bible, the church, and the Holy Spirit, may view the Old Testament method as mechanical and limited. But we must not lose sight of the fact that almost three thousand years ago there were people who thought it was important to seek the counsel of God concerning the actions they were considering. The fact that David had access to the counsel of God is one of the significant advantages which he had over Saul.

When David asked God whether he should attempt to rescue the city of Keilah from the Philistines, the answer was yes. But when he told his men what they were about to do, they expressed doubt at the wisdom of the attack and asked him to seek God's counsel again. When the question was put to the priest again the answer was the same, so both captain and soldiers moved into battle and saved Keilah (vv. 4–6). David's willingness to go back to the priests at the request of his soldiers indicated that he had a much more wholesome relationship with his men than Saul had with his. The deliverance of that city must have helped David with the people of his country, because it pictured him as a true Israelite fighting his country's persistent enemy.

It was at Keilah that David learned to be realistic about human nature and also to be unselfish in dealing with people who were indebted to him. Saul learned where David was and planned an attack upon the city feeling that *"God has delivered him into my hand"* (v. 7). (It's always a little confusing for Christians when opposing sides on issues both claim God's hand in either their thinking or their actions.) When David learned that Saul was coming, he turned to Abiathar with a question for God, *"Will the men of Keilah deliver me into his hand?"* (v. 11), and the answer came back, *"They will deliver you"* (v. 12).

David's response was to gather his band of six hundred men and leave. He was wise enough to know that he was endangering them if he stayed, and he certainly didn't want to feel responsible for another massacre such as the one that occurred at Nob. His action created an interesting contrast between David and Saul. David was playing the role of a king in delivering the city, and they were more threatened by Saul than by their traditional enemies, the Philistines. When the word spread of David's actions on behalf of the city, it must have helped to neutralize the talk about what happened at Nob.

## HELP FROM UNEXPECTED SOURCES

14 And David stayed in strongholds in the wilderness, and remained in the mountains in the Wilderness of Ziph. Saul sought him every day, but God did not deliver him into his hand. 15 So David saw that Saul had come out to seek his life. And David was in the Wilderness of Ziph in a forest. 16 Then Jonathan, Saul's son, arose and went to David in the woods and strengthened his hand in God. 17 And he said to him, "Do not fear, for the hand of Saul my father shall not find you. You shall be king over Israel, and I shall be next to you. Even my father Saul knows that." 18 So the two of them made a covenant before the LORD. And David stayed in the woods, and Jonathan went to his own house.

19 Then the Ziphites came up to Saul at Gibeah, saying, "Is David not hiding with us in strongholds in the woods, in the hill of Hachilah, which is on the south of Jeshimon? 20 Now therefore, O king, come down according to all the desire of your soul to come down; and our part shall be to deliver him into the king's hand."

21 And Saul said, "Blessed are you of the LORD, for you have compassion on me. 22 Please go and find out for sure, and see the place where his hideout is, and who has seen him there. For I am told he is very crafty. 23 See therefore, and take knowledge of all the lurking places where he hides; and come back to me with certainty, and I will go with you. And it shall be, if he is in the land, that I will search for him throughout all the clans of Judah."

24 So they arose and went to Ziph before Saul. But David and his men were in the Wilderness of Maon, in the plain on the south of Jeshimon. 25 When Saul and his men went to seek him, they told David. Therefore he went down to the rock, and stayed in the Wilderness of Maon. And when Saul heard that, he pursued David in the Wilderness of Maon. 26 Then Saul went on one side of the mountain, and David and his men on the other side of the mountain. So David made haste to get away from Saul, for Saul and his men were encircling David and his men to take them.

27 But a messenger came to Saul, saying, "Hurry and come, for the Philistines have invaded the land!"
28 Therefore Saul returned from pursuing David, and went against the Philistines; so they called that place the Rock of Escape. 29 Then David went up from there and dwelt in strongholds at En Gedi.

*—1 Samuel 23:14–29*

These verses cover Saul's chase of David from Keilah to the Wilderness of Ziph to En Gedi (vv. 14, 29). It was a move from a walled city to a barren waste to the edge of the Dead Sea, with Saul's pursuit so persistent that David feared for his life. The Ziphites, who had less reason to be supportive of David, followed the pattern of the men of Keilah and told Saul of David's whereabouts and promised to deliver him into Saul's hands (vv. 19–20). Evidently the information flowed two ways because as the Ziphites furnished details of David's moves (vv. 21–23), someone kept David informed enough of Saul's plans for him to move on to the Wilderness of Maon (v. 24). Saul followed David there and was in the process of encircling him when a Philistine invasion of the land forced Saul to withdraw, allowing David to escape (vv. 25–28).

In these verses two incidents dramatize God's care for David in a most desperate time. First, Jonathan came to David to encourage him (vv. 16–18). The contrast between Saul and his son is so amazing: The father sought to kill David and Jonathan risked his life to encourage him. Saul was hunting everywhere for David, and his son *"went to David in the woods"* (v. 16). Besides the encouragement of his presence, Jonathan discussed with David his feeling that his father would not find David. He also told David that even his father knew that David would become king of Israel (v. 17). At such a low ebb for David, these were words of great encouragement.

As Barnabas has the reputation for being the great encourager in the New Testament, Jonathan models this virtue in the Old Testament. Everyone experiences times when they need to be encouraged—about themselves, their gifts or talents, their work, their children, or their relationship with God. And everyone needs to develop the gift of encouragement, because it is one of the most powerful forces in human relationships. The second event that reminds the reader of God's care for David was performed not by his best friend but by his worst enemies, the Philistines. Just as Saul had David almost surrounded and was almost ready to spring his trap, word came to him with an urgent appeal for help because the Philistines had launched an invasion of the land (v. 27). One interpreter of this passage referred to the invasion as a miracle, not so much in the event as in the timing. For the Philistines to invade Israel was a common occurrence, but that they should attack at that particular moment was a miracle. The narrative was probably preserved because it was a reminder that God can use both friends and enemies to further His purpose.

In the next chapter the conflict between Saul and David continues with a strange twist—David has an opportunity to kill Saul and won't do it, nor will he allow his men to harm Saul. There's even what seems to be a reconciliation, at least for a moment. But mainly, there is growth and maturation on David's part on the slow road to becoming king.

## RESPECTING GOD'S ANOINTED

**24:1** Now it happened, when Saul had returned from following the Philistines, that it was told him, saying, "Take note! David is in the Wilderness of En Gedi." [2] Then Saul took three thousand chosen men from all Israel, and went to seek David and his men on the Rocks of the Wild Goats. [3] So he came to the sheepfolds by the road, where there was a cave; and Saul went in to attend to his needs. (David and his men were staying in the recesses of the cave.) [4] Then the men of David said to him, "This is the day of which the

LORD said to you, 'Behold, I will deliver your enemy into your hand, that you may do to him as it seems good to you.'" And David arose and secretly cut off a corner of Saul's robe. 5 Now it happened afterward that David's heart troubled him because he had cut Saul's robe. 6 And he said to his men, "The LORD forbid that I should do this thing to my master, the LORD's anointed, to stretch out my hand against him, seeing he is the anointed of the LORD." 7 So David restrained his servants with these words, and did not allow them to rise against Saul. And Saul got up from the cave and went on his way.

*—1 Samuel 24:1–7*

Chapter 24 records the first of two accounts where David had an opportunity to kill Saul and refused to do so. The other is in 1 Samuel 26. While the account was probably originally preserved to further establish the innocence of David in his relationship with Saul, it deals also with the themes of forgiveness and reconciliation. David's unwillingness to be the instrument of God's judgment upon Saul raises probing questions about individuals taking vengeance upon those who have harmed them. David's defense of his innocence is magnificent and Saul's emotional response is full of pathos and tragedy.

This incident took place after Saul had dealt with the Philistine threat and had resumed the chase. All it took to return him to his obsession was hearing *"David is in the Wilderness of En Gedi"* (v. 1). If David still had his six hundred men, then he would have been outnumbered fivefold by Saul's *"three thousand chosen men"* (v. 2). The area was in the hilly country just west of the Dead Sea and the nature of its terrain was suggested by the *"Rocks of the Wild Goats"* where David and his men were hiding.

The event around which the whole story organized itself was when Saul withdrew from his men and went into the shelter of a cave to relieve himself, not realizing that David and his men were *"staying in the recesses of the cave"* (v. 3). It was not uncommon for the entrances of caves to be large enough for sheltering herds of animals during storms, and often the cave branched in several different directions from the entrance. The circumstance was one in which Saul was totally vulnerable to David and his men.

The situation provides the reader a classic example of how different people can look at the same situation and come to totally different conclusions about the role that God had in it. David's men were sure that David's enemy had been delivered into his hand (v. 4). But David saw it as a temptation to do evil—to stretch forth his hand against *"God's anointed"* (v. 6). The refusal to slay Saul was not based on a magnanimous spirit but on David's deeply rooted belief that it was wrong to harm one whom God had anointed. Even though he felt that Saul deserved death, he could not bring himself to be his executioner. His feelings were so strong about not harming God's anointed that later he slew the Amalekite who said that he had slain Saul (2 Sam. 1:1–16).

Since the contemporary Christian does not usually face enemies who have been anointed by God through one of the prophets, there is a tendency to limit the term "God's anointed" to the ordained leadership of the church. Insecure leadership has often used this concept to protect themselves from any criticism and from the responsibility of being accountable for their actions. But the idea of "God's anointed" needs a much broader application than to Old Testament kings and the professional clergy. It needs to apply to every person. The knowledge that each person is made in the image of God, is the object of God's eternal love, is capable of fellowship with God, and is one for whom Christ died ought to make him one of "God's anointed."

The text does not tell how David was able to cut off *"a corner of Saul's robe"* (v. 4) without being detected. Nor does it explain his troubled conscience afterward (v. 5). It could have been a matter of face or ridicule or embarrassment that was symbolized by such an act. In his speech to Saul later David used the act as proof that he had been close enough to Saul to have killed him (v. 11).

In this whole story of David's sparing of Saul's life there is evidence of a continuing deep personal feeling that David has toward Saul. One needs only take the phrases which are used in referring to Saul from David's conversation with his own men and from his speech to Saul. In addition to "the LORD's anointed" there is *"my master"* (v. 6), *"my lord the king"* (v. 8), and *"my father"* (v. 11). David's experience is a painful reminder that all of us will know in life what it is to love someone who thinks of himself as our enemy.

## A CASE FOR INNOCENCE

8 David also arose afterward, went out of the cave, and called out to Saul, saying, "My lord the king!" And when Saul looked behind him, David stooped with his face to the earth, and bowed down. 9 And David said to Saul: "Why do

you listen to the words of men who say, 'Indeed David seeks your harm'? [10] Look, this day your eyes have seen that the LORD delivered you today into my hand in the cave, and someone urged me to kill you. But my eye spared you, and I said, 'I will not stretch out my hand against my lord, for he is the LORD's anointed.' [11] Moreover, my father, see! Yes, see the corner of your robe in my hand! For in that I cut off the corner of your robe, and did not kill you, know and see that there is neither evil nor rebellion in my hand, and I have not sinned against you. Yet you hunt my life to take it. [12] Let the LORD judge between you and me, and let the LORD avenge me on you. But my hand shall not be against you. [13] As the proverb of the ancients says, 'Wickedness proceeds from the wicked.' But my hand shall not be against you. [14] After whom has the king of Israel come out? Whom do you pursue? A dead dog? A flea? [15] Therefore let the LORD be judge, and judge between you and me, and see and plead my case, and deliver me out of your hand."

*—1 Samuel 24:8–15*

This chapter contains one of the few times when David and Saul communicated face to face after David left the court. These verses contain David's personal plea for Saul to acknowledge his innocence. After Saul was a safe distance from the cave, David showed himself and called out to Saul. Knowing the soldiers who were at Saul's disposal meant this was an act of courage. When the king was able to see him, *"David stooped with his face to the earth, and bowed down"* (v. 8). From the tone of the speech that followed, his homage appears sincere.

His strong rhetoric had several points. First, he blamed the problem on the king's listening to David's critics (v. 9). People's conclusions are usually controlled by those whose information they listen to, and Saul had listened to the wrong people. Second, he called on the fact that he cut off the corner of the robe instead of slaying Saul, as a witness to the fact that he has never meant any harm to the king (vv. 10–11). Often when we cannot hear the good sense people make with their words we can see it in their actions. Third, David plays down his significance with his *"Whom do you pursue? A dead dog? A flea?"* (v. 14). But David's most powerful point he saved to the end when he turned the case over to God to take care of (vv. 12, 15). Judgment was coming, but David assured Saul that it would come from God and not from himself.

## AN EFFORT AT RECONCILIATION

16 So it was, when David had finished speaking these words to Saul, that Saul said, "Is this your voice, my son David?" And Saul lifted up his voice and wept. 17 Then he said to David: "You are more righteous than I; for you have rewarded me with good, whereas I have rewarded you with evil. 18 And you have shown this day how you have dealt well with me; for when the LORD delivered me into your hand, you did not kill me. 19 For if a man finds his enemy, will he let him get away safely? Therefore may the LORD reward you with good for what you have done to me this day. 20 And now I know indeed that you shall surely be king, and that the kingdom of Israel shall be established in your hand. 21 Therefore swear now to me by the LORD that you will not cut off my descendants after me, and that you will not destroy my name from my father's house."

22 So David swore to Saul. And Saul went home, but David and his men went up to the stronghold.

—*1 Samuel 24:16–22*

David's words deeply moved Saul and he referred to him tenderly as *"my son David"* (v. 16). His awareness of his own narrow escape and his reaction to David's words combined to give him a moment of clarity of thought and of judgment. Although his later actions do not match his words because of the radical shift of his moods and behavior, the words that he spoke here put Saul in line with his children and the prophets and the priests concerning David.

First, Saul clearly confessed David's innocence of intending him harm (vv. 17–18). It is a wonderful thing to be able to see when our understandings have been wrong because it opens the doors to new relationships. Next, Saul formally blessed David saying, *"May the LORD reward you with good for what you have done to me this day"* (v. 19). It was that strange reversal of heart where Saul was blessing the one he had been cursing. Then he acknowledged that it was God's will for David to be king. He put into words what he had feared to believe and had hoped to prevent. Finally, he asked David to enter into a covenant with him to *"not cut off my descendants after me"* (v. 21). It was a similar covenant to the one between Jonathan and David.

David swore the oath to Saul and Saul departed to his home, introducing a temporary time of calm for both of their lives. What existed was more a lack of war than real reconciliation, however. There was no possibility now of David's returning to court, so he stayed with his men in his stronghold. It would be but a brief time before the chase would resume (1 Sam. 26).

The next chapter briefly records the death of Samuel and then devotes itself to telling how David came to have Abigail for one of his wives. But it gives the reader a good picture of how David and his men lived during the days before he was officially made king. It also introduces a character, Nabal, who seems almost as unpleasant as Doeg the Edomite.

## SAMUEL'S DEATH

> **25:1** Then Samuel died; and the Israelites gathered together and lamented for him, and buried him at his home in Ramah. And David arose and went down to the Wilderness of Paran.
>
> *—1 Samuel 25:1*

This chapter gives us insight into the conditions under which David and his men lived during that period, tells how he came to meet and marry Abigail, and gives more information about his rise to the throne. But it begins with the detached note about the death of Samuel (v. 1), an announcement which is repeated in 1 Samuel 28:11ff.

Samuel played such a significant role in the life of Israel that his death must have been the occasion of great grief and mourning. As a judge he had settled disputes. As a priest he had interceded with God on behalf of the people. As a prophet he had anointed kings, counseled them, and also deposed one. Just as his life embodied the themes of this book, more than anyone else Samuel symbolized the idea of God's overruling purpose for Israel. The news of his death must have shaken the people and created an uncertainty about their future.

Once I drove through an area of great forest where the timber which had grown there for more than a century had been harvested and the whole mountainside had been planted with seedlings. While I understood our need for lumber to build homes and make furniture for people and was delighted to know that the company that cut down the trees had planted other trees for future generations, there was still a sadness in looking at those enormous stumps, some of them ten feet across, surrounded by tiny seedlings not yet an inch in diameter. It is a sadder day when one of the giants dies, whether they were politicians, teachers, scholars, businesspeople, or leaders in the church.

## WHEN WEALTH AND POWER BREED CONTEMPT

2 Now there was a man in Maon whose business was in Carmel, and the man was very rich. He had three thousand sheep and a thousand goats. And he was shearing his sheep in Carmel. 3 The name of the man was Nabal, and the name of his wife Abigail. And she was a woman of good understanding and beautiful appearance; but the man was harsh and evil in his doings. He was of the house of Caleb.

4 When David heard in the wilderness that Nabal was shearing his sheep, 5 David sent ten young men; and David said to the young men, "Go up to Carmel, go to Nabal, and greet him in my name. 6 And thus you shall say to him who lives in prosperity: 'Peace be to you, peace to your house, and peace to all that you have! 7 Now I have heard that you have shearers. Your shepherds were with us, and we did not hurt them, nor was there anything missing from them all the while they were in Carmel. 8 Ask your young men, and they will tell you. Therefore let my young men find favor in your eyes, for we come on a feast day. Please give whatever comes to your hand to your servants and to your son David.'"

9 So when David's young men came, they spoke to Nabal according to all these words in the name of David, and waited.

10 Then Nabal answered David's servants, and said, "Who is David, and who is the son of Jesse? There are many servants nowadays who break away each one from his master. 11 Shall I then take my bread and my water and my meat that I have killed for my shearers, and give it to men when I do not know where they are from?"

*—1 Samuel 25:2–11*

This story of David's request and Nabal's response illustrates the kind of dilemma David faced in making provisions for his warriors, who now numbered six hundred men. While Nabal's response was not typical, it reminds us of the delicate situation David experienced constantly, because he was totally dependent upon the people of the area for food. The story can also serve as a warning to those of us who tend to underestimate the effect that affluence can have upon our character.

The one who preserved the story wanted readers to know two things about Nabal: that he was very rich and that he was very different from his wife. The description of his wealth makes him sound like Job before disaster struck. While in those days it was generally assumed that great wealth was God's reward for one's obedience, this was not the case with Nabal. His name meant "fool" and he is described as harsh and evil (v. 3). A casual reading of the narrative would also reveal that he was arrogant, insensitive, self-centered, lacking discipline, and not terribly bright. In contrast, his wife Abigail is described as both intelligent and beautiful (v. 3). From her actions one might conclude that she was shrewd and decisive and might well have been used as a model for the ideal woman in Proverbs 31. This is another example in the Old Testament where a gifted and wise woman was used by God in a significant way.

The account of David's request of Nabal needs to be seen in contrast to the response (vv. 4–8). The ten warriors were sent at the time of the shearing of the sheep. It was a festive time, a time when the people enjoyed the fellowship of working together. It was a time when people were more disposed to be generous. It was an ideal time to make a request such as David did.

David, who was growing in his knowledge of how to deal with people, gave specific instructions for asking for the gift of food. They were not to come with demands or threats or even try to make Nabal feel guilty for being so rich. They were to come with words of blessing and in a posture of peace (v. 6). David's men were not in the "protection" business as some have suggested, but present circumstances prevented them from sustaining themselves in any other way.

They also presented evidence that they were deserving of help because of services that they had rendered to Nabal's shepherds in the past. They considered themselves worthy to be helped and asked Nabal to verify their claim by checking with his own servants. Having once lived in a western city where two main highways intersected, where people were constantly coming to the little church there with pleas for help, I remember how nice it was when the one who made the request was able to give us a way to verify that they were who they claimed to be and that their need was real and not just a racket.

David's men made no suggestion to Nabal as to how many men were to be fed or as to what they felt he ought to give them. This was left completely to Nabal's generosity, or to his "supposed generosity." His response must have taken them by surprise. Often when I have been trying to get money to buy food or clothing for the very poor, I have been surprised by the caring spirit and the generous gifts of those who did not have much more than those for whom we were taking the offering. And I have also at times been shocked by those who could have rendered great help but gave nothing. Nabal's kind have continued to proliferate.

In three terse verses (vv. 9–11) we learn that wealth does not automatically create generosity. The story also reminds us that there are worse things than saying no to a request, and that is treating those who ask for help with contempt and derision. Since he made the men wait for an answer, the response more likely reflected Nabal's character and feeling rather than a momentary loss of temper. What he did was deliberate and a thing in which he seemed to take delight.

He showed his contempt by pretending never to have heard of David, the son of Jesse. He fueled the insult by suggesting that David might be some runaway slave. He insulted their intelligence by suggesting that giving to them would be tantamount to taking food from his own servants' mouths. Nabal's problem had moved beyond being stingy or lacking generosity. He had become mean-spirited and hurtful in his dealing with people. Later the Scriptures will describe a paralysis which immobilized him, but long before that time his heart was frozen and his spirit calloused.

## WHEN WISDOM INTERRUPTS ANGER

12 So David's young men turned on their heels and went back; and they came and told him all these words. 13 Then David said to his men, "Every man gird on his sword." So every man girded on his sword, and David also girded on his sword. And about four hundred men went with David, and two hundred stayed with the supplies.

14 Now one of the young men told Abigail, Nabal's wife, saying, "Look, David sent messengers from the wilderness to greet our master; and he reviled them. 15 But the men were very good to us, and we were not hurt, nor did we miss anything as long as we accompanied them, when we were in the fields. 16 They were a wall to us both by night and day, all the time we were with them keeping the sheep. 17 Now therefore, know and consider what you will do, for harm is determined against our master and against all his household. For he is such a scoundrel that one cannot speak to him."

18 Then Abigail made haste and took two hundred loaves of bread, two skins of wine, five sheep already dressed, five seahs of roasted grain, one hundred clusters of raisins, and two hundred cakes of figs, and loaded them on donkeys. 19 And she said to her servants, "Go on before me; see, I am coming after you." But she did not tell her husband Nabal.

20 So it was, as she rode on the donkey, that she went down under cover of the hill; and there were David and his men, coming down toward her, and she met them. 21 Now David had said, "Surely in vain I have protected all that this fellow has in the wilderness, so that nothing was missed of all that belongs to him. And he has repaid me evil for good. 22 May God do so, and more also, to the enemies of David, if I leave one male of all who belong to him by morning light."

23 Now when Abigail saw David, she dismounted quickly from the donkey, fell on her face before David, and bowed down to the ground. 24 So she fell at his feet and said: "On me, my lord, on me let this iniquity be! And please let your maidservant speak in your ears, and hear the words of your maidservant. 25 Please, let not my lord regard this scoundrel Nabal. For as his name is, so is he: Nabal is his name, and folly is with him! But I, your maidservant, did not see the young men of my LORD whom you sent. 26 Now therefore, my lord, as the LORD lives and as your soul lives, since the Lord has held you back from coming to bloodshed and from avenging yourself with your own hand, now then, let your enemies and those who seek harm for my lord be as Nabal. 27 And now this present which your maidservant has brought to my lord, let it be given to the young men who follow my lord. 28 Please forgive the trespass of your maidservant. For the LORD will certainly make for my lord an enduring house, because my lord fights the battles of the LORD, and evil is not found in you throughout your days. 29 Yet a man has risen to pursue you and seek your life, but the life of my lord shall be bound in the bundle of the living with the LORD your God; and the lives of your enemies He shall sling out, as from the pocket of a sling. 30 And it shall come to pass, when the LORD has done for my lord according to all the good that He has spoken concerning you, and has appointed you ruler over Israel, 31 that this will be no grief to you, nor offense of heart to my lord, either that you

have shed blood without cause, or that my lord has avenged himself. But when the LORD has dealt well with my lord, then remember your maidservant."

32 Then David said to Abigail: "Blessed is the LORD God of Israel, who sent you this day to meet me! 33 And blessed is your advice and blessed are you, because you have kept me this day from coming to bloodshed and from avenging myself with my own hand. 34 For indeed, as the LORD God of Israel lives, who has kept me back from hurting you, unless you had hurried and come to meet me, surely by morning light no males would have been left to Nabal!" 35 So David received from her hand what she had brought him, and said to her, "Go up in peace to your house. See, I have heeded your voice and respected your person."

—1 Samuel 25:12–35

The way the story has been told, readers have already been prepared for David's response to Nabal's churlish behavior and understand the implications of *"each of you gird on his sword"* (v. 13) and tend to sympathize with the proposed action. The feeling that Nabal needs to be taught a lesson comes quite naturally. It isn't until David and Abigail meet that we learn that David has made a vow to God that he will utterly destroy Nabal and every male child and servant (vv. 21–22). David had concluded that Nabal's rejection of his request was in essence a rejection of God, making his action against Nabal the "judgment of God" rather than David's revenge.

That David eventually thanked God for sending Abigail to deter him from his intentions (v. 32) is a clear indication that David's plan had been colored more by his desire for revenge than he himself had realized. One of the great dangers Christians face, even the most dedicated, is that it is too easy to confuse our own agenda with God's.

During my graduate studies I once spent an afternoon in a room of the library which contained all of the library, writings, and personal correspondence of a very notorious preacher. His grandson, feeling that the material had historical significance and wanting to preserve the memory of his grandfather after his death, donated the materials to the school. In book after book, article after article, and in much of his personal correspondence there was the common belief—that anyone who opposed him was opposing God and that an effort to destroy his personal enemies was actually helping God with his work. Yet even as I found myself reacting so strongly to his rationalizing his attitudes and actions, I realized that each of us has this tendency and needs to seek God's help lest we forget the difference between the Creator and the creature.

Abigail's response to her husband's foolish action can serve as a model for all who are not content to face with benign resignation the problems that are created by others. First, she was willing to hear the truth from servants. She based her plan on the information she received from the servants who had not been consulted by her husband. Second, she moved immediately to honor David's request with provisions for his men. While what was to be given didn't make a dent in Nabal's wealth, it did take time and effort to gather and transport food for six hundred persons. Finally, she designed a plan to meet David and to dissuade him from retaliating against the whole household because of Nabal's foolishness. Abigail could function as the patron saint of those who meet difficult situations with clear thinking, decisive action, and risk-taking efforts at reconciliation. What she did took both discernment and courage, but it was the only thing that could redeem a bad situation.

Her speech to David is a classic effort at reconciliation and a model of tact. While the main reason the story was preserved was related to its insights into the acceptance by the populace that David was indeed God's choice for king and how David was able to build support among the Calebites by his marriage to Abigail, there are also lessons for defusing potentially dangerous conflict between people. Since most of our unhappiness comes from conflict with people, and because so many people have an aversion to dealing directly with anything that creates tension, Abigail offers some help for us all.

Her first act was to accept responsibility for what had happened—*"On me let this iniquity be"* (v. 24). She was keenly aware that with the blame came also the punishment. She held herself responsible for not seeing or hearing David's servants when they came (v. 25). The changing of the target from the harsh and foolish Nabal to his intelligent and beautiful wife took David completely by surprise, and he was willing to halt his action and listen to her request. Those who are able to accept judgment for things they didn't do are much more apt to set things right than those who are always trying to blame others for their own actions. It's the principle of the Cross, and it opens doors for peace.

While Abigail made no effort to cover up her husband's actions, she separated herself from it and asked David to consider the source (v. 25). Her whole posture was one in which she treated

David as a rightful king and argued that her husband's slight of David was only the expected response of a man whose very name meant "fool." There was the suggestion that David and his warriors against a fool was a needless mismatch.

One of the most helpful things that Abigail did was to help David evaluate the consequences of his planned action. She even suggested that she might be saving him from doing something that would haunt him in the days to come and that rather than carrying out the judgment of God, what he planned might even thwart God's purpose (v. 31). A lot of tension is created in our lives by wanting both to be affirmed in all we think and do and also to be told the truth. While David was angry and felt justified in his plans, there must have been some small cloud of doubt in the back side of his mind about what he was doing or he would not have responded the way he did. Wise friends often don't tell us what we ought to do as much as they help us to recognize and act on what we already know and have ignored.

But the argument that cinched her case was that since David was under God's care then he could trust God to punish Nabal. She used as her analogy of God's care for David a practice she had witnessed often—the placing of valuable jewels and pieces of silver and gold on a cloth, rolling it, and tying it so that the possessions might be stored or transported without danger (v. 29). Her words had the power to transport David from the trying circumstances of the moment and remind him that what Abigail said was true. Since the day Samuel had anointed him he had been in God's hands. Each of us needs constantly to be reminded that our lives are in God's hands and we can trust Him ultimately to make things right.

With the assumption that God would take care of Nabal and would eventually make David ruler of Israel (v. 30), Abigail's last request was for herself. She pled, *"When the Lord has dealt well with my lord, then remember your maidservant"* (v. 31). David's response was like a doxology in which he praised God for the whole experience and the difference it was going to make (vv. 32–33). He received the gift and spared the household (v. 35). It was to David's credit that he responded the way he did. Since so many people are allergic to logic and common sense and ideas that didn't originate with themselves, it is encouraging to find a great and powerful man who is able to take good counsel. We all have impulses that need to be denied, plans that need to be rethought, and feelings that ought not be translated into action. We all need to ask God to give us the ability to recognize wisdom that is of Him, whatever the human source.

## THE SOLIDIFYING OF SUPPORT

[36] Now Abigail went to Nabal, and there he was, holding a feast in his house, like the feast of a king. And Nabal's heart was merry within him, for he was very drunk; therefore she told him nothing, little or much, until morning light. [37] So it was, in the morning, when the wine had gone from Nabal, and his wife had told him these things, that his heart died within him, and he became like a stone. [38] Then it happened, after about ten days, that the LORD struck Nabal, and he died.

[39] So when David heard that Nabal was dead, he said, "Blessed be the LORD, who has pleaded the cause of my reproach from the hand of Nabal, and has kept His servant from evil! For the LORD has returned the wickedness of Nabal on his own head."

And David sent and proposed to Abigail, to take her as his wife. [40] When the servants of David had come to Abigail at Carmel, they spoke to her saying, "David sent us to you, to ask you to become his wife."

[41] Then she arose, bowed her face to the earth, and said, "Here is your maidservant, a servant to wash the feet of the servants of my lord." [42] So Abigail rose in haste and rode on a donkey, attended by five of her maidens; and she followed the messengers of David, and became his wife.
[43] David also took Ahinoam of Jezreel, and so both of them were his wives.

[44] But Saul had given Michal his daughter, David's wife, to Palti the son of Laish, who was from Gallim.

*1 Samuel 25:36–44*

The events described in these verses wrap up the loose ends of the story and show their effect upon David's move toward the throne. The first event was the death of Nabal (vv. 36–38). When his wife returned from her successful negotiations with David, her husband was holding a great festival banquet and was too drunk for her to expect to communicate with him. When some of the effects of the alcohol had worn off the next day, she told him all that had happened. Upon hearing it, Nabal had either a serious stroke or a massive heart attack. Within ten days he was dead. While a modern-day autopsy would have probably discovered a natural cause for his death, it was the conclusion of everyone that it was the Lord who had *"struck Nabal"* (v. 38).

Upon hearing of Nabal's death, David rejoiced that God had vindicated his own cause and sent a proposal of marriage to Nabal's widow, which she quickly accepted (vv. 39–42). While David was impressed with her beauty and intelligence and was grateful for the role she had played in keeping him from making a grave mistake, the marriage had strong political implications. Being married to the richest widow in the area of the Calebites both eased his financial dilemma and solidified his support in the area. Mentioning David's marriage to Ahinoam of Jezreel immediately after the announcement of his marriage to Abigail would add strength to this political view of David's marriages.

First Samuel 26 tells of another incident in which David spared Saul's life. It is again obvious that the material that has been preserved has not considered chronological sequence of great importance. What was important was to show how God brought David to the throne. Ultimately, the most important part of a person's story is how God is able to work through many events and experiences to accomplish His purpose for our lives.

## ENEMIES WHO NEVER GIVE UP

**26:1** Now the Ziphites came to Saul at Gibeah, saying, "Is David not hiding in the hill of Hachilah, opposite Jeshimon?" 2 Then Saul arose and went down to the Wilderness of Ziph, having three thousand chosen men of Israel with him, to seek David in the Wilderness of Ziph. 3 And Saul encamped in the hill of Hachilah, which is opposite Jeshimon, by the road. But David stayed in the wilderness, and he saw that Saul came after him into the wilderness. 4 David therefore sent out spies, and understood that Saul had indeed come.

5 So David arose and came to the place where Saul had encamped. And David saw the place where Saul lay, and Abner the son of Ner, the commander of his army. Now Saul lay within the camp, with the people encamped all around him. 6 Then David answered, and said to Ahimelech the Hittite and to Abishai the son of Zeruiah, brother of Joab, saying, "Who will go down with me to Saul in the camp?"

And Abishai said, "I will go down with you."

7 So David and Abishai came to the people by night; and there Saul lay sleeping within the camp, with his spear

stuck in the ground by his head. And Abner and the people lay all around him. ⁸ Then Abishai said to David, "God has delivered your enemy into your hand this day. Now therefore, please, let me strike him at once with the spear, right to the earth; and I will not have to strike him a second time!"

⁹ But David said to Abishai, "Do not destroy him; for who can stretch out his hand against the LORD's anointed, and be guiltless?" ¹⁰ David said furthermore, "As the LORD lives, the LORD shall strike him, or his day shall come to die, or he shall go out to battle and perish. ¹¹ The LORD forbid that I should stretch out my hand against the LORD's anointed. But please, take now the spear and the jug of water that are by his head, and let us go." ¹² So David took the spear and the jug of water by Saul's head, and they got away; and no man saw or knew it or awoke. For they were all asleep, because a deep sleep from the LORD had fallen on them.

*—1 Samuel 26:1–12*

People reading through 1 Samuel for the first time frequently come to chapter 26 and have the feeling that they had read this story before. While there are a number of significant differences between chapters 24 and 26, the similarities are so striking that many scholars have concluded that they are really two different accounts of the same incidents, the differences being explained by the perspectives of those who preserved the separate accounts. But there are other scholars who in spite of all the similarities feel that the two chapters refer to two separate incidents in the struggle between Saul and David. The historian whom God used to preserve the material we have in the Scripture was much more interested in the testimony it gave to the legitimacy of David's claim to the throne than to its sequence.

One of the mistakes many Christians make in studying the Bible is to try to find meaning for their lives today without first trying to discover the original context of the events described and the purpose for which these stories were preserved in their present form. When we ignore this very basic principle for "rightly dividing the word of truth" (2 Tim. 2:15), we are apt to spend our time trying to solve problems that were not problems for those whom God used to preserve the Scriptures.

Both chapters fulfill the compiler's purpose; namely, they declare David's innocence of any treachery or treason against Saul.

This fact would counteract any effort by David's enemies to besmirch his reputation or to undermine the people's confidence in his leadership. Both chapters stress God's protection of David and that Saul no longer enjoyed that status. This is dramatized by the fact that although Saul is the pursuer in both stories and that his forces are five times the size of David's, no harm comes to David. Both chapters emphasize the fact both that vengeance belongs to God and that we should not harm those whom God anoints. Both chapters are a reminder that during this period David was constantly harassed. All these points were central to the intention of the one who compiled the material that we have.

Despite efforts at reconciliation and times when Saul seemed to abandon his pursuit of David, it didn't take much for Saul to take up the chase again. This time it was news from the people of the Wilderness of Zith that David was *"hiding in the hill of Hachilah"* (v. 1). I was an idealistic teenager the first time I read this story and could not imagine why they would betray the man who had become a national hero as a result of his exploits against the Philistines and others of Israel's enemies. Now I realize that it wasn't that they did not like David. They were afraid of Saul, of what he would do to them if David were in their part of the land and they did not tell the king. They remembered the massacre at Nob, where Saul had slain the priests, their families, and every living thing that they owned because they had helped David (1 Sam. 22:19).

While most of us never have to deal with the level of violence described in these stories, we all have our actions more controlled by fear than we realize. And most of it isn't motivated by a low threshold for pain but by a desire to be liked by everyone. People sit quietly while their friends' reputations are attacked and say nothing because they "don't want to cause trouble." Others with genuine convictions on issues critical to society or to the church refuse to allow them to surface because they have seen what happens to those who do and they are afraid. We are not really too different from the people of Zith who had been so terrorized by Saul's violence that they would betray David. We need to discover an antidote for fear in our relationship with God. Paul, writing to young Timothy, reminded us all that "God has not given us a spirit of fear, but of power and of love and of a sound mind" (2 Tim. 1:7).

Saul had hardly made camp with his three thousand soldiers before spies brought the news to David (v. 4). Because the encampment was in the open, it was possible for David's men to take positions where they could look down on it and discern that Saul was bedded down at the very center of the camp, surrounded by his soldiers and guarded by his general, Abner (v. 5). One of David's most courageous soldiers, Abishai, volunteered to accompany David into the camp. Under normal circumstances, this would have been considered a suicide mission. It's not until the adventure was over that the narrator reveals that *"a deep sleep from the LORD had fallen on them"* (v. 12), helping us to understand how they were able to carry out their feat undetected.

The compiler of the story wanted to be sure that his readers would realize that Saul's efforts were frustrated by God's activity, not David's cunning. One of the most natural and dangerous tendencies of many Christians is to ask for God's help in our difficult times and afterward to act like we made it on our own.

When David and his men came across Saul in the cave, they urged David to kill him (24:4). At the encampment, Abishai also felt that God had delivered Saul into their hands and offered to kill Saul with perhaps the very spear with which Saul had sought to pin David to the wall. Because of his feeling about the sin involved in laying hands on "God's anointed," David refused Abishai's request (v. 9). His feeling was that whether Saul died of some disease, or of old age, or in some battle, that it was in God's hands and not his own (vv. 10–11). This ability to continue to trust God with his life was one of the dominant characteristics of David's life. Sometimes it seems easier to try to "help God" make things happen rather than trust in God's timetable.

While he wouldn't allow physical harm to come to Saul, David felt the need to prove what he could have done, so he took the spear and a tiny canteenlike water jug and retreated to a spot above and away from the camp (v. 12).

## WHEN THERE'S TALK WITHOUT COMMUNICATION

13 Now David went over to the other side, and stood on the top of a hill afar off, a great distance being between them. 14 And David called out to the people and to Abner the son of Ner, saying, "Do you not answer, Abner?"

Then Abner answered and said, "Who are you, calling out to the king?"

15 So David said to Abner, "Are you not a man? And who is like you in Israel? Why then have you not guarded your lord the king? For one of the people came in to destroy your lord the king. 16 This thing that you have done is not

good. As the Lord lives, you deserve to die, because you have not guarded your master, the Lord's anointed. And now see where the king's spear is, and the jug of water that was by his head."

[17] Then Saul knew David's voice, and said, "Is that your voice, my son David?"

David said, "It is my voice, my lord, O king." [18] And he said, "Why does my lord thus pursue his servant? For what have I done, or what evil is in my hand? [19] Now therefore, please, let my lord the king hear the words of his servant: If the Lord has stirred you up against me, let Him accept an offering. But if it is the children of men, may they be cursed before the Lord, for they have driven me out this day from sharing in the inheritance of the Lord, saying, 'Go, serve other gods.' [20] So now, do not let my blood fall to the earth before the face of the Lord. For the king of Israel has come out to seek a flea, as when one hunts a partridge in the mountains."

[21] Then Saul said, "I have sinned. Return, my son David. For I will harm you no more, because my life was precious in your eyes this day. Indeed I have played the fool and erred exceedingly."

[22] And David answered and said, "Here is the king's spear. Let one of the young men come over and get it. [23] May the Lord repay every man for his righteousness and his faithfulness; for the Lord delivered you into my hand today, but I would not stretch out my hand against the Lord's anointed. [24] And indeed, as your life was valued much this day in my eyes, so let my life be valued much in the eyes of the Lord, and let Him deliver me out of all tribulation."

[25] Then Saul said to David, "May you be blessed, my son David! You shall both do great things and also still prevail."

So David went on his way, and Saul returned to his place.

*—1 Samuel 26:13–25*

If we were to make a study of all the dialogues between David and Saul that occurred after David was driven from the palace, we would probably discover that little meaningful conversation ever really took place. This dialogue began between David and Abner, who was the king's representative and the one personally responsible for Saul's safety. Surprisingly, David condemns Abner and all the soldiers for not doing a better job of guarding the *"LORD's anointed"* (vv. 14–16). To prove that they had neglected their duty he showed them the spear and jug that he and Abishai had brought back from the camp. The whole point of the story was that those who had come hunting David had themselves been found by David, and he could have killed their king had he desired. This would counteract any effort to paint David as a person who had betrayed his king.

It was Saul who first recognized David's voice and called out to him. David acknowledged him as *"my lord, O king"* (v. 17). The heart of the chapter is found in David's appeal to Saul (vv. 18–20). David insisted that he was innocent of any wrongdoing and pleaded with Saul to tell him of any wrong that he had done (v. 18). As was true in other such requests, Saul not only had no charges to make but freely admitted that he had wronged David and promised never again to seek to harm him (v. 21). While the promises didn't last long, that they were made serves as a reminder of David's innocence and of Saul's inability to control his deeply rooted hatred of David. There may have been a time when Saul could have kept the resolve of his heart, but that was long ago. His pathetic condition is a reminder that habits of thought and action that we willfully introduce into our lives, thinking all along that we can control them, can remain long enough and get such a grip upon us that we are no longer able to exorcise them.

There are two very interesting aspects of this particular plea to Saul. First, David tries to explore with Saul the source of his feelings about David. In the speech recorded in chapter 24, there is the hint that maybe evil men have planted false rumors in Saul's mind (v. 9). But David in this speech wonders if maybe it is God who has stirred Saul and offers to make a sacrifice to God and to ask for forgiveness (v. 19). If the source isn't God, then David suggests that they will be cursed before the Lord (v. 19). While his name isn't called, there is a strong inference that Saul is the one to suffer God's judgment.

David's plea not to *"let my blood fall to the earth before the face of the LORD"* (v. 20) reflects his feeling that Saul's pursuit has driven him from his friends, from the normal pursuits of life, and even away from the places where God is worshiped in Judah. When Israel had been in the wilderness God related to them as a covenant community not connected to place. When they arrived in the Promised Land, one of the natural temptations would have been to limit God to that place. My grandmother never referred to the place where we worshiped as the "church" but as the "meeting house." Her contention was that the church was the community of believers and the meeting house was where it met to worship. That is a good distinction to make but not always an easy one.

After Saul's confession and promise never to pursue David again, the spear is returned to the king (v. 22). No mention is made of the jar. The chapter closes with David's reminder that he has again spared Saul's life and with the prayer that God may be as good to David as David has been to Saul (v. 24). If a person did not know the true dynamic of the relationship he would be moved by Saul's reference to David as *"my son David"* (v. 25), but the real situation is revealed by *"David went on his way, and Saul returned to his place"* (v. 25). Nothing had changed, and nothing would change in the relationship.

When I study the Scriptures I try to find myself in the stories. Even as I have written about Saul's hatred of David, I have thought of people who hate me and who try to do me harm. And as I have written about David's transparency in his efforts to be reconciled to Saul, I think of those times I have reached out to people without success. But even as I had these thoughts I had to admit that I wasn't being entirely honest with myself. For just as often I have played Saul's role. I've harbored feelings that I was afraid to analyze, have found it hard to admit that I might be wrong in my evaluation, and often collect only material that substantiates conclusions I have no intention of abandoning. My prayer is that God will not abandon me to my prejudices and my stubbornness, but will work to keep me open to the possibilities of getting rid of an enemy by becoming a friend.

# CHAPTER TEN—LIFE AMONG THE PHILISTINES

## I SAMUEL 27:1—31:13

*Scripture Outline*

This chapter begins the tale of a period of exile that continues into the first chapter of 2 Samuel. The lad who slew Goliath, the Philistine champion, now takes his soldiers and their families into the land of the Philistines. While these chapters serve well the compiler's goal to show how God brought David to the throne in spite of seemingly insurmountable obstacles, many of his activities create problems for the modern reader who brings a New Testament ethic to these chapters. But there is more to be learned here than Jewish history.

These stories are a reminder that God always works in the context of history, whether dealing with a nation or an individual.

This is why an understanding of the history and culture into which God's self-revelation is given is so important to the understanding of Scripture. These accounts also remind us that when we are interpreting stories in the Old Testament, it is necessary to judge their ethical concepts by God's supreme revelation in Jesus Christ. If we fail to do these two things, we will unconsciously use our own cultural standards as a basis for interpreting a totally different culture, and we will be tempted to adopt ethical norms that do not measure up to Christ's teachings or standards.

## FINDING SAFETY WITH ENEMIES

**27:1** And David said in his heart, "Now I shall perish someday by the hand of Saul. There is nothing better for me than that I should speedily escape to the land of the Philistines; and Saul will despair of me, to seek me anymore in any part of Israel. So I shall escape out of his hand." 2 Then David arose and went over with the six hundred men who were with him to Achish the son of Maoch, king of Gath. 3 So David dwelt with Achish at Gath, he and his men, each man with his household, and David with his two wives, Ahinoam the Jezreelitess, and Abigail the Carmelitess, Nabal's widow. 4 And it was told Saul that David had fled to Gath; so he sought him no more.

5 Then David said to Achish, "If I have now found favor in your eyes, let them give me a place in some town in the country, that I may dwell there. For why should your servant dwell in the royal city with you?" 6 So Achish gave him Ziklag that day. Therefore Ziklag has belonged to the kings of Judah to this day. 7 Now the time that David dwelt in the country of the Philistines was one full year and four months.

8 And David and his men went up and raided the Geshurites, the Girzites, and the Amalekites. For those nations were the inhabitants of the land from of old, as you go to Shur, even as far as the land of Egypt. 9 Whenever David attacked the land, he left neither man nor woman alive, but took away the sheep, the oxen, the donkeys, the camels, and the apparel, and returned and came to Achish. 10 Then Achish would say, "Where have you made a raid today?" And David would say, "Against the southern area of Judah, or against the southern area of the Jerahmeelites, or against the southern area of the Kenites." 11 David would

save neither man nor woman alive, to bring news to Gath, saying, "Lest they should inform on us, saying, 'Thus David did.'" And thus was his behavior all the time he dwelt in the country of the Philistines. [12] So Achish believed David, saying, "He has made his people Israel utterly abhor him; therefore he will be my servant forever."

—*1 Samuel 27:1–12*

As chapter 27 begins, David seems to be at the end of his tether. He and his men can go nowhere without Saul's pursuing them. David is aware that, in spite of Saul's words promising change, nothing has really changed in the relationship. There is a lot of "health and success" preaching today which implies that when we serve God and trust Him, then only good things can happen to us. But that didn't happen in David's experience. God did not protect David from experiencing difficult periods in his life, but He did work through those experiences to prepare him for the throne. The religion that equates God's love with a life without problems will crumble as it crashes against life's realities, but a faith that turns to God whatever the circumstances will grow and prevail.

There was a certain amount of courage shown in David's choosing the land of the Philistines as his refuge. On a previous trip he met with such hostility that he had to feign madness to escape with his life (1 Sam. 21:10–15). But this time there were several differences. At the time of his earlier visit he was still remembered as the one who had "slain his ten thousands," most of whom had been Philistines. But by now the word had come of Saul's total disaffection with David. And this time, instead of coming alone, he had six hundred seasoned warriors. Their number posed no real threat to the Philistines since they had potential as mercenaries—a common practice in those days. The account is so familiar to those who know the Bible stories that the radical nature of David's decision is missed. If one of our generals was out of favor with the Joint Chiefs of Staff and suddenly took all of his top aides and moved to an enemy nation, the media would be full of stories about the "defection."

This decision also accomplished David's purpose, of going somewhere Saul was not likely to follow. He could have gone to Moab, which would have been a neutral place, but Saul would probably have followed. But when he went to the land of the Philistines and the word reached Saul, *he sought him no more* (v. 4). The story does not give many details as to how David negotiated with Achish, who was the king's son. But he leased Ziklag, which was on the border with Judah, probably in exchange for military services or for a portion of the plunder from his raids. Many feel that David's request for a separate city, rather than staying in the capital, was to give him more freedom to carry out his plan of operating within the land of the Philistines but continuing to espouse the cause of Judah.

David's men supported themselves by raiding various people and gathering plunder. Achish and his people thought they were raiding the villages of Judah, and David nursed that misconception by making sure there were no prisoners or survivors from his raids who might enlighten Achish. David was so successful in his deception that a larger problem was created later—Achish decided that David was so trustworthy that he would make him and his men a part of the Philistine army (1 Sam. 28:1–3).

This story was preserved to show how God was able to bless David even as he lived among Israel's enemies. When the story was told later in the Jewish households, everyone would have been delighted at David's successful guile in deceiving the enemy. While what David did was considered normal in his day, modern-day readers may have difficulty with the unashamed deceit and extreme cruelty. American soldiers faced criminal charges for killing all the women and children in a Vietnamese village because they felt they had harbored the Viet Cong. Yet David massacred whole villages to cover up his deceit. To keep us from feeling morally superior to David, we need to remember that the same type of cruelty still goes on today, some of it sponsored by our own government and supported by some Christian groups.

The compiler could not have anticipated that this tale might become a stumbling block to people reading it centuries later. The main purpose of this story is to tell how God put David beyond the reach of Saul and how he was able to survive, even in the land of the enemy. Earlier I mentioned how God is able to take the difficult experiences of our lives and salvage good from them. It was probably a result of his living outside Judah that David was so successful in negotiating treaties with Judah's neighbors when he was king. It also shows how God works with us, not only in the context of our culture, but in spite of a limited knowledge of His nature and purpose. We need to remember always that God has to overlook our inadequacies in order to work in any of our lives.

## WHEN DECEIT WORKS TOO WELL

**28:1** Now it happened in those days that the Philistines gathered their armies together for war, to fight with Israel.

And Achish said to David, "You assuredly know that you
will go out with me to battle, you and your men."

² So David said to Achish, "Surely you know what your
servant can do."

And Achish said to David, "Therefore I will make you
one of my chief guardians forever."

*—1 Samuel 28:1–2*

Chapter 28 pictures the full tragedy of Saul's life. After his fall
from favor for not honoring the ban on Amalek (15:16–31), he experienced one failure after another while David knew only success.
This chapter also contains one of the most unusual episodes in the
life of King Saul—his consulting a witch in an effort to seek the advice of the dead prophet Samuel. This chapter turns the tables in the
Saul/David conflict. On the surface, driving David into exile seemed
to end any hope David had for ascending the throne and appeared
to secure for Saul a firm grip on political power. Here, however, we
learn that Saul is at the end of his career and that, even in exile, God
has blessed David. Our story begins with David's being trapped in
the web of his own deceit and ends with Saul's trudging back to a
battle that he knew he could not win, having been judged for his disobedience and his flawed character.

In the previous chapter, the compiler celebrated the clever way
in which David was able to convince Achish that he had been
attacking Israelite villages when actually he had been destroying
Israel's enemies. There is a price tag, however, for that deceit. As
the Philistines gathered their army for a major offensive against
Saul and his army, Achish decided that David had proved to be
such a trustworthy ally that he would include him and his men
among those who would attack the Israelite army (v. 1).

Achish's plans posed a terrible dilemma for David. He couldn't
refuse because that would have revealed his true loyalties and
brought about his death. Neither could he go against his own people in battle. In his helplessness, David makes a very ambiguous
statement, *"Surely you know what your servant can do"* (v. 2). Taking
his statement as consent, Achish gave David and his men one of
the most important places in his company—his bodyguard. Up to
this point, David had always cleverly covered his deceit. Now he
was helpless and would have to rely on someone else to deliver
him from his dilemma.

While the purpose of preserving this event in the Scriptures
was to show how God was able to bring David to the throne, there

is an interesting lesson to be learned about the price of deceit. There is no more natural temptation than to pretend to be what we aren't. We do this throughout life for a variety of reasons: to get people to like us, to avoid conflict, to get a job we're not qualified for, or to cover up some wrong we've done. By its nature, deceit is self-serving and abuses trust, makes real communication impossible, confuses everyone, and fragments the identity of the one who pretends to be what he isn't. Once it is adopted as a way of life, deceit leads further and further away from reality and creates conflict, hostility, and all sorts of pain. How David was rescued from his dilemma is revealed in chapter 29.

## A LEADER WITHOUT CONFIDENCE

<sup>3</sup> Now Samuel had died, and all Israel had lamented for him and buried him in Ramah, in his own city. And Saul had put the mediums and the spiritists out of the land.
<sup>4</sup> Then the Philistines gathered together, and came and encamped at Shunem. So Saul gathered all Israel together, and they encamped at Gilboa. <sup>5</sup> When Saul saw the army of the Philistines, he was afraid, and his heart trembled greatly.
<sup>6</sup> And when Saul inquired of the LORD, the LORD did not answer him, either by dreams or by Urim or by the prophets.
<sup>7</sup> Then Saul said to his servants, "Find me a woman who is a medium, that I may go to her and inquire of her."

And his servants said to him, "In fact, there is a woman who is a medium at En Dor."

*—1 Samuel 28:3–7*

These verses picture a desperate man. Saul faced an enemy he wasn't sure he could defeat. He sought the advice of God without success. He seemed to be plunging headlong into a fate he didn't seem able to avoid. Therefore, all of his actions need to be understood in the light of these circumstances.

The compiler begins this section by presenting two facts that are important if the reader is going to understand Saul's amazing action which follows. Although Samuel's death had been reported in chapter 25, it is noted here as an explanation of Saul's behavior. The other fact was that, as a part of his faithfulness to God, Saul had made it illegal to try to communicate with the dead. There is in the Bible an uncompromising prohibition of the use of mediums (Deut. 18:11; Lev. 20:6, 27).

Saul was driven to seek a message from beyond the grave because he faced the most powerful threat the Philistines had posed to his kingdom since he had been king. As the armies faced each other he was terrified. Saul had exiled the only warrior he had who could have led Israel into battle with any hope of victory. His fears were multiplied because when he made efforts to seek God's counsel *"the LORD did not answer him"* (v. 6) by any of the usual ways in which God communicated with His children—no dreams with religious meaning, no priest to inquire of God, no prophet to speak the word of God. Samuel was dead and Saul could still feel the sting of his last message (ch. 15) and missed having his counsel. Saul had killed the priests for assisting David, and Abiathar, the sole survivor, had defected to David, taking with him the ephod. When Saul had lain down and slept in sacred places, no dreams had come from God.

This story is a classic example of a person who has rejected God's guidance. When he suffers the consequences of his action, he is without resource or help. Saul had "made his bed," but now he didn't want to "sleep in it." We live in a society that does not see the relationship between our decisions and what happens to us. Even the religious community seems to feel that no matter what we do with God's instruction for our lives, at any moment we can repent and turn to God. Naturally He will not only forgive us but will relieve us of the consequences of our actions. God does forgive graciously, and grace causes our relationship to be restored, but that does not mean that we can start afresh without having to live with the results of our action. An abusive father or an alcoholic mother may discover God's love and forgiveness, but that does not undo the damage done to children who have been scarred physically and emotionally by past actions and experiences. For Saul to be forced to go into battle alone was nothing more than the natural results of his decisions and actions.

## WHEN DESPERATION RULES

[8] So Saul disguised himself and put on other clothes, and he went, and two men with him; and they came to the woman by night. And he said, "Please conduct a séance for me, and bring up for me the one I shall name to you."

[9] Then the woman said to him, "Look, you know what Saul has done, how he has cut off the mediums and the spiritists from the land. Why then do you lay a snare for my life, to cause me to die?"

10 And Saul swore to her by the LORD, saying, "As the LORD lives, no punishment shall come upon you for this thing."

11 Then the woman said, "Whom shall I bring up for you?"

And he said, "Bring up Samuel for me."

12 When the woman saw Samuel, she cried out with a loud voice. And the woman spoke to Saul, saying, "Why have you deceived me? For you are Saul!"

13 And the king said to her, "Do not be afraid. What did you see?"

And the woman said to Saul, "I saw a spirit ascending out of the earth."

14 So he said to her, "What is his form?"

And she said, "An old man is coming up, and he is covered with a mantle." And Saul perceived that it was Samuel, and he stooped with his face to the ground and bowed down.

15 Now Samuel said to Saul, "Why have you disturbed me by bringing me up?"

And Saul answered, "I am deeply distressed; for the Philistines make war against me, and God has departed from me and does not answer me anymore, neither by prophets nor by dreams. Therefore I have called you, that you may reveal to me what I should do."

16 Then Samuel said: "So why do you ask me, seeing the LORD has departed from you and has become your enemy? 17 And the LORD has done for Himself as He spoke by me. For the LORD has torn the kingdom out of your hand and given it to your neighbor, David. 18 Because you did not obey the voice of the LORD nor execute His fierce wrath upon Amalek, therefore the LORD has done this thing to you this day. 19 Moreover the LORD will also deliver Israel with you into the hand of the Philistines. And tomorrow you and your sons will be with me. The LORD will also deliver the army of Israel into the hand of the Philistines."

*—1 Samuel 28:8–19*

While consulting witches was legislated against in the Scriptures and had been made illegal by the edict of Saul himself, the king's servants had no problem locating one. The servants located a "lady of ghosts," which is a literal translation of "witches." She lived at En Dor, which was about seventeen miles from Saul's camp at Gilboa. Going to her involved both exposing Saul to the Philistines and involving himself in an illegal act. One of the great temptations of all authority figures is to feel that laws are good for the people but do not apply to themselves. They say, "I am above the law."

These six verses raise all sorts of questions that neither they nor those who have made a vocation of studying them are able to answer to everyone's satisfaction. There is little benefit in using this incident as a basis of discussing whether there really are those who can talk with the dead on our behalf. The compiler was mainly interested in showing the degree to which Saul had sunk and the almost total deterioration of the man on the eve of the day on which he was to lead Israel into battle against her ancient foe.

Saul went at night because it was easier to avoid being seen by the Philistines and because it was believed that it was easier for the mediums to contact the dead in Sheol at night. (At that time Sheol was thought of as a watery place beneath the earth where all the dead experienced a shadowy existence—a place of rest but not one of either reward or punishment.) He dressed in a disguise so neither the Philistines nor the woman would know who he was. In the whole episode the woman seemed to have a higher ethic than God's anointed king, first in her reciting the law to him and later in ministering to him in his despondency. The form of the dialogue would indicate that Saul only heard the voice and it was the witch who described what she saw.

Most people feel that Saul's desperate move to contact Samuel was an effort to know the future just as foolish people today read horoscopes in an effort to know ahead of time what will happen to them. It was the common belief that dead people know the future. I'm inclined to think that Saul already knew the future and that he wanted Samuel to intercede with God to bring him back into His grace and favor and change the future.

Whatever Saul's expectations were for his attempted meeting with Samuel, nothing good came from it. There was no I-have-good-news-and-bad-news format: It was all bad news. First, Samuel reiterated what he had told Saul previously concerning God's having torn the kingdom from him (v. 17) and reminding him of the reason for God's action (v. 18). Then Samuel's message struck Saul with two blows: the announcement both of the defeat of Israel and of the death of Saul and his sons (v. 19). This was the final word of rejection and Saul fell to the ground and lay there "dreadfully afraid" (v. 20) for he had heard and understood at the deepest level that all was gone for him. There is not a sadder picture of despair and hopelessness in the Bible.

## SMALL COMFORT FROM A STRANGE SOURCE

20 Immediately Saul fell full length on the ground, and was dreadfully afraid because of the words of Samuel. And there was no strength in him, for he had eaten no food all day or all night.
21 And the woman came to Saul and saw that he was severely troubled, and said to him, "Look, your maidservant has obeyed your voice, and I have put my life in my hands and heeded the words which you spoke to me. 22 Now therefore, please, heed also the voice of your maidservant, and let me set a piece of bread before you; and eat, that you may have strength when you go on your way."
23 But he refused and said, "I will not eat."
So his servants, together with the woman, urged him; and he heeded their voice. Then he arose from the ground and sat on the bed. 24 Now the woman had a fatted calf in the house, and she hastened to kill it. And she took flour and kneaded it, and baked unleavened bread from it. 25 So she brought it before Saul and his servants, and they ate. Then they rose and went away that night.

—*1 Samuel 28:20–25*

This chapter ends with a very touching sequel. The woman who—at great risk—had joined the king in an illegal activity was moved by Saul's helplessness. In contrast with Saul from whom all strength had fled, she took firm measures and forced him to eat *"that you may have strength when you go on your way"* (v. 22). Her action ought to serve as a gentle reminder that there can be in every human being, whatever their state, the capacity for compassion for another human being. She took from her larder the best she had to offer and prepared what was probably Saul's last meal before his death. While we know neither her motives nor her name, she performed a moving act. It stands in such contrast to the scene of Saul and his servants as they began a nightlong walk back to their camp in order to be there to fight a battle they could not win.

## BEING SAVED BY OUR ENEMIES

29:1 Then the Philistines gathered together all their armies at Aphek, and the Israelites encamped by a fountain which is in Jezreel. 2 And the lords of the Philistines passed in review by hundreds and by thousands, but David and his men passed in review at the rear with Achish. [3] Then the princes of the Philistines said, "What are these Hebrews doing here?"

And Achish said to the princes of the Philistines, "Is this not David, the servant of Saul king of Israel, who has been with me these days, or these years? And to this day I have found no fault in him since he defected to me."

[4] But the princes of the Philistines were angry with him; so the princes of the Philistines said to him, "Make this fellow return, that he may go back to the place which you have appointed for him, and do not let him go down with us to battle, lest in the battle he become our adversary. For with what could he reconcile himself to his master, if not with the heads of these men? [5] Is this not David, of whom they sang to one another in dances, saying:

'Saul has slain his thousands,
And David his ten thousands'?"

[6] Then Achish called David and said to him, "Surely, as the LORD lives, you have been upright, and your going out and your coming in with me in the army is good in my sight. For to this day I have not found evil in you since the day of your coming to me. Nevertheless the lords do not favor you. [7] Therefore return now, and go in peace, that you may not displease the lords of the Philistines."

[8] So David said to Achish, "But what have I done? And to this day what have you found in your servant as long as I have been with you, that I may not go and fight against the enemies of my lord the king?"

[9] Then Achish answered and said to David, "I know that you are as good in my sight as an angel of God; nevertheless the princes of the Philistines have said, 'He shall not go up with us to the battle.' [10] Now therefore, rise early in the morning with your master's servants who have come with you. And as soon as you are up early in the morning and have light, depart."

[11] So David and his men rose early to depart in the morning, to return to the land of the Philistines. And the Philistines went up to Jezreel.

*—1 Samuel 29:1–11*

The person whom God used to compile these materials certainly had a flair for telling a story in such a way as to keep our attention. He told of the dilemma David faced (28:1–2) when it looked as though he and his men were to be a part of a Philistine army marching to battle against the Israelites. Just when the reader decided that there was no way out for David, the story was interrupted by the account of Saul's visit to the witch of En Dor. Now in these eleven verses we discover what happened to prevent David from having to do battle against his own people. God solved the problem by using David's enemies.

The whole of the Philistine army was gathered at Aphek, a very important military outpost. In the process of preparing to move out to battle, each commander came by to review his troops (vv. 1–2). David and his men were at the end of the processional, next to the king. The Philistine commanders immediately protested the very idea of allowing David and his men to fight alongside the Philistines. Achish defended the decision on the basis of how David had performed since *"he defected to me"* (v. 3). Achish took great pride in the fact that King Saul's son-in-law had become his vassal. This pride, however, made him vulnerable to David's deceit, causing him to trust David with the most important of tasks—serving as the king's bodyguard (28:2). It is a sad truth that many of us are deceived in life because we want to believe certain things or people so much that we don't face facts. We are all too easily fooled when we want to believe something.

While Achish was naive about David's true loyalties, his men were not. They had remained free from the spell of David's charm and were better judges of his heart than their king. They remembered Goliath and the humiliation of his death. Some remembered when David had fooled them with his feigned madness. All of them remembered the song that had been sung about David's prowess as a mighty warrior (v. 5). Some may have even known of David's passing up opportunities to kill Saul because he did not want to harm God's anointed. In spite of what seemed to be circumspect behavior since coming over to the other side, Achish's commanders felt that the pattern of David's life suggested that in a showdown between Israel and the Philistines there was no way that David would be loyal to the Philistines—and they were right.

In evaluating the character of people most of us need to develop greater spiritual discernment. We should not be taken in by holy words when they stand in conflict with the pattern of one's life. The old saying is true: If it looks like a duck, quacks like a duck, and swims in the pond with ducks, then it's probably a duck. To the Philistine commanders David looked like an Israelite, and they didn't want to risk their lives with him by their side in battle.

Finally Achish gave in to the pressure and came to David with great apologies for the necessity of sending him home to Ziklag, but as he did so he reaffirmed his absolute confidence in David's integrity. David protested his innocence, renewed his vows to Achish, and then led his men home to Ziklag. There was some ambiguity in his reverence to *"my lord the king"* (v. 8). Achish could have thought that it was a reference to himself, but David could have been thinking of Saul. The story does not give us any idea of what David would have done had he been accepted by the commanders. Maybe he had a plan to betray the Philistines and win a victory for his people. The story, however, seems to indicate that God is able to use people who are not His own people to advance His cause.

In stark contrast to Saul, for whom nothing goes right, here is a story of David who is trapped one moment in a dilemma from which he cannot extricate himself and then in the next moment he is sent home with his men and has remained in the favor of a great Philistine ruler. It's another example of God's intervention in the ordinary affairs of men to bring His anointed to the throne. Sensitive Christians who look over their shoulders at how things have worked out in their lives will often note that God has been at work even when they were not aware of it—sometimes using people who don't like us or trust us to accomplish God's will for our lives.

The next chapter follows David home to a crisis situation and shows him victorious in a battle against the Amalekites. It brings us to the concluding battle between Israel and the Philistines, a battle which brings the story of Saul to its tragic end.

## A DISASTROUS HOMECOMING

**30:1** Now it happened, when David and his men came to Ziklag, on the third day, that the Amalekites had invaded the South and Ziklag, attacked Ziklag and burned it with fire, **2** and had taken captive the women and those who were there, from small to great; they did not kill anyone, but carried them away and went their way. **3** So David and his men came to the city, and there it was, burned with fire; and their wives, their sons, and their daughters had been taken captive. **4** Then David and the people who were with him lifted up their voices and wept, until they had no more power to weep. **5** And David's two wives, Ahinoam the Jezreelitess, and Abigail the widow of Nabal the Carmelite, had been taken captive. [6] Now David was greatly distressed, for the people spoke of stoning him, because the soul of all the people was grieved, every man for his sons and his daughters. But David strengthened himself in the LORD his God.

*—1 Samuel 30:1–6*

The historian decides to keep his readers in suspense about the big battle impending between the Philistines and the Israelites while he follows the fortunes of David. David had been saved by the distrust of the Philistine commanders from having to fight against his own people and had been sent back to Ziklag. While it might seem inappropriate to turn from the preparations for a great battle to cover the activities of a soldier who was not planning to participate in the battle, it fits perfectly into the historian's purpose—to show how the hand of God continued to be in everything David did and how each event prepared him to ascend the throne.

The Amalekites were the persistent enemies of all the settled villages. When all men of fighting age in Israel and Philistia were gathered into two warring armies, the time was ideal for raiding the unprotected towns. So the Amalekites attacked Ziklag, David's headquarters, took everyone captive, and burned the city to the ground. They took the women and children with them, probably intending to sell them as slaves or make them their own slaves.

For David, this homecoming delivered a double blow. It was bad enough to find the city sacked and burned, and it was even worse to find that all the families had been taken—including David's two wives. But the second blow was that David's men turned on him and threatened to kill him. Whether it was anger over his having left the town unguarded or the normal scapegoating of a leader, which people often do when things go wrong, we don't know.

This incident is a reminder of the hazards that are inherent to responsible leadership and also of how fickle human nature is. The David who was usually the object of their hero worship became in a moment of great frustration the object of their deadly wrath. Our Lord tasted the same swing of moods when He heard the hosannas on Palm Sunday and from the same lips a few days later heard them chant "Crucify him." David was in a corner again, but this time it was by his own men and not the Philistine commanders. In the predicament he turned to the Lord for counsel.

## WHEN PEOPLE TURN TO GOD

[7] Then David said to Abiathar the priest, Ahimelech's son, "Please bring the ephod here to me." And Abiathar brought the ephod to David. [8] So David inquired of the LORD, saying, "Shall I pursue this troop? Shall I overtake them?"

And He answered him, "Pursue, for you shall surely overtake them and without fail recover all."

[9] So David went, he and the six hundred men who were with him, and came to the Brook Besor, where those stayed who were left behind. [10] But David pursued, he and four hundred men; for two hundred stayed behind, who were so weary that they could not cross the Brook Besor.

*—1 Samuel 30:7–10*

There is a sense in which David had nowhere else to turn. He had no idea where the women and children had been taken or if there was any possibility of finding them and rescuing them. It is also true that David had made it a habit of his life to seek God's counsel in critical times. He continued to do that during his lifetime, with one or two disastrous exceptions. When we seek God's guidance for our lives in the daily routines, then it's easier to turn to Him in the real crises of life.

David's method of seeking a word from God may seem strange to today's Christian, but to him it represented a way of getting answers to problems from God. Abiathar the priest carried sacred stones in the ephod that could be cast and could get answers to questions which could be answered with a yes or a no. They were called Urim and Thummim. The two questions that David asked of the Lord were *"Shall I pursue this troop?"* and *"Shall I overtake them?"* (v. 8). The answer came back that David was to go after them, that he would catch them, and that he would recover everything. It was in this knowledge which God gave him that David found the courage to lead his men after the Amalekites.

Although the casting of lots to discern God's will persisted into the New Testament era and was actually used to determine who would succeed Judas as an apostle (Acts 1:26), most Christians today would seek God's guidance in their lives through different means. Christians have many resources not available to David—the written Scriptures which contain the teachings of Christ, the Holy Spirit which is in each believer, the insights of the church as the body of Christ, the counsel of Christian friends, and the resources of prayer.

Yet David's example of seeking God's guidance in his life is still an inspiration to us.

With God's promise of success in his venture, David and his army of six hundred men immediately began their efforts to recover their families and their property. The decision to leave two hundred of the most weary men behind at the brook of Besor may reflect David's military strategy or it may have been a show of confidence in God's ability to deliver a superior enemy into his hands by His power. It did create an occasion for the beginning of a tradition in Israel concerning the division of the spoils of battle that still existed at the time the historian compiled the records which make up 1 Samuel.

## THE HAND OF GOD

11 Then they found an Egyptian in the field, and brought him to David; and they gave him bread and he ate, and they let him drink water. 12 And they gave him a piece of a cake of figs and two clusters of raisins. So when he had eaten, his strength came back to him; for he had eaten no bread nor drunk water for three days and three nights.
13 Then David said to him, "To whom do you belong, and where are you from?"

And he said, "I am a young man from Egypt, servant of an Amalekite; and my master left me behind, because three days ago I fell sick. 14 We made an invasion of the southern area of the Cherethites, in the territory which belongs to Judah, and of the southern area of Caleb; and we burned Ziklag with fire."

15 And David said to him, "Can you take me down to this troop?"

So he said, "Swear to me by God that you will neither kill me nor deliver me into the hands of my master, and I will take you down to this troop."

*—1 Samuel 30:11–15*

David and his men probably interrogated everyone they saw between Ziklag and the brook of Besor as to which direction the marauding army had taken. Upon crossing the brook they came upon a half-starved, sick Egyptian who was a cast off slave of one of the Amalekites. Having neither eaten or drunk for three days, he was possibly not even conscious. From the way they treated him he must have seemed to be the best source of information they had found. After they gave him water and bread, they fed him a *"cake of figs and two clusters of raisins"* (v. 12).

He was a wonderful source of information for David because he knew all the places that the Amalekites had raided in addition to Ziklag (v. 14). He also knew the direction the raiders had taken but refused to share the information until David had sworn that he would neither kill him nor turn him over to his former masters (v. 15).

While the compiler makes no comment about the significant role which the slave played, it is obvious that he was not there by accident. In retrospect it was but another example of the way in which God was looking out for David and bringing him to the throne. Many Christians have looked over their shoulders at events that, at the time, seemed almost accidental and which they have later seen as the hand of God.

The most spectacular incident of this sort happened to me when I was a college student struggling with rheumatoid arthritis. I just "happened" to move to New Mexico to live with an aunt and just "happened" to be under the care of a certain rheumatologist when he received a grant to test the extensive use of steroids on arthritis patients. At the time I felt lucky to have been chosen and grateful that my response to the medicine allowed me to finish college and go on to the seminary. Looking back now, though, I see God's hand in it all, even when I was not aware of the ways in which He was working things out for me.

In our reading of these last few chapters of 1 Samuel, we should be struck by the contrast between Saul and David. Saul gets no answer when he calls upon God; David gets the best possible response. Saul gets the witch of En Dor to call up Samuel and learns that Israel will be defeated and he and his sons will be killed; David picks up a half-dead slave from the desert and gets invaluable information that allows him to rescue the families of his people and recapture their property. It's as though nothing Saul does is right and nothing David does can go wrong. This is the message that is intended—that when God's hand is upon one, nothing can keep His purpose from being accomplished.

## RECOVERING EVERYTHING

16 And when he had brought him down, there they were, spread out over all the land, eating and drinking and dancing, because of all the great spoil which they had taken from the land of the Philistines and from the land of Judah.

17 Then David attacked them from twilight until the evening of the next day. Not a man of them escaped, except four hundred young men who rode on camels and fled. 18 So David recovered all that the Amalekites had carried away, and David rescued his two wives. 19 And nothing of theirs was lacking, either small or great, sons or daughters, spoil or anything which they had taken from them; David recovered all. 20 Then David took all the flocks and herds they had driven before those other livestock, and said, "This is David's spoil."

21 Now David came to the two hundred men who had been so weary that they could not follow David, whom they also had made to stay at the Brook Besor. So they went out to meet David and to meet the people who were with him. And when David came near the people, he greeted them. 22 Then all the wicked and worthless men of those who went with David answered and said, "Because they did not go with us, we will not give them any of the spoil that we have recovered, except for every man's wife and children, that they may lead them away and depart."

23 But David said, "My brethren, you shall not do so with what the LORD has given us, who has preserved us and delivered into our hand the troop that came against us. 24 For who will heed you in this matter? But as his part is who goes down to the battle, so shall his part be who stays by the supplies; they shall share alike." 25 So it was, from that day forward; he made it a statute and an ordinance for Israel to this day.

26 Now when David came to Ziklag, he sent some of the spoil to the elders of Judah, to his friends, saying, "Here is a present for you from the spoil of the enemies of the LORD"— 27 to those who were in Bethel, those who were in Ramoth of the South, those who were in Jattir, 28 those who were in Aroer, those who were in Siphmoth, those who were in Eshtemoa, 29 those who were in Rachal, those who were in the cities of the Jerahmeelites, those who were in the cities of the Kenites, 30 those who were in Hormah, those who were in Chorashan, those who were in Athach, 31 those who were in Hebron, and to all the places where David himself and his men were accustomed to rove.

—*1 Samuel 30:16–31*

David and his warriors came upon the Amalekites because the raiders had stopped to celebrate their recent victories. With a great battle looming to the north there was no reason for them to expect the kind of pursuit David and his men had given. The Amalekites were caught completely by surprise. Only those mounted on camels escaped the sword, and all the people and property were recovered—plus what had been taken from the other villages which had been raided. Everything had gone as God had promised David.

When the army came to the Brook Besor, driving all the animals before them, David greeted those who had stayed behind. At this point a very nasty spirit manifested itself and David's leadership was challenged again. Some of those who had fought resented those who had stayed with the baggage and wanted them not only to be deprived of any share in the spoil but suggested that they be given their families and put out of the company (v. 22). But David decided that everyone would share alike whether they had gone to the battle or had kept the baggage; it was such a popular judgment that it became a statute (vv. 23–25).

The principle is the same as the one which the apostle Paul presents when he is discussing the different parts of the body of Christ in his letter to the Corinthians (1 Cor. 12). His point is that just as the body has many parts and all are so interrelated that each is needed, so then all the diverse gifts of the church are needed and important to the cause of Christ. When I was a college student I heard a great preacher preach a memorable sermon on this 1 Samuel text entitled "They Who Stay by the Stuff." It spoke to David's decision—that everyone who participates in God's work should share in the honor and victory.

The chapter closes with a second act of generosity by David. If the decision that all would share in the spoil solidified him with his army, the decision to send gifts to the Judean villages that had been raided must have communicated to them that he was loyal to them. Instead of using his larger share to enrich himself, David used it to help others and to establish himself as a kingly leader. It was an act that helped pave the way for his acceptance by them later as king.

The final chapter of 1 Samuel brings to an end the tragic story of Saul and lays the foundation for David to ascend the throne. The battle on Mount Gilboa presents God's final act in tearing the kingdom from Saul. The day is full of tragedy, but no surprise. It is the logical result of actions taken and judgments pronounced long before.

## THE INEVITABLE END

**31:1** Now the Philistines fought against Israel; and the men of Israel fled from before the Philistines, and fell slain on Mount Gilboa. [2] Then the Philistines followed hard after Saul and his sons. And the Philistines killed Jonathan, Abinadab, and Malchishua, Saul's sons. [3] The battle became fierce against Saul. The archers hit him, and he was severely wounded by the archers.

[4] Then Saul said to his armorbearer, "Draw your sword, and thrust me through with it, lest these uncircumcised men come and thrust me through and abuse me."

But his armorbearer would not, for he was greatly afraid. Therefore Saul took a sword and fell on it. [5] And when his armorbearer saw that Saul was dead, he also fell on his sword, and died with him. [6] So Saul, his three sons, his armorbearer, and all his men died together that same day.

[7] And when the men of Israel who were on the other side of the valley, and those who were on the other side of the Jordan, saw that the men of Israel had fled and that Saul and his sons were dead, they forsook the cities and fled; and the Philistines came and dwelt in them. [8] So it happened the next day, when the Philistines came to strip the slain, that they found Saul and his three sons fallen on Mount Gilboa. [9] And they cut off his head and stripped off his armor, and sent word throughout the land of the Philistines, to proclaim it in the temple of their idols and among the people. [10] Then they put his armor in the temple of the Ashtoreths, and they fastened his body to the wall of Beth Shan.

[11] Now when the inhabitants of Jabesh Gilead heard what the Philistines had done to Saul, [12] all the valiant men arose and traveled all night, and took the body of Saul and the bodies of his sons from the wall of Beth Shan; and they came to Jabesh and burned them there. [13] Then they took their bones and buried them under the tamarisk tree at Jabesh, and fasted seven days.

*—1 Samuel 31:1–13*

This short chapter reports the death and burial of King Saul and brings 1 Samuel to a close. It concludes the story begun in chapter 28, then interrupted to narrate David's escape from having to fight against his own people (ch. 29) and his battle to recover the families and property of his warriors (ch. 30). Again David's military conquest in the far south of the country stands in contrast to the scenario on Mount Gilboa where Saul and his army are suffering a smashing defeat. The only relief from the tragic events is found in the heroism of the men of Jabesh Gilead.

The narrator gives few details of the battle—who attacked, tactics used, or skirmishes fought. It's as though knowing what the outcome was going to be made the details of the confrontation unimportant. Yet the outcome is reported in almost heroic fashion. First, Saul's men fled before the Philistines so he was without an army (v. 1). Then his sons were killed so that he was without a family (v. 2). (One son, Ishbosheth, was either not present at the battle or had escaped for he appears later as a successor to Saul in 2 Samuel 2:8.) His last confidant was his armorbearer, a position held at one time by David. In the last moments of his life he was a man to be pitied.

Saul's request of his armorbearer to kill him didn't mean that he was afraid of death at the hand of the enemy. He was rather afraid that they would not kill him and that he would be used as a mockery to Israel as Samson had been (Judg. 16:25ff.). The refusal of the armorbearer was probably linked to his fear of laying hands on God's anointed. His devotion to Saul was evidenced by his following his master in death by his own hand. When the people realized that Saul was dead, they fled the villages on the east of the Jordan River and in the Jezreel Valley—opening the whole area up to Philistine occupation. In terms of territory, Israel was back almost where she had been at the beginning of the monarchy.

In those days it was a common practice for the victors to strip the slain for plunder. So on the following day the Philistines came to claim the prizes of war. Because Saul was the king, they cut off his head as David had done to Goliath. They put his armor in the temple of Ashtoreth, their female deity, nailed his body to the wall at Beth Shan, and sent word throughout the land of their victory. It was a sad end for a man who had only been searching for his father's donkeys when he was chosen to be the first king of Israel.

The only moment of light in this chapter is found in the response of the people of Jabesh Gilead to what the Philistines had done to Saul's body. Like many others in Israel, they had a reason to be grateful to Saul. Early in Saul's reign their city had been under siege by Nahash the Ammonite, whose price for surrender was the right eye of each man. They had asked for seven days in which to consider the surrender and had sent word to Saul for help. Saul had rallied the men of the country and had demolished the Ammonite army, freeing the city (ch. 11). The people of the city had not forgotten their indebtedness to Saul and decided to show their gratitude in a concrete way. During the night they marched to Beth Shan and at great risk to themselves took the bodies of Saul and his sons from the wall, carried them to Jabesh, and gave them proper burial. Their action was commended by David later (2 Sam. 2:5–6), and he eventually removed the bones and buried them in the family tomb (2 Sam. 21:14). So many of the things that are done for us are quickly forgotten. This story is a reminder of what a noble virtue gratitude is.

At this point it's impossible to make a balanced assessment of Saul and his reign. While at his death all looks bleak for the country, the people of God are moving slowly from their past tribal organization toward a united nation. The Second Book of Samuel is but a continuation of the story, and after pausing to interpret the death of Saul and Jonathan it moves on to continue the story of how God deals with people. The Book of 2 Samuel is one of my favorite books in the Old Testament because each of its stories sheds more light upon God's nature and His purpose and how He wants us to respond to His revelation. Sometimes these ancient events come alive with frightening application to our lives and our world today. David captures the stage completely in 2 Samuel and in his growth, his failures, and his triumphs we find our own journey of faith made richer.

# THE STORY OF DAVID

*2 SAMUEL 1:1—20:26*

# CHAPTER ELEVEN—THE MAN WHO WOULD BE KING

## 2 SAMUEL 1:1—5:5

*Scripture Outline*

The Book of 1 Samuel closed with the burial of the bones of Saul and Jonathan under a tamarisk tree at Jabesh and the beginning of a seven-day fast (1 Sam. 31:13). The Book of 2 Samuel opens with David's learning of Israel's defeat and of the deaths of Saul and Jonathan. Even the casual reader senses the continuity of the events that were recorded in 1 Samuel. David's presence in Ziklag is explained by the events in 1 Samuel 30, and the report brought from the front by the Amalekite is a continuation of the events recorded in 1 Samuel 31:1–7. The division between the two books is artificial and was not made until the Old Testament was translated into Greek centuries later.

As the division stands, 1 Samuel closes with the end of Saul's reign and 2 Samuel opens with the beginning of David's reign, with this first chapter serving as a transition. The chapter has two natural parts. The first sixteen verses tell of the report of Saul's death and the response it evoked. Of special interest is the conflicting account of Saul's death and the rationale for killing the messenger who brought the report. The concluding eleven verses are a dirge or an elegy that David composed in response to the death of the king and his son.

## WHEN THOSE WHO HATE US DIE

**1:1** Now it came to pass after the death of Saul, when David had returned from the slaughter of the Amalekites, and David had stayed two days in Ziklag, ² on the third day, behold, it happened that a man came from Saul's camp with his clothes torn and dust on his head. So it was, when he came to David, that he fell to the ground and prostrated himself.

³ And David said to him, "Where have you come from?"

So he said to him, "I have escaped from the camp of Israel."

⁴ Then David said to him, "How did the matter go? Please tell me."

And he answered, "The people have fled from the battle, many of the people are fallen and dead, and Saul and Jonathan his son are dead also."

⁵ So David said to the young man who told him, "How do you know that Saul and Jonathan his son are dead?"

⁶ Then the young man who told him said, "As I happened by chance to be on Mount Gilboa, there was Saul, leaning on his spear; and indeed the chariots and horsemen followed hard after him. ⁷ Now when he looked behind him, he saw me and called to me. And I answered, 'Here I am.' ⁸ And he said to me, 'Who are you?' So I answered him, 'I am an Amalekite.' ⁹ He said to me again, 'Please stand over me and kill me, for anguish has come upon me, but my life still remains in me.' ¹⁰ So I stood over him and killed him, because I was sure that he could not live after he had fallen. And I took the crown that was on his head and the bracelet that was on his arm, and have brought them here to my lord."

<sup>11</sup> Therefore David took hold of his own clothes and tore them, and so did all the men who were with him.
<sup>12</sup> And they mourned and wept and fasted until evening for Saul and for Jonathan his son, for the people of the LORD and for the house of Israel, because they had fallen by the sword.
<sup>13</sup> Then David said to the young man who told him, "Where are you from?"

And he answered, "I am the son of an alien, an Amalekite."

<sup>14</sup> So David said to him, "How was it you were not afraid to put forth your hand to destroy the LORD's anointed?" <sup>15</sup> Then David called one of the young men and said, "Go near, and execute him!" And he struck him so that he died. <sup>16</sup> So David said to him, "Your blood is on your own head, for your own mouth has testified against you, saying, 'I have killed the LORD's anointed.'"

—*2 Samuel 1:1–16*

When the runner arrived in Ziklag to bring the first report of the disastrous battle between Israel and the Philistines, his appearance sent the message before him. His garments were torn and his head was covered with dust, the traditional posture for mourning. There is the possibility, however, that beneath the clothes of grief he was full of hope that the news he brought and the articles that he carried would bring both praise and a reward from David. While the messenger was an Amalekite, he had a special status in Israel as an alien or sojourner. In some way not described here, he may have been attached to Saul's camp. He knew of Saul's hatred of David and of the energy Saul had spent trying to locate and kill him. It was this knowledge which made him think that David would be glad to hear that his old and persistent enemy was now dead. He also knew that many people felt that David would be Saul's successor. He carried in his hand both the crown that Saul had worn into battle and Saul's arm bracelet, both of which he intended to give to David. In his own mind it was impossible for the messenger to imagine the response that he got to his story.

Had he limited himself to the results of the battle he probably could have joined David and his men in their grief. Saul's death would have been accepted as the judgment of God and no guilt would have been attached to the messenger. But when he was asked by David *"How do you know that Saul and Jonathan his son are dead also?"* (v. 5), the man gave a different account of Saul's death than the one recorded in 1 Samuel 31:1–7. That account records that Saul was mortally wounded by the archers. Because he did not want to fall into the hands of the Philistines while still alive for several reasons, Saul asked his armorbearer to kill him with his sword. When his aide refused to kill him, Saul killed himself by falling on his own sword. The armorbearer, upon seeing that Saul was dead, killed himself.

In the Amalekite's version of the story he had come upon Saul who was in a state of utter fatigue and about to be run down by Philistine chariots and horsemen. Realizing that he was finished and not wanting to be captured by the Philistines Saul asked the Amalekite to kill him, which he did, and he had in his hand the crown and the bracelet as proof that his story was true. Serious Bible students have struggled to know what to do with the Amalekite's story. Many feel that it was a fabrication on his part to ingratiate himself to David. Some have seen it as a different version of Saul's death which had been preserved. Others have tried to weave the two stories together in such a way that all the parts fit. We must not let our modern desire to reconcile every detail of the story keep us from seeing the main truth being taught in David's response to the account.

When David and his men heard the details of the lost battle and Saul's death, they began to tear their own clothes and to mourn. The text says that they *"wept and fasted until evening for Saul and for Jonathan his son, for the people of the LORD and for the house of Israel, because they had fallen by the sword"* (v. 12). The intensity of the lament must have confused the messenger who, in spite of his outward garb of mourning, might have expected a different response. And he was totally unprepared for David's probing question, *"How was it you were not afraid to put forth your hand to destroy the Lord's anointed?"* (v. 14). That Saul had asked to be killed or that Saul would have been taken by the Philistines meant nothing to David. Twice he had spared Saul's life when he could have taken it (1 Sam. 24 and 26). On those occasions David's men felt that Saul had been delivered into David's hands by God and had urged him to kill Saul.

David had refused because of a very special feeling that he had about God's anointed. He felt that since God had anointed Saul to be king of Israel, then God would have to be the one who removed him. If Saul were to be slain by the Philistines or were to kill himself, David could have accepted that as God's judgment.

But after having spared Saul twice, David felt completely justified in judging the Amalekite by his own words and having him slain. The sentence may seem harsh to our modern sensitivities but behind David's motive is a concept that needs to be recovered—a respect for those whom God anoints. This means leaving judgment with God. It means having respect for an office even when the officeholder may not act respectably. It means trusting God with His plan for your life and not feeling that you need to take things into your own hands.

## A SONG OF SADNESS

17 Then David lamented with this lamentation over Saul and over Jonathan his son, 18 and he told them to teach the children of Judah the Song of the Bow; indeed it is written in the Book of Jasher:

19 "The beauty of Israel is slain on your high places!
How the mighty have fallen!

20 Tell it not in Gath,
Proclaim it not in the streets of Ashkelon—
Lest the daughters of the Philistines rejoice,
Lest the daughters of the uncircumcised triumph.

21 "O mountains of Gilboa,
Let there be no dew nor rain upon you,
Nor fields of offerings.
For the shield of the mighty is cast away there!
The shield of Saul, not anointed with oil.

22 From the blood of the slain,
From the fat of the mighty,
The bow of Jonathan did not turn back,
And the sword of Saul did not return empty.

23 "Saul and Jonathan were beloved and pleasant in their lives,
And in their death they were not divided;
They were swifter than eagles,
They were stronger than lions.

24 "O daughters of Israel, weep over Saul,
Who clothed you in scarlet, with luxury;
Who put ornaments of gold on your apparel.

25 "How the mighty have fallen in the midst of the battle!
Jonathan was slain in your high places.

26 I am distressed for you, my brother Jonathan;

You have been very pleasant to me;
Your love to me was wonderful,
Surpassing the love of women.
27 "How the mighty have fallen,
And the weapons of war perished!"

*—2 Samuel 1:17–27*

There is nothing more natural than to grieve the death of a friend. Often I'm with persons who have suffered the loss of a loved one and yet feel guilty about their grief. They have been taught—in error—that people who have faith in God should not grieve. As a result they have added to their natural pain a sense of guilt for hurting. The ability to grieve is God's gift which allows us to process our loss in such a way that we can go on living without a sense of guilt. Our Lord stood at the tomb of Lazarus with the sisters, Mary and Martha, and wept (John 11:35). And so David and his men began to grieve when they heard of the slaughter of the soldiers and of the deaths of Saul and Jonathan.

David wrote an elegy for the occasion that he told them to teach to the children of Judah in order that the names of Saul and Jonathan might not be forgotten. It is one of the longest and most moving elegies found in the Old Testament and takes up the remaining verses of the first chapter. The language and form are poetic so that much is lost in a word-by-word exegesis. There is a little bit of background, however, to some of the phrases that will make it easier to read and appreciate. After reading these brief comments and getting a better grasp of the context in which David first sang the dirge, the reader ought to read the poem aloud several times with animation and feeling.

The theme that keeps repeating itself during the elegy is "How the mighty have fallen." It appears in verses 19, 25, and 27. It gathers up all of the loss that Israel suffered on one day into one haunting phrase. I stood one day in the middle of a national cemetery in Hawaii where those who died at Pearl Harbor on December 7, 1941, are buried. My heart was heavy with the awareness of the loss that was represented there. I watched an older couple from the Midwest stand for the first time at the grave of their son and their tears could not be held back. They would have understood the theme of David's lament.

At the heart of the poem was the wish that the joy of the Philistines in their victory would be short-lived. His prayer that the news would not reach Gath or Ashkelon, two principle Philistine cities, was because he knew what the rituals of victory were. He feared:

> "Lest the daughters of the Philistines rejoice,
> Lest the daughters of the uncircumcised triumph."
>
> —*verse 20*

David could remember when he and Saul and Jonathan and the army had come home victorious and had been met in the villages and towns by women dancing in the streets and singing their songs of victory. It was just such an occasion that had triggered Saul's jealousy as they had sung their song:

> "Saul has slain his thousands,
> And David his ten thousands."
>
> —*1 Samuel 18:7*

On this day David was a part of the vanquished.

David's next thoughts were of the range of mountains where the battle had taken place, *"O mountains of Gilboa"* (v. 21). His prayer was that it would suffer an extreme drought so that nothing would grow there. His mind wandered over the battlefield, and he envisioned in the midst of the spilled blood the weapons of his lost friends—Saul's shield and Jonathan's bow. In the words of the lament the feeling is projected that a place where such defeat had come to the Lord's people ought never be the same again. His prayer almost had the force of a curse.

The closing stanzas of the song focus on Saul and Jonathan and are considered by many to be the most beautiful part of the lament. David appropriately left out whatever differences existed between Saul and Jonathan and voiced that *"in their death they were not divided"* (v. 23). While it is true that Jonathan did not share his father's animosity for David—still he never left his father to join David and died at his father's side in battle. David was right to paint the two in a partnership of intimacy in life, in battle, and in death. A lesser person than David might have magnified the differences rather than the things that they had in common. David had fought by their sides in battle enough to know that the imagery of "eagles" and "lions" was an apt description of his warrior friends when living.

David's call on the daughters of Israel to weep over Saul was tied to the fact that they had shared in the bounty after battle:

> "Who clothed you in scarlet, with luxury;
> Who put ornaments of gold on your apparel."
>
> —*verse 24*

David had been there when the finery taken from the enemy had been shared with the women who danced in the street. Now he wanted them to remember Saul in his death. Those who bless us in their lifetime should be mourned when they die.

The last stanza of the lament is devoted to Jonathan, who was the best friend whom David would have in his lifetime. They had met on the day on which David had slain the Philistine giant and had become instant friends. That relationship had developed and matured through the years and had survived many challenges, most of which were created by Saul's insane jealousy of David. They had made pledges to each other before God and those pledges were to be kept even after Jonathan's death. Our day is always tying the word "love" to sexual love and that makes it hard to understand David's declaration of his love for Jonathan. What David is describing is a friendship that was long-lasting, consistent, loyal, selfless, responsible, and realistic. It was a friendship that ennobled their lives while they were both living and a relationship which enriched David's memory after Jonathan was dead. Many people live their lives without experiencing a friendship of this dimension and are diminished as a result.

In the next chapter David at last becomes king, but only of the tribe of Judah. While there was no plan of succession established by tradition, a struggle for power began that would not be easily resolved. Abner, the commander of Saul's army, set up one of Saul's surviving sons as a puppet king over Israel. This created a conflict with David's men, led by Joab. While Samuel had anointed David to be king when he was a shepherd lad, it would be awhile before he would serve as king over all Israel. God's purpose is always sure, but it often takes longer to become reality than we think it will.

## DAVID ANOINTED KING OF JUDAH

**2:1** It happened after this that David inquired of the Lord, saying, "Shall I go up to any of the cities of Judah?"
And the Lord said to him, "Go up."
David said, "Where shall I go up?"
And He said, "To Hebron."
² So David went up there, and his two wives also, Ahinoam the Jezreelitess, and Abigail the widow of Nabal the Carmelite. ³ And David brought up the men who were with him, every man with his household. So they dwelt in the cities of Hebron.

<sup></sup>4 Then the men of Judah came, and there they anointed David king over the house of Judah. And they told David, saying, "The men of Jabesh Gilead were the ones who buried Saul." 5 So David sent messengers to the men of Jabesh Gilead, and said to them, "You are blessed of the LORD, for you have shown this kindness to your lord, to Saul, and have buried him. 6 And now may the LORD show kindness and truth to you. I also will repay you this kindness, because you have done this thing. 7 Now therefore, let your hands be strengthened, and be valiant; for your master Saul is dead, and also the house of Judah has anointed me king over them."

—*2 Samuel 2:1–7*

With the death of King Saul and Crown Prince Jonathan there was no functioning government for Israel. Into the vacuum moved two strong high-ranking soldiers—Abner, who was Saul's cousin and commander of the army, and David, who was Saul's son-in-law and a strong warrior with an army of his own. Those who live in countries that have stable institutions and which experience orderly transfer of power during a change of leaders do not realize how often in younger and less stable countries the death of a leader creates a climate of total uncertainty. This was the case with Israel after the deaths of Saul and Jonathan.

This chapter tells of David's enthronement as Judah's king in Hebron, records David's communication with the citizens of Jabesh Gilead, and chronicles the first battles of the civil war which will continue until Israel is finally united under David. In the midst of what seems to be of interest only to students of the history of the monarchy, there are some valuable insights for Christians today who are struggling with knowing God's will, dealing with power, and learning to make peace in an imperfect world.

As the kingdom was divided between two strong leaders, the historian was careful to point out the significant differences between the men and how they moved to positions of power. It could have been assumed that once Saul was dead, David would have moved to take over the throne. It was for this purpose that Samuel had anointed him while he was still a shepherd lad in his father's household (1 Sam. 16:13). With Israel in disarray after Saul's death, David could have marched home from Ziklag to take over as God's chosen successor. Instead, he asked God, *"Shall I go up to any of the cities of Judah?"* (v. 1). Abiathar, who was a priest of the line of Eli, was still with David giving him a word from God. David did not want to make a move toward the throne unless God was in the move. He stands in contrast to his competitor Abner, who seized power without any religious sanction.

While the mechanism for discerning the will of God was very primitive in David's day, the motivation behind the request of God was very profound—to find God's leadership in the day-by-day decisions of life. Today's Christian has much more help for discerning God's will than David had. We have the Bible's written word which gives insight into God's nature and purpose, moral and ethical stances which Christians ought to take, and the recorded history of how God had dealt with His people in similar circumstances. In addition we have the Holy Spirit which is God's gift to all who become His children. In addition to prayer there is the counsel of the community of faith, the church. Yet with all this help, often people make decisions about their lives without seeking insight through their relationship with God. In Paul's letter to the Romans he urged those who belonged to God to learn to "discern the will of God" (Rom. 12:2, NEB).

God's answer to David was affirmative, and when asked whether or not he should go to Hebron, the answer was yes again. A look at the map reveals Hebron's central location. (Some have wondered why the Philistines, who were very much in charge, would allow David to move to Hebron. Although he had lived with them, he had never been totally trusted, and they may have liked the idea of Abner and his puppet king having competition.) Hebron had historical significance for a king. It was where Abraham and his wife Sarah were buried (Gen. 23 and 25). It was an ancient royal city (Josh. 10) and had been captured and occupied by Caleb when Israel entered the Promised Land (Josh. 15). It was also an area to which David had sent gifts from his raids upon the enemy while he lived in Ziklag (1 Sam. 30:26ff.). It was the perfect place for David, his family, his soldiers, and their families to move.

It was in Hebron where the men of Judah came and *"anointed David king over the house of Judah"* (v. 4). It was a different David whom the elders of Judah anointed than the young naive lad whom Samuel had set aside after God had rejected Saul. During his years as a fugitive fleeing from Saul's wrath and his years in exile with the Philistines he had experienced life with all its ups and downs and had discovered God was with him in the most extreme of circumstances. He had developed in his understanding

226

of himself and of others. He had become a leader with knowledge, experience, and skills he would never have developed in the palace. He fled the palace an idealistic and inexperienced young man and he marched to Hebron as a king.

Many of us fail to understand that the distance is often great between the time God puts a dream in our heart about our life and the fulfillment of that dream. We have lived too long with the "instant" culture, where time is short-circuited. Just as we enjoy instant potatoes and instant coffee, we also want instant character, instant maturity, and instant fulfillment. David's experience is a reminder that there is no shortcut from where God meets us with a plan for our life and the fulfilling of that plan.

I first met Lawanda after she had finished college. She was a registered nurse doing her year of seminary studies before taking an appointment with the mission board to serve in a hospital in Africa. What those who didn't know her well failed to understand was that the dream of serving God as a missionary had come to her when she was in a mission study group at her church when she was a fourth grader. Still to come were years of schooling, some hard decisions, and a maturing of the call. It was an inexperienced, idealistic, little child who said, "I think God wants me to be a missionary." It was a mature woman who sailed to Africa as a medical missionary. This is how God works in the lives of His children.

David's first act as the new king of Judah was to send a message to the men of Jabesh Gilead. He had learned from the men of Judah that they were the men who had given proper burial to Saul and Jonathan. (The details of their brave exploit are recorded in 1 Samuel 31.) They were located in northern Israel, some fifteen miles from Ishbosheth's capital at Mahanaim. Some saw David's message as opportunistic, but that is probably too harsh a judgment. He had several reasons for sending the message. First, he wanted to express gratitude for their loyalty to Saul and their rescuing his body from the wall of Beth Shan (1 Sam. 31:12). While Saul had been David's enemy, David had never been Saul's enemy, and he was genuinely moved by what they had done. Second, he wanted to commend their conduct to God and ask God's blessing upon them for what they bad done. Third, he wanted to remind them that Saul was dead and that he had been anointed king of Judah. He did not ask them to serve him, but he was looking ahead. This incident was probably preserved by the historian as a reminder that David's anointing at Hebron was not the final step in God's plan.

## A RIVAL KING

8 But Abner the son of Ner, commander of Saul's army, took Ishbosheth the son of Saul and brought him over to Mahanaim; 9 and he made him king over Gilead, over the Ashurites, over Jezreel, over Ephraim, over Benjamin, and over all Israel. 10 Ishbosheth, Saul's son, was forty years old when he began to reign over Israel, and he reigned two years. Only the house of Judah followed David. 11 And the time that David was king in Hebron over the house of Judah was seven years and six months.

*—2 Samuel 2:8–11*

It would have been so simple had all of Israel united under David's leadership, but it didn't for very understandable reasons. The primary reason was named Abner. He had been Saul's cousin and the commander of Israel's army. With Saul gone, his career was also gone. So in a pure power play he put Saul's only surviving son on the throne, with his headquarters in Mahanaim, which was on the east side of the Jordan, a place in which the Philistines had shown little interest. Ishbosheth was a weak king of a weak kingdom set up by a strong man for his own selfish purposes. That there were no religious sanctions stands in contrast to David's seeking God's will, and that the men of Judah anointed David stands in contrast to Abner's anointing Ishbosheth king of Israel.

David's rule was over a group of six tribes, not all of which were Israelites. *"All Israel"* (v. 9) merely describes everyone north of Jerusalem and east of the Jordan River. It is possible that both David and Ishbosheth ruled almost as vassals with the permission of the Philistines who were delighted to have opposing camps among the Israelites. There is some question about Saul's son being forty at the time since David was but thirty years of age and a contemporary of Jonathan, who was Saul's oldest son. There is also some question about the length of Ishbosheth's reign, many thinking that it was more than two years. What the historian who collected the material was anxious to show was the fact that though David was now king of Judah, there were still obstacles to be faced before there could be a united kingdom under David.

## THE BEGINNING OF CIVIL WAR

12 Now Abner the son of Ner, and the servants of Ishbosheth the son of Saul, went out from Mahanaim to Gibeon. 13 And Joab the son of Zeruiah, and the servants of

David, went out and met them by the pool of Gibeon. So they sat down, one on one side of the pool and the other on the other side of the pool. [14] Then Abner said to Joab, "Let the young men now arise and compete before us."

And Joab said, "Let them arise."

[15] So they arose and went over by number, twelve from Benjamin, followers of Ishbosheth the son of Saul, and twelve from the servants of David. [16] And each one grasped his opponent by the head and thrust his sword in his opponent's side; so they fell down together. Therefore that place was called the Field of Sharp Swords, which is in Gibeon. [17] So there was a very fierce battle that day, and Abner and the men of Israel were beaten before the servants of David.

[18] Now the three sons of Zeruiah were there: Joab and Abishai and Asahel. And Asahel was as fleet of foot as a wild gazelle. [19] So Asahel pursued Abner, and in going he did not turn to the right hand or to the left from following Abner.

[20] Then Abner looked behind him and said, "Are you Asahel?"

He answered, "I am."

[21] And Abner said to him, "Turn aside to your right hand or to your left, and lay hold on one of the young men and take his armor for yourself." But Asahel would not turn aside from following him. [22] So Abner said again to Asahel, "Turn aside from following me. Why should I strike you to the ground? How then could I face your brother Joab?" [23] However, he refused to turn aside. Therefore Abner struck him in the stomach with the blunt end of the spear, so that the spear came out of his back; and he fell down there and died on the spot. So it was that as many as came to the place where Asahel fell down and died, stood still.

[24] Joab and Abishai also pursued Abner. And the sun was going down when they came to the hill of Ammah, which is before Giah by the road to the Wilderness of Gibeon. [25] Now the children of Benjamin gathered together behind Abner and became a unit, and took their stand on top of a hill. [26] Then Abner called to Joab and said, "Shall the sword devour forever? Do you not know that it will be bitter in the latter end? How long will it be then until you tell the people to return from pursuing their brethren?"

[27] And Joab said, "As God lives, unless you had spoken, surely then by morning all the people would have given up

pursuing their brethren." [28] So Joab blew a trumpet; and all the people stood still and did not pursue Israel anymore, nor did they fight anymore. [29] Then Abner and his men went on all that night through the plain, crossed over the Jordan, and went through all Bithron; and they came to Mahanaim.

[30] So Joab returned from pursuing Abner. And when he had gathered all the people together, there were missing of David's servants nineteen men and Asahel. [31] But the servants of David had struck down, of Benjamin and Abner's men, three hundred and sixty men who died. [32] Then they took up Asahel and buried him in his father's tomb, which was in Bethlehem. And Joab and his men went all night, and they came to Hebron at daybreak.

*—2 Samuel 2:12–32*

The war that would preoccupy all Israel for several years began almost as a game which accelerated into a full-scale war. Most conflicts that separate families or churches or lands often begin over laughable differences and then grow into disastrous engagements. The most efficient peacemakers are not those who know how to stop raging wars but those who recognize the dangers in the small engagements and refuse to let them grow.

The problem with Abner and Joab was that they both led armies of men who were spoiling for a fight. The text does not tell us how they happened to meet at the pool at Gibeon nor does it explain adequately what was going on when twelve young men from each side met to compete. Some feel that it was something as innocent as a wrestling match for the entertainment of the troops. Most students do not feel that it was "representative combat" as when Goliath represented the Philistines and David represented Israel. More people feel that there was some sort of deceit planned by Abner in which the Benjaminites took advantage of Judah's young men. Whatever really happened, a fierce battle followed, and that battle resulted in conflicts that haunted David's efforts to build a united kingdom.

The casualty that created the most problems was the death of Asahel, who was David's nephew and Joab's brother. Israel's soldiers were being beaten and were in retreat. Asahel had a reputation for being fleet of foot and ran in pursuit of Abner who was slower but a superior soldier. Upon learning who he was, Abner tried to talk Asahel into pursuing someone more in his league, but Asahel continued. When Asahel caught up with Abner, Abner *"struck him in the stomach with the blunt end of the spear"* (v. 23) and killed him. What is sad about the young man's death was that Abner didn't want to kill him and tried to avoid the conflict. Some feel Asahel's persistence was somehow tied to an act of deception at the pool of Gibeon which had so infuriated him that he couldn't stop. Others think that Asahel became enamored with the idea of slaying the opposing general. Whatever the reason, it created a continuing tragedy.

As Joab and Abishai pursued their brother's killer, Abner made a move for peace with them, and his cry is one which needs to be heard in this age of violence in which we live: *"Shall the sword devour forever? Do you not know that it will be bitter in the latter end? How long will it be then until you tell the people to return from pursuing their brethren?"* (v. 26). While his plea accomplished a temporary halt in the battle, it created no lasting peace. But it is still a question worth pursuing. This is a haunting question for a world in which people are starving to death and others are dying of diseases for which cures are available, and still the world's nations impoverish themselves by spending billions of dollars on weapons of war. It's also a good question for those troubled spots of the world where people are dying daily in racial and religious conflicts.

In the skirmishes David's men had been clearly victorious, suffering only 19 casualties in contrast to 360. But the deepest wound was not visible. Asahel's death had created a hatred in Joab's heart for Abner that would surface at a time when peace was within David's grasp and would jeopardize both the peace and David's integrity. There are few things more destructive than hatred that is nourished within a heart. It can destroy marriages and families, churches and denominations, and even countries. More than anything else, hatred poisons the soul of the one who carries it in his or her heart.

Second Samuel 3 continues the events begun in this chapter. It tells of David's expanding family and of the fact that Saul's house grew weaker and weaker. It tells of Abner's break with Ishbosheth and his decision to join forces with David and to bring all of Israel with him. It closes with the murder of Abner and David's mourning his death with his immortal "a prince and a great man has fallen this day in Israel" (3:38). These are chapters full of political intrigue and assassinations. But in the midst of it all there is the awareness that God is able to work His will in the midst of our sinful history and to move Israel forward toward His ultimate purpose.

## LOOKING LIKE A KING

**3:1** Now there was a long war between the house of Saul and the house of David. But David grew stronger and stronger, and the house of Saul grew weaker and weaker.

² Sons were born to David in Hebron: His firstborn was Amnon by Ahinoam the Jezreelitess; ³ his second, Chileab, by Abigail the widow of Nabal the Carmelite; the third, Absalom the son of Maacah, the daughter of Talmai, king of Geshur; ⁴ the fourth, Adonijah the son of Haggith; the fifth, Shephatiah the son of Abital; ⁵ and the sixth, Ithream, by David's wife Eglah. These were born to David in Hebron.

*—2 Samuel 3:1–5*

This chapter tells of the event that brought Israel into David's hands. It is a story of three powerful men and a puppet king. Abner was a relative of Saul's and a powerful personality. Joab was David's nephew and the chief of his army. Abner controlled Israel's king and Joab could not be controlled by David. The amount of detail given indicates that the historian sensed that this was a major event in David's career. It is a story full of conflict, intrigue, deceit, and violence, yet it is told in such a way as to communicate the fact that God was at work through it all working out His larger plan for David and for Israel.

These verses describe the gradual shift of power from Saul's house to David's house (v. 1). They also list six sons of David by six different wives. Like others in that time, David used marriage as a political tool and often wives were symbols of alliances that consolidated power. The fact that Absalom's mother was the *"daughter of Talmai, king of Geshur"* (v. 3) suggests that David's relationship to Maacah represented more than romance. In these verses only the firstborn are mentioned and none of the daughters were listed.

Additional children are listed in 2 Samuel 5:13–16. After stating that David took "more concubines and wives from Jerusalem" and that "more sons and daughters were born to David," the text lists the names of eleven additional children, including Solomon. A united list is printed in 1 Chronicles 3:1–9. That text lists nineteen sons and one daughter and calls attention to sons by concubines without giving any names. The listing here in 2 Samuel 3 is not meant to detail David's family relationships but to show how in this sphere also David was growing stronger. Not only was he growing stronger in the field of battle, but he was gathering wives who were producing potential heirs. The compiler of the material intended for these verses to point out yet another way in which God was preparing David to rule over all Israel.

## ABNER JOINS FORCES WITH DAVID

[6] Now it was so, while there was war between the house of Saul and the house of David, that Abner was strengthening his hold on the house of Saul.

[7] And Saul had a concubine, whose name was Rizpah, the daughter of Aiah. So Ishbosheth said to Abner, "Why have you gone in to my father's concubine?"

[8] Then Abner became very angry at the words of Ishbosheth, and said, "Am I a dog's head that belongs to Judah? Today I show loyalty to the house of Saul your father, to his brothers, and to his friends, and have not delivered you into the hand of David; and you charge me today with a fault concerning this woman? [9] May God do so to Abner, and more also, if I do not do for David as the LORD has sworn to him— [10] to transfer the kingdom from the house of Saul, and set up the throne of David over Israel and over Judah, from Dan to Beersheba." [11] And he could not answer Abner another word, because he feared him.

[12] Then Abner sent messengers on his behalf to David, saying, "Whose is the land?" saying also, "Make your covenant with me, and indeed my hand shall be with you to bring all Israel to you."

[13] And David said, "Good, I will make a covenant with you. But one thing I require of you: you shall not see my face unless you first bring Michal, Saul's daughter, when you come to see my face." [14] So David sent messengers to Ishbosheth, Saul's son, saying, "Give me my wife Michal, whom I betrothed to myself for a hundred foreskins of the Philistines." [15] And Ishbosheth sent and took her from her husband, from Paltiel the son of Laish. [16] Then her husband went along with her to Bahurim, weeping behind her. So Abner said to him, "Go, return!" And he returned.

[17] Now Abner had communicated with the elders of Israel, saying, "In time past you were seeking for David to be king over you. [18] Now then, do it! For the LORD has spoken of David, saying, 'By the hand of My servant David, I will save My people Israel from the hand of the Philistines and the hand of all their enemies.'" [19] And Abner also spoke in

the hearing of Benjamin. Then Abner also went to speak in the hearing of David in Hebron all that seemed good to Israel and the whole house of Benjamin.

20 So Abner and twenty men with him came to David at Hebron. And David made a feast for Abner and the men who were with him. 21 Then Abner said to David, "I will arise and go, and gather all Israel to my lord the king, that they may make a covenant with you, and that you may reign over all that your heart desires." So David sent Abner away, and he went in peace.

*—2 Samuel 3:6–21*

When the scene moves from David's house to Ishbosheth's there is a striking difference. While David's house was expanding, Ishbosheth was not able to maintain control of the wives and concubines that he had inherited from his father. While Abner's role in the death of Asahel plays an important part in the events of the chapter, the amount of detail that is given is tied to the way in which Abner played a part in undermining Ishbosheth's power and preparing Israel to accept David's rule.

This section of the chapter is divided into three parts: the quarrel between Abner and Ishbosheth (vv. 6–11), Abner's negotiations with David (vv. 12–16), and the establishing of a solid basis for the allegiance of all Israel to David (vv. 17–21).

Abner appears in the first section as a powerful, ambitious kingmaker, who may have decided that he wanted to be king. It was he who had made Ishbosheth into a puppet king. Now in these verses we see the inevitable conflict between the two. We don't know what it was that Abner really did, only that he was accused of being sexually intimate with Rizpah, who had been one of Saul's concubines (v. 7). Rizpah later was the heroine whom David honored for her role in protecting the bones of the sons of Saul who had been put to death in order to settle the claim of the Gibeonites (2 Sam. 21:1–14).

Since a king's wives and concubines became the property of his successor, for Abner to take one of Saul's concubines was an act of treason. It meant that he was claiming to be king. When Absalom was in rebellion against David and took his concubines it was to demonstrate that he was his father's successor (2 Sam. 16:22). When David's son Adonijah requested one of David's consorts it cost him his life (1 Kin. 2:13–25). Of course, the accusation could have been the result of court gossip begun by someone who was jealous of

Abner's power and who knew that the king didn't have enough power to stop the rumor. What we do know is that it was the event that precipitated a split between Abner and the king.

Abner's strong answer (vv. 8–10) to Ishbosheth documents the fact that the king was little more that a puppet put there and controlled by Abner. The compiler wants the readers to see the whole passage in the light of God's working out His plan in history through imperfect people and less than ideal circumstances. This is easier to do when we are looking at events that took place thousands of years ago, especially when we know the outcome. But when we see power struggles split churches and the personal agendas of strong personalities fragment denominations, it's hard to see God's being able to accomplish His will. We tend to think that maybe God can do good in spite of such circumstances, but we find it very hard to believe that God's purpose can be realized even through these happenings. Yet if God can bring good out of a quarrel over a concubine, then maybe He can still salvage something out of the fragmentation of the church or the ego-driven leaders who often plague the work.

In his confrontation with Ishbosheth, Abner suggested that maybe David's claim that God had anointed him king was true (v. 9), and he threatened to transfer the kingdom from the house of Saul to the *"throne of David"* (v. 10). In this section (vv. 12–16), Abner begins negotiations with David that would turn his threat into reality. He first sent envoys promising that if David would make a covenant with him, then he would bring all Israel to him. David quickly agrees to make a covenant but added the return of his wife Michal as a precondition even to talking (v. 13). (The unusual circumstances of David's marriage to Saul's daughter Michal are recorded in 1 Samuel 18:20–29.) So Michal was taken from her husband, Paltiel, and sent to David, causing great grief to Paltiel who followed weeping until Abner ordered him to return home (v. 16). David's demand probably had nothing to do with love but was another way to lay claim to being Saul's successor. Ishbosheth may have been Saul's son, but David was his son-in-law and one of his valiant warriors.

The final verses of this section (vv. 17–21) tell of the establishment of a firm basis for bringing all Israel under David's rule. Abner portrays the elders of Israel as having wanted for some time to have David as their king (v. 17). Abner also reminded the elders that the Lord had spoken to David promising to use his hand to deliver Israel from the Philistines (v. 18). No reason is given for

Abner's making a separate approach to the tribe of Benjamin unless it was that it was Saul's and his tribe. While David and Abner came to an agreement, nothing is said about what David had to promise to Abner for his bringing Israel into the fold. In light of Abner's ambition and power, David probably had to promise some role of great prominence in his administration. The safe conduct that David gave to Abner ties this part of the story to the next.

## JOAB MURDERS ABNER

22 At that moment the servants of David and Joab came from a raid and brought much spoil with them. But Abner was not with David in Hebron, for he had sent him away, and he had gone in peace. 23 When Joab and all the troops that were with him had come, they told Joab, saying, "Abner the son of Ner came to the king, and he sent him away, and he has gone in peace." 24 Then Joab came to the king and said, "What have you done? Look, Abner came to you; why is it that you sent him away, and he has already gone? 25 Surely you realize that Abner the son of Ner came to deceive you, to know your going out and your coming in, and to know all that you are doing."

26 And when Joab had gone from David's presence, he sent messengers after Abner, who brought him back from the well of Sirah. But David did not know it. 27 Now when Abner had returned to Hebron, Joab took him aside in the gate to speak with him privately, and there stabbed him in the stomach, so that he died for the blood of Asahel his brother.

28 Afterward, when David heard it, he said, "My kingdom and I are guiltless before the LORD forever of the blood of Abner the son of Ner. 29 Let it rest on the head of Joab and on all his father's house; and let there never fail to be in the house of Joab one who has a discharge or is a leper, who leans on a staff or falls by the sword, or who lacks bread." 30 So Joab and Abishai his brother killed Abner, because he had killed their brother Asahel at Gibeon in the battle.

*—2 Samuel 3:22–30*

While David was making a deal with Abner, his men were involved in a raid. This gives insight into their activity. Though they had moved their headquarters to Hebron, they still supported themselves from the spoils of the raids on enemy villages and countryside.

Joab and the other warriors arrived soon after Abner had left and were told immediately not only that Abner had been there but that David had allowed him to depart in peace (v. 23). This infuriated Joab, and he went directly to David to register his disapproval and to question the wisdom of the decision. It was impossible for Joab to think of Abner as anything but an enemy, and with this perspective he suggested that the only reason for Abner's presence was to scout out the camp for a possible future raid (v. 25). David's response is not recorded in this passage. In all likelihood there was a vigorous discussion in which the whole dialogue between David and Abner was shared without lessening Joab's anger or changing his mind. When people wrap their conclusions in deep emotions they are hard to reason with. Joab's thoughts and words are recorded as an explanation for his action that follows.

This passage is a classic example of a person getting trapped by mixed motives. Joab's claim to David was that Abner was guilty of deceit in his peace plan. Since Abner died within hours, there is no way to determine what he would have done had he lived. But every indication is that Joab could have had several motives other than worrying about Abner's character. First, he could have feared Abner as a rival in David's house. Although there is no record as to what he asked in exchange for leading Israel over to David's side, Abner was ambitious enough and experienced enough to have made a good deal for himself. It may have been not knowing what David had promised Abner that bothered Joab. There is in most people the capacity to be territorial, to be defensive about what we consider to be "our turf."

Second, Joab's strongest motive behind his attitude probably was tied to the fact that Abner had killed his brother Asahel. The text indicated this as the prime motive, *"so that he died for the blood of Asahel his brother"* (v. 27). That Abner had not really wanted to kill the young man and did everything he could to dissuade Asahel was completely lost on Joab. The tribal morality of that time required Joab to avenge his brother's death—and he did. It is a natural tendency for us to try to hide our real motives from others and sometimes even from ourselves. Joab's slaying of Abner is a sad picture of a person allowing his own personal agenda to take precedence and thereby jeopardize God's larger purpose. It happens in families, in churches, in businesses, and in the life of a nation. Personal ambition and the desire for revenge both introduce an agenda into life that undermines God's purpose for our lives and for the kingdom.

Many of the scholars who have studied this incident wonder if David were as innocent of the death of Abner as he claimed and as helpless in controlling his general as he seemed. Some even wonder if David "allowed" it to happen. Others have suggested that David could have "used" Joab's feelings to take Abner out of the picture. He would not have been the first person to orchestrate something from a distance and then publicly denounce the action. Nothing in the text itself would indicate anything other than David's anger at Joab and his genuine grief at the death of Abner. For David to pronounce a curse upon the house of Joab in perpetuity (v. 29) would indicate that David's anger was real and that this was not just a slap on the wrist. David's mourning Abner's death, which is described in the last section of the chapter, would indicate that it had been his genuine intention to deal with Abner along the lines of their agreement.

## DAVID'S MOURNING FOR ABNER

31 Then David said to Joab and to all the people who were with him, "Tear your clothes, gird yourselves with sackcloth, and mourn for Abner." And King David followed the coffin. 32 So they buried Abner in Hebron; and the king lifted up his voice and wept at the grave of Abner, and all the people wept. 33 And the king sang a lament over Abner and said:

"Should Abner die as a fool dies?
34 Your hands were not bound
Nor your feet put into fetters;
As a man falls before wicked men, so you fell."
Then all the people wept over him again.

35 And when all the people came to persuade David to eat food while it was still day, David took an oath, saying, "God do so to me, and more also, if I taste bread or anything else till the sun goes down!" 36 Now all the people took note of it, and it pleased them, since whatever the king did pleased all the people. 37 For all the people and all Israel understood that day that it had not been the king's intent to kill Abner the son of Ner. 38 Then the king said to his servants, "Do you not know that a prince and a great man has fallen this day in Israel? 39 And I am weak today, though anointed king; and these men, the sons of Zeruiah, are too harsh for me. The LORD shall repay the evildoer according to his wickedness."

*—2 Samuel 3:31–39*

These nine verses give a rather detailed description of Abner's funeral. Although he had been the general of his rival to the throne, David ordered a full schedule of mourning for Abner, including fasting. Because of the fact that Joab was both David's nephew and his chief soldier it was only natural that some would question whether or not David had been involved in Abner's death. David's role in the funeral erased any question anyone may have had, and what had potential for being very divisive actually served as a unifying event.

David's lament (vv. 33–34) is probably only a fragment of a much longer eulogy that he delivered. In its entirety it moved the people to tears. The part that was preserved in this text points the accusing finger at his slayer. After the burial, when all the people were participating in the feast that was a part of the ritual of burial, David continued his fast as a sign of his grief and refused to touch food until the sun had set. More than anything else this was the event which convinced the people that David was innocent of any involvement (v. 37).

David's greatest tribute to Abner came in conversation with his servants when he said, *"Do you not know that a prince and a great man has fallen this day in Israel?"* (v. 38). In this statement David gave to the church a wonderful text for the funeral of a great leader. I followed in the pastorate a man who had been pastor of the church for a third of a century. In addition to being a national leader in his denomination, he had been recognized as a force for righteousness in the life of the city. When he died, I was asked to conduct his funeral. I knew that in addition to his immediate family and church family that there would be people attending from a broad spectrum of religious and civic life. David's words about Abner seemed to be the best words for understanding the occasion.

As this chapter closes with the funeral of Israel's strongest person the next chapter gives the account of the death of Israel's puppet king, Ishbosheth. His death would remove the last remaining obstacle to David's reigning over all Israel. Each of these incidents was preserved so we could see how God used all the events that took place to bring David to the throne of Israel.

## THE MURDER OF ISHBOSHETH

**4:1** When Saul's son heard that Abner had died in Hebron, he lost heart, and all Israel was troubled. **2** Now Saul's son had two men who were captains of troops. The name of one was Baanah and the name of the other Rechab, the sons of Rimmon the Beerothite, of the children of Benjamin. (For Beeroth also was part of Benjamin, 3 because the Beerothites fled to Gittaim and have been sojourners there until this day.)

4 Jonathan, Saul's son, had a son who was lame in his feet. He was five years old when the news about Saul and Jonathan came from Jezreel; and his nurse took him up and fled. And it happened, as she made haste to flee, that he fell and became lame. His name was Mephibosheth.

5 Then the sons of Rimmon the Beerothite, Rechab and Baanah, set out and came at about the heat of the day to the house of Ishbosheth, who was lying on his bed at noon. 6 And they came there, all the way into the house, as though to get wheat, and they stabbed him in the stomach. Then Rechab and Baanah his brother escaped. 7 For when they came into the house, he was lying on his bed in his bedroom; then they struck him and killed him, beheaded him and took his head, and were all night escaping through the plain. 8 And they brought the head of Ishbosheth to David at Hebron, and said to the king, "Here is the head of Ishbosheth, the son of Saul your enemy, who sought your life; and the LORD has avenged my lord the king this day of Saul and his descendants."

9 But David answered Rechab and Baanah his brother, the sons of Rimmon the Beerothite, and said to them, "As the LORD lives, who has redeemed my life from all adversity, 10 when someone told me, saying, 'Look, Saul is dead,' thinking to have brought good news, I arrested him and had him executed in Ziklag—the one who thought I would give him a reward for his news. 11 How much more, when wicked men have killed a righteous person in his own house on his bed? Therefore, shall I not now require his blood at your hand and remove you from the earth?" 12 So David commanded his young men, and they executed them, cut off their hands and feet, and hanged them by the pool in Hebron. But they took the head of Ishbosheth and buried it in the tomb of Abner in Hebron.

*—2 Samuel 4:1–12*

This chapter of only twelve verses tells of the murder of Saul's son Ishbosheth by two of his own soldiers. Ishbosheth's death removed the one remaining obstacle to David's becoming king over all the tribes. The story was preserved in this account both to explain why the Israelites came and asked David to become their king (2 Sam. 5:1) and to vindicate David of any involvement in the murder of his rival. It is also a reminder that God is able to work His purpose both through the deeds and the misdeeds of people.

Abner's influence in Israel is witnessed to by the effect that his death had on the king and the people. Losing their only real leader robbed them of their courage and created a political vacuum. The king had been put on the throne by Abner and functioned like a puppet. While he resented Abner's heavy-handedness, he was dependent upon him. The people looked to Abner for protection against their traditional enemies. While none thought that Ishbosheth could lead Israel, they were all aware that as long as he was king they couldn't approach David about being their king. The circumstances were ripe for intrigue and violence.

Ishbosheth's death is a story of betrayal and opportunism. The description and the deed take only six verses (vv. 2–3, 5–8) but give us a clear picture of two of the most repulsive people in the Old Testament. They were brothers who felt their hour had come. They were both captains of raiding parties and were accustomed to making quick judgments and acting on them. Some authors suggest that there may have been a family score to settle with the house of Saul. It's possible that they sensed the mood of the people—the resentment of the fact that a weak and despondent king stood in the way of David's being their king—and decided to take things into their own hands. The more likely scenario is that they were opportunists. They knew that Ishbosheth was through and decided to act quickly in order to ingratiate themselves to David and possibly collect a reward. They felt no loyalty to anyone but themselves, so they set their sails to the prevailing winds for their own good. We live in a society where more people make decisions on the basis of self-interest than out of deep convictions. As a result every structure of society is weakened.

The account of how Jonathan's son came to be crippled (v. 4) doesn't seem to relate to the story, thus raising a question as to what it's doing here. Several suggestions have been made. It may have been placed at this place to indicate that after the death of Ishbosheth there wasn't really a suitable claimant to Saul's throne. It could also be here to point to a subsequent story connected with Saul's grandson (2 Sam. 9). It could also be here to contrast the treachery of the two brothers with David's later treatment of

Jonathan's son. It does introduce an interesting person who will figure in David's keeping a promise to a friend and a name—Mephibosheth—that has been tripped over by everyone who ever tried to pronounce it.

While the original language makes it difficult to know exactly how the brothers were able to gain access to the king's chamber, the success of their effort is clear. They struck the king, beheaded him, and then took the head with them as a proof for David of the king's death. The speech that they made to David (v. 8) would indicate that they expected both praise and a reward for what they had done. There was a time when I would read stories like this in the Old Testament and think how horrible it would have been to live in such an era. Yet violence in our homes, political murders, and escalating acts of terrorism have led me to believe that the light of God's revelation in Christ still needs to shine in places of darkness in our world.

David's reaction was swift and decisive. First, he reminded the brothers of his response to the man who claimed to have slain Saul (v. 10). Second, he accused them of being worse than the one who had slain God's anointed. Saul had been wounded in battle and had asked to be killed. Ishbosheth had been asleep in his own home. David did not refer to Ishbosheth as God's anointed, for it was common knowledge that no prophet had anointed him and that Abner had put him on the throne as an expression of his own ambition. People who cannot be king but would be kingmakers have been around for a long time. David, however, did call him *"a righteous person"* (v. 11) and ordered his murderers slain and mutilated (v. 12). This meant that they were to be treated like common criminals whose bodies were exhibited and not buried. In contrast, David had the head of Ishbosheth buried in Abner's tomb (v. 12).

The story was preserved for a purpose. David's judgment of the brothers was a severe reminder that vengeance belongs to God. It was also a way in which David could distance himself from both their motives and their actions. It sent a clear message that even though God had anointed him to be king, he didn't approve of coming to power in that way. He had passed up several opportunities to kill Saul. While David repudiated the action, he must have been aware that the brothers had removed the only obstacle which lay between him and ruling over all Israel. Like many of the incidents that precede this one, it shows how God stood over the events of history, good or bad, in order to bring David to the throne and to accomplish his purpose in history.

The next chapter will find David reigning over all Israel, capturing Jerusalem, and leading Israel in a major defeat of their enemy, the Philistines.

## DAVID REIGNS OVER ALL ISRAEL

5:1 Then all the tribes of Israel came to David at Hebron and spoke, saying, "Indeed we are your bone and your flesh. 2 Also, in time past, when Saul was king over us, you were the one who led Israel out and brought them in; and the LORD said to you, 'You shall shepherd My people Israel, and be ruler over Israel.'" 3 Therefore all the elders of Israel came to the king at Hebron, and King David made a covenant with them at Hebron before the LORD. And they anointed David king over Israel. 4 David was thirty years old when he began to reign, and he reigned forty years. 5 In Hebron he reigned over Judah seven years and six months, and in Jerusalem he reigned thirty-three years over all Israel and Judah.

*—2 Samuel 5:1–5*

Chapter 5 is a collection of incidents that are not arranged in the sequence in which they took place but are arranged to make clear the message that the monarchy was united, recognized, growing, and able to defend itself against its enemies. Permeating it all is the idea that God is the one who has brought it about.

When the representatives of all the tribes gathered to ask David to be their king, they had three compelling reasons. First, they were family. In the larger sense they were all children of Jacob. In a more specific sense, David was Saul's son-in-law. It didn't make sense for people who were family to continue to be at war with each other. Second, David was already a proven leader of Israel. The people remembered the times when David had led Saul's army into battle and defeated their enemies. Saul's jealousy had been fed by the people's love for David and a fear that they would turn to him as their king. Third, they felt that the Lord had chosen David. Some may have known of Samuel's anointing of David (1 Sam. 16:13) but more of them probably had witnessed God's blessing of David and accepted that as a sign of God's anointing. Everything seemed right in their request.

There was a very simple principle at work in the logic of the elders. They turned their back on all of their differences and focused on the things they had in common, the things that could unite them. Our world would live more peacefully if its leaders could learn to look for common interests and common concerns as a basis for unity instead of allowing our many differences to be magnified and divisive. The cause of Christ's kingdom would be helped if Christians could learn to celebrate what they have in common rather than arguing over their areas of differences. Even in the brokenness of our society and in our churches we need to live with the dream of unity when "all in heaven and on earth, might be brought into a unity in Christ" (Eph. 1:10, NEB).

David made a covenant with the tribal elders (v. 3) that stipulated the nature of the kingship. There were two aspects of David's covenant with the elders that are significant to understanding the story and which have application to us today. First, it was a covenant that laid out the obligations of both parties. While there may have been things that David wanted the people to agree to concerning their commitments to him, there were also his obligations to the people. A wise attorney once told me that both parties win in any good agreement. There are too many people in the world today who have forgotten the mutual aspect of covenant relationships and this continually undermines businesses, international relationships, and relationships between people.

The second element in David's covenant with the elders was that it was made *"before the LORD"* (v. 3). They made a religious ceremony out of the agreement. This underlined the seriousness with which they made their commitment. It acknowledged God's part in bringing them together. It sought God's continued leadership in the affairs of Israel. Our lives are given their meaning by the covenants we make and keep. Becoming a follower of Jesus Christ means entering into a covenant with God. It is a relationship with obligations on God's part and on ours. Getting married is entering into a sacred covenant about the most important of all human relationships. All of us need to learn to see the covenants that we make as "before God" and to find resources in God for keeping those covenants.

David's anointing as king was probably done by a priest—although none is mentioned—at the instruction of the elders of Israel. That ceremony brought to fruition what had been anticipated when Samuel had visited the house of Jesse and anointed David while he was just a lad in the presence of his brothers (1 Sam. 16:13). This should serve as a reminder to us that there is often a great distance between the beginning of a dream and its fulfillment. There must have been times when David seriously doubted that he was God's anointed because of the trials he went through as a fugitive and an exile. We live in a society that is obsessed with instant everything. This mentality has also affected how we view the Christian life. We often want now what it takes God time to create. The fruits of the spirit do not become ours from a hurried-up, crash course on Christian living. The dream that Joseph had as a youth took almost twenty years to fulfill and included abuse, slavery, temptation, prison, and betrayal. Often we think only of the destination that God has for us and forget the journey. David's pilgrimage had included both adulation and persecution, deep friendships and dedicated enemies, but in it all God was moving David's life forward toward its goal.

# CHAPTER TWELVE—THE CONSOLIDATION OF THE KINGDOM OF DAVID

2 SAMUEL 5:6—10:19

*Scripture Outline*

The two most significant events of chapter 5 are David's being made king of a united Israel and Jerusalem's being made the nation's capital. Although Israel was never a major world power and Jerusalem was never compared to Babylon or Rome, the religious significance of the nation and the city has been profound for the world. David's line of kings lasted four hundred years. It was the beginning of a golden age out of which came the expectations for the messianic age. Jerusalem became the religious capital both for Jews and Christians.

## CONQUEST OF JERUSALEM

⁶ And the king and his men went to Jerusalem against the Jebusites, the inhabitants of the land, who spoke to

David, saying, "You shall not come in here; but the blind and the lame will repel you," thinking, "David cannot come in here." ⁷ Nevertheless David took the stronghold of Zion (that is, the City of David).

⁸ Now David said on that day, "Whoever climbs up by way of the water shaft and defeats the Jebusites (the lame and the blind, who are hated by David's soul), he shall be chief and captain." Therefore they say, "The blind and the lame shall not come into the house."

⁹ Then David dwelt in the stronghold, and called it the City of David. And David built all around from the Millo and inward. ¹⁰ So David went on and became great, and the LORD God of hosts was with him.

¹¹ Then Hiram king of Tyre sent messengers to David, and cedar trees, and carpenters and masons. And they built David a house. ¹² So David knew that the LORD had established him as king over Israel, and that He had exalted His kingdom for the sake of His people Israel.

¹³ And David took more concubines and wives from Jerusalem, after he had come from Hebron. Also more sons and daughters were born to David. ¹⁴ Now these are the names of those who were born to him in Jerusalem: Shammua, Shobab, Nathan, Solomon, ¹⁵ Ibhar, Elishua, Nepheg, Japhia, ¹⁶ Elishama, Eliada, and Eliphelet.

*—2 Samuel 5:6–16*

While the action of these eleven verses focuses on the capture of Jerusalem, it also contains the story of a gift of a palace from a neighboring king and an account of the expansion of David's family. These separate events are gathered together in this place in the Scripture to show all the ways God is blessing David in his new role as king over all Israel. There are times when it is good to do with our own lives what the compiler has done here—to take a handful of the good things that God has done in our lives and think about them and talk about them. Often when the problems with which I'm dealing are getting me down, I will stop what I'm doing, take a sheet of paper, and write down as many of God's blessings in my life as I can think of. It never fails to put things in perspective.

There is a sparsity of details about David's capture of the city of Jerusalem for his new capital. It was a thousand years old. Because of its location on a high ridge above sheer cliffs it was considered impregnable. The words, *"the blind and the lame shall repel you"* (v. 6) was probably a proverb that indicated that the city was so well located that it could even be defended by the blind and the lame in the city. Scholars are confused as to what the other references to the blind and lame might mean (v. 8). The story does not give details as to how David's men were able to climb the water shaft (v. 8). Over the centuries scholars have written pages of speculation as to how it was done. The main truth recorded was *"David took the stronghold of Zion"* (v. 7). One reason for so little detail about this battle and the two with the Philistines probably related to the fact that they were considered to be God's battles, with Israel functioning as God's agent. Conquering Jerusalem gave David a stronghold for his capital that was perfectly located between the two groups who had united behind him as king.

A second sign of God's blessing came in the response of the king of Tyre (v. 11). Later Hiram will play a significant part in the building of the temple under Solomon, but in this instance he builds a palace for David's household. One author has suggested that Hiram may have been motivated by the fact that Tyre shared a common enemy with Israel in the Philistines. David's perspective on the event was that it made him know "that the LORD had established him as king over Israel, for his kingdom was highly exalted for the sake of His people Israel" (1 Chr. 14:2). It was a sign to David that God had given him standing in the eyes of the surrounding people. What was happening did not go unnoticed by the Philistines either, as the latter part of the chapter discloses.

A third sign of God's blessing that is recorded in this passage deals with the expansion of David's family (vv. 13–16). An oriental king was known by the size of his harem, and David enlarged his by adding both wives and concubines, lesser wives. Many of these didn't come from Jerusalem, as the text seems to indicate, but were added while he was in Jerusalem. Most of the women brought into his household were parts of political arrangements rather than any romantic attachment. Many sons and daughters were born of these arrangements and the names of eleven sons are listed (vv. 14–16). In David's time nothing was a greater sign of God's blessing than many children. In our more urban industrial society we attach no spiritual significance to the number of children born into a family. Our tendency is to view the materialistic success symbols of a secular society as a sign of God's blessing.

## THE PHILISTINES DEFEATED

<sup>17</sup> Now when the Philistines heard that they had anointed David king over Israel, all the Philistines went up to search for David. And David heard of it and went down to the stronghold. <sup>18</sup> The Philistines also went and deployed themselves in the Valley of Rephaim. <sup>19</sup> So David inquired of the LORD, saying, "Shall I go up against the Philistines? Will You deliver them into my hand?"

And the LORD said to David, "Go up, for I will doubtless deliver the Philistines into your hand."

<sup>20</sup> So David went to Baal Perazim, and David defeated them there; and he said, "The LORD has broken through my enemies before me, like a breakthrough of water." Therefore he called the name of that place Baal Perazim. <sup>21</sup> And they left their images there, and David and his men carried them away.

<sup>22</sup> Then the Philistines went up once again and deployed themselves in the Valley of Rephaim. <sup>23</sup> Therefore David inquired of the LORD, and He said, "You shall not go up; circle around behind them, and come upon them in front of the mulberry trees. <sup>24</sup> And it shall be, when you hear the sound of marching in the tops of the mulberry trees, then you shall advance quickly. For then the LORD will go out before you to strike the camp of the Philistines." <sup>25</sup> And David did so, as the LORD commanded him; and he drove back the Philistines from Geba as far as Gezer.

*—2 Samuel 5:17–25*

The events depicted in these verses probably follow directly after the anointing of David as king (v. 3). Most scholars believe that they happened before the capture of Jerusalem and that the stronghold referred to in verse 17 was the one from which he had been operating previously; namely, Hebron. The text makes it clear that when the Philistines *"heard that they had anointed David king over Israel"* (v. 17) they decided to attack. As long as the two rival groups of Israelite tribes were fighting with each other they were no threat to anyone. Now that they were unified the Philistines were concerned and moved against David quickly before he had time to consolidate his resources. Christians ought to learn lessons from this event. As long as we use up our energy competing with each other, the world isn't going to worry about us. This is probably why the world tends to be so patronizing of the church. When God's children join their considerable resources to do God's work, they always get a reaction from the world that operates with different values and goals.

One aspect of the two battles featured in the text is that David did not make a move against the Philistines without consulting God (vv. 19, 23). He sought God's guidance through the priest of God who cast lots to get a yes-or-no answer to the questions that David composed. Knowing what questions to ask God is a part of spiritual wisdom. In the first battle, David's request was probably two questions—the first asking if he should engage the Philistines and the second asking whether he would win. In his second inquiry, the questions related to strategy. One battle called for a frontal attack and the other for a flanking movement. The capturing of the Philistine's idols was an answer to the Philistines previously capturing the ark of the covenant (1 Sam. 4—5). In both cases it was assumed that it was God's battle and that God was going before them into battle (v. 24). Often God's children make the mistake of thinking that the work is theirs and that it must be done in their own strength.

The point of the whole chapter is summarized by verse 10, *"So David went on and became great, and the LORD God of hosts was with him."* Chapter 6 tells of David's moving the ark of God to Jerusalem. It's a story of joy and celebration, of tragedy and questioning, of music and dancing, of adoration and worship, and of tension and strife. Most of us have lived too long with the awareness of God's presence everywhere to fully appreciate what the ark meant to Israel as a symbol of God's presence. There are many lessons to be learned by today's Christians in the ancient stories of the early days of the Israelite monarchy.

## FIRST STAGE OF THE ARK'S MOVE

6:1 Again David gathered all the choice men of Israel, thirty thousand. [2] And David arose and went with all the people who were with him from Baale Judah to bring up from there the ark of God, whose name is called by the Name, the LORD of Hosts, who dwells between the cherubim. [3] So they set the ark of God on a new cart, and brought it out of the house of Abinadab, which was on the hill; and Uzzah and Ahio, the sons of Abinadab, drove the new cart. [4] And they brought it out of the house of Abinadab, which was on the hill, accompanying the ark of God; and Ahio went before the ark. [5] Then David and all the house of Israel played music before the LORD on all kinds of instruments of fir wood, on harps, on stringed instruments, on tambourines, on sistrums, and on cymbals.

6 And when they came to Nachon's threshing floor, Uzzah put out his hand to the ark of God and took hold of it, for the oxen stumbled. 7 Then the anger of the LORD was aroused against Uzzah, and God struck him there for his error; and he died there by the ark of God. 8 And David became angry because of the LORD's outbreak against Uzzah; and he called the name of the place Perez Uzzah to this day.

9 David was afraid of the LORD that day; and he said, "How can the ark of the LORD come to me?" 10 So David would not move the ark of the LORD with him into the City of David; but David took it aside into the house of Obed-Edom the Gittite. 11 The ark of the LORD remained in the house of Obed-Edom the Gittite three months. And the LORD blessed Obed-Edom and all his household.

—*2 Samuel 6:1–11*

While the moving of the ark to Jerusalem relates closely to the establishment of the monarchy, this story also needs to be seen as a sequel to the capture and return of the ark by the Philistines (1 Sam. 4:3—7:2). The earlier story grew out of the incident when the children of Israel brought the ark into a battle that they were losing in hopes of turning the tide the other way. In that battle the Israelites lost 30,000 men, including the two sons of Eli, and the ark was captured (1 Sam. 4:10–11). The Philistines connected the ark with all the bad things that happened to them after its capture, so they got rid of it by taking it to Kiriath Jearim, to the house of Abinadab, whose son Eleazar took care of it (1 Sam. 7:1–2). It had remained there for years. The military dominance of the Philistines in the area was probably the main reason that it remained there so long. David's two victories over the Philistines and the capturing of their idols cleared the way for the ark to be moved without opposition from the Philistines. To understand the mood of victory and celebration that surrounded the moving of the ark, 1 Samuel 4—6 ought to be read as background.

The ark was a symbol of the presence of God. Moving it to the new capital was David's first step in making Jerusalem into a religious capital. It was where David reigned and he wanted God to reign there also. It is also true that for the Israelites the ark had both religious and patriotic symbolism. This mixture is understandable since they had so recently had God for their king and Samuel as His prophet. But in the twenty-first century it is surprising to find people who confuse their patriotism and their religion. While the duties of Christian citizenship are clearly taught in the Scriptures, the Bible is equally clear about the fact that all nations stand before God as the object of His love and judgment. The temptation to feel that one's nation is "God's pet" is natural, but wrong.

The moving of the ark is made in two stages. While the dominant mood of the occasion is joy and celebration, there is a troubling incident connected with each stage. The death of Uzzah, who touched the ark as it was about to fall (v. 7), created such fear that the journey was halted for ninety days. Then Michal's reaction of contempt for David's behavior (v. 20) created an estrangement between David and his wife that was permanent. But even these two "dark clouds" over an otherwise joyous occasion have lessons to teach.

While the ark had been neglected for years and may have looked like nothing more than an ornate box, the events reported in these verses reminded all the participants of God's holy power for both disaster and blessing. David decided not merely to send some of his servants to bring the ark to Jerusalem. Rather he chose to make it a national affair with pomp and ceremony. This was probably wise for more than one reason. First, the ark had been lost as the whole nation had been engaged in battle, so it would be appropriate for the nation to be involved in its recovery. Of even more significance, however, was what participating in the ceremony would do for religious unity in Israel. While we know that God is a Spirit who can enter into the heart of any person who believes, it is also true that large groups of believers gathering for religious events can serve as reinforcement for one's faith.

It's interesting that David took as many men with him to recover the ark as had been killed when the ark was taken. The house of Abinadab was located approximately seven miles southwest of Jerusalem. The ark was placed on a new cart, one that could not have been defiled. This is what the Philistines did when they moved it because of their sense of the danger of holiness (1 Sam. 6:7–8). It was accompanied by Uzzah and Ahio, who were Abinadab's sons. Nothing is said about Eleazer, Abinadab's son who originally cared for the ark when the Philistines delivered it there.

A great celebration preceded the ark on its journey toward Jerusalem (v. 5). It was more like the return of a victorious army from battle than a solemn procession. There was music, singing, and dancing all along the way. It was a much less inhibited expression of joy and celebration than most of us associate with church and worship. This type of personal total involvement is more likely to take place at a rock concert or a sporting event than in our worship. Most of the musical instruments mentioned are listed in Psalm 150. It's interesting to notice that centuries ago God's people used every known musical instrument in praise and that today we still have churches who feel that there is something irreligious about guitars or drums in worship.

The mood was changed instantly by an incident that took the life of Uzzah, one of the brothers accompanying the ark (v. 7). This event is a troubling one to a modern reader who lives in a world in which the sense of the holy has been almost lost. Those who were there probably wondered why everyone hadn't been smitten. They knew of the seventy who had been slain for not rejoicing with the others when the ark was welcomed to Beth Shemesh (1 Sam. 6:19–20). Detailed instructions had been given for the moving of the ark in Numbers 4, and it was clearly stated that the penalty for touching the ark was death (Num. 4:15).

A part of this lesson was that people were not to be too familiar with the holy—that God can't be owned or manipulated. One scholar reminds us that the event was interpreted and not photographed. The result of the incident was the fresh recognition of God's awesome power, but David reacted to Uzzah's death with anger (v. 8). One of the most common characteristics of Israel's worship was a worshiper's willingness to complain to God about His action or inaction (Ps. 13 or 22 would be a good example). Yet underlying their complaint was the deep conviction that God cared for them and was able to change things.

David was also frightened by what had happened (v. 9). He wondered if Uzzah's death might be a message to him. He wondered whether he might be unworthy to be in God's presence. This new vision of the holiness of God made him doubt whether he ought to take the ark into Jerusalem. This was behind his decision to leave the ark at the house of Obed-Edom the Gittite (vv. 10–11). He needed time to see if the presence of the ark would be a blessing or a curse. The text reports that *"the LORD blessed Obed-Edom and all his household"* (v. 11). This usually meant material blessings of family, crops, livestock, and other possessions. This sent a clear message to David that there was more to be gained than feared from the presence of God in the ark.

## THE ARK'S MOVE TO JERUSALEM

12 Now it was told King David, saying, "The LORD has blessed the house of Obed-Edom and all that belongs to him,

254

because of the ark of God." So David went and brought up the ark of God from the house of Obed-Edom to the City of David with gladness. [13] And so it was, when those bearing the ark of the LORD had gone six paces, that he sacrificed oxen and fatted sheep. [14] Then David danced before the LORD with all his might; and David was wearing a linen ephod. [15] So David and all the house of Israel brought up the ark of the LORD with shouting and with the sound of the trumpet.

[16] Now as the ark of the LORD came into the City of David, Michal, Saul's daughter, looked through a window and saw King David leaping and whirling before the LORD; and she despised him in her heart. [17] So they brought the ark of the LORD, and set it in its place in the midst of the tabernacle that David had erected for it. Then David offered burnt offerings and peace offerings before the LORD. [18] And when David had finished offering burnt offerings and peace offerings, he blessed the people in the name of the LORD of hosts. [19] Then he distributed among all the people, among the whole multitude of Israel, both the women and the men, to everyone a loaf of bread, a piece of meat, and a cake of raisins. So all the people departed, everyone to his house.

[20] Then David returned to bless his household. And Michal the daughter of Saul came out to meet David, and said, "How glorious was the king of Israel today, uncovering himself today in the eyes of the maids of his servants, as one of the base fellows shamelessly uncovers himself!"

[21] So David said to Michal, "It was before the LORD, who chose me instead of your father and all his house, to appoint me ruler over the people of the LORD, over Israel. Therefore I will play music before the LORD. [22] And I will be even more undignified than this, and will be humble in my own sight. But as for the maidservants of whom you have spoken, by them I will be held in honor."

[23] Therefore Michal the daughter of Saul had no children to the day of her death.

*—2 Samuel 6:12–23*

The first verse in this section summarizes the whole story in one sentence. *"So David went and brought up the ark of God from the house of Obed-Edom to the City of David with gladness"* (v. 12). The verses that follow fill in the details (vv. 13–19). The decision to make the move was precipitated by David's hearing how God was blessing the house where the ark was being kept. The story of the move is an exciting one marked by a sacrifice, energetic worship, and the placing of the ark in a special tabernacle that *"David had erected for it"* (v. 17).

Unlike the first stage of the move, this time the ark was carried by men rather than transported on a cart. When they had moved but six paces, David had them stop and then he made a sacrifice of *"oxen and fatted sheep"* (v. 13). Whether this was the only time this was done or whether a similar ritual was followed at given intervals is not known. In it all David functioned as both priest and king. Again David danced *"before the LORD"* (v. 14) as a part of the worship of God and as a celebration of God's presence.

It would be hard to overestimate the importance both to David's leadership and to Israel's religion of bringing the ark of God to Jerusalem. While the revelation of God in Jesus Christ promises the Spirit of God to everyone who believes, there is still the need in the world for places especially associated with the presence of God. I don't know a person who would equate the presence of God with a building to the degree that the Israelites associated God's presence with the ark, but when people go to a place for Bible study, worship, and Christian fellowship over a period of years, they begin to associate the building with their experiences with God. As a result they find it easier to experience the presence of God at that place. Even though we live with the assurance of God's abiding presence with us, we still need special places to meet God.

Just as the death of Uzzah marred the first stage of the ark's move, the reaction of Michal to David's dancing was a cloud over the celebration of the final move of the ark to Jerusalem (vv. 20–23). Although she was David's wife, she is referred to as *"Saul's daughter"* three times in this chapter (vv. 16, 20, and 23). While there are some who feel that her only criticism was that David's actions were too undignified for a king, others feel that there must have been more to her attitude since her own father had danced naked with the prophets (1 Sam. 19:24). David's defense of his activity was that it was before the very Lord who had rejected her father and had chosen him (v. 20). This confrontation put to rest any dream anyone had for a child who would bring together the lines of Saul and David. The ensuing estrangement left Michal barren.

Chapter 7 introduces the dialogue between David and God concerning David's desire to build a house for God. David's desire was to be fulfilled by his son Solomon, but this chapter deals with

David's religious development as it records David in a time of worship that is pure thanksgiving.

## GOD'S COVENANT WITH DAVID

7:1 Now it came to pass when the king was dwelling in his house, and the LORD had given him rest from all his enemies all around, 2 that the king said to Nathan the prophet, "See now, I dwell in a house of cedar, but the ark of God dwells inside tent curtains."

3 Then Nathan said to the king, "Go, do all that is in your heart, for the LORD is with you."

4 But it happened that night that the word of the LORD came to Nathan, saying, 5 "Go and tell My servant David, 'Thus says the LORD: "Would you build a house for Me to dwell in? 6 For I have not dwelt in a house since the time that I brought the children of Israel up from Egypt, even to this day, but have moved about in a tent and in a tabernacle. 7 Wherever I have moved about with all the children of Israel, have I ever spoken a word to anyone from the tribes of Israel, whom I commanded to shepherd My people Israel, saying, 'Why have you not built Me a house of cedar?'"'

8 Now therefore, thus shall you say to My servant David, 'Thus says the LORD of hosts: "I took you from the sheepfold, from following the sheep, to be ruler over My people, over Israel. 9 And I have been with you wherever you have gone, and have cut off all your enemies from before you, and have made you a great name, like the name of the great men who are on the earth. 10 Moreover I will appoint a place for My people Israel, and will plant them, that they may dwell in a place of their own and move no more; nor shall the sons of wickedness oppress them anymore, as previously, 11 since the time that I commanded judges to be over My people Israel, and have caused you to rest from all your enemies. Also the LORD tells you that He will make you a house.

12 "When your days are fulfilled and you rest with your fathers, I will set up your seed after you, who will come from your body, and I will establish his kingdom. 13 He shall build a house for My name, and I will establish the throne of his kingdom forever. 14 I will be his Father, and he shall be My son. If he commits iniquity, I will chasten him with the rod of men and with the blows of the sons of men.

¹⁵ But My mercy shall not depart from him, as I took it from Saul, whom I removed from before you. ¹⁶ And your house and your kingdom shall be established forever before you. Your throne shall be established forever."'"

¹⁷ According to all these words and according to all this vision, so Nathan spoke to David.

*—2 Samuel 7:1–17*

This chapter marks a climax of events. Jerusalem had been conquered, the Philistines had been defeated, and the ark had been enshrined in a tent. The events of this chapter assume the victories that are recorded in the following chapters (chs. 8, 10—12). The compiler was more interested in showing the tie between the bringing of the ark to Jerusalem and David's desire to build a permanent home for it than to recite the events in their historical sequence. The two critical questions being raised were: What is to be the future of the Jerusalem shrine? Who would be David's successor on the throne of Israel? This chapter addresses both questions.

Chapter 7 also introduces the prophet Nathan, who appears three times in the Scriptures. His last appearance is at the accession of Solomon to the throne (1 Kin. 1). In that account Nathan reminded David of God's intention, which is recorded in this chapter. His second appearance is his confrontation of David with God's displeasure over the king's relationship with Bathsheba (2 Sam. 12). In this chapter Nathan presents two different oracles from God to David, tied together by a play on the word "house." David wants to build a house for God; God instead intends to build David's house.

It's a wonderful thing to dream of doing something to honor God. Now for the first time since ascending the throne David was in a position to do something that had probably been in his heart for a long time. He was now established in his new house and secure from his Philistine enemies. Often people come to this place in their lives and become bored and restless. Rather than using their stability as a base from which to do good, they focus on themselves in an effort to become more established and more secure. David was at that place in his life where he wanted to use his time, resources, and knowledge to honor God. I have known a score of Christians who have come to a place in their lives where they wanted to do something special for God. One became wealthy in the scrap metal business. After selling his business he used a large amount of his money to erect a children's building for his inner-city church. He has lived to see hundreds of children's lives salvaged as a result.

David was very conscious of God's presence in his life. One of the factors that caused him to declare his interest and intention to Nathan was the contrast between the house in which he now lived and the tent that he had provided for the ark of God. He was now living in a beautiful house of cedar, built for him as a gift from Hiram, the king of Tyre (2 Sam. 5:11–12). Not everyone is bothered by the contrast between their opulent lifestyle and the neglect of the church. David's attitude would have thrilled the prophet Haggai who railed against God's people because they built for themselves "paneled houses" while the temple lay in ruins (Hag. 1:2–4). It isn't hard to see why Nathan was impressed by David's desire and gave his blessing to the project (v. 3).

But God did not intend for David to build the temple and communicated that fact through Nathan. The Hebrew word that is translated "house" is used in this passage two different ways. When it is used in the rhetorical question *"Would you build a house for Me to dwell in?"* (v. 5), it means "temple." When God is promising to establish David's house (v. 16), it means "dynasty." In essence God's message to David was "I will not let you build for Me a house, but I will build your house." This is so characteristic of God's dealings with His children, where our desire to do things for Him are constantly outstripped by His plans to bless us.

The main reason given in this chapter for David's not building the temple was that it wasn't necessary. God's argument reaches back into the history of His relationship with Israel; namely, when the tribes came out of Egypt and the ark was housed in a tent and moved when the people did (vv. 6–7). The virtue of that tent shrine was its mobility. This wilderness tradition was strong and God didn't want them to lose the pilgrim quality of their religious heritage. If that dynamic were lost, there would be the danger of thinking that God could be captured in a building—or a creed or a program. To illustrate, God reminded David that the lack of a permanent place hadn't hindered God from calling him and from blessing Israel (vv. 8–11).

Although it wasn't preserved in this account, the Scriptures give another reason for David's not being allowed to build the temple (1 Chr. 22:6–10). In that passage, David shares with his son Solomon the fact that he had wanted to build the temple but that God had forbidden it because he had "shed much blood and have made great wars" (1 Chr. 22:8). This seems to reflect a much later position on war because the battles in which David participated were considered to be God's battles and the subsequent victories were considered to be God's and not Israel's. The main thrust of the 2 Samuel account was that the building of the temple was not necessary, not that David had disqualified himself by being a soldier.

Nor was there an inference that the temple should never be built. David was allowed to make many of the preparations—choosing the site, gathering materials, finding skilled craftsmen, and clearing the way with other officials. David's spirit is revealed in the fact that he was willing to lay foundations on which others would ultimately have the privilege of building. The world has too many people who won't plant trees unless they are going to be around to eat the apples. The church needs more people who are planning and praying with the future needs of the church in mind. There are many things we would like to do and can't, but all of us can be a part of laying the foundations for the future of our children.

The Scripture indicates that God blesses not just the things we do but the things we would like to do. God blesses our intentions. When the temple had been built and the ark was being brought to its new home, Solomon made a speech in which he told how God had blessed his father David because it was in his heart "to [build] a house for My name" (1 Kin 8:18). This is an early reminder that God's interest is not just in our actions but in the interests of our hearts. The kingdom needs scores of people who fill their minds with things they would like to do for God.

With the questions of the temple laid to rest, Nathan's second message from God dealt with the matter of succession. God's answer to David's desire to build a house for Him was to promise to build David's household. God promised David what Saul had been denied, that is, that a son would succeed him (v. 12). More than that, God promised the *"throne of his kingdom forever"* (v. 13). As the phrase is used it could be a synonym for "a very long time," which in the case of David's heirs was fulfilled with four hundred years of reigning. Since Christ came from David's lineage, the "forever" is also fulfilled. Every Christian participates in the fulfillment of God's promise to David.

Nathan's message to David is a reminder that God's larger purpose isn't always tied to our particular dreams. Sometimes we try to give ourselves to things that seem right but which do not reflect God's priority. We are all too bound by the present time and fail to realize that with us, as with David, God's purposes for our lives reach into eternity. This portion of the chapter gives us a beautiful picture of God's inverting the sequence. David had a dream of something big he wanted to do for God, but God had a much larger dream of something He wanted to do for David.

## DAVID'S THANKSGIVING TO GOD

18 Then King David went in and sat before the LORD; and he said: "Who am I, O LORD God? And what is my house, that You have brought me this far? 19 And yet this was a small thing in Your sight, O LORD God; and You have also spoken of Your servant's house for a great while to come. Is this the manner of man, O LORD God? 20 Now what more can David say to You? For You, LORD God, know Your servant. 21 For Your word's sake, and according to Your own heart, You have done all these great things, to make Your servant know them. 22 Therefore You are great, O LORD God. For there is none like You, nor is there any God besides You, according to all that we have heard with our ears. 23 And who is like Your people, like Israel, the one nation on the earth whom God went to redeem for Himself as a people, to make for Himself a name—and to do for Yourself great and awesome deeds for Your land—before Your people whom You redeemed for Yourself from Egypt, the nations, and their gods? 24 For You have made Your people Israel Your very own people forever; and You, LORD, have become their God.

25 "Now, O LORD God, the word which You have spoken concerning Your servant and concerning his house, establish it forever and do as You have said. 26 So let Your name be magnified forever, saying, 'The LORD of hosts is the God over Israel.' And let the house of Your servant David be established before You. 27 For You, O LORD of hosts, God of Israel, have revealed this to Your servant, saying, 'I will build you a house.' Therefore Your servant has found it in his heart to pray this prayer to You.

28 "And now, O LORD God, You are God, and Your words are true, and You have promised this goodness to Your servant. 29 Now therefore, let it please You to bless the house of Your servant, that it may continue before You forever; for You, O LORD God, have spoken it, and with Your blessing let the house of Your servant be blessed forever."

—2 Samuel 7:18–29

These verses are a prayer of thanksgiving borne as a natural response to God's promises. The phrase *"David went in and sat before the LORD"* (v. 18) probably means that he went into the tent shrine and sat down before the ark of God. The characteristics of this response might serve as a model for any Christian who has been overwhelmed by a sense of God's grace. It anticipates in spirit many of the psalms of thanksgiving.

There is a genuine sense of humility. David picked up on God's reminder that He had taken him "from the sheepfold" (v. 8) and raised the question many reflective Christians raise: *"Who am I . . . that You have brought me this far?"* (v. 18). Sitting before the Lord, David's mind ran back to the beginning, to Samuel's visit to his father's house. He was overwhelmed at the memory of all the good things which God had done from that day on to bring him to the throne in Jerusalem and to bring peace and prosperity to Israel. One of our great temptations is to take the blessings of God for granted. It is good for our spiritual life to sit before God and remember how far He has brought us.

There is a sense of gratitude for God's promises. David had lived through a period of great uncertainty, not sure whether he would ever be king over Israel. He softened God's "forever" (v. 16) to *"a great while to come"* (v. 19). He was speechless before God, *"What more can David say to You? For You, LORD God, know Your servant"* (v. 20). He recovers sufficiently to compare the God of Israel with the gods of the other nations (vv. 22–24) as he places God's gifts to him in a historical context. Then he rehearses the promises that God has made to him (vv. 25–29), not so much to remind God but to remind himself once again of the greatness of God as reflected in His promises.

The next chapter deals with the conquests that brought the peace to Israel which is reflected in this chapter. It lists the different groups and their leaders whom David defeated as a way of showing the extent of strength and stability Israel was coming to enjoy. It also gives a first glimpse of David's growing skill as an administrator.

## DAVID'S FURTHER CONQUESTS

8:1 After this it came to pass that David attacked the Philistines and subdued them. And David took Metheg Ammah from the hand of the Philistines.

2 Then he defeated Moab. Forcing them down to the ground, he measured them off with a line. With two lines he measured off those to be put to death, and with one full line those to be kept alive. So the Moabites became David's servants, and brought tribute.

³ David also defeated Hadadezer the son of Rehob, king of Zobah, as he went to recover his territory at the River Euphrates. ⁴ David took from him one thousand chariots, seven hundred horsemen, and twenty thousand foot soldiers. Also David hamstrung all the chariot horses, except that he spared enough of them for one hundred chariots.

⁵ When the Syrians of Damascus came to help Hadadezer king of Zobah, David killed twenty-two thousand of the Syrians. ⁶ Then David put garrisons in Syria of Damascus; and the Syrians became David's servants, and brought tribute. So the LORD preserved David wherever he went. ⁷ And David took the shields of gold that had belonged to the servants of Hadadezer, and brought them to Jerusalem. ⁸ Also from Betah and from Berothai, cities of Hadadezer, King David took a large amount of bronze.

⁹ When Toi king of Hamath heard that David had defeated all the army of Hadadezer, ¹⁰ then Toi sent Joram his son to King David, to greet him and bless him, because he had fought against Hadadezer and defeated him (for Hadadezer had been at war with Toi); and Joram brought with him articles of silver, articles of gold, and articles of bronze. ¹¹ King David also dedicated these to the LORD, along with the silver and gold that he had dedicated from all the nations which he had subdued—¹² from Syria, from Moab, from the people of Ammon, from the Philistines, from Amalek, and from the spoil of Hadadezer the son of Rehob, king of Zobah.

¹³ And David made himself a name when he returned from killing eighteen thousand Syrians in the Valley of Salt. ¹⁴ He also put garrisons in Edom; throughout all Edom he put garrisons, and all the Edomites became David's servants. And the LORD preserved David wherever he went.

*—2 Samuel 8:1–14*

Chapter 8 picks up the story that was left off in 2 Samuel 5. The events recorded here tell of the growth of David's kingdom and describe how extensive this kingdom was. Consequently there is quite a change in mood from the conversation with God on which the previous chapter ended and the bloody battles of this chapter. The key to understanding the point of this chapter is found in verse 13, *"And David made himself a name."* Two factors were involved in the rapid growth of his empire and his great renown. First, David was skilled both in politics and in war. Whether negotiating with the ruler of another country or leading his men into battle, he had no equal in his time. Second, the Lord helped him. If there is one theme that runs through all of his exploits it is that God was blessing his efforts. What David was able to accomplish in so short a time can only be explained by these factors.

While the *"After this"* of verse 1 meant to refer directly to God's promises in the previous chapter, it also ties onto 2 Samuel 5:17–25. That passage details the battle referred to only casually here. It is meant to convey the fact that David began his other conquests after the Philistines were subdued. Nowhere does the Scripture indicate that David placed garrisons in the midst of the Philistines and collected tribute. Rather he pushed them back along the coast and contained them there before expanding his reign in the other directions. While what may have precipitated the various battles isn't detailed here, David's two motivations were defense and consolidation. The country had to be made safe from its enemies and trade routes had to be established and maintained if Israel was to survive.

While the accounts are given to show how Israel came to peace and stability, there are both unanswered questions and interesting insights in these verses. No one seems to know exactly why David dealt so harshly with the Moabites—killing two-thirds of the men whom he captured after defeating them. It was probably a picture of the cruelty of war during that period. What makes the treatment especially interesting is David's connections with Moab. His great-grandmother was a Moabitess (Ruth 4:17; Matt. 1:5–6). David also sent his parents to Moab while he was in exile (1 Sam. 22:3). For contemporary Christians the account is a good reminder of how important it is for students of the Scriptures to employ principles of interpretation lest they use the Bible to promulgate nonbiblical teachings.

The account of David's defeat of Hadadezer, the king of Zobah, and of the Syrians who attempted to rescue Hadadezer gives insight into how David managed those whom he conquered (vv. 3–8). Where he intended to collect tribute, he left garrisons of soldiers to protect against rebellion and assure the prompt payment of the tribute. When the major cities were raided they took booty from the battle. David's crippling of most of the horses he captured indicated both that his army was still mainly infantry and that David did not fully realize the worth of the horses as his son Solomon would. His taking of the gold shields and the large amounts of bronze would suggest that he understood metals. The broad range of David's conquests is suggested by the fact that David dedicated all the silver and gold *"from all the nations which he had subdued"* (vv. 11–12).

## DAVID'S ADMINISTRATION

[15] So David reigned over all Israel; and David administered judgment and justice to all his people. [16] Joab the son of Zeruiah was over the army; Jehoshaphat the son of Ahilud was recorder; [17] Zadok the son of Ahitub and Ahimelech the son of Abiathar were the priests; Seraiah was the scribe; [18] Benaiah the son of Jehoiada was over both the Cherethites and the Pelethites; and David's sons were chief ministers.

*—2 Samuel 8:15–18*

These four verses read as though they had been copied from official lists, and they inform us of who the leading men were at David's court. It is a small but significant group, and their names and responsibilities give us insight into how David managed to absorb all the new subjects and to rule over new territories acquired during the period of great expansion. Anything that grows requires the involvement of other people, whether it is a church, a company—or David's kingdom. A part of David's success was his ability to rule Israel through responsible people who shared the task of leadership.

While these four verses list several members of the administration, it was David who was the supreme judge. The office of judge was of great importance in the history of Israel. It was a judge, Samuel, who anointed David to be king of Israel. David was interested in justice for all the people and accepted the responsibility for hearing their cases.

Most of those who were listed would play a prominent part in the life of Israel. Joab, who was the first to enter the city of Jerusalem during its conquest (1 Chr. 11:6), became the commander of Israel's army (v. 16). Jehoshaphat was listed as the *"recorder"* (v. 16). He was probably David's secretary of state, serving as consultant and confidential adviser. Zadok (v. 17) may have been a priest of the Jebusite shrine who was promoted to his position for political reasons. Seraiah, who was the scribe (v. 17), handled correspondence, but his was not a position of power. Benaiah (v. 18) was in charge of mercenaries, most likely made up of Philistines and Cretans, who served as guards in David's house. All the names and their various responsibilities suggest better organization and a more complex monarchy than had existed under Saul.

The next chapter contains one of the most touching incidents of David's early reign in Israel—his keeping of his promise to his friend Jonathan. It also introduces a remarkable servant from the household of Saul by the name of Ziba, a man who may have had more honor than his master. This chapter is a delightful interlude before David's resumption of battle with the Ammonites and Syrians (2 Sam. 10).

## DAVID'S KINDNESS TO MEPHIBOSHETH

**9:1** Now David said, "Is there still anyone who is left of the house of Saul, that I may show him kindness for Jonathan's sake?"

2 And there was a servant of the house of Saul whose name was Ziba. So when they had called him to David, the king said to him, "Are you Ziba?"

He said, "At your service!"

3 Then the king said, "Is there not still someone of the house of Saul, to whom I may show the kindness of God?"

And Ziba said to the king, "There is still a son of Jonathan who is lame in his feet."

4 So the king said to him, "Where is he?"

And Ziba said to the king, "Indeed he is in the house of Machir the son of Ammiel, in Lo Debar."

5 Then King David sent and brought him out of the house of Machir the son of Ammiel, from Lo Debar.

6 Now when Mephibosheth the son of Jonathan, the son of Saul, had come to David, he fell on his face and prostrated himself. Then David said, "Mephibosheth?"

And he answered, "Here is your servant!"

7 So David said to him, "Do not fear, for I will surely show you kindness for Jonathan your father's sake, and will restore to you all the land of Saul your grandfather; and you shall eat bread at my table continually."

8 Then he bowed himself, and said, "What is your servant, that you should look upon such a dead dog as I?"

9 And the king called to Ziba, Saul's servant, and said to him, "I have given to your master's son all that belonged to Saul and to all his house. 10 You therefore, and your sons and your servants, shall work the land for him, and you shall bring in the harvest, that your master's son may have food to eat. But Mephibosheth your master's son shall eat bread at my table always." Now Ziba had fifteen sons and twenty servants.

<sup>11</sup> Then Ziba said to the king, "According to all that my lord the king has commanded his servant, so will your servant do."

"As for Mephibosheth," said the king, "he shall eat at my table like one of the king's sons." <sup>12</sup> Mephibosheth had a young son whose name was Micha. And all who dwelt in the house of Ziba were servants of Mephibosheth. <sup>13</sup> So Mephibosheth dwelt in Jerusalem, for he ate continually at the king's table. And he was lame in both his feet.

—*2 Samuel 9:1–13*

This chapter is the story of the keeping of a promise. It is the first of a dozen chapters that deal with the question of the succession to David's throne. Half of them relate to Absalom and his attempt to wrest the throne from his father. While the event reported in this chapter is tied to the question of whether there was a possibility of claimants for the throne from Saul's household, the story pictures David as a keeper of promises.

At our best we are all keepers of promises. We make promises to God, to others, and to ourselves. These promises predict actions and they anticipate relationships that cover the whole range of our lives. Our day, however, tends to make light of promises. For the Christian, the whole idea of the sacredness of promises comes from the way God treats His promises to us. This story gives us classic insight into what is really involved in keeping the promises that we make.

David's inquiry as to whether there was still *"anyone who is left of the house of Saul"* (v. 1) probably came immediately after the events detailed in 2 Samuel 21 took place. Those events related to a famine in the land that David believed had been caused because of Saul's act of treachery against the Gibeonites. Because of this unresolved grievance against Saul, the Gibeonites asked that all of Saul's seed be destroyed. All the sons by Saul's wives were already dead, but they wanted the sons by the concubines slain as well. They also wanted Saul's grandson, by Jonathan, to be killed. To right the wrong that had been done to them, David allowed seven descendants to be killed, but he would not allow them to touch Mephibosheth.

If this is the sequence of events it is easy to see why David's declared intention to *"show him kindness for Jonathan's sake"* (v. 1) might have been suspect. It was the common practice to destroy the household of one's predecessor rather than lift it up. Others suggest that while David did not kill Mephibosheth, bringing him to his table was a way of keeping an eye on him. Ziba's announcement that Jonathan's son was *"lame in his feet"* (v. 3) seemed to be a way of suggesting that he represented no threat to David. There is a sense in which David was in a bind as to what to do with Mephibosheth. He had an obligation to safeguard his position as a trust from God. This might dictate destroying anyone who posed a potential, future threat. On the other hand, he needed to honor his covenant with Jonathan, which was made before God (1 Sam. 20:14–15). In this incident David put the keeping of his word above other considerations and models for us some of the dynamic involved in keeping one's promises.

Often the circumstances under which promises are made are different from those in which they must be kept. When the covenant was made, Saul was the king, Jonathan was a prince, and David was a fugitive who posed little if any danger to anyone. When the promise was fulfilled, Saul and Jonathan had been dead for years and David was king of Israel with absolute power over the lives of his subjects. Yet the change of circumstances did not make any difference to David in the keeping of his promise. For many people in our day, any change in circumstances becomes a valid reason for breaking contracts and for forgetting our promises.

Often the keeping of our promises seems against our own self-interests. All the property involved in the estate rightfully belonged to David as the successor—but this was the lesser cost of his action. David found himself restoring to a place of prominence one who could potentially hurt him. Mephiboseth was not just any unfortunate person: He was Saul's grandson. When Absalom revolted and David was forced to flee from Jerusalem, Mephibosheth did not go with him, and the reasons are not entirely clear. His servant, Ziba, appeared more loyal to the king than this one whom David had honored. This was a risk that David knowingly took, feeling that not keeping the promise posed greater risk to his character and to his relationship with God.

The next chapter is a reminder that things always change in relationships between both people and nations. After the death of the king of Ammon, David's effort to show kindness was rebuffed and his messengers humiliated. That precipitated a new war which eventually involved the Syrians. It deals not so much with the question of succession as with the strength of David's position both as a soldier and a king.

## THE AMMONITES AND SYRIANS DEFEATED

**10:1** It happened after this that the king of the people of Ammon died, and Hanun his son reigned in his place. [2] Then David said, "I will show kindness to Hanun the son of Nahash, as his father showed kindness to me."

So David sent by the hand of his servants to comfort him concerning his father. And David's servants came into the land of the people of Ammon. [3] And the princes of the people of Ammon said to Hanun their lord, "Do you think that David really honors your father because he has sent comforters to you? Has David not rather sent his servants to you to search the city, to spy it out, and to overthrow it?"

[4] Therefore Hanun took David's servants, shaved off half of their beards, cut off their garments in the middle, at their buttocks, and sent them away. [5] When they told David, he sent to meet them, because the men were greatly ashamed. And the king said, "Wait at Jericho until your beards have grown, and then return."

[6] When the people of Ammon saw that they had made themselves repulsive to David, the people of Ammon sent and hired the Syrians of Beth Rehob and the Syrians of Zoba, twenty thousand foot soldiers; and from the king of Maacah one thousand men, and from Ish-Tob twelve thousand men. [7] Now when David heard of it, he sent Joab and all the army of the mighty men. [8] Then the people of Ammon came out and put themselves in battle array at the entrance of the gate. And the Syrians of Zoba, Beth Rehob, Ish-Tob, and Maacah were by themselves in the field.

[9] When Joab saw that the battle line was against him before and behind, he chose some of Israel's best and put them in battle array against the Syrians. [10] And the rest of the people he put under the command of Abishai his brother, that he might set them in battle array against the people of Ammon. [11] Then he said, "If the Syrians are too strong for me, then you shall help me; but if the people of Ammon are too strong for you, then I will come and help you. [12] Be of good courage, and let us be strong for our people and for the cities of our God. And may the LORD do what is good in His sight."

[13] So Joab and the people who were with him drew near for the battle against the Syrians, and they fled before

him. [14] When the people of Ammon saw that the Syrians were fleeing, they also fled before Abishai, and entered the city. So Joab returned from the people of Ammon and went to Jerusalem.

[15] When the Syrians saw that they had been defeated by Israel, they gathered together. [16] Then Hadadezer sent and brought out the Syrians who were beyond the River, and they came to Helam. And Shobach the commander of Hadadezer's army went before them. [17] When it was told David, he gathered all Israel, crossed over the Jordan, and came to Helam. And the Syrians set themselves in battle array against David and fought with him. [18] Then the Syrians fled before Israel; and David killed seven hundred charioteers and forty thousand horsemen of the Syrians, and struck Shobach the commander of their army, who died there. [19] And when all the kings who were servants to Hadadezer saw that they were defeated by Israel, they made peace with Israel and served them. So the Syrians were afraid to help the people of Ammon anymore.

—*2 Samuel 10:1–19*

This account of the Ammonites was incorporated into the story of the succession to David's throne because it provides the setting for the story of David and Bathsheba. This particular passage supplements the account of David's military action reported in 2 Samuel 8. It deals mainly with the Ammonites, a small kingdom located to the north of Moab and Edom.

The event that precipitated the war must have happened very early in David's reign. At a later time, when Israel was a force to be reckoned with by all, no one would have dared treat envoys in such a disrespectful way. When Nahash the Ammonite king died, in an effort to show his kindness to his son Hanun who had succeeded him, David sent special envoys. While Saul had been Nahash's enemy, for some reason David was friendly. It's possible that while David was a fugitive he had been befriended by the Ammonite king. Nahash would have been anxious to give support to one of Saul's enemies.

The princes who advised the young king convinced him that David's envoys were not really there to comfort the king about his father's death but to *"search the city, to spy it out, and to overthrow it"* (v. 3). This lack of trust between leaders has a rather modern tone to it. It shows how a war can be started over nothing more than an unfounded misunderstanding. What is true of nations applies equally to families and to churches.

What the Ammonites did to David's envoys was tantamount to declaring war. They shaved off half of each man's beard. Then they cut each man's garment so that he was indecently exposed (v. 4). The first was the ultimate insult because the beard was the oriental's glory, a symbol of seniority, dignity, and rank. As they made their way home they were probably ridiculed by all who saw them. The men were so ashamed they were allowed to remain in Jericho until their beards had grown back (v. 5).

Even before David had time to react to the insult, the people of Ammon realized that they had *"made themselves repulsive to David"* (v. 6). The metaphor that they used had to do with odor and meant that they realized that what they did "smelled." Yet rather than attempt to rectify their mistake and make peace, they hired soldiers from Beth Rehob and Zoba to help them face David (v. 6). David sent Joab and *"all the army of the mighty men"* (v. 7) to meet the Ammonites and their mercenaries. The mighty men were a force of 600 seasoned, professional soldiers who had fought with David in many battles. When Joab realized that they were about to be trapped in a pincer movement, he deployed his troops accordingly (vv. 9–12). The code they were to follow was that whoever needed help was to get it from the others (v. 11), an approach that has application in all of life. As a result, Joab and the men were able to win the battle and return to Jerusalem (v. 14).

The account of the battle recorded in the latter verses of the chapter (vv. 15–19) might just be a second account of David's battle that is recorded in chapter 8. There are many similarities and the differences are not significant. What is communicated is that the Syrians decided to serve Israel (v. 19) and exchanged one master for another.

# CHAPTER THIRTEEN—THE BEGINNING OF THE END

## 2 SAMUEL 11:1—12:31

*Scripture Outline*

    David, Bathsheba, and Uriah (11:1–27)

    Nathan's Parable and David's Confession (12:1–15a)

    The Death of David's Son (12:15b–23)

    Solomon Is Born and the War Ends (12:24–31)

This section deals with one of the most familiar stories in this part of the Old Testament, with the possible exception of the story of David and Goliath. It is the story of David's disastrous affair with Bathsheba and its implications for David and for the monarchy. The story is told with candor and honesty in order that the reader may understand some of the things that follow in David's family. Notwithstanding, the story of David and Bathsheba is much more than a history lesson for the modern student. It offers amazing insight into the elements that make us spiritually vulnerable.

### DAVID, BATHSHEBA, AND URIAH

**11:1** It happened in the spring of the year, at the time when kings go out to battle, that David sent Joab and his servants with him, and all Israel; and they destroyed the people of Ammon and besieged Rabbah. But David remained at Jerusalem.

² Then it happened one evening that David arose from his bed and walked on the roof of the king's house. And from the roof he saw a woman bathing, and the woman was very beautiful to behold. ³ So David sent and inquired about

the woman. And someone said, "Is this not Bathsheba, the daughter of Eliam, the wife of Uriah the Hittite?" 4 Then David sent messengers, and took her; and she came to him, and he lay with her, for she was cleansed from her impurity; and she returned to her house. 5 And the woman conceived; so she sent and told David, and said, "I am with child."

6 Then David sent to Joab, saying, "Send me Uriah the Hittite." And Joab sent Uriah to David. 7 When Uriah had come to him, David asked how Joab was doing, and how the people were doing, and how the war prospered. 8 And David said to Uriah, "Go down to your house and wash your feet." So Uriah departed from the king's house, and a gift of food from the king followed him. 9 But Uriah slept at the door of the king's house with all the servants of his lord, and did not go down to his house. 10 So when they told David, saying, "Uriah did not go down to his house," David said to Uriah, "Did you not come from a journey? Why did you not go down to your house?"

11 And Uriah said to David, "The ark and Israel and Judah are dwelling in tents, and my lord Joab and the servants of my lord are encamped in the open fields. Shall I then go to my house to eat and drink, and to lie with my wife? As you live, and as your soul lives, I will not do this thing."

12 Then David said to Uriah, "Wait here today also, and tomorrow I will let you depart." So Uriah remained in Jerusalem that day and the next. 13 Now when David called him, he ate and drank before him; and he made him drunk. And at evening he went out to lie on his bed with the servants of his lord, but he did not go down to his house.

14 In the morning it happened that David wrote a letter to Joab and sent it by the hand of Uriah. 15 And he wrote in the letter, saying, "Set Uriah in the forefront of the hottest battle, and retreat from him, that he may be struck down and die." 16 So it was, while Joab besieged the city, that he assigned Uriah to a place where he knew there were valiant men. 17 Then the men of the city came out and fought with Joab. And some of the people of the servants of David fell; and Uriah the Hittite died also.

18 Then Joab sent and told David all the things concerning the war, 19 and charged the messenger, saying, "When you have finished telling the matters of the war to

the king, [20] if it happens that the king's wrath rises, and he says to you: 'Why did you approach so near to the city when you fought? Did you not know that they would shoot from the wall? [21] Who struck Abimelech the son of Jerubbesheth? Was it not a woman who cast a piece of a millstone on him from the wall, so that he died in Thebez? Why did you go near the wall?'—then you shall say, 'Your servant Uriah the Hittite is dead also.'"

[22] So the messenger went, and came and told David all that Joab had sent by him. [23] And the messenger said to David, "Surely the men prevailed against us and came out to us in the field; then we drove them back as far as the entrance of the gate. [24] The archers shot from the wall at your servants; and some of the king's servants are dead, and your servant Uriah the Hittite is dead also."

[25] Then David said to the messenger, "Thus you shall say to Joab: 'Do not let this thing displease you, for the sword devours one as well as another. Strengthen your attack against the city, and overthrow it.' So encourage him."

[26] When the wife of Uriah heard that Uriah her husband was dead, she mourned for her husband. [27] And when her mourning was over, David sent and brought her to his house, and she became his wife and bore him a son. But the thing that David had done displeased the LORD.

*—2 Samuel 11:1–27*

Second Samuel 11—12 tells the whole story of what has been called "David's sin." Even the casual reader will not have difficulty in seeing why Hollywood was interested in it. The central characters are interesting: a passionate warrior-king, a beautiful but passive woman, a pious and trusting husband, an obedient but amoral general, and a prophet of God without fear. The events in the story would give the plot broad appeal: lust, adultery, deceit, murder, potential blackmail, confrontation, and tragedy. The movie would be rated PG (parental guidance) and the advertisements would probably be lurid.

One of the first questions that comes to mind is why the compiler included this particular incident, since such great effort has been taken to show how God had brought David to the throne. The two Books of Chronicles, which wanted to show David in a better light, eliminated the incident from their record. The story, which doesn't gloss over anything, does dramatize David's humanness in an unforgettable way. It also reminds us that in accomplishing His purpose God always is forced to use fallible people. It could warn against presumption upon position and status, that all people are vulnerable, and that none is above God's law.

The more likely reason for the inclusion of this story, which shows David in such a bad light, is in order to explain the events that come in the succeeding chapters as a result of God's judgment upon David. The repercussions of David's sins do not end with the death of the child but seem to lay the foundation for a whole series of tragic events—rape, murder, and insurrection. The shock waves that began in a lustful heart on a rooftop were still being felt when David lay dying and was being pressured to make Solomon his successor on the throne.

The first verse sets the backdrop for the story. It was that time of the year after the agricultural chores had been taken care of and before the heat of summer. The army of Israel had laid siege to the capital of Ammon, Rabbah. The kingdom had grown to the place where David delegated to Joab the leadership of the army in the field and usually came to the scene of battle when victory was imminent. It was a time when many of David's goals had been reached and he was experiencing fulfillment and satisfaction. Israel was united, the borders had been expanded, the country was prospering, and David was now firmly established in the minds and hearts of the people. Having the pressure off may have made David more vulnerable to temptation.

The sin that set the whole chain of events into motion was lust. It was the cool of the late afternoon. David had risen from a nap that he had taken during the heat of the day and took a walk on the flat roof of his palace to catch the cool evening breeze. As his eyes scanned the rooftops and gardens of the houses located below the ridge on which the palace had been built he saw a beautiful woman bathing. Most scholars think that it was a ritual bath marking the end of her menstrual period. The Scriptures report that *"the woman was very beautiful to behold"* (v. 2). David now had leisure he was not equipped to enjoy. He was a man of action with a bit of time on his hands, a warrior who now took naps in the afternoon, and he may have felt the need for some excitement, for a new interest, or for an escape.

David's sin could have stopped with nothing more than an erotic fantasy, but it didn't. David was now the most powerful person in the kingdom and had grown accustomed to getting whatever he wanted, so he followed up his physical desire with an inquiry *"about the woman"* (v. 3). The answer came in the form of a question suggesting that David may have met her previously, although he had not recognized her from his roof. Each part of the question was a statement that should have said "Off Limits!" That she was *"the daughter of Eliam"* should have given David pause. That she was *"the wife of Uriah the Hittite"* should have stopped him cold, because this meant that she was married to one of David's mighty men. Their answer about Bathsheba's identity implied that she was not just a beautiful woman whom David desired but a person in a family with commitments to another.

As though that were not enough, David had his own role as the king, priest, and judge to consider, but in the heat of the moment he regarded these roles as nothing. The two verses that describe the whole affair have David sending for Bathsehba, their having sexual intercourse, and Bathsheba returning to her house and later sending word that she was pregnant (vv. 4–5). Knowing how scriptural accounts are often condensed, some scholars wonder if the affair might not have been of longer duration with the account giving the minimal facts. The account tells nothing about Bathsheba's feelings. Although I have heard sermons that tried to fix the blame on Bathsheba for bathing where she could be seen by David, the Scripture account lays the blame on David.

The marriage bond was considered sacred and the punishment for adultery was severe (Lev. 20:10). David could have been put to death for what he did, but there was even then a double standard for men and women. Kings made the laws for the people, but they did not always feel the need to obey the laws themselves. This happens today in our country. It has always been a temptation for people in authority through the years. One of the ways in which power corrupts is by making those who have it think that they are above the rules that guide the conduct of ordinary people.

When word came to David that Bathsheba was pregnant, rather than coming to his senses and facing up to his sins, he immediately made plans to hide his wrongdoing. He sent a message to Joab instructing that Uriah be sent to the palace, where he inquired of him about Joab, the people, and the battle (vv. 6–7). Since the only reason for getting Uriah back was to attribute the paternity of the child to him, David suggested that Uriah go home and wash his feet (v. 8). Although some have tried to read sexual inference into the statement, most scholars think it meant little more than "go home and relax." To encourage compliance with his wish, David sent a gift of food after Uriah, which must have seemed unusual.

Discovering that Uriah had slept *"at the door of the king's house"* (v. 9), David questioned him about his activities and discovered that Uriah's devotion to God and to his country took precedence over his own personal desires (vv. 10–11). After this David got Uriah drunk in one last effort to entice him to go home, but again he failed (v. 13). Some have wondered if Uriah might have heard rumors about his wife's affair with David and refused to go home as a way of forcing David to live with the situation that he had created. Since David had used servants in arranging the liaisons, there is little likelihood that his liaison had been kept a secret and word could have made its way to Uriah. The Scriptures tell us nothing of what Uriah felt or knew, only what he did. He is presented as a faithful and pious soldier who had more respect for the law of God when he was drunk than his king did when he was sober. David's efforts to manipulate his own subject is a sad picture indeed.

Once David began his effort to cover up his sin, each step seemed inevitable: first lust, then adultery, then deceit, and finally murder. Our day has had its share of highly placed people who made matters worse as they sought to cover up their wrongdoing. To show how calloused David had become, he sent the letter which plotted the Hittite's death by Uriah himself (vv. 14–15). The plan he suggested was to put Uriah in the front of an intense battle, then withdraw so he would be killed. While Joab had no qualms about accomplishing David's goal, he amended his plan as having too great a risk both for Joab and David. It would have been too obvious to everyone and would have made many of those who fought under Joab's command doubt his commitment to them. So Joab led an attack against a part of the city where he knew the resistance would be great. In the process of that battle he lost several men, including Uriah (vv. 16–17).

Joab knew that he needed to let the king know that his objective had been accomplished without revealing to anyone else that the two of them had murdered Uriah in such a way that it looked like just another casualty of war. He also knew that when David heard the report of the battle that he would immediately recognize that Joab had taken unnecessary risks and would object. So the messenger was told that after David raised his objections he was to reveal to him that *"your servant Uriah the Hittite is dead also"* (vv. 18–21). Since Joab had altered the plan, David might not have recognized the battle as one that his own desire to be rid of Uriah had caused, but he reacted exactly as Joab had anticipated. The news of Uriah's death calmed him and in the message that he sent back to Joab, David covered their treachery with pious words, *"the sword devours one as well as another"* (v. 25).

Two verses end the chapter but not the story. When Bathsheba heard of Uriah's death, *"she mourned for her husband"* (v. 26). We still are not given any indication of her feelings, since the words may be a reference to the prescribed ritual of mourning for the dead. It could have been as little as a week. We are, however, told of her becoming David's wife and bearing him a son. This could have been the end of the story. It was true that David had broken at least three of the basic commandments that God had given Israel for relating to God and to fellowmen. He had coveted another man's wife, committed adultery, and killed. Yet who can judge the judge, who can question the actions of the king? The answer comes in the final verse of the chapter in words that suggest that no one stands above the law of God. What seemed to David a happy ending to what could have been a very sticky situation is but the beginning of problems because *"the thing that David had done displeased the LORD"* (v. 27).

The next chapter begins the story of God's response to David's sin. It contains two well-known incidents in David's life: the confrontation by the prophet Nathan with his parable of the poor man's lamb and the story of the death of the child born of the adulterous relationship. The chapter will close with the birth of Solomon and with David's presence at the fall of Rabbah.

## NATHAN'S PARABLE AND DAVID'S CONFESSION

**12:1** Then the LORD sent Nathan to David. And he came to him, and said to him: "There were two men in one city, one rich and the other poor. ² The rich man had exceedingly many flocks and herds. ³ But the poor man had nothing, except one little ewe lamb which he had bought and nourished; and it grew up together with him and with his children. It ate of his own food and drank from his own cup and lay in his bosom; and it was like a daughter to him. ⁴ And a traveler came to the rich man, who refused to take from his own flock and from his own herd to prepare one for the wayfaring man who had come to him; but he took the poor man's lamb and prepared it for the man who had come to him."

⁵ So David's anger was greatly aroused against the man, and he said to Nathan, "As the LORD lives, the man who has done this shall surely die! ⁶ And he shall restore fourfold for the lamb, because he did this thing and because he had no pity."

⁷ Then Nathan said to David, "You are the man! Thus says the LORD God of Israel: 'I anointed you king over Israel, and I delivered you from the hand of Saul. ⁸ I gave you your master's house and your master's wives into your keeping, and gave you the house of Israel and Judah. And if that had been too little, I also would have given you much more! ⁹ Why have you despised the commandment of the LORD, to do evil in His sight? You have killed Uriah the Hittite with the sword; you have taken his wife to be your wife, and have killed him with the sword of the people of Ammon. ¹⁰ Now therefore, the sword shall never depart from your house, because you have despised Me, and have taken the wife of Uriah the Hittite to be your wife.' ¹¹ Thus says the LORD: 'Behold, I will raise up adversity against you from your own house; and I will take your wives before your eyes and give them to your neighbor, and he shall lie with your wives in the sight of this sun. ¹² For you did it secretly, but I will do this thing before all Israel, before the sun.'"

¹³ So David said to Nathan, "I have sinned against the LORD."

And Nathan said to David, "The LORD also has put away your sin; you shall not die. ¹⁴ However, because by this deed you have given great occasion to the enemies of the LORD to blaspheme, the child also who is born to you shall surely die." ¹⁵ Then Nathan departed to his house.

*—2 Samuel 12:1–15a*

David's marriage to Bathsheba after her period of mourning seemed to be the end of the story but for one small detail, "the thing that David had done displeased the LORD" (2 Sam. 11:27). The events of chapter 12, however, are a reminder that how we live is of concern to God and that no one shows contempt for God's commandments with impunity. It pictures the prophet Nathan in his finest moment. The judgments pronounced by Nathan are acted out in succeeding chapters. While this chapter is full of judgment it is also full of forgiveness and promise.

This passage pictures one of the most dramatic moments in the Old Testament, a God who cares challenging the action of one of His children. A year had passed and even the gossips at the palace had quit talking about what David had done. A few cynics were still complaining, "I told you nothing would happen." David's sin, however, did not go unnoticed nor unchallenged by God. He had been preparing His prophet Nathan to speak to David. During the year Nathan had listened to the gossip, sorted out the truth, observed the changes taking place, planned his approach, and waited for an opportunity to speak to David. The prophets were not just dictation machines into whom God dictated messages He wanted transcribed and delivered; they were people who were especially sensitive to God, dedicated to justice for all, and alert to everything that went on as well as their implications.

On other occasions Nathan had come to David in his role as judge with some problem or another in the land, so his appearance at court would not have created suspicion in itself. This time, however, he came to David with what has come to be one of the best-known parables in the Old Testament. It was a parable designed to penetrate the facade of self-righteousness with which David had covered himself. It drew upon Nathan's belief that there was still enough of a sense of fairness and justice in David for him to be able to see how his actions looked from God's perspective.

One reason that it was easy for David to get involved in the story was that it did not focus on lust or adultery or murder, but rather upon greed, selfishness, and a meanness of spirit. The contrast between the rich man who grew sheep for the market and the poor man whose lamb was almost a member of the family was skillfully drawn. By the time Nathan had finished the story David was ready with judgment, *"the man who has done this shall surely die!"* (v. 5). Nathan paused to let David's words soak in and then looking into the king's face pronounced God's judgment, *"You are the man!"* (v. 7). Reading the words centuries later, we want to applaud, but Nathan risked his life to tell the king what no one else had dared tell him, that what he had done was an offense to God. What David heard was not just the voice of his people, or the voice of a preacher who didn't like the way he had been acting: David heard the voice of God and he knew it.

Then Nathan began to pronounce God's judgment for David's action. He started first with the privileges that David had abused. Rather than starting with a list of David's sins, the prophet began the judgment with a list of God's blessings. He reminded him of his anointing, of his delivery from Saul, of his other blessings that had come at God's hand (vv. 7–8). Since it was lust for a woman that had started everything, he reminded David of all the women who had become his as a result of succeeding Saul (v. 8). Nathan wanted David to see what he had done in the light of God's purpose for his life. Had all God's protection from his enemies, provision for his needs, and unlimited interest and resources not been enough? It's good to look at our disobedience against the backdrop of God's love. The thoughts of God's goodness were enough to drive David to repentance.

Nathan next reduced David's actions to their essence—he had *"despised the commandment of the LORD"* (v. 9). Three things were mentioned: killing Uriah the Hittite, stealing his wife, and using the sword of the enemy to commit his crime (v. 9). While David's sin devastated his family, destroyed Uriah, compromised his general, embarrassed Israel, and caused Israel's enemies to blaspheme, when his sin was reduced to its essence, it was against God. That David accepted the fact that he had sinned against God is reflected in the penitential psalm (Ps. 51). There can never be genuine repentance nor restoration where the nature of our offense is not faced and responsibility accepted.

It wasn't until he had set David's actions in the context of God's blessings and the true nature of his sin that Nathan pronounced God's judgment upon David. In his impulsive response to Nathan's parable David had passed judgment by the law of retaliation, which itself reflected the impossibility of retribution in kind. David suggested fourfold retribution. Nathan pronounced three judgments. The first judgment was a play on the fact that David had killed Uriah with the *"sword of the people of Ammon"* (v. 9). Therefore God's judgment was that *"the sword shall never depart from your house, because you have despised Me"* (v. 10). For the rest of his life David would witness violence and death in his own household, with three of his sons dying violent deaths.

The second judgment was that there would be trouble in the family. Nathan then invokes two basic principles of justice. First, that the punishment should fit the crime. Just as David had been guilty of adultery and murder, lust and violence would afflict his house. Second, justice needs to be witnessed. Just as David had taken another man's wife as his own and created an open scandal, others would take David's wives. This prediction would be fulfilled by Absalom when he openly claimed his father's wives during the insurrection (2 Sam. 16:20–21).

The third judgment upon David came after his repentance and forgiveness. After the second judgment David broke the silence with one sentence, *"I have sinned against the LORD"* (v. 13). He made no excuses for himself. There was no effort to rationalize the responsibility for his actions. He didn't try to blame the times, or his age, or Bathsheba. Rather he acknowledged his guilt and made no complaint concerning the judgment. That God accepted his repentance and forgave David is reflected in Nathan's words: *"The LORD also has put away your sin; you shall not die"* (v. 13).

Then the final word of judgment came, *"the child also who is born to you shall surely die"* (v. 14). With that word Nathan left the palace and went to his home. His presence had been a reminder that God does not take our actions lightly and that even when we are forgiven, we must live with the effects of the sins we have committed. Nathan's presence bore witness to a God who cares enough to confront us in our sins in order to call us back into relationship with Him.

## THE DEATH OF DAVID'S SON

15 And the LORD struck the child that Uriah's wife bore to David, and it became ill. 16 David therefore pleaded with God for the child, and David fasted and went in and lay all night on the ground. 17 So the elders of his house arose and went to him, to raise him up from the ground. But he would not, nor did he eat food with them. 18 Then on the seventh day it came to pass that the child died. And the servants of David were afraid to tell him that the child was dead. For they said, "Indeed, while the child was alive, we spoke to him, and he would not heed our voice. How can we tell him that the child is dead? He may do some harm!"

19 When David saw that his servants were whispering, David perceived that the child was dead. Therefore David said to his servants, "Is the child dead?"

And they said, "He is dead."

20 So David arose from the ground, washed and anointed himself, and changed his clothes; and he went into the house of the LORD and worshiped. Then he went to his own house; and when he requested, they set food before him, and he ate. 21 Then his servants said to him, "What is this that you have done? You fasted and wept for the child while he was alive, but when the child died, you arose and ate food."

22 And he said, "While the child was alive, I fasted and wept; for I said, 'Who can tell whether the LORD will be gracious to me, that the child may live?' 23 But now he is dead;

why should I fast? Can I bring him back again? I shall go to him, but he shall not return to me."

—*2 Samuel 12:15b–23*

This section of the chapter begins with a statement that causes problems for readers, *"the LORD struck the child . . . and it became very ill"* (v. 15). That the child should be punished for what David did seems wrong. We need to remind ourselves, however, that even today innocent children suffer from the things their parents do. The more pointed question deals with whether God should be credited with the cause of the suffering. I sat once at the funeral of a child who had been accidentally killed by a drunk man riding through the community on a motorcycle. In the funeral message the minister tried to convince those of us present that God had a purpose in the child's death as though it were something God had planned. I was revolted by what he said because he took an evil event and made God the cause. In understanding Nathan's interpretation of the child's illness we need to separate the physical cause and the religious interpretation or application. Whatever the child's illness, both Nathan and David saw it as connected with David's sin and raised no questions about it as we do.

The fascinating aspect of this incident is David's reaction to the child's illness and to his death. He inverted the usual sequence of reaction: He mourned while the child was still living (vv. 16–17) and ceased mourning when the child died (v. 20), just as everyone else was beginning to mourn. His actions were so unusual that the servants questioned him about it (v. 21). His explanation may be helpful to those today who face great loss and need to be able to find resources for going on with their lives.

David had done what he did as a prayer to God for the child's life. He loved the child with his whole heart. His inner relief at being forgiven for his sins gave way to a sense of guilt as to his possible role in the child's illness. He went into mourning and displayed all the trappings of grief, complete self-abasement. He wouldn't eat, covered himself with sackcloth and ashes, and slept on the floor (v. 16). All this was done as a prayer of intercession for the child with the hope that the Lord might let the child live (v. 22).

When the child died, David accepted it without complaint and went back to living. He washed, anointed himself, put on clean clothes, went to worship, and came home and ate (v. 20). All of us suffer loss in our lives, and we need to learn the lesson that David models in this story. Learning to turn loose of what we cannot change is one of the Christian's most needful lessons. David's lesson for us is that when we have done all we can and it's out of our hands, we need to accept it as a fact and turn loose. This is how God frees us to go on living.

## SOLOMON IS BORN AND THE WAR ENDS

24 Then David comforted Bathsheba his wife, and went in to her and lay with her. So she bore a son, and he called his name Solomon. Now the LORD loved him, 25 and He sent word by the hand of Nathan the prophet: So he called his name Jedidiah, because of the LORD.

26 Now Joab fought against Rabbah of the people of Ammon, and took the royal city. 27 And Joab sent messengers to David, and said, "I have fought against Rabbah, and I have taken the city's water supply. 28 Now therefore, gather the rest of the people together and encamp against the city and take it, lest I take the city and it be called after my name." 29 So David gathered all the people together and went to Rabbah, fought against it, and took it. 30 Then he took their king's crown from his head. Its weight was a talent of gold, with precious stones. And it was set on David's head. Also he brought out the spoil of the city in great abundance. 31 And he brought out the people who were in it, and put them to work with saws and iron picks and iron axes, and made them cross over to the brick works. So he did to all the cities of the people of Ammon. Then David and all the people returned to Jerusalem.

*—2 Samuel 12:24–31*

The birth of another child was a comfort to Bathsheba for the loss of the first child and a sign to David that God had truly forgiven him. The child was named Solomon, probably meaning "peace." The prophet Nathan gave the child a second name, Jedidiah. Literally it meant "beloved of Yahweh." The name that God gave the child was tantamount to announcing that he had been chosen to succeed David on the throne. It's interesting that the same prophet who announced the judgment of God on David's action was the one who brought the promise of a successor to the throne.

The final verses of the chapter tell of the end of the war with Ammon. This conflict had lasted close to two years and framed the incidents covered in these two chapters. When the city was ready to fall, Joab sent word to David to gather the people and come (vv. 27–28). David arrived for the taking of the city and supervised the taking of the treasures and booty. He also took those who had humiliated his envoys and made them laborers working *"with saws and iron picks and iron axes"* (v. 31).

The next chapter is the first of several that tell of the results of David's action on his family. It is a story of rape and murder within David's family, the beginning of a deterioration that will climax with open insurrection. David's sins have been forgiven and his relationship with God restored, but the effect of his wrongdoing will hang over the family, as Nathan predicted, like a sword.

# CHAPTER FOURTEEN—CIVIL WAR
## 2 SAMUEL 13:1—19:8

*Scripture Outline*

Solomon, whose birth was recorded in 2 Samuel 12, is not mentioned again in 2 Samuel. His story is resumed in 1 Kings. For seven chapters Absalom is the focus of the story, but Absalom's story does not begin with himself but with the rape of his beautiful sister Tamar. While sexual abuse in the family is a familiar story in today's world, the casual reader will probably wonder what a sordid story like this, told in such vivid detail, is doing in the Bible. When the rape of Tamar is put in the context of the whole story there are several obvious reasons for its being included.

First, this story of sexual violence describes part of the punishment that Nathan had prophesied. He had said that the sword would never depart from David's house (2 Sam. 12:10), and this story tells of one of his sons murdering another. He had prophesied that adversity would rise up in David's own household (2 Sam. 12:11), and this is the incident that creates the original rupture in the relationship between Absalom and David. Nathan had promised that what David had done in secret would be seen by all Israel (2 Sam. 12:12), and David's two sons recreated their father's sins for all to see. Amnon modeled his father's unbridled passion when he took Bathsheba, and Absalom modeled his father's deceit and cunning when he arranged the death of Uriah the Hittite.

There are many people who think the idea of being punished for our sins is an Old Testament idea that has no relevance for today—but they are wrong. David's story ought to be a reminder that one of the ways in which God punishes us is by allowing our children to copy our sins. It was a painful experience for David to have Nathan hold his sins before him, but it was much worse to see them acted out in the lives of his children.

A second reason for including this incident in the Scriptures is that it helps us to understand subsequent relationships between David and Absalom. David almost lost his throne to his son Absalom. The story behind Absalom's armed rebellion against his father began with Tamar's rape. Many breakdowns in relationships within a family have a beginning in a single incident that could have been dealt with at the time. When the problem is neglected, it has a tendency to fester and lay the foundation for further trouble. A divorce or an estrangement seldom occurs as a result of one argument or slight or misunderstanding. More likely it is the result of an accumulation of problems that had a simple beginning.

Probably the main reason for this story is to give added focus to the matter of succession to David's throne. The natural thing would have been for the eldest son to succeed David, except Nathan had left the impression that Solomon had been chosen (2 Sam. 12:24–25). Amnon was the eldest son; Absalom was David's third son. This chapter gives us the reasons both as to why they didn't succeed David and why they shouldn't have succeeded their father. Since the historian wanted to explain why Solomon came to the throne instead of his older brothers, the inclusion of this story was necessary. The perspective of history helps us to see what must have been very difficult for those who were closer to these incidents. We need to be thankful to God for the ways in which He is looking out for His children even when they are not aware of it at the time.

Completely apart from these historical reasons for this story, this part of the succession narrative shows us the historical consequences of what seems to be a purely private act. We live in a day that has tried hard to separate character from performance in the public arena. Some have gone so far as to suggest that to probe into the private morality of a person seeking employment or public office is an invasion of privacy. Yet the scandals that have rocked the nation as leaders in business and government and religion have betrayed their trust ought to remind us that the kind of persons we are will be reflected in what we do. This is why God's first step in a different kind of world is the creation of a different kind of people.

## AMNON AND TAMAR

**13:1** After this Absalom the son of David had a lovely sister, whose name was Tamar; and Amnon the son of David loved her. 2 Amnon was so distressed over his sister Tamar that he became sick; for she was a virgin. And it was improper for Amnon to do anything to her. 3 But Amnon had a friend whose name was Jonadab the son of Shimeah, David's brother. Now Jonadab was a very crafty man. 4 And he said to him, "Why are you, the king's son, becoming thinner day after day? Will you not tell me?"

Amnon said to him, "I love Tamar, my brother Absalom's sister."

5 So Jonadab said to him, "Lie down on your bed and pretend to be ill. And when your father comes to see you, say to him, 'Please let my sister Tamar come and give me food, and prepare the food in my sight, that I may see it and eat it from her hand.'" 6 Then Amnon lay down and pretended to be ill; and when the king came to see him, Amnon said to the king, "Please let Tamar my sister come and make a couple of cakes for me in my sight, that I may eat from her hand."

7 And David sent home to Tamar, saying, "Now go to your brother Amnon's house, and prepare food for him." 8 So Tamar went to her brother Amnon's house; and he was lying down. Then she took flour and kneaded it, made cakes in his sight, and baked the cakes. 9 And she took the pan

and placed them out before him, but he refused to eat. Then Amnon said, "Have everyone go out from me." And they all went out from him. ¹⁰ Then Amnon said to Tamar, "Bring the food into the bedroom, that I may eat from your hand." And Tamar took the cakes which she had made, and brought them to Amnon her brother in the bedroom. ¹¹ Now when she had brought them to him to eat, he took hold of her and said to her, "Come, lie with me, my sister."

¹² But she answered him, "No, my brother, do not force me, for no such thing should be done in Israel. Do not do this disgraceful thing! ¹³ And I, where could I take my shame? And as for you, you would be like one of the fools in Israel. Now therefore, please speak to the king; for he will not withhold me from you." ¹⁴ However, he would not heed her voice; and being stronger than she, he forced her and lay with her.

¹⁵ Then Amnon hated her exceedingly, so that the hatred with which he hated her was greater than the love with which he had loved her. And Amnon said to her, "Arise, be gone!"

¹⁶ So she said to him, "No, indeed! This evil of sending me away is worse than the other that you did to me."

But he would not listen to her. ¹⁷ Then he called his servant who attended him, and said, "Here! Put this woman out, away from me, and bolt the door behind her." ¹⁸ Now she had on a robe of many colors, for the king's virgin daughters wore such apparel. And his servant put her out and bolted the door behind her.

¹⁹ Then Tamar put ashes on her head, and tore her robe of many colors that was on her, and laid her hand on her head and went away crying bitterly. ²⁰ And Absalom her brother said to her, "Has Amnon your brother been with you? But now hold your peace, my sister. He is your brother; do not take this thing to heart." So Tamar remained desolate in her brother Absalom's house.

²¹ But when King David heard of all these things, he was very angry. ²² And Absalom spoke to his brother Amnon neither good nor bad. For Absalom hated Amnon, because he had forced his sister Tamar.

*—2 Samuel 13:1–22*


While the rape of Tamar is out of an ancient culture and separated from us by many ages, it has a frighteningly modern ring to it.

Ours is an age becoming increasingly aware of sexual abuse both in the marketplace and in the home. The most casual reader of the story can understand what happened with little or no help from biblical scholars. Only in a place or two is the insight enriched by a greater knowledge of the traditions of the culture. Amnon was David's eldest son, greatly loved by his father and heir to the throne, but he was dominated by lust for his half-sister Tamar. Like his father at the time of his encounter with Bathsheba, he was dominated by sensuality. His passion made him sick. Any person who goes into the average video rental store today will realize from looking at the covers of the offerings that our country already has a lot of Amnons on its hands and is creating more and more each year. I do not believe those who say that the entertainment media does not create a moral climate but merely reflects what already exists. The media participates in creating both interest in and approval for a life given totally to the gratifying of every appetite whatever the cost to self or others.

Had she been any other girl, Amnon would probably have sent for her as his father had sent for Bathsheba. Since Tamar was the daughter of the king, however, and had great political value as the possible wife of the son of a potential ally, she was carefully guarded. Evidently David suspected nothing when Amnon implemented the plot that his cousin Jonadab suggested to him. There may have been a standing friendship relationship between Amnon and Tamar, but as with the case of Bathsheba we are told nothing about her feelings. The scene was set for the crime by getting rid of the servants who would have been witnesses. When they were alone all pretense was laid aside and Amnon said to his sister, *"Come, lie with me"* (v. 11).

Amnon had not anticipated that she would refuse his advances and articulate both why she wouldn't do it and why he shouldn't. Her reasoning is reminiscent of Joseph's rationale for refusing the advances of Potiphar's wife. She gave three reasons why it would be wrong and then gave an alternative: It violated the moral standards of Israel, it disgraced Amnon, and it shamed Tamar. Her alternative was that if he really loved her, he should ask his father for her to be his wife. While marriage between a brother and a sister was later forbidden in Israel, it was still practiced at this time. Although Tamar's reasoning was strong, Amnon was physically stronger and he forced himself upon her. Most incidents like this remain unreported for fear of worse violence, but this crime is known by everyone because Amnon followed the rape with an act even more cruel.

At this point in the story Tamar probably felt that she now belonged to Amnon; she was no longer a virgin and couldn't be married to one of her father's potential allies. Rather than loving her and claiming her for his own once he had made love to her, the Scriptures record that Amnon hated her now more strongly than he had loved her before (v. 15). No explanation is given for his sudden rejection of her. Some feel it was her refusal to willingly lie with him. Others suggest that her reasoning might have pricked his conscience. It may have been that he was only drawn to her because she was not available. Now having "conquered" her, he had no more use for her. His throwing her out was both a refusal to acknowledge his own guilt and a suggestion that she was the aggressor in the affair.

It was not the last time that the victim was made to look guilty for the crime that had been committed against her. After centuries, our society today is only beginning to treat this kind of crime as a violent act. She was reduced to being a widow who had never had a husband and went into mourning. When her brother Absalom saw her and discerned what had happened, he took her into his house for protection. His counsel for her not to say anything didn't bring comfort to her and she remained desolate. Although he said nothing to anyone about it, a deep hatred for his brother was created in Absalom's heart because of what Amnon had done.

## ABSALOM MURDERS AMNON

23 And it came to pass, after two full years, that Absalom had sheepshearers in Baal Hazor, which is near Ephraim; so Absalom invited all the king's sons. 24 Then Absalom came to the king and said, "Kindly note, your servant has sheepshearers; please, let the king and his servants go with your servant."

25 But the king said to Absalom, "No, my son, let us not all go now, lest we be a burden to you." Then he urged him, but he would not go; and he blessed him.

26 Then Absalom said, "If not, please let my brother Amnon go with us."

And the king said to him, "Why should he go with you?" 27 But Absalom urged him; so he let Amnon and all the king's sons go with him.

28 Now Absalom had commanded his servants, saying, "Watch now, when Amnon's heart is merry with wine, and when I say to you, 'Strike Amnon!' then kill him. Do not be

afraid. Have I not commanded you? Be courageous and valiant." [29] So the servants of Absalom did to Amnon as Absalom had commanded. Then all the king's sons arose, and each one got on his mule and fled.

[30] And it came to pass, while they were on the way, that news came to David, saying, "Absalom has killed all the king's sons, and not one of them is left!" [31] So the king arose and tore his garments and lay on the ground, and all his servants stood by with their clothes torn. [32] Then Jonadab the son of Shimeah, David's brother, answered and said, "Let not my lord suppose they have killed all the young men, the king's sons, for only Amnon is dead. For by the command of Absalom this has been determined from the day that he forced his sister Tamar. [33] Now therefore, let not my lord the king take the thing to his heart, to think that all the king's sons are dead. For only Amnon is dead."

[34] Then Absalom fled. And the young man who was keeping watch lifted his eyes and looked, and there, many people were coming from the road on the hillside behind him. [35] And Jonadab said to the king, "Look, the king's sons are coming; as your servant said, so it is." [36] So it was, as soon as he had finished speaking, that the king's sons indeed came, and they lifted up their voice and wept. Also the king and all his servants wept very bitterly.

[37] But Absalom fled and went to Talmai the son of Ammihud, king of Geshur. And David mourned for his son every day. [38] So Absalom fled and went to Geshur, and was there three years. [39] And King David longed to go to Absalom. For he had been comforted concerning Amnon, because he was dead.

*—2 Samuel 13:23–39*

At this point in the story the reader's attention moves from Amnon to Absalom whose needs and reactions were much more complex. If Amnon's action seemed to be copying his father's treatment of Bathsheba, Absalom's response to Amnon was more like his father's dealing with Uriah the Hittite, Bathsheba's husband whom David had murdered. No mention is given as to why David did not punish Amnon in any way for what he had done. The Greek translation of this passage adds half a verse missing from the Hebrew text and suggests that it was because he was his eldest son and he loved him. It is entirely possible that David failed to understand that love that did not discipline would be interpreted by his son not as love but as indifference. While children who are disciplined can be expected to complain at the moment, they eventually interpret the punishment as an act of love. This is God's motive for punishment.

A second reason why David didn't punish Amnon could have been that it is hard for a parent to punish a child for what the child sees the parent do. Children take their cues from their parents— how honest they are, how they treat people, and what their values and goals are. The child assumes that it's all right to do what the parents do. When the model for the act has been the parent, it's hard to criticize the child. David was in a bind and did nothing. There is no way we can know how the history of his relationship with Absalom would have been different had David punished Amnon for violating Tamar. There is a timing to life. Once the moment has passed when something could have been done, we do not get it back. What happened to Absalom is a powerful argument for dealing with problems in a family at the time they arise and not letting them slide until it's too late.

The biblical account of Absalom's murder of Amnon gives us insight into his tragic character. He was capable of sustained hatred. Most people will get angry at someone or something and then get over it with time. Absalom nursed his hatred of his brother and it grew. The destructive power of hatred was seen first in the story of Cain and Abel. Even our Lord warned that murder begins in the heart (Matt. 5:21–22). Absalom was also patient and cold-blooded in his approach to revenge. He waited two years for just the right moment. Had his father David accepted his invitation to the sheepshearing, he would have waited for the next opportunity to present itself. It would have been more understandable had Absalom slain his brother in an act of rage upon discovering what had been done to his sister, but his elaborate deceitful plan reveals a frightening flaw in his character. He had taken his father's faults and refined them.

The gathering at which the killing took place was a festive occasion—the annual shearing of the sheep. More space is given to Absalom's instructions to the servants than to the actual event itself. David's first news that all the sons had been slain was corrected by his nephew Jonadab, who had been the one who had given Amnon the scheme for seducing Tamar. In all of life there are people like Jonadab, those who ingratiate themselves to powerful people by their practical insights, although they are often without ethical or moral values. They live to serve the interests of their sponsor without respect to right or wrong.

While the surviving sons made their way to Jerusalem, Absalom fled to the house of his grandfather, Talmai, king of Geshur. He remained there for three years while his father mourned the death of Amnon. Finally, after a time David began to long to see his son Absalom. The next chapter tells how Joab worked with David to arrange the return of Absalom to the court.

## ABSALOM'S RETURN TO JERUSALEM

**14:1** So Joab the son of Zeruiah perceived that the king's heart was concerned about Absalom. <sup>2</sup> And Joab sent to Tekoa and brought from there a wise woman, and said to her, "Please pretend to be a mourner, and put on mourning apparel; do not anoint yourself with oil, but act like a woman who has been mourning a long time for the dead. <sup>3</sup> Go to the king and speak to him in this manner." So Joab put the words in her mouth.

<sup>4</sup> And when the woman of Tekoa spoke to the king, she fell on her face to the ground and prostrated herself, and said, "Help, O king!"

<sup>5</sup> Then the king said to her, "What troubles you?"

And she answered, "Indeed I am a widow, my husband is dead. <sup>6</sup> Now your maidservant had two sons; and the two fought with each other in the field, and there was no one to part them, but the one struck the other and killed him. <sup>7</sup> And now the whole family has risen up against your maidservant, and they said, 'Deliver him who struck his brother, that we may execute him for the life of his brother whom he killed; and we will destroy the heir also.' So they would extinguish my ember that is left, and leave to my husband neither name nor remnant on the earth."

<sup>8</sup> Then the king said to the woman, "Go to your house, and I will give orders concerning you."

<sup>9</sup> And the woman of Tekoa said to the king, "My lord, O king, let the iniquity be on me and on my father's house, and the king and his throne be guiltless."

<sup>10</sup> So the king said, "Whoever says anything to you, bring him to me, and he shall not touch you anymore."

<sup>11</sup> Then she said, "Please let the king remember the LORD your God, and do not permit the avenger of blood to destroy anymore, lest they destroy my son."

And he said, "As the LORD lives, not one hair of your son shall fall to the ground."

12 Therefore the woman said, "Please, let your maidservant speak another word to my lord the king."

And he said, "Say on."

13 So the woman said: "Why then have you schemed such a thing against the people of God? For the king speaks this thing as one who is guilty, in that the king does not bring his banished one home again. 14 For we will surely die and become like water spilled on the ground, which cannot be gathered up again. Yet God does not take away a life; but He devises means, so that His banished ones are not expelled from Him. 15 Now therefore, I have come to speak of this thing to my lord the king because the people have made me afraid. And your maidservant said, 'I will now speak to the king; it may be that the king will perform the request of his maidservant. 16 For the king will hear and deliver his maidservant from the hand of the man who would destroy me and my son together from the inheritance of God.' 17 Your maidservant said, 'The word of my lord the king will now be comforting; for as the angel of God, so is my lord the king in discerning good and evil. And may the LORD your God be with you.'"

18 Then the king answered and said to the woman, "Please do not hide from me anything that I ask you."

And the woman said, "Please, let my lord the king speak."

19 So the king said, "Is the hand of Joab with you in all this?" And the woman answered and said, "As you live, my lord the king, no one can turn to the right hand or to the left from anything that my lord the king has spoken. For your servant Joab commanded me, and he put all these words in the mouth of your maidservant. 20 To bring about this change of affairs your servant Joab has done this thing; but my lord is wise, according to the wisdom of the angel of God, to know everything that is in the earth."

21 And the king said to Joab, "All right, I have granted this thing. Go therefore, bring back the young man Absalom."

22 Then Joab fell to the ground on his face and bowed himself, and thanked the king. And Joab said, "Today your servant knows that I have found favor in your sight, my

lord, O king, in that the king has fulfilled the request of his servant." 23 So Joab arose and went to Geshur, and brought Absalom to Jerusalem. 24 And the king said, "Let him return to his own house, but do not let him see my face." So Absalom returned to his own house, but did not see the king's face.

*—2 Samuel 14:1–24*

This chapter begins with Absalom in exile and ends with his experiencing the kiss of forgiveness from his father David in the palace in Jerusalem. The incident that was used to bring about the reconciliation provides the substance of the chapter and it continues the theme of this section of the book—the succession to the throne.

For a second time David is tricked into condemning his own action by someone who comes to him for judgment on a matter that appears to be unrelated to David's life. This was the method used by the prophet Nathan when he confronted David about his affair with Bathsheba (2 Sam. 12). Both Nathan and the wise woman from Tekoa were attempting to get David to change his attitude on something significant and it wasn't easy. Both of them used a technique that Christ later used—the telling of a story. When people get involved in the story of others they often think more clearly about their own story. This proved to be the case with David.

The person most responsible for Absalom's return to Jerusalem was Joab, David's commander in chief. Joab's reasons for interceding are not given, but there are several possibilities. The king's attitude toward Absalom was softening (v. 1), yet Joab knew that David was unlikely to initiate any action without some help. Joab probably admired the younger Absalom and saw him, at least at this time, as a logical heir to the throne. Being a power-oriented man, Joab would have been concerned over the potential instability created by an aging king without a clearly designated successor. Joab had probably broached the subject with David on occasion, without success, and thus decided on an indirect approach. While subsequent events would prove that Joab's judgment of Absalom was wrong, this action was taken in the light of his best insights.

While the actress in the drama was a woman of Tekoa, Joab was the writer and producer. The text says that he *"put the words in her mouth"* (v. 3). That she would have access to David indicates both that she was a wise woman of some reputation in the community and that David was still functioning as a judge in certain cases. While the story is more about succession than parenting, it is sad that a woman whom David had never met, with a story that had been fabricated for the occasion, was able to get his attention concerning the son and heir whom he had not seen for three years. A friend of mine came to his office one day and while checking with his secretary about his schedule discovered that his teenaged daughter had made an appointment to see him. He didn't have to be told why because when he saw her name on his calender he realized that the people with whom he worked were getting more of his time than his own child.

On the surface it would seem that David would have recognized immediately that the story was about himself and Absalom, but he probably didn't for good reason. The teller of the story was a very convincing woman who got special sympathy because of the "widow's weeds" in which she was dressed. The story she told of the bitter rivalry between her two sons who were always fighting and the resulting death of one was a common problem among the Bedouin families around Tekoa. Even the fact that when two important principals were in conflict with each other a higher authority would be sought seemed natural for David for he was *the* judge in Israel. The issue seemed to be so concretized in the fervent plea of the woman that her last *"ember"* should not be allowed to be extinguished (v. 7) that it never occurred to David that she was talking about Israel and not her own family. The woman was also helped in her deception by the fact that David had so successfully rationalized his act that he was not aware even of the need for a change of attitude. This is human nature.

The two principles in conflict were articulated clearly. The son who had killed his brother deserved the punishment of death and the clan was calling for that. The other principle was the fact that to carry out the punishment would bring her line to an end and make her childless, which would also impoverish her because the clan would claim all her possessions. As was the case with Nathan's parable, where David interrupted the storyteller to pronounce judgment on the rich man (2 Sam. 12), David quickly decided that the remaining son should not be executed and that his mother would be protected from any who would dispute that judgment (vv. 8–11). What he could not see in his own family he saw so clearly in the woman's family. It is human nature that we all tend to apply judgment more wisely to others than to ourselves.

After David committed himself to the woman, she knew that she had succeeded in her purpose, so she dropped all pretense that the issue she was discussing was personal. That she saw David's action against Absalom as against *"the people of God"* (v. 13) indicates that both she and Joab saw the issue as political and not personal. They felt, as many people probably did, that it was in Israel's best interest for Absalom to be restored to his place as heir. When we read chapter 15 we will realize that this popular opinion was wrong and that their advice was bad. While it is true that hindsight is always more accurate, we should be reminded by this story that the majority is often wrong and that the person who on the surface seems most fitted for a position is often the worst choice. These chapters about Absalom are probably preserved here as a reminder that God's great wisdom was shown in choosing Solomon instead of either Amnon or Absalom. It would be good if we could have God's wisdom in choosing our leaders instead of being so manipulated by media consultants who create images that often bear little or no resemblance to the candidates. Even churches often call the wrong leader on the basis of first impressions upon hearing one sermon.

When the woman showed her hand to David he immediately recognized Joab's part in the plot because this was an issue they had probably discussed before. The woman told David the truth and left. David than called Joab in and announced his decision and gave him the authority to carry it out. No explanation is given as to why Absalom was not allowed to see David. It could mean that David had not fully forgiven him for the death of Amnon or it could mean that David had not decided to name Absalom as his successor. From the knowledge we get from the events that follow, if David had not intended to see his son he probably would have been wiser to leave him in exile.

## DAVID FORGIVES ABSALOM

25 Now in all Israel there was no one who was praised as much as Absalom for his good looks. From the sole of his foot to the crown of his head there was no blemish in him. 26 And when he cut the hair of his head—at the end of every year he cut it because it was heavy on him—when he cut it, he weighed the hair of his head at two hundred shekels according to the king's standard. 27 To Absalom were born three sons, and one daughter whose name was Tamar. She was a woman of beautiful appearance.

28 And Absalom dwelt two full years in Jerusalem, but did not see the king's face. 29 Therefore Absalom sent for Joab, to send him to the king, but he would not come to him. And when he sent again the second time, he would not come. 30 So he said to his servants, "See, Joab's field is near mine, and he has barley there; go and set it on fire." And Absalom's servants set the field on fire.

31 Then Joab arose and came to Absalom's house, and said to him, "Why have your servants set my field on fire?"

32 And Absalom answered Joab, "Look, I sent to you, saying, 'Come here, so that I may send you to the king, to say, "Why have I come from Geshur? It would be better for me to be there still."' Now therefore, let me see the king's face; but if there is iniquity in me, let him execute me."

33 So Joab went to the king and told him. And when he had called for Absalom, he came to the king and bowed himself on his face to the ground before the king. Then the king kissed Absalom.

*—2 Samuel 14:25–33*

The biographical material that the historian inserted here (vv. 25–27) gives the first description of Absalom. The purpose for interrupting the narrative was to picture him as a strong and attractive personality. The description of the hair is not as much a comment on his personal attractiveness as a tribute to his virility and power. That culture so prized a good head of hair that in this case they announced how much it weighed when it was cut. The Greek translation of the Old Testament gave the weight of the cut hair at half of the four and a half pounds of our text. The mention of his three sons seems to contradict the later account in which Absalom says that he had no sons (2 Sam. 18:18). Evidently he named his daughter after his sister whom he loved. David referred to him as a young man in his conversation with Joab (v. 21), but the picture of Absalom is that of a person with property and family and a strong following among the people. If that were not so it would be impossible to explain the number who followed him in his revolt.

This brief section also gives us insight into the character and personality of Absalom. While he showed great patience in biding his time before taking revenge upon Amnon, he resented being in Jerusalem and not having access to the king, his father. When Joab did not respond to his requests to see him, Absalom instructed his servants to set Joab's field on fire. This got his attention and tells us that Absalom was a man of action, not intimidated by influential people like Joab. There was a kind of arrogance in his demanding a trial before his father if he were guilty of anything. His treatment of Joab—who had been his only advocate at court and who had played the father role for Absalom in David's absence—was harsh and it may have been the beginning of Joab's changing his mind about Absalom's future. The perspective of history allows the reader of this story to see what those close to it couldn't, that many potential leaders have flaws that can be seen in the ways they try to get attention and in the ways they treat the people who help them.

The scene in which David and Absalom see each other for the first time in five years is tense and moving. If this were the end of the story it would make a wonderful illustration of forgiveness and reconciliation. Subsequent events, however, indicate that whatever may have been in David's heart at the time of receiving his son back, Absalom never recovered from the way he had been treated and used his new status to undermine his father. The next chapter tells the story of Absalom's treason, a move in which he almost succeeded in taking the throne from his father.

## ABSALOM'S TREASON

**15:1** After this it happened that Absalom provided himself with chariots and horses, and fifty men to run before him. ² Now Absalom would rise early and stand beside the way to the gate. So it was, whenever anyone who had a lawsuit came to the king for a decision, that Absalom would call to him and say, "What city are you from?" And he would say, "Your servant is from such and such a tribe of Israel." ³ Then Absalom would say to him, "Look, your case is good and right; but there is no deputy of the king to hear you." ⁴ Moreover Absalom would say, "Oh, that I were made judge in the land, and everyone who has any suit or cause would come to me; then I would give him justice." ⁵ And so it was, whenever anyone came near to bow down to him, that he would put out his hand and take him and kiss him. ⁶ In this manner Absalom acted toward all Israel who came to the king for judgment. So Absalom stole the hearts of the men of Israel.

⁷ Now it came to pass after forty years that Absalom said to the king, "Please, let me go to Hebron and pay the vow which I made to the LORD. ⁸ For your servant took a vow while I dwelt at Geshur in Syria, saying, 'If the LORD

indeed brings me back to Jerusalem, then I will serve the LORD.'"

⁹ And the king said to him, "Go in peace." So he arose and went to Hebron.

¹⁰ Then Absalom sent spies throughout all the tribes of Israel, saying, "As soon as you hear the sound of the trumpet, then you shall say, 'Absalom reigns in Hebron!'" ¹¹ And with Absalom went two hundred men invited from Jerusalem, and they went along innocently and did not know anything.

¹² Then Absalom sent for Ahithophel the Gilonite, David's counselor, from his city—from Giloh—while he offered sacrifices. And the conspiracy grew strong, for the people with Absalom continually increased in number.

*—2 Samuel 15:1–12*

Chapter 15 depicts one of the most painful experiences in the life of David, and one of the critical times in the life of Israel: the conflict between David and Absalom for the throne. After Absalom's return to court and to his father's favor he seemed to be in line to eventually inherit the throne. We are not told why he decided not to wait. The decisions that people make are usually the result of many influences. We are told, however, exactly how he went about stealing the hearts of the people. Apart from his love for his sister Tamar, Absalom comes across in these accounts as cunning, cold, and ruthless. Those who later read this material would have no difficulty figuring out why God turned away from Absalom as Israel's ruler. The reader of this material must remember that the historian telescopes events in this account in order to give a better sense of what really happened.

The two elements that laid the foundation for Absalom's successful revolt were time and his skillful manipulating of people. Sometime after his father had returned him to favor, the text does not fix the time precisely, Absalom created for himself the air of a ruler with chariots, horses, and a group of men who made up the equivalent of a private army (v. 1). While this princely show of status was not normal, it could have been excused as the way in which Absalom was compensating for having had to cool his heels for two years before his father would even see him. This was Absalom's way of indicating how he saw himself—as the heir apparent of the throne. Often the outward appearances that seem so important to people speak more about their own self-perception than about external realities.

The really damaging thing that Absalom did with great success, and the thing that explains best his popularity with the people, was his politicking with the ordinary people (vv. 2–6). His was a familiar pattern. He sought first to undermine the people's confidence in his father. Then he always put himself forward as the solution to their situation. Each day he would rise early and stand where the people were waiting to get a judgment on some grievance or another. He showed an interest in people, who they were, what city they came from, and the nature of their complaint. Then he would suggest that were he to be given authority to judge their case that they would have an advocate at the court. By using this approach over a period of four years Absalom was able to create allies to his cause in every village in the land and he was able to do it, not by actually helping them, but by leaving the impression that he would if he could. (Where the NKJV says in verse 7 that Absalom approached David forty years after his return from exile, many of our best manuscripts say that he did so four years after his return.)

If the pattern seems slightly familiar it's because it is used constantly by politicians who are running for offices that someone else holds. They create a base of support for themselves by making their opponents responsible for all the flaws in society and presenting themselves as the hope for change. A person can accumulate a following in any organization, whether a club, a business, or a church, by whispering in the ear of the unhappy what he would do if he were in charge.

Absalom's success might also indicate that there was sufficient neglect of the people and delay in justice that his words touched a sore spot with the populace. Although David still saw people, these delays became longer as the kingdom grew and became more complex. This is what created such a morale problem for Moses (Ex. 18:13ff.). If there were no real problem, Absalom created one; if the problem *were* real, he magnified it.

The saddest part of his whole routine is that there is no indication that he was really interested in justice or that he cared for the people. He was himself a murderer of his own brother who had not been punished and nothing in his life, with the exception of his relationship to his sister, indicates that he cared for anyone but himself. He is a classic example of a person without ideals who uses the talking of lofty ideals as a means of manipulating people and getting power for himself.

Absalom covered his plan to claim the throne at his birthplace in Hebron by asking permission from the king to worship in Hebron in order to keep a vow that he had made to God when he was returned to the court four years before (vv. 7–8). David evidently did not suspect anything, just as he had suspected nothing when Absalom had requested that Amnon be sent to the festive occasion where he had made plans for his murder (ch. 13). One wonders if Absalom had been so clever that there were no rumors of a possible rebellion. Could David have been so out of touch with what was going on that he suspected nothing? It's a fact that he found it hard to be objective about the actions of his children. He could sense that something was going on and assumed that it might be a part of God's punishment as announced by the prophet Nathan.

Throughout history many terrible things have been done by individuals who were motivated by a lust for power. Especially despicable are those who dressed their ambitions in the clothing of religion. Much harm has been done to the cause of Christ when we try to disguise our own selfish goals as being done for the sake of the kingdom of God.

Absalom's move was swift and met with great initial success. Spies were sent throughout the land with the word that on a certain signal it would be announced that *"Absalom reigns in Hebron"* (v. 10). The two hundred guests who had been invited to worship with Absalom were completely innocent of the plot, but they were trapped (v. 11). If they had tried to leave, they could have been killed. Yet by staying there it seemed that they were in on the rebellion. Had Absalom been compelled to conquer Jerusalem, they would probably have been used as hostages. While Absalom was popular with the people, the only significant person who went over to him was Ahithophel, one of David's most trusted counselors. No reason is given for his defection. He was Bathsheba's grandfather, but that seems an unlikely reason since his grandson, Solomon, was mentioned by many as a possible successor. That he was sent for at Giloh may mean that David was not using him at the time. The one sure thing was that his wise counsel was most valuable to Absalom, and David was aware of it and anxious to counteract it.

## DAVID'S ESCAPE FROM JERUSALEM

13 Now a messenger came to David, saying, "The hearts of the men of Israel are with Absalom."

14 So David said to all his servants who were with him at Jerusalem, "Arise, and let us flee, or we shall not escape from Absalom. Make haste to depart, lest he overtake us sud-

denly and bring disaster upon us, and strike the city with the edge of the sword."

15 And the king's servants said to the king, "We are your servants, ready to do whatever my lord the king commands." 16 Then the king went out with all his household after him. But the king left ten women, concubines, to keep the house. 17 And the king went out with all the people after him, and stopped at the outskirts. 18 Then all his servants passed before him; and all the Cherethites, all the Pelethites, and all the Gittites, six hundred men who had followed him from Gath, passed before the king.

19 Then the king said to Ittai the Gittite, "Why are you also going with us? Return and remain with the king. For you are a foreigner and also an exile from your own place. 20 In fact, you came only yesterday. Should I make you wander up and down with us today, since I go I know not where? Return, and take your brethren back. Mercy and truth be with you."

21 But Ittai answered the king and said, "As the LORD lives, and as my lord the king lives, surely in whatever place my lord the king shall be, whether in death or life, even there also your servant will be."

22 So David said to Ittai, "Go, and cross over." Then Ittai the Gittite and all his men and all the little ones who were with him crossed over. 23 And all the country wept with a loud voice, and all the people crossed over. The king himself also crossed over the Brook Kidron, and all the people crossed over toward the way of the wilderness.

24 There was Zadok also, and all the Levites with him, bearing the ark of the covenant of God. And they set down the ark of God, and Abiathar went up until all the people had finished crossing over from the city. 25 Then the king said to Zadok, "Carry the ark of God back into the city. If I find favor in the eyes of the LORD, He will bring me back and show me both it and His dwelling place. 26 But if He says thus: 'I have no delight in you,' here I am, let Him do to me as seems good to Him." 27 The king also said to Zadok the priest, "Are you not a seer? Return to the city in peace, and your two sons with you, Ahimaaz your son, and Jonathan the son of Abiathar. 28 See, I will wait in the plains of the wilderness until word comes from you to inform me." 29 Therefore Zadok and Abiathar carried the ark of God back to Jerusalem. And they remained there.

30 So David went up by the Ascent of the Mount of Olives, and wept as he went up; and he had his head covered and went barefoot. And all the people who were with him covered their heads and went up, weeping as they went up. 31 Then someone told David, saying, "Ahithophel is among the conspirators with Absalom." And David said, "O LORD, I pray, turn the counsel of Ahithophel into foolishness!"

32 Now it happened when David had come to the top of the mountain, where he worshiped God—there was Hushai the Archite coming to meet him with his robe torn and dust on his head. 33 David said to him, "If you go on with me, then you will become a burden to me. 34 But if you return to the city, and say to Absalom, 'I will be your servant, O king; as I was your father's servant previously, so I will now also be your servant,' then you may defeat the counsel of Ahithophel for me. 35 And do you not have Zadok and Abiathar the priests with you there? Therefore it will be that whatever you hear from the king's house, you shall tell to Zadok and Abiathar the priests. 36 Indeed they have there with them their two sons, Ahimaaz, Zadok's son, and Jonathan, Abiathar's son; and by them you shall send me everything you hear."

37 So Hushai, David's friend, went into the city. And Absalom came into Jerusalem.

*—2 Samuel 15:13–37*

Unlike most rebellions or coups, this takeover did not begin with a battle but rather with an announcement: *"The hearts of the men of Israel are with Absalom"* (v. 13). Over a period of time, explained in the discussion of the first verses of this chapter, the allegiance of the people had been transferred from David to Absalom. In the account that we have, David made no effort to question or deny what had happened but made plans to leave the city of Jerusalem immediately. He didn't want to be surprised by Absalom's forces and he wanted to spare the city the devastation that a siege might bring. He also could have feared treachery. With people of the significance of Ahithophel defecting, he might have feared others. He obviously did not want to risk a battle with Absalom until a more accurate assessment of the situation could be made. The only escape route was to the east toward the wilderness.

The story of David's abandoning Jerusalem spans 2 Samuel 15:13—16:14 and should be seen as one unit that pulls together many persons and events. They show two things. First, David was not without significant friends. These included support from the military, the priests, and from outstanding statesmen. More than anything else, however, these incidents give us a picture of David's attitude toward what was happening to himself and to Israel as a result of his son's rebellion. While David is not without faults, his reactions to the tragic event gives insight into his relationship with God and with the people that suggests that on his worst day he was preferable to his son as a leader.

There are two strains in his actions that are complementary but not contradictory. There was a very deep trust in God's ability to bring things to the right conclusion. This is shown most vividly in his ordering the ark back to Jerusalem. There is in his *"If I find favor in the eyes of the LORD"* (v. 25) a willingness to surrender himself to God's will for his life. There is also a willingness to plan wisely to meet the demands of the situation. This is shown in the same incident when he enlisted the priests to be an intelligence-gathering group in Jerusalem (vv. 27–28).

The same pattern is seen in David's reaction to Ahithophel's defection and Hushai's decision to be loyal. David prayed to God that He would *"turn the counsel of Ahithophel into foolishness!"* (v. 31). To help God answer his prayer, David sent Hushai, his most trusted adviser, back to Jerusalem with instructions as to how he could become Absalom's adviser. He needed him both to pass information to the priests about what Absalom's plans were and to counteract the counsel of Ahithophel to Absalom (vv. 33–35).

David's exchange with Ittai the Gittite indicates that he was not without soldiers who were loyal to him. In spite of David's gracious offer to release Ittai from any pledge he may have made because of the changing circumstances, he refused the offer and pledged himself to David anew. The loyalty of the band of six hundred mercenaries stands in contrast to the betrayal of David's own son. David did not yet know who was loyal to him and who would follow his son, but those who were with him represented a real military presence. David's offer to release them had only drawn them closer, revealing that his ability to command loyalty wasn't entirely gone.

The saddest picture in the chapter is that of the mighty king climbing the Mount of Olives barefoot, his head covered, weeping (v. 30). For David it was a time of penance but there would come a day when Jesus would weep in that place for the sins of the whole world. The chapter ends with the simple statement *"And

*Absalom came into Jerusalem"* (v. 37). In verse 1 he is an ambitious prince; in the final verse he occupies the city as its king.

The next chapter continues the list of people who interacted with David as he fled the city—Ziba, the servant of Jonathan's son, Mephibosheth, and Shimei, who threw rocks at David and cursed him. Chapter 16 also tells of Absalom's behavior upon entering Jerusalem.

## MEPHIBOSHETH'S SERVANT

**16:1** When David was a little past the top of the mountain, there was Ziba the servant of Mephibosheth, who met him with a couple of saddled donkeys, and on them two hundred loaves of bread, one hundred clusters of raisins, one hundred summer fruits, and a skin of wine.
2 And the king said to Ziba, "What do you mean to do with these?"

So Ziba said, "The donkeys are for the king's household to ride on, the bread and summer fruit for the young men to eat, and the wine for those who are faint in the wilderness to drink."

3 Then the king said, "And where is your master's son?"

And Ziba said to the king, "Indeed he is staying in Jerusalem, for he said, 'Today the house of Israel will restore the kingdom of my father to me.'"

4 So the king said to Ziba, "Here, all that belongs to Mephibosheth is yours."

And Ziba said, "I humbly bow before you, that I may find favor in your sight, my lord, O king!"

*—2 Samuel 16:1–4*

This chapter records the rest of David's escape from Jerusalem and closes with the arrival at the banks of the Jordan River where he plans to await reports about Absalom's plans from Zadok and the priests who are loyal to him. The events of this chapter are as discouraging as the previous chapter was encouraging. In chapter 15 we learned that David still had many friends—soldiers, priests, and statesmen. The incidents of this chapter remind us that David still has formidable enemies, although there are a couple of bright spots. The first verses of this chapter (vv. 1–14) should be seen as a continuation of the narrative of David's escape and the rest of the chapter (vv. 15–23) details the beginning of Absalom's activities in his effort to claim the throne.

As David and his party were just beyond the edge of the Mount of Olives they were met by Ziba, whom David had appointed to be servant to Mephibosheth, Jonathan's son and Saul's grandson (2 Sam. 9). He came bearing gifts of food and transportation for the king and his household (v. 2) as a sign of his loyalty to David. His gifts were reminiscent of the gifts of Abigail, now David's wife (1 Sam. 25:18). When asked by David where his master was he indicated that Mephibosheth had stayed in Jerusalem in the hopes of having Saul's kingdom restored to him (v. 3). Most scholars agree that there was little likelihood for that to happen whatever the fate of David or Absalom. Many believe that Ziba's report is not the truth but his own effort to ingratiate himself to David whom he thinks will be the victor in the conflict with Absalom.

At the moment, David believed him and delivered to him all the possessions that had been given previously to Mephibosheth (v. 4). It was a moment of crisis and those who were willing to commit themselves before the outcome was certain were welcomed. So many people sit on the fence during troubled times waiting to see who will win before they commit themselves and thus gain in the spoils of war without personal risk in the battle. Also, Saul's household was not totally reconciled to David, as the incident that follows indicates, and the presence of the grandson of Saul, even if he were crippled, could have provided a rallying point against both David and Absalom. Besides, Ziba was believable and his timing was perfect. He came when he was needed. Our lives come into contact with many people who make no impression, but we always remember favorably those who came to us in our times of crisis. Even if David would later listen to Mephibosheth's story and spare him, he still remembered and rewarded Ziba for his thoughtfulness and loyalty as he fled the city.

## SHIMEI CURSES DAVID

5 Now when King David came to Bahurim, there was a man from the family of the house of Saul, whose name was Shimei the son of Gera, coming from there. He came out, cursing continuously as he came. 6 And he threw stones at David and at all the servants of King David. And all the people and all the mighty men were on his right hand and on his left. 7 Also Shimei said thus when he cursed: "Come out! Come out! You bloodthirsty man, you rogue! 8 The LORD has brought upon you all the blood of the house of Saul, in whose place you have reigned; and the LORD has delivered the kingdom into the hand of Absalom your son. So now

you are caught in your own evil, because you are a blood-thirsty man!"

9 Then Abishai the son of Zeruiah said to the king, "Why should this dead dog curse my lord the king? Please, let me go over and take off his head!"

10 But the king said, "What have I to do with you, you sons of Zeruiah? So let him curse, because the LORD has said to him, 'Curse David.' Who then shall say, 'Why have you done so?'"

11 And David said to Abishai and all his servants, "See how my son who came from my own body seeks my life. How much more now may this Benjamite? Let him alone, and let him curse; for so the LORD has ordered him. 12 It may be that the LORD will look on my affliction, and that the LORD will repay me with good for his cursing this day."
13 And as David and his men went along the road, Shimei went along the hillside opposite him and cursed as he went, threw stones at him and kicked up dust. 14 Now the king and all the people who were with him became weary; so they refreshed themselves there.

—*2 Samuel 16:5–14*

This final scene that took place during David's escape from the city is the more important of these two incidents because it gives the reader an understanding of how David's enemies felt about him. It again pictures David's sense of surrender to the judgment of God for his sins.

Shimei was a distant relative of Saul's. He may have been mad with rage, but he had courage to run along the ridge cursing the king and throwing rocks and dirt on the group while David had several hundred crack troops with him. His basic accusations against David were that he was a murderer or *"bloodthirsty man"* and that he was a usurper of the throne of Saul (v. 8). As he ranted and raved and threw debris down upon them he claimed that Absalom's rebellion was nothing less than God's punishment upon David for his sins (v. 8). To have come from the palace where his word was absolute to be exposed to the rantings of a man mad with hatred for him indicates how the fortunes of David had changed so drastically.

There were two reactions to Shimei in the group. Abishai, who was Joab's brother, asked the king's permission to kill Shimei (v. 9). His was the power solution. He sounds quite modern since we live in a world that tries to deal with all crises in terms of physical power. They want to silence all the voices of disagreement and are woefully unaware of the forces of moral and spiritual truth. It was this mentality that had brought the death of Abner and others for whom David was now being given blame.

The second attitude toward Shimei's ravings was David's, and he not only refused to allow him to be silenced but rebuked his soldier for even suggesting it (v. 10). David's reasoning is very interesting—maybe God had told him to curse David (v. 11). This is an interesting theological view, that coming from the hate-filled rantings of an apparent madman might be the voice of God to David. The willingness to listen to one's critics and even to one's enemies may be the only way to discover the truth of God. The natural tendency is to surround ourselves with friends who are often reluctant to tell us the things we need to know. This opens the possibility that we may do well at times to listen to people who wish us harm but tell us the truth. Here again we see David's willingness to expose himself to God's word for his life and to God's judgment upon his life.

## THE ADVICE OF AHITHOPHEL

15 Meanwhile Absalom and all the people, the men of Israel, came to Jerusalem; and Ahithophel was with him. 16 And so it was, when Hushai the Archite, David's friend, came to Absalom, that Hushai said to Absalom, "Long live the king! Long live the king!"

17 So Absalom said to Hushai, "Is this your loyalty to your friend? Why did you not go with your friend?"

18 And Hushai said to Absalom, "No, but whom the LORD and this people and all the men of Israel choose, his I will be, and with him I will remain. 19 Furthermore, whom should I serve? Should I not serve in the presence of his son? As I have served in your father's presence, so will I be in your presence."

20 Then Absalom said to Ahithophel, "Give advice as to what we should do."

21 And Ahithophel said to Absalom, "Go in to your father's concubines, whom he has left to keep the house; and all Israel will hear that you are abhorred by your father. Then the hands of all who are with you will be strong."

22 So they pitched a tent for Absalom on the top of the house, and Absalom went in to his father's concubines in the sight of all Israel.

23 Now the advice of Ahithophel, which he gave in those days, was as if one had inquired at the oracle of God. So was all the advice of Ahithophel both with David and with Absalom.

17:1 Moreover Ahithophel said to Absalom, "Now let me choose twelve thousand men, and I will arise and pursue David tonight. 2 I will come upon him while he is weary and weak, and make him afraid. And all the people who are with him will flee, and I will strike only the king. 3 Then I will bring back all the people to you. When all return except the man whom you seek, all the people will be at peace." 4 And the saying pleased Absalom and all the elders of Israel.

*—2 Samuel 16:15—17:4*

This last section of the chapter contains good news and bad news for David and describes an incident in which Absalom takes an irrevocable step. The good news was the establishment of Hushai as David's agent at the side of Absalom. Hushai was totally loyal to David and had intended to leave Jerusalem with him but had been sent to Absalom by David as a means of counteracting the counsel of Ahithophel (2 Sam. 15:32–34). Hushai had returned to the city and was there to greet Absalom with *"Long live the king! Long live the king!"* (v. 16). When asked why he had not been loyal to David he replied that his responsibility lay with the one whom both God and the people had chosen and that nothing would be more natural for one who had served the father than to also serve the son (vv. 18–19). The man who had ingratiated himself to the people with flattery proved that he himself was also susceptible to it, so Absalom accepted Hushai among his counselors. It was a tragic mistake, as succeeding events would confirm, because he had compromised his best weapon, the counsel of Ahithophel.

The first advice that Ahithophel gave Absalom was to take David's concubines as his own (v. 21). This would be such a humiliation to his father that it would break any bond that might still be left. It would be a clear claim to the throne that all the people could understand and would possibly bring to his side some who were waiting to see just how far he would go. It would also mean that there would be no turning back. In his wisdom, Ahithophel realized that Absalom's only chance of winning lay in his willingness to totally commit himself to his goal and this one act demonstrated that commitment. It also fulfilled the prophecy of Nathan (2 Sam. 12:11) that others would lie with David's wives in full view of others.

The tribute to the quality of Ahithophel's advice is almost unequalled in the Scriptures (v. 23). It referred not just to sound judgment but to having words with power to influence events. In those days there were considered to be three sources of insight: priestly directives, prophetic words, and wise counsel. Ahithophel was Absalom's greatest resource and had his advice been followed things would have been different. History is replete with the stories of driven leaders who lost their cause because they did not know how to listen to the advice of those who are wise.

We are not told why Ahithophel decided to go with Absalom in his revolt against David, only that he did and that he gave him the same good advice that he had given to David. He knew David well from their long years of association and he also was aware that David's flight with his soldiers had been slowed by the families he had taken with him. He was sure that peace could be accomplished quickly and with a minimum loss of life if Absalom were to follow his advice.

The plan was to take a band of soldiers and make a night march in order to catch up with David before he crossed the Jordan River. He felt that the surprise of such a move had the possibility of isolating David where it would be possible to kill him and demoralize all his followers, effectively destroying all opposition to Absalom. Ahithophel assumed that Absalom could declare an amnesty for those who had followed David and unite all Israel under his leadership. It's interesting that in Ahithophel's counsel he referred to David as *"the king"* (v. 2) and *"the man"* (v. 3) but never as Absalom's father. It's a sad thing when our ambition makes us forget the relationships that ought to bind us together.

Ahithophel was not just wise in discerning what needed to be done but showed great skill in communicating with Absalom. His counsel was full of vivid imagery that must have given it appeal. His painting of David as weary and weak from his flight minimized the danger of the plan he was suggesting. His use of the wedding imagery must have appealed to Absalom's ambition as he spoke of bringing all Israel to him as a bride to her husband (v. 3). The only possible flaw in the advice was that he offered to lead the soldiers himself rather than suggesting that Absalom do it. For at that time the first essential for a king of Israel was his military ability. Other than that the advice was flawless. It took into consideration both immediate needs and future consequences and it depended upon a quick decision and decisive action. What was done with the advice is a testimony to the fact that we need more than good counsel to be successful in the ventures of life. We also need the ability to accept it and act upon it. All of the histories of World War II indicate that Hitler went down to defeat not for lack of good counsel from his generals but from his inability to accept their advice and act upon it.

The stage is set for Absalom's ultimate defeat. The first phase of the revolt was a great success with the capital being occupied without even a skirmish being fought. The only negative was that Absalom had arrived in Jerusalem too late to catch David. But David, whose flight had been slowed by the women and children who were traveling with him, was within a hard night's march of Absalom's army. The revolt was now ready for its second stage, but it ended up being a war of words as Absalom was faced with opposing counsel as to what he would do next. So much of the success or failure in life is tied to our ability to use discernment when we are faced with conflicting choices. Absalom's response is a model of a bad decision and a reminder that life's choices are important. The chapter also contains the story of the escape of the spies and their success in warning David of Absalom's plans. This section closes with the armies grouped for battle amid signs that the tide has already turned toward David. Permeating the chapter is the theme that has characterized all these accounts: God's hand was in Absalom's problems and in David's increased fortunes.

## THE ADVICE OF HUSHAI

5 Then Absalom said, "Now call Hushai the Archite also, and let us hear what he says too." 6 And when Hushai came to Absalom, Absalom spoke to him, saying, "Ahithophel has spoken in this manner. Shall we do as he says? If not, speak up."

7 So Hushai said to Absalom: "The advice that Ahithophel has given is not good at this time. 8 For," said Hushai, "you know your father and his men, that they are mighty men, and they are enraged in their minds, like a bear robbed of her cubs in the field; and your father is a man of war, and will not camp with the people. 9 Surely by now he is hidden in some pit, or in some other place. And it will be, when some of them are overthrown at the first, that whoever hears it will say, 'There is a slaughter among the people who follow Absalom.' 10 And even he who is valiant,

whose heart is like the heart of a lion, will melt completely. For all Israel knows that your father is a mighty man, and those who are with him are valiant men. [11] Therefore I advise that all Israel be fully gathered to you, from Dan to Beersheba, like the sand that is by the sea for multitude, and that you go to battle in person. [12] So we will come upon him in some place where he may be found, and we will fall on him as the dew falls on the ground. And of him and all the men who are with him there shall not be left so much as one. [13] Moreover, if he has withdrawn into a city, then all Israel shall bring ropes to that city; and we will pull it into the river, until there is not one small stone found there."

[14] So Absalom and all the men of Israel said, "The advice of Hushai the Archite is better than the advice of Ahithophel." For the LORD had purposed to defeat the good advice of Ahithophel, to the intent that the LORD might bring disaster on Absalom.

*—2 Samuel 17:5–14*

It was assumed by Ahithophel that his counsel would be acted upon immediately, but it wasn't. While the text indicated that the *"saying pleased Absalom and all the elders of Israel"* (v. 4), Absalom decided to get a second opinion from Hushai, who was actually acting as David's agent in the camp. This was Absalom's fatal mistake because it caused sufficient delay for David to flee across the Jordan and to organize himself and his defenses. There are many times in life when indecision has the effect of being a decision not to act. When I was a student my pastor would often say during an evangelistic invitation that "not to decide is to decide no." Absalom's decision to seek further counsel had that effect.

Hushai's successful effort to counter the advice of Ahithophel is a classic use of the principles of rhetoric being used to convince a person to take a certain action. He appealed to fear, to the desire for military glory, and to Absalom's strong desire for personal achievement. He created fear by referring to David and his men not as "weary and weak" but as being enraged *"like a bear robbed of her cubs"* (v. 8), and he reminded Absalom of David's experience as a soldier and of the caution he was bound to have taken. The use of fear is one of the emotions often used in motivating people to action—even by the church. Hushai built upon his theme by suggesting that David was probably already hidden and that a battle that cost lives but did not capture the king would start the rumor that *"there is a slaughter among the people who follow Absalom"* (v. 9) and that it might take the heart out of many of his followers (v. 10). He cinched his building of fear with another reminder of what a mighty man David was and what valiant men followed him (v. 10). This passage is a classic example of the fact that the person who can make you afraid can eventually control you. This is why a religion built upon fear alone never creates the liberating experience that authentic faith has as its goal.

Hushai's whole plan was full of exaggeration and no part more than his suggestion that Absalom wait until he could put together a great army. He pictured it as being so extensive that it would be like *"the sand that is by the sea"* (v. 11). He painted a picture for Absalom of a military force so large that it would be as irresistible as the dew that *"falls on the ground"* (v. 12). He pictured a conquest so complete that of all the men with David *"there shall not be left so much as one"* (v. 12). He even suggested that if David had withdrawn to a city, the walls could be pulled down and after the battle *"not one small stone"* would be found there (v. 13).

The suggestion that tied them all together was that Absalom was the only person who could lead such an army into battle. Nothing was said about the contrast with Ahithophel's advice on this point, but it is likely that Hushai had sensed that Ahithophel had not been sensitive enough to Absalom's enlarged ego and decided to take advantage of it. The need to flatter those whom you would like to manipulate is also universal, and people whose need for flattery is strong can always be controlled by others. Hushai knew what he wanted to do—delay any action against David. He also knew how to do it—play on Absalom's fears and his ego. He was successful because as a result of his eloquent appeal the advice of Ahithophel was rejected. That decision sealed the fate of the revolt.

This section ends with a phrase that reminds the reader of God's part in the bad decision: *"For the LORD had purposed to defeat the good counsel of Ahithophel"* (v. 14). The theme that permeates all of these events is that it was God who brought David to the throne and in these accounts it is God who was responsible for preserving the throne for David. In this case God used Absalom's lack of discernment and good judgment. It's a reminder that counsel is never any better than the person who hears it and when one's character is tainted with hatred or ambition or pride it is harder to make wise choices. The passage is also a stern reminder of God's overriding sovereignty in the affairs of mankind.

## HUSHAI WARNS DAVID TO ESCAPE

15 Then Hushai said to Zadok and Abiathar the priests, "Thus and so Ahithophel advised Absalom and the elders of Israel, and thus and so I have advised. 16 Now therefore, send quickly and tell David, saying, 'Do not spend this night in the plains of the wilderness, but speedily cross over, lest the king and all the people who are with him be swallowed up.'" 17 Now Jonathan and Ahimaaz stayed at En Rogel, for they dared not be seen coming into the city; so a female servant would come and tell them, and they would go and tell King David. 18 Nevertheless a lad saw them, and told Absalom. But both of them went away quickly and came to a man's house in Bahurim, who had a well in his court; and they went down into it. 19 Then the woman took and spread a covering over the well's mouth, and spread ground grain on it; and the thing was not known. 20 And when Absalom's servants came to the woman at the house, they said, "Where are Ahimaaz and Jonathan?"

So the woman said to them, "They have gone over the water brook."

And when they had searched and could not find them, they returned to Jerusalem. 21 Now it came to pass, after they had departed, that they came up out of the well and went and told King David, and said to David, "Arise and cross over the water quickly. For thus has Ahithophel advised against you." 22 So David and all the people who were with him arose and crossed over the Jordan. By morning light not one of them was left who had not gone over the Jordan.

23 Now when Ahithophel saw that his advice was not followed, he saddled a donkey, and arose and went home to his house, to his city. Then he put his household in order, and hanged himself, and died; and he was buried in his father's tomb.

24 Then David went to Mahanaim. And Absalom crossed over the Jordan, he and all the men of Israel with him. 25 And Absalom made Amasa captain of the army instead of Joab. This Amasa was the son of a man whose name was Jithra, an Israelite, who had gone in to Abigail the daughter of Nahash, sister of Zeruiah, Joab's mother. 26 So Israel and Absalom encamped in the land of Gilead.

27 Now it happened, when David had come to Mahanaim, that Shobi the son of Nahash from Rabbah of the people of Ammon, Machir the son of Ammiel from Lo Debar, and Barzillai the Gileadite from Rogelim, 28 brought beds and

basins, earthen vessels and wheat, barley and flour, parched grain and beans, lentils and parched seeds, [29] honey and curds, sheep and cheese of the herd, for David and the people who were with him to eat. For they said, "The people are hungry and weary and thirsty in the wilderness."

*—2 Samuel 17:15–29*

This section of the chapter tells how the advantage begins to turn toward David, who seemed such a hopeless underdog when the revolt began. It begins with the successful escape of the two spies and David's acting upon the information that they brought (vv. 15–22). The text gives the details as to how the spy operation was carried out—the two sons staying outside the city and information being carried to them by a servant girl (vv. 17–18). It also reminds us that not everyone was supportive of Absalom or else the two spies would not have been hidden in a well until it was safe for them to travel (vv. 19–21). The message that Hushai sent would indicate that he still wasn't sure whose advice Absalom might follow (vv. 1–2). Unlike Absalom who couldn't make up his mind how to use the advice that had been given to him, David acted immediately on the word that he received and by morning had all his people safely across the Jordan (v. 22).

The second thing in this passage that indicated that the tide was turning is Ahithophel's suicide. The story is told in one pointed verse (v. 23). He didn't kill himself because his advice hadn't been followed. There had probably been other times when the king had not listened. He killed himself because he knew that Absalom's delay meant that the revolt would fail. He didn't want to wait for David to hunt him down and execute him for his part in the rebellion, so he killed himself. When leadership consistently turns its back on the sound advice of its wisest adherents it is doomed to failure. When we operate out of fear or ignorance and turn away from the insights of our best minds we also fail.

The three verses that tell of the general preparation for the impending battle also suggest that Absalom is no longer functioning as a favorite (vv. 24–26). Because of the information supplied by the two spies David was able to cross the Jordan and then occupy the city of Mahanaim, which had been Ishbosheth's headquarters after the death of Saul. It was a walled city and could be defended. In contrast Absalom's men were in the open and were led by a less-experienced soldier, Amasa, who was Absalom's cousin and David's nephew. The time that had been bought by Hushai's counsel to Absalom had been used well and now David's position seemed superior.

On the surface the concluding verses of the chapter seem to have nothing to do with the conflict, but they are a reminder that David has the support of significant people in the area. The rich men of the region were willing to befriend him and provide provisions for his army. This would indicate both that David had more support than many had thought at the beginning of the revolt and that these men, who were astute judges of situations, had come to the conclusion that David was going to win. Of special interest in the group is Machir, a close friend of Mephibosheth, Jonathan's son and Saul's grandson. He probably had been impressed by David's earlier generosity. While Absalom had stood in the gate and whispered promises in the ears of the people, David had been building relationships with people and that investment provided significant support in his hour of need.

The next chapter records the battle in which Absalom is slain and the revolt smashed. David's strategy for the battle reflects his years of experience. The most interesting thing in the chapter is the contrast between Joab's and David's attitudes toward Absalom—with David functioning more as a father and Joab as a soldier. It closes on one of the saddest notes in David's life, when as a broken-hearted father he sobs out his grief at the death of his son whom he had really lost years before.

## ABSALOM'S DEFEAT AND DEATH

**18:1** And David numbered the people who were with him, and set captains of thousands and captains of hundreds over them. ² Then David sent out one third of the people under the hand of Joab, one third under the hand of Abishai the son of Zeruiah, Joab's brother, and one third under the hand of Ittai the Gittite. And the king said to the people, "I also will surely go out with you myself."

³ But the people answered, "You shall not go out! For if we flee away, they will not care about us; nor if half of us die, will they care about us. But you are worth ten thousand of us now. For you are now more help to us in the city."

⁴ Then the king said to them, "Whatever seems best to you I will do." So the king stood beside the gate, and all the people went out by hundreds and by thousands. ⁵ Now the king had commanded Joab, Abishai, and Ittai, saying, "Deal gently for my sake with the young man Absalom." And all

the people heard when the king gave all the captains orders concerning Absalom.

6 So the people went out into the field of battle against Israel. And the battle was in the woods of Ephraim. 7 The people of Israel were overthrown there before the servants of David, and a great slaughter of twenty thousand took place there that day. 8 For the battle there was scattered over the face of the whole countryside, and the woods devoured more people that day than the sword devoured.

9 Then Absalom met the servants of David. Absalom rode on a mule. The mule went under the thick boughs of a great terebinth tree, and his head caught in the terebinth; so he was left hanging between heaven and earth. And the mule which was under him went on. 10 Now a certain man saw it and told Joab, and said, "I just saw Absalom hanging in a terebinth tree!"

11 So Joab said to the man who told him, "You just saw him! And why did you not strike him there to the ground? I would have given you ten shekels of silver and a belt."

12 But the man said to Joab, "Though I were to receive a thousand shekels of silver in my hand, I would not raise my hand against the king's son. For in our hearing the king commanded you and Abishai and Ittai, saying, 'Beware lest anyone touch the young man Absalom!' 13 Otherwise I would have dealt falsely against my own life. For there is nothing hidden from the king, and you yourself would have set yourself against me."

14 Then Joab said, "I cannot linger with you." And he took three spears in his hand and thrust them through Absalom's heart, while he was still alive in the midst of the terebinth tree. 15 And ten young men who bore Joab's armor surrounded Absalom, and struck and killed him.

16 So Joab blew the trumpet, and the people returned from pursuing Israel. For Joab held back the people. 17 And they took Absalom and cast him into a large pit in the woods, and laid a very large heap of stones over him. Then all Israel fled, everyone to his tent.

18 Now Absalom in his lifetime had taken and set up a pillar for himself, which is in the King's Valley. For he said, "I have no son to keep my name in remembrance." He called the pillar after his own name. And to this day it is called Absalom's Monument.

*—2 Samuel 18:1–18*

Chapter 18 is full of contrasts. It begins with David's making plans for the battle that will end the revolt and ends with that same David immobilized with grief over the death of his son Absalom. The most interesting study in the chapter is the contrast between the attitudes of Joab and David concerning the fate of Absalom. The chapter also gives the reader an unforgettable picture of a brokenhearted father—a man to whom what was the best of news to him as a king was the worst of news to him as a father. The chapter opens with Absalom planning his final assault upon the king and closes with Absalom buried in a pit underneath a pile of stones.

The very way in which David prepared for battle exuded confidence of victory. His son's revolt had shaken him and he had fled the capital in a hurried manner. Now he was in control and showed his skill as a strategist as he divided his soldiers into three groups, with Joab and his brother Abishai in command of two groups and his faithful mercenary Ittai in charge of the other (vv. 1–2). They were disciplined and battle-experienced soldiers led by skilled officers, and they would prove to be too much for the loosely organized citizens' army of Absalom.

It had been David's intention to lead the army into battle, but the people persuaded him that it was not in the best interest of their cause for him to go (v. 3). They knew that in spite of all the people involved, the conflict was between two men: Absalom and David. They also knew that if a stray arrow should fell David that the kingdom would be lost, so David agreed to stay in the city and stand by the gate and inspect the troops as they went forth to battle (v. 4). He knew that his future and the future of Israel rested with their loyalty and their skill.

David's final instruction to his troops was to *"deal gently for my sake with the young man Absalom"* (v. 5). While the instruction showed confidence in the outcome of the battle it also revealed that David's concerns as a father were keeping him from being in touch with political reality. Our lives cannot be broken into compartments that we can keep completely separated. In David's heart there was still the hope for reconciliation with his son, and he was still treating the trouble between them as some sort of a misunderstanding that could be resolved. He was willing to risk his own life and wanted Absalom to be safe, but Joab had decided to keep David safe and to kill Absalom.

The encounter took place in rough, wooded terrain that was as dangerous for flight as it was for battle (vv. 6, 8), and the entire account of Absalom's defeat is given in one sentence: *"The people of Israel were overthrown there before the servants of David"* (v. 7). More detail is given to the fate of Absalom who led the revolt. According to the text, as he rode under the thick, low-hanging boughs of a tree, *"his head caught"* in the branches (v. 9). As a youth I heard a number of sermons that dealt with this text and every one of them pictured Absalom as having caught the hair he was so proud of in the branches of the tree, but the text says he caught his head and hung there helpless as the mule on which he had been riding ran on without him.

The soldier who discovered Absalom told Joab, who reprimanded him for not taking advantage of the situation and then offered him a reward for killing Absalom (v. 11). The loyalty to the king's command and the simple logic of the man showed both character and courage. First, he reminded Joab of the king's clear order to spare his son (v. 12). Then he suggested that if he were to kill Absalom the king would find out since *"There is nothing hidden from the king"* (v. 13). His courage came in suggesting to Joab that if David sought to avenge his son's death that even Joab who ordered it probably wouldn't defend him (v. 13). The soldier showed a knowledge of human nature because history is full of the stories of those who betrayed those who carried out their commands. While the soldier lacked the political sophistication of Joab, he displayed a kind of loyalty to his king's wishes that is admirable.

In disgust Joab dismissed him with the phrase, *"I cannot linger with you"* (v. 14), and turned to do what the soldier refused to do. A more literal translation than *"three spears"* would be "three sticks." They were not so much meant to kill Absalom as they were a symbolic act of killing by Joab which the ten soldiers finished. Joab knew that to spare the son would please the father but that as long as Absalom was alive the kingdom would be in peril, so he assumed the responsibility for his death. His concern was for the nation and not for himself. He had been an early admirer of Absalom and had been his advocate with his father. It is to Joab's credit that although he had once thought that Absalom should succeed his father on the throne that he was able to change his mind in the light of changed circumstances. The most notable aspect of this act is that Joab was willing to expose himself to David's potential wrath in order to serve David's best interests. It was a wise and courageous choice.

With Absalom dead Joab concluded that the revolt was over and called the troops back from pursuing the Israelites (v. 16).

Then he threw the body into a large pit and covered it with stones as all of Absalom's followers *"fled, everyone to his tent"* (v. 17). Ahithophel had rightly judged that when "the man" had been killed, Israel would be united. He was wrong only in which man it would be. It was a sad end to a man who showed so much potential but seemed born to lose.

## DAVID HEARS OF ABSALOM'S DEATH AND MOURNS

19 Then Ahimaaz the son of Zadok said, "Let me run now and take the news to the king, how the LORD has avenged him of his enemies."

20 And Joab said to him, "You shall not take the news this day, for you shall take the news another day. But today you shall take no news, because the king's son is dead."
21 Then Joab said to the Cushite, "Go, tell the king what you have seen." So the Cushite bowed himself to Joab and ran.

22 And Ahimaaz the son of Zadok said again to Joab, "But whatever happens, please let me also run after the Cushite."

So Joab said, "Why will you run, my son, since you have no news ready?"
23 "But whatever happens," he said, "let me run."

So he said to him, "Run." Then Ahimaaz ran by way of the plain, and outran the Cushite.

24 Now David was sitting between the two gates. And the watchman went up to the roof over the gate, to the wall, lifted his eyes and looked, and there was a man, running alone. 25 Then the watchman cried out and told the king. And the king said, "If he is alone, there is news in his mouth." And he came rapidly and drew near.

26 Then the watchman saw another man running, and the watchman called to the gatekeeper and said, "There is another man, running alone!"

And the king said, "He also brings news."
27 So the watchman said, "I think the running of the first is like the running of Ahimaaz the son of Zadok."

And the king said, "He is a good man, and comes with good news."

28 So Ahimaaz called out and said to the king, "All is well!" Then he bowed down with his face to the earth before the king, and said, "Blessed be the LORD your God, who has delivered up the men who raised their hand against my lord the king!"

²⁹ The king said, "Is the young man Absalom safe?"

Ahimaaz answered, "When Joab sent the king's servant and me your servant, I saw a great tumult, but I did not know what it was about."

³⁰ And the king said, "Turn aside and stand here." So he turned aside and stood still.

³¹ Just then the Cushite came, and the Cushite said, "There is good news, my lord the king! For the LORD has avenged you this day of all those who rose against you."

³² And the king said to the Cushite, "Is the young man Absalom safe?"

So the Cushite answered, "May the enemies of my lord the king, and all who rise against you to do harm, be like that young man!"

³³ Then the king was deeply moved, and went up to the chamber over the gate, and wept. And as he went, he said thus: "O my son Absalom—my son, my son Absalom—if only I had died in your place! O Absalom my son, my son!"

—*2 Samuel 18:19–33*

In the previous verses more time was spent on how Absalom was killed than how the army of Israel was routed, and in this section more details are given as to how David received word of the battle than were devoted to the battle and to his son's death. This whole section gets its mood from the plaintive request that David made to each of the messengers, *"Is the young man Absalom safe?"* (vv. 29, 32). He had totally lost sight of what was at stake for himself and those who were loyal to him and was absorbed in his concern for his son. He sat at the gate waiting for good news from the battlefield, and when it finally came it was to him the worst of news.

As soon as the battle was over Ahimaaz asked permission to take the news to the king (v. 19). He was the son of Zadok the priest and had been instrumental in bringing David the intelligence that had allowed him to escape across the Jordan. Now he wanted to tell the king how the Lord had *"avenged him of his enemies"* (v. 19). Evidently he did not know what had happened in the past to messengers who brought messages to David that upset him (2 Sam. 1:15; 4:5ff.). Joab's reluctance to let him go was probably based on his desire to protect Ahimaaz's relationship with the king. Instead he sent an African slave whom he referred to as the Cushite, because he was from Cush, which is south of Egypt (v. 21). As a foreigner and a servant of David he would have little to fear from delivering the message.

When Ahimaaz persisted in his request that he also be allowed to run, Joab relented and let him go (vv. 22–23). By taking an easier route he was able to outrun the Cushite and arrive first with the message, *"All is well!"* and bowing down before the king he proclaimed: *"Blessed be the LORD your God, who has delivered up the men who raised their hand against my lord the king"* (v. 28). When the king ignored the news of the battle and asked only about the safety of his son, Ahimaaz must have suddenly realized the wisdom of what Joab had said to him so he feigned ignorance of what had happened to Absalom. He was asked to stand to the side and wait with the king for the second messenger. His discretion probably saved his life.

When the Cushite arrived his message was almost identical to that of Ahimaaz and the king hit him with the same question about the safety of Absalom. While his answer was not direct, the king understood it and was devastated. The text gives no record of any effort on David's part to get details of his son's death or to discover who had killed him or why his orders had not been obeyed. It tells rather how he left his place at the gate and went to a chamber over the gate and began the process of grieving. As he went, he wept and said over and over again, *"O my son Absalom—my son, my son Absalom—if only I had died in your place! O Absalom my son, my son!"* (v. 33). It was the beginning of a grief process that immobilized the king.

The next chapter tells of David's putting his life back together, with the aid of Joab, and of his beginning the process of bringing healing to Israel after a time of strife. The incidents show a quality of mercy and kindness and wisdom that may have been a part of what David salvaged from the experience. One of the most valuable lessons of faith is that no experience, however painful, need be wasted, but that there are lessons to be learned that have the potential of enriching our lives.

## GRIEF THAT IMMOBILIZES

**19:1** And Joab was told, "Behold, the king is weeping and mourning for Absalom." [2] So the victory that day was turned into mourning for all the people. For the people heard it said that day, "The king is grieved for his son." [3] And the people stole back into the city that day, as people who are ashamed steal away when they flee in battle. [4] But the king covered his face, and the king cried out with a loud voice, "O my son Absalom! O Absalom, my son, my son!"

[5] Then Joab came into the house to the king, and said, "Today you have disgraced all your servants who today have

saved your life, the lives of your sons and daughters, the lives of your wives and the lives of your concubines, [6] in that you love your enemies and hate your friends. For you have declared today that you regard neither princes nor servants; for today I perceive that if Absalom had lived and all of us had died today, then it would have pleased you well. [7] Now therefore, arise, go out and speak comfort to your servants. For I swear by the LORD, if you do not go out, not one will stay with you this night. And that will be worse for you than all the evil that has befallen you from your youth until now." [8] Then the king arose and sat in the gate. And they told all the people, saying, "There is the king, sitting in the gate." So all the people came before the king.

For everyone of Israel had fled to his tent.

*—2 Samuel 19:1–8*

The failure of the revolt didn't automatically restore the country to David's control. There were many things that needed to be done immediately: Thank those who had been loyal, court those who had stayed neutral, convince those who had followed his son that there would not be a bloodbath, and try not to alienate one group while placating another. The problem was that David was doing none of these. He was in his chamber over the gate mourning the death of his son. This so devastated his people that they *"stole back into the city that day, as people who are ashamed steal away when they flee in battle"* (v. 3). They had come back from battle expecting to participate in a victory celebration and instead found their king weeping and crying *"O my son Absalom! O Absalom, my son, my son!"* (v. 4).

Joab confronted the king with what he was doing. He was ignoring those who had stood between him and Absalom's ruthlessness (v. 5). Grief has a way of temporarily making us forget the living to whom we are indebted. David couldn't distinguish between his friends and his enemies (v. 6). He had completely forgotten about the larger implications of his situation. Only the shock of Joab's warning that his people would desert him unless he met with them shook him out of his preoccupation about his personal losses and sent him to the gate to greet those who had fought to save him (vv. 7–8).

In life each of us experiences losses great and small that cause grief which is natural, healthy, and healing. Occasionally something happens that within itself is not that different from other things which have happened, but we can't get over it.

These things that we ordinarily could have handled knock us down and we can't seem to get up. This is what happened to David. A closer look at why Absalom's death affected him this way may help us with our own bouts with grief when it threatens to immobilize us.

David was no stranger to violence and death, even the death of children. His reaction to this death, however, was unhealthy. Instead of his grief over Absalom being cleansing, it was contagious, and all the people came down with it. It inverted reality. There had to be more to this grief than the death of a son. Healthy grief will free us to go on living, but unhealthy grief usually has something else mixed with it. For David it was a mixture of grief and guilt, and that was a volatile mixture. When we can't get over some loss it's usually because there is a larger agenda than grief alone.

David was mourning that he had not disciplined his children. He was having second thoughts too late. He was seeing his own sins duplicated in his sons' lives. He felt betrayed by Joab. He was discovering too late how much more his family had meant to him than he had previously realized. He was facing the fact that Absalom's popularity wouldn't have been possible without the vacuum created by his own neglect. His unwillingness to let Absalom grow up in life made it impossible for him to turn him loose in death.

When something gets us down we need a friend who will confront us, remind us of who our friends are, of the blessings of God in our lives, of others who need us, and call us to go back to living. For David, God sent Joab. For us there are wise people who love us enough to tell us the truth whether we want to hear it or not.

# CHAPTER FIFTEEN—PUTTING THE PIECES BACK TOGETHER

## 2 SAMUEL 19:9—20:26

*Scripture Outline*

While chapter 19 begins with David's coming to grips with his grief over Absalom's death, the bulk of this chapter is about his efforts to recapture the hearts of the people. In it we meet people we have met before, such as Shimei, who threw rocks at David and cursed him as he left Jerusalem, and Ziba, who provided provisions for David in his flight, and Mephibosheth, who did not flee with David. The actions in this chapter capture both David's magnanimity to his enemies and his capacity to be caustic with his best friends. Most of all the chapter dramatizes the degree to which David had lost the hearts of the people and the uphill battle he had in his effort to unite Israel and Judah.

### DAVID'S RETURN TO JERUSALEM

⁹ Now all the people were in a dispute throughout all the tribes of Israel, saying, "The king saved us from the hand of our enemies, he delivered us from the hand of the

Philistines, and now he has fled from the land because of Absalom. ¹⁰ But Absalom, whom we anointed over us, has died in battle. Now therefore, why do you say nothing about bringing back the king?"

¹¹ So King David sent to Zadok and Abiathar the priests, saying, "Speak to the elders of Judah, saying, 'Why are you the last to bring the king back to his house, since the words of all Israel have come to the king, to his very house? ¹² You are my brethren, you are my bone and my flesh. Why then are you the last to bring back the king?' ¹³ And say to Amasa, 'Are you not my bone and my flesh? God do so to me, and more also, if you are not commander of the army before me continually in place of Joab.'" ¹⁴ So he swayed the hearts of all the men of Judah, just as the heart of one man, so that they sent this word to the king: "Return, you and all your servants!"

¹⁵ Then the king returned and came to the Jordan. And Judah came to Gilgal, to go to meet the king, to escort the king across the Jordan. ¹⁶ And Shimei the son of Gera, a Benjamite, who was from Bahurim, hurried and came down with the men of Judah to meet King David. ¹⁷ There were a thousand men of Benjamin with him, and Ziba the servant of the house of Saul, and his fifteen sons and his twenty servants with him; and they went over the Jordan before the king. ¹⁸ Then a ferryboat went across to carry over the king's household, and to do what he thought good.

*—2 Samuel 19:9–18a*

This passage describes what was almost a second inaugural for David. Since David had fled before Absalom, and since Absalom had been crowned but was now dead, the people were at loose ends as to what to do (vv. 9–10). When Israel invited David to return to the throne, David took the initiative with the leaders of Judah and chided them about their being so slow in returning the throne to him (vv. 11–12).

Then he made a most remarkable move: He named Amasa, who had been Absalom's commander during the revolt, commander of the army instead of Joab. Some feel it was his way of punishing Joab for having slain his son. Others feel it was a political move to show the Israelites he wasn't going to purge Absalom's supporters. Some feel that it was an indefensible move on David's part since Joab was a blood relative and had been loyal to him. They failed to see the wisdom of punishing the commander and promoting the man who led the revolt. Whatever we might think, David recaptured the hearts of the people so that they sent word for him to return (v. 14) and sent a delegation to meet him as he came back over the Jordan River (v. 15).

The concluding verses of this section introduce again the characters who were last seen as David fled the city: Shimei, who had cursed David and thrown rocks at him and his people, and Ziba, who was Mephibosheth's servant and who had brought provisions for David's family as they had fled. That the circumstances have changed is indicated by the fact that Shimei has come with a thousand Benjamites to greet David (vv. 16–17). Some suggest that Ziba's coming with all his servants and his sons (v. 17) indicates that he was anxious to reinforce his version of the events before David met with Mephibosheth. Human nature is such that there is a flow of people to the winner when conflicts between opposing camps are settled. David had crossed the river in haste to escape his enemies. He returned on a ferryboat with everyone wanting to entertain him (v. 18).

## DAVID'S MERCY TO SHIMEI

18b Now Shimei the son of Gera fell down before the king when he had crossed the Jordan. 19 Then he said to the king, "Do not let my lord impute iniquity to me, or remember what wrong your servant did on the day that my lord the king left Jerusalem, that the king should take it to heart. 20 For I, your servant, know that I have sinned. Therefore here I am, the first to come today of all the house of Joseph to go down to meet my lord the king."

21 But Abishai the son of Zeruiah answered and said, "Shall not Shimei be put to death for this, because he cursed the LORD's anointed?"

22 And David said, "What have I to do with you, you sons of Zeruiah, that you should be adversaries to me today? Shall any man be put to death today in Israel? For do I not know that today I am king over Israel?" 23 Therefore the king said to Shimei, "You shall not die." And the king swore to him.

—*2 Samuel 19:18b–23*

These verses both contrast David's station as he left and as he returned to Jerusalem. As he left he was subjected to the verbal abuse of a hate-filled man, but on his return he enjoys this man's allegiance. The account also contrasts David's mercy upon Shimei with Abishai's suggestion that he should be slain for cursing one of the Lord's anointed (v. 21). The same suggestion had been made as they had fled Jerusalem and been subjected to Shimei's rantings and ravings (2 Sam. 16:9).

Shimei gave David two reasons for his asking for forgiveness. First, he freely confessed that he had been wrong in what he had done and asked the king's forgiveness (v. 19). Then, he claimed that he had been the first person from the tribe *"of Joseph"* who had come down to pledge his allegiance to David. In rejecting the suggestion that Shimei should be slain David seemed to infer that on such a day, one in which he had been assured that he was still king over Israel, no blood should be shed (v. 22). Therefore he pardoned Shimei with the words *"You shall not die"* (v. 23).

While David kept his promise not to kill Shimei, his subsequent actions indicate that the decision to spare him had been political, a decision made because David needed to do everything possible to build a following, especially among the Benjamites. This interpretation is supported by the report that among David's instructions to Solomon when he became king was a request that he kill Shimei for having cursed David as he was fleeing Jerusalem (1 Kin. 2:8–9), and one of Solomon's first acts was to have Shimei killed (1 Kin. 2:36–46). The whole event is a reminder that people may speak words of mercy when they have hatred in their heart. The story is also a reminder of the pressures to act out of expedience rather than conviction.

### DAVID AND MEPHIBOSHETH MEET

24 Now Mephibosheth the son of Saul came down to meet the king. And he had not cared for his feet, nor trimmed his mustache, nor washed his clothes, from the day the king departed until the day he returned in peace. 25 So it was, when he had come to Jerusalem to meet the king, that the king said to him, "Why did you not go with me, Mephibosheth?"

26 And he answered, "My lord, O king, my servant deceived me. For your servant said, 'I will saddle a donkey for myself, that I may ride on it and go to the king,' because your servant is lame. 27 And he has slandered your servant to my lord the king, but my lord the king is like the angel of God. Therefore do what is good in your eyes. 28 For all my

father's house were but dead men before my lord the king. Yet you set your servant among those who eat at your own table. Therefore what right have I still to cry out anymore to the king?"

29 So the king said to him, "Why do you speak anymore of your matters? I have said, 'You and Ziba divide the land.'"

30 Then Mephibosheth said to the king, "Rather, let him take it all, inasmuch as my lord the king has come back in peace to his own house."

*—2 Samuel 19:24–30*

Mephibosheth's appearance was that of a mourner, having suspended all efforts to keep himself groomed *"from the day the king departed until the day he came back"* (v. 24). There is no way of knowing whether his grief was real or feigned. The king went immediately to the heart of his concerns by asking, *"Why did you not go with me, Mephibosheth?"* (v. 25). His answer appears lame: His servant both tricked him and then slandered him to David (vv. 26–27). Mephibosheth then recited David's kindness to his father's house and put himself at David's mercy (v. 28). From reading the text it isn't possible to decide whether or not David believed him. It may be that being unable to decide between them was David's reason for saying, *"You and Ziba divide the land"* (v. 29). Or mercy may have been shown, not because David believed him, but because, like Shimei, he was a Benjamite. For David it was more a time for building fences than for punishing those who had been unfaithful to him. This whole series of events pictures David's graciousness on his return to the throne.

## DAVID'S KINDNESS TO BARZILLAI

31 And Barzillai the Gileadite came down from Rogelim and went across the Jordan with the king, to escort him across the Jordan. 32 Now Barzillai was a very aged man, eighty years old. And he had provided the king with supplies while he stayed at Mahanaim, for he was a very rich man. 33 And the king said to Barzillai, "Come across with me, and I will provide for you while you are with me in Jerusalem."

34 But Barzillai said to the king, "How long have I to live, that I should go up with the king to Jerusalem? 35 I am

today eighty years old. Can I discern between the good and bad? Can your servant taste what I eat or what I drink? Can I hear any longer the voice of singing men and singing women? Why then should your servant be a further burden to my lord the king? 36 Your servant will go a little way across the Jordan with the king. And why should the king repay me with such a reward? 37 Please let your servant turn back again, that I may die in my own city, near the grave of my father and mother. But here is your servant Chimham; let him cross over with my lord the king, and do for him what seems good to you."

38 And the king answered, "Chimham shall cross over with me, and I will do for him what seems good to you. Now whatever you request of me, I will do for you." 39 Then all the people went over the Jordan. And when the king had crossed over, the king kissed Barzillai and blessed him, and he returned to his own place.

—*2 Samuel 19:31–39*

These verses turn happily from people whose motives were questionable to Barzillai, a Gileadite, who had provided the king with supplies while he was in Mahanaim (v. 32). Out of his appreciation for what had been done for him David offered to bring Barzillai to Jerusalem so David could now provide for him (v. 33). The offer is a reminder that David was capable of great generosity to those who had been his friends in times of trouble. He might spare Shimei or believe Mephibosheth for political reasons, but he wouldn't neglect this old man who had shared his riches with him.

Barzillai's answer is a study in wisdom and grace. He had no interest in trading the comfort of his old age in his own house and land for the excitement of life at court. He pled his case by reciting those things that his age no longer allowed him to do (v. 35). He wanted to end life where he had begun it and where he had lived it (v. 37). To soften his rejection of the king's offer he sent his son Chimham (v. 38) back with David as the king started over the Jordan.

Often I have watched people who, after years of living in one community, move to a totally different part of the country in retirement. They did it without realizing the support system for life that they had built at work, at church, with relatives, and in the neighborhood. Barzillai's rationale for not accepting David's offer has wisdom in it for people today. New experiences can be exciting, but as we get older we need to preserve and use the support systems we have built during our lives.

While David was not allowed to reward his friend Barzillai, he had the privilege of honoring his friend's son. Often the best way of expressing gratitude to those who have befriended you is to look for opportunities to be of assistance to their children. Every time David saw Chimham at court he must have been reminded of Barzillai's kindness to him at a critical time in life.

## THE QUARREL ABOUT THE KING

40 Now the king went on to Gilgal, and Chimham went on with him. And all the people of Judah escorted the king, and also half the people of Israel. 41 Just then all the men of Israel came to the king, and said to the king, "Why have our brethren, the men of Judah, stolen you away and brought the king, his household, and all David's men with him across the Jordan?"

42 So all the men of Judah answered the men of Israel, "Because the king is a close relative of ours. Why then are you angry over this matter? Have we ever eaten at the king's expense? Or has he given us any gift?"

43 And the men of Israel answered the men of Judah, and said, "We have ten shares in the king; therefore we also have more right to David than you. Why then do you despise us— were we not the first to advise bringing back our king?"

Yet the words of the men of Judah were fiercer than the words of the men of Israel.

*—2 Samuel 19:40–43*

The country's situation had not yet stabilized. David had barely crossed the Jordan before a rivalry arose between the men of Judah and the men of Israel. The men of Israel accused the men of Judah of stealing the king from them (v. 41) and the men of Judah denied favoritism, claiming only that they were close relatives (v. 42). As the argument continued, the men of Judah prevailed. That is what is meant by their *"words . . . were fiercer"* (v. 43). The historian probably recorded the events to remind the reader of the precarious position that David occupied as he sought to unite the country.

The next chapter tells the story of the rebellion of Sheba, another Benjamite. Almost incidental in the story, but not out of

335

character, is Amasa's murder by Joab. The chapter closes with another list of David's officers in the new government.

## THE REBELLION OF SHEBA

**20:1** And there happened to be there a rebel, whose name was Sheba the son of Bichri, a Benjamite. And he blew a trumpet, and said:

"We have no share in David,
Nor do we have inheritance in the son of Jesse;
Every man to his tents, O Israel!"

2 So every man of Israel deserted David, and followed Sheba the son of Bichri. But the men of Judah, from the Jordan as far as Jerusalem, remained loyal to their king.

3 Now David came to his house at Jerusalem. And the king took the ten women, his concubines whom he had left to keep the house, and put them in seclusion and supported them, but did not go in to them. So they were shut up to the day of their death, living in widowhood.

4 And the king said to Amasa, "Assemble the men of Judah for me within three days, and be present here yourself." 5 So Amasa went to assemble the men of Judah. But he delayed longer than the set time which David had appointed him. 6 And David said to Abishai, "Now Sheba the son of Bichri will do us more harm than Absalom. Take your lord's servants and pursue him, lest he find for himself fortified cities, and escape us." 7 So Joab's men, with the Cherethites, the Pelethites, and all the mighty men, went out after him. And they went out of Jerusalem to pursue Sheba the son of Bichri. 8 When they were at the large stone which is in Gibeon, Amasa came before them. Now Joab was dressed in battle armor; on it was a belt with a sword fastened in its sheath at his hips; and as he was going forward, it fell out. 9 Then Joab said to Amasa, "Are you in health, my brother?" And Joab took Amasa by the beard with his right hand to kiss him. 10 But Amasa did not notice the sword that was in Joab's hand. And he struck him with it in the stomach, and his entrails poured out on the ground; and he did not strike him again. Thus he died.

Then Joab and Abishai his brother pursued Sheba the son of Bichri. 11 Meanwhile one of Joab's men stood near Amasa, and said, "Whoever favors Joab and whoever is for David—follow Joab!" 12 But Amasa wallowed in his blood in the middle of the highway. And when the man saw that all the people stood still, he moved Amasa from the highway to the field and threw a garment over him, when he saw that everyone who came upon him halted. [13] When he was removed from the highway, all the people went on after Joab to pursue Sheba the son of Bichri.

[14] And he went through all the tribes of Israel to Abel and Beth Maachah and all the Berites. So they were gathered together and also went after Sheba. [15] Then they came and besieged him in Abel of Beth Maachah; and they cast up a siege mound against the city, and it stood by the rampart. And all the people who were with Joab battered the wall to throw it down.

[16] Then a wise woman cried out from the city, "Hear, hear! Please say to Joab, 'Come nearby, that I may speak with you.'" [17] When he had come near to her, the woman said, "Are you Joab?"

He answered, "I am."

Then she said to him, "Hear the words of your maidservant."

And he answered, "I am listening."

[18] So she spoke, saying, "They used to talk in former times, saying, 'They shall surely seek guidance at Abel,' and so they would end disputes. [19] I am among the peaceable and faithful in Israel. You seek to destroy a city and a mother in Israel. Why would you swallow up the inheritance of the LORD?"

[20] And Joab answered and said, "Far be it, far be it from me, that I should swallow up or destroy! [21] That is not so. But a man from the mountains of Ephraim, Sheba the son of Bichri by name, has raised his hand against the king, against David. Deliver him only, and I will depart from the city."

So the woman said to Joab, "Watch, his head will be thrown to you over the wall." [22] Then the woman in her wisdom went to all the people. And they cut off the head of Sheba the son of Bichri, and threw it out to Joab. Then he blew a trumpet, and they withdrew from the city, every man to his tent. So Joab returned to the king at Jerusalem.

*—2 Samuel 20:1–22*

Another revolt broke out before David reached Jerusalem. The historian recorded it as a further example of David overcoming opposition. It is almost an appendix to Absalom's rebellion and has a direct tie to the contention recorded in the previous chapter (2 Sam. 19:40–43). The revolt seemed at first more of a threat than really materialized, with a minimum of bloodshed, in contrast to Absalom's revolt which had been crushed in a great battle with many lives lost.

Woven into the account of the pursuit of Sheba is the story of Amasa's murder by Joab. As the picture of Joab's character unfolds it becomes more apparent that David had more reason to replace Joab than his killing of Absalom. David needed a broader base of followers than that which could be commanded by a professional army. There is no doubt that Joab was intensely loyal to David, but he had a very constricted vision of the kingdom. Often some of the people who love the church the most keep it from fulfilling its mission because of the narrowness of their vision.

Little is known about Sheba except that he was of the tribe of Benjamin, which was Saul's and Shimei's tribe. Whether he was of the house of Saul isn't known. The text refers to him as *"worthless,"* but this is not so much a description of his character as a reference to what he did in rebelling. The climate for the revolt was created by the quarrel between the men of Israel and the men of Judah (2 Sam. 19:40–43), and Sheba took advantage of the situation. There continue to be people who will exploit the differences between others for their own advantage.

He blew the ram's horn and issued his poetic call to arms: *"Every man to his tents, O Israel!"* (v. 1). He did not plan to attack David or make himself king but to stop Israel from crowning David as their king. It was characteristic for the northern tribes to repudiate the Davidic line. It's interesting how attitudes can come to be characteristic of a people or a geographical area and can be passed on from generation to generation. At the time of Solomon's death this hostility between the north and south would culminate in a permanent division.

As David arrived in Jerusalem, his action toward the ten concubines who had been left in the city to care for things is recorded in a parenthetical verse (v. 3). These were the women with whom Absalom had sexual intercourse as a public and symbolic way of making his claim to the throne (2 Sam. 16:22). Because they were considered defiled, they were isolated and shunned by all men. It was a human tragedy and David's action closed the story of Absalom's revolt.

Sheba's revolt gave David an opportunity to implement a policy that he had initiated when he made Amasa his commander in place of Joab: reliance on a civilian militia rather than a professional army. So he instructed Amasa to quickly assemble the men of Judah (v. 4). Because it took him more than the three days which had been predicted, David turned the task over to Abishai, Joab's brother (vv. 6–7). It isn't known whether Amasa was not able to enlist the men needed in the time allotted or whether he may have been trying on his own to take advantage of the situation to continue Absalom's revolt. Whatever it was, it wasn't a healthy situation.

The Hebrew in the verses that describe Amasa's murder is confusing but the overall picture is clear. The act was preconceived by Joab and he used trickery to pull it off. Had Joab met Amasa in battle he would have slain him. Once David had replaced Joab with another commander the die had been cast. The historian preserved the account not so much to exalt the act but to show clearly that it was Joab and not David who was responsible for the death of Absalom's commander. The feigning of friendship accompanied by the cold-blooded act is similar to his murder of Abner (2 Sam. 3:27). Even the dragging of the body to the side of the road and covering it so his men wouldn't have to see it as they went by sends a shiver down one's spine (vv. 11–13).

While the account lays the crime at Joab's feet, no judgment was ever passed on him for it. In contrast, he became the leader of the army immediately. While David continued to complain about the "sons of Zeruiah" (2 Sam. 19:22), he continued to depend upon them in times of crisis. It was a contradictory relationship and not unlike relationships seen today, where a leader will publicly decry the methods of people he privately encourages.

David sent the professional soldiers in an effort to catch Sheba before he was able to *"find for himself fortified cities"* (v. 6), but his fears materialized when Sheba entered a city in the north of Palestine named Abel of Beth Maachah (vv. 13–14). Joab and the combined armies laid siege to the city and the only thing that saved it from destruction was the wise counsel of a good woman who was a citizen of the city.

In a chapter full of intrigue and murder the dialogue between the woman and Joab is a wonderful relief. It is reminiscent of David's talk with the wise woman from Tekoa (2 Sam. 14). She was a woman of peace and she knew how to plead her cause. She reminded Joab that her city was known for its wisdom and evidently quoted a proverb to that effect, although the text makes it difficult to translate (v. 18). Evidently it was a city that prided itself in its attachment to traditional Israelite values. Then she personified the city Joab was about to destroy as *"a mother in Israel"* (v. 19) and suggested that he was about to swallow up *"the inheritance of the LORD."*

Joab denied vigorously his intentions to destroy the city and stated his sole objective: to capture Sheba (vv. 20–21). He promised that if Sheba's head were delivered, he would depart. No account is given as to how she was able to get the city to agree to the demands. With no allies it was probably the sensible thing to do, but people don't always do the sensible thing unless there is strong rational leadership provided by someone. In a society that has come to look upon war making more as a business than a moral problem, we need more people like this wise woman whose action crushed a rebellion and saved a city and all its people.

## DAVID'S GOVERNMENT OFFICERS

<sup>23</sup> And Joab was over all the army of Israel; Benaiah the son of Jehoiada was over the Cherethites and the Pelethites; <sup>24</sup> Adoram was in charge of revenue; Jehoshaphat the son of Ahilud was recorder; <sup>25</sup> Sheva was scribe; Zadok and Abiathar were the priests; <sup>26</sup> and Ira the Jairite was a chief minister under David.

*—2 Samuel 20:23–26*

This list of those who played key roles in David's government needs to be compared with similar lists in 2 Samuel 8:15–18 and 1 Kings 4:1–6. Most of the names are the same. Joab is commander of the army again. Benaiah is still in charge of David's personal bodyguard. Jehoshaphat is still the recorder. Zodak and Abiathar are still priests. The name of Sheva, the scribe, is recorded in 2 Samuel 8:17 as Seraiah, but it refers to the same person. The only new office seems to be that of Adoram who was in charge of forced labor, which is called *"revenue"* in the New King James (v. 24). This office was much more prominent in the times of Solomon. Not much is known about Ira the Jairite or the nature of his office.

The concluding four chapters of 2 Samuel are considered as appendixes. The next chapter tells of David's repaying the Gibeonites for wrongs that they had suffered under Saul. It also records a story of a confrontation with a Philistine giant that sounds like the same story in which David became Israel's hero. Chapter 22 is a song of praise to God for deliverance. Chapter 23 records David's last words, and the final chapter records a story of sin and restoration.

## SECTION FIVE

# APPENDIXES
## 2 SAMUEL 21:1—24:25

# CHAPTER SIXTEEN—EXTRA THREADS ON THE HISTORICAL TAPESTRY

## 2 SAMUEL 21:1–22

*Scripture Outline*

The Gibeonites Avenged (21:1–14)

Philistine Giants Destroyed (21:15–22)

The last four chapters of 2 Samuel are set between the revolt of Sheba and Adonijah's bid for the throne (1 Kin. 1) and serve as an appendix to the story of David. Much of the material would fit much earlier chronologically. For instance, Shimei probably had in mind the slaying of Saul's sons when he accused David of being a "bloodthirsty man" (2 Sam. 16:7). The historian probably included the story of the vengeance of the Gibeonites to explain David's action against the house of Saul as a mandate from God to relieve the famine. As has been true before, the intention of the chapter is to show David sympathetically.

## THE GIBEONITES AVENGED

**21:1** Now there was a famine in the days of David for three years, year after year; and David inquired of the LORD. And the LORD answered, "It is because of Saul and his bloodthirsty house, because he killed the Gibeonites." [2] So the king called the Gibeonites and spoke to them. Now the Gibeonites were not of the children of Israel, but of the remnant of the Amorites; the children of Israel had sworn protection to them, but Saul had sought to kill them in his zeal for the children of Israel and Judah.

[3] Therefore David said to the Gibeonites, "What shall I do for you? And with what shall I make atonement, that you may bless the inheritance of the LORD?"

<sup>4</sup> And the Gibeonites said to him, "We will have no silver or gold from Saul or from his house, nor shall you kill any man in Israel for us."

So he said, "Whatever you say, I will do for you."

<sup>5</sup> Then they answered the king, "As for the man who consumed us and plotted against us, that we should be destroyed from remaining in any of the territories of Israel, <sup>6</sup> let seven men of his descendants be delivered to us, and we will hang them before the LORD in Gibeah of Saul, whom the LORD chose."

And the king said, "I will give them."

<sup>7</sup> But the king spared Mephibosheth the son of Jonathan, the son of Saul, because of the LORD's oath that was between them, between David and Jonathan the son of Saul. <sup>8</sup> So the king took Armoni and Mephibosheth, the two sons of Rizpah the daughter of Aiah, whom she bore to Saul, and the five sons of Michal the daughter of Saul, whom she brought up for Adriel the son of Barzillai the Meholathite; <sup>9</sup> and he delivered them into the hands of the Gibeonites, and they hanged them on the hill before the LORD. So they fell, all seven together, and were put to death in the days of harvest, in the first days, in the beginning of barley harvest.

<sup>10</sup> Now Rizpah the daughter of Aiah took sackcloth and spread it for herself on the rock, from the beginning of harvest until the late rains poured on them from heaven. And she did not allow the birds of the air to rest on them by day nor the beasts of the field by night.

<sup>11</sup> And David was told what Rizpah the daughter of Aiah, the concubine of Saul, had done. <sup>12</sup> Then David went and took the bones of Saul, and the bones of Jonathan his son, from the men of Jabesh Gilead who had stolen them from the street of Beth Shan, where the Philistines had hung them up, after the Philistines had struck down Saul in Gilboa. <sup>13</sup> So he brought up the bones of Saul and the bones of Jonathan his son from there; and they gathered the bones of those who had been hanged. <sup>14</sup> They buried the bones of Saul and Jonathan his son in the country of Benjamin in Zelah, in the tomb of Kish his father. So they performed all that the king commanded. And after that God heeded the prayer for the land.

*—2 Samuel 21:1–14*

Many readers will find this passage hard to understand from several perspectives. The idea of blood-guilt seems archaic in the light of Christ's command to love our enemies. Our heightened sense of individual responsibility makes the idea of children and grandchildren being punished because of Saul's action seem wrong. The growing dependence upon science to explain our world makes a culture that sees a direct tie between God and the events of nature seem almost naive. This story is a good example as to why it is necessary to understand the age and the culture that provides the setting of the biblical account so as to understand what the message may be for our day. We need to remember that the story is included to explain David's action against Saul's sons.

The first verse sets the whole scene. There had been a three-year famine, most likely from a lack of rain which caused a crop failure. Since the people assumed a tie between God and the weather, they concluded that the bad weather must be punishment for some sin. They were right to connect sin and punishment, a truth that many modern people have forgotten. They were wrong, as Christ later taught, to tie every illness to sin on the part of the one who suffered (John 9). As the people turned to David for the reason for the famine, David turned to God through an oracle, a method of discerning God's will by a series of questions that could be answered yes or no. They needed a religious reason for what was happening.

God's answer was that the famine had been caused because of Saul's slaughter of the Gibeonites (v. 1). The Scriptures do not record the incident nor give insight into Saul's motives. We do know of a treaty that Joshua made with the Gibeonites which allowed them to coexist with Israel (Josh. 9). God's fixing of the blame cleared both the Israelites and David of being the cause for the famine. The point of the story is that treaties and promises that are made are to be kept. The breaking of a treaty, however, was the cause of this natural disaster. When I read a story like this I immediately think of all the treaties that the U.S. government made with the American Indians and then promptly broke. While there may have been a primitive understanding of the world in the Old Testament times, there was a very high value placed on keeping promises, a virtue that needs to be recovered today.

The story that was introduced in the first verse is fleshed out in the following verses (vv. 2–6). The Gibeonites were *a remnant of the Amorites"* (v. 2). Although they were not of the children of Israel, they were allowed to live by the treaty made with Joshua.

Because of what Saul had done to them, David allowed them to define what it would take to make things right, to prescribe the nature of the retribution (v. 3).

They wouldn't settle for money but asked for the lives of Saul's sons. While David would not give them Mephibosheth because of his promise to Jonathan, he did turn over two of Saul's sons and five of his grandsons to the Gibeonites. They were probably ritually executed and their bodies were left exposed and unburied.

The concluding verses of this section of the chapter tell of the long vigil of Rizpah, the mother of the two sons and one of Saul's concubines who was very loyal to the house of Saul. Her faithfulness in watching over the bodies until it rained moved David to bury the bodies as an act of piety. The story seems to answer any who had questions about David's treatment of the house of Saul—it had been done at God's instruction to save the people from famine.

## PHILISTINE GIANTS DESTROYED

15 When the Philistines were at war again with Israel, David and his servants with him went down and fought against the Philistines; and David grew faint. 16 Then Ishbi-Benob, who was one of the sons of the giant, the weight of whose bronze spear was three hundred shekels, who was bearing a new sword, thought he could kill David. 17 But Abishai the son of Zeruiah came to his aid, and struck the Philistine and killed him. Then the men of David swore to him, saying, "You shall go out no more with us to battle, lest you quench the lamp of Israel."

18 Now it happened afterward that there was again a battle with the Philistines at Gob. Then Sibbechai the Hushathite killed Saph, who was one of the sons of the giant. 19 Again there was war at Gob with the Philistines, where Elhanan the son of Jaare-Oregim the Bethlehemite killed the brother of Goliath the Gittite, the shaft of whose spear was like a weaver's beam.

20 Yet again there was war at Gath, where there was a man of great stature, who had six fingers on each hand and six toes on each foot, twenty-four in number; and he also was born to the giant. 21 So when he defied Israel, Jonathan the son of Shimea, David's brother, killed him.

22 These four were born to the giant in Gath, and fell by the hand of David and by the hand of his servants.

—*2 Samuel 21:15–22*

This passage and the list of David's mighty men (2 Sam. 23:8–39) clearly come from an earlier period in David's life, the latter listing Uriah the Hittite whom David had killed (2 Sam. 23:39). Most of the names are unknown to modern readers although the original readers would have seen in these lists the names of their forbears. These are the stories of men who earned the right to be remembered by their heroic acts on behalf of their country. These lists are verbal memorials of their contribution to the establishment and defense of the kingdom. Nations, institutions, and churches need to find ways to preserve the memory of the host of people who have contributed to their existence.

This passage tells of three battles of limited interest to the modern reader. The first gives us a phrase that dramatizes the importance of the leader in any enterprise. In this particular battle with the Philistines, David had grown faint and was about to be killed by "one of the giants. He was rescued by Abishai, Joab's brother, and after the close call with death the men suggested that David no longer go with them into battle *"lest you quench the lamp of Israel"* (v. 17). The lamp burned constantly in the temple as a symbol of God's presence with the people. The men felt that David symbolized their contact with God and without him they would be leaderless, in darkness, without a light. Ours is a culture that seems to have lost sight of the importance of leaders. Rather than protect them, we seem to try to bring them down.

The second thing of interest is the account of Elhanan's slaying of the brother of the giant Goliath (v. 19). Whether this is a similar event to the one described earlier in which David is described as slaying Goliath (1 Sam. 17) or a different version of the same event is not certain.

The next chapter is a song of praise unto God that David sang on the occasion of his deliverance from the hands of his enemies and from the hand of Saul. By its nature it could just as easily have been placed in the Book of Psalms. It gives insight into the heart of the king and his relationship with God.

# Chapter Seventeen—The Poetic Side of a Warrior-King and the Exploits of His Mighty Men

## 2 Samuel 22:1—23:39

*Scripture Outline*
>  Praise for God's Deliverance (22:1–51)
>  David's Last Words (23:1–7)
>  David's Mighty Men (23:8–39)

Except for the first verse, which is introductory, this chapter is a song of praise to God. Often in thinking of David as a mighty warrior or as an administrator we forget that he was also a musician and a poet. One of the early pictures of David has him playing the harp and soothing the troubled soul of Saul (1 Sam. 16:23). His skill as a poet was noted in the lamentation that he prepared to mark the death of Saul and Jonathan (2 Sam. 1:19–27). While there is little relevance in David's accomplishments as a warrior or king for today's reader, the psalms of David continue to enrich the spiritual lives of those who read them. They reflect with honesty the relationship of a man with the living God and thus become models for us.

This poem of thanksgiving to God is almost identical to Psalm 18, with only minor differences. The language is pictorial and it relates not just to one experience, as some of the other psalms do, but to a variety of situations. It begins and ends with praise to the Lord (vv. 2–4, 47–51).

### PRAISE FOR GOD'S DELIVERANCE

**22:1** Then David spoke to the Lord the words of this song, on the day when the Lord had delivered him from the hand of all his enemies, and from the hand of Saul. ² And he said:

349

"The LORD is my rock and my fortress and my
deliverer;
3 The God of my strength, in whom I will trust;
My shield and the horn of my salvation,
My stronghold and my refuge;
My Savior, You save me from violence.
4 I will call upon the LORD, who is worthy to be
praised;
So shall I be saved from my enemies.
5 "When the waves of death surrounded me,
The floods of ungodliness made me afraid.
6 The sorrows of Sheol surrounded me;
The snares of death confronted me.
7 In my distress I called upon the LORD,
And cried out to my God;
He heard my voice from His temple,
And my cry entered His ears.
8 "Then the earth shook and trembled;
The foundations of heaven quaked and were
shaken,
Because He was angry.
9 Smoke went up from His nostrils,
And devouring fire from His mouth;
Coals were kindled by it.
10 He bowed the heavens also, and came down
With darkness under His feet.
11 He rode upon a cherub, and flew;
And He was seen upon the wings of the wind.
12 He made darkness canopies around Him,
Dark waters and thick clouds of the skies.
13 From the brightness before Him
Coals of fire were kindled.
14 "The LORD thundered from heaven,
And the Most High uttered His voice.
15 He sent out arrows and scattered them;
Lightning bolts, and He vanquished them.
16 Then the channels of the sea were seen,
The foundations of the world were uncovered,
At the rebuke of the LORD,
At the blast of the breath of His nostrils.
17 "He sent from above, He took me,
He drew me out of many waters.

18 He delivered me from my strong enemy,
From those who hated me;
For they were too strong for me.

19 They confronted me in the day of my calamity,
But the LORD was my support.

20 He also brought me out into a broad place;
He delivered me because He delighted in me.

21 "The LORD rewarded me according to my righteousness;
According to the cleanness of my hands
He has recompensed me.

22 For I have kept the ways of the LORD,
And have not wickedly departed from my God.

23 For all His judgments were before me;
And as for His statutes, I did not depart from them.

24 I was also blameless before Him,
And I kept myself from my iniquity.

25 Therefore the LORD has recompensed me according
to my righteousness,
According to my cleanness in His eyes.

26 "With the merciful You will show Yourself merciful;
With a blameless man You will show Yourself
blameless;

27 With the pure You will show Yourself pure;
And with the devious You will show Yourself
shrewd.

28 You will save the humble people;
But Your eyes are on the haughty, that You may
bring them down.

29 "For You are my lamp, O LORD;
The LORD shall enlighten my darkness.

30 For by You I can run against a troop;
By my God I can leap over a wall.

31 As for God, His way is perfect;
The word of the LORD is proven;
He is a shield to all who trust in Him.

32 "For who is God, except the LORD?
And who is a rock, except our God?

33 God is my strength and power,
And He makes my way perfect.

34 He makes my feet like the feet of deer,
And sets me on my high places.

35 He teaches my hands to make war,
So that my arms can bend a bow of bronze.
36 "You have also given me the shield of Your salvation;
Your gentleness has made me great.
37 You enlarged my path under me;
So my feet did not slip.
38 "I have pursued my enemies and destroyed them;
Neither did I turn back again till they were destroyed.
39 And I have destroyed them and wounded them,
So that they could not rise;
They have fallen under my feet.
40 For You have armed me with strength for the battle;
You have subdued under me those who rose against me.
41 You have also given me the necks of my enemies,
So that I destroyed those who hated me.
42 They looked, but there was none to save;
Even to the LORD, but He did not answer them.
43 Then I beat them as fine as the dust of the earth;
I trod them like dirt in the streets,
And I spread them out.
44 "You have also delivered me from the strivings of my people;
You have kept me as the head of the nations.
A people I have not known shall serve me.
45 The foreigners submit to me;
As soon as they hear, they obey me.
46 The foreigners fade away,
And come frightened from their hideouts.
47 "The LORD lives!
Blessed be my Rock!
Let God be exalted,
The Rock of my salvation!
48 It is God who avenges me,
And subdues the peoples under me;
49 He delivers me from my enemies.
You also lift me up above those who rise against me;
You have delivered me from the violent man.
50 Therefore I will give thanks to You, O LORD, among the Gentiles,

And sing praises to Your name.
51 "He is the tower of salvation to His king,
And shows mercy to His anointed,
To David and his descendants forevermore."

*—2 Samuel 22:1–51*

The poem begins with an expression of confidence in God's deliverance (vv. 2–7). In expressing God's power and protection David piles words on top of words: rock, fortress, strength, shield, salvation, stronghold, and refuge (vv. 2–4). While these verses do not describe a single experience in his life, they easily recall those days in which he was a fugitive trying to escape Saul's grasp. He recalls the enemy that he faced in terms of death: waves of death, sorrows of Sheol, and snares of death (vv. 5–6). Obviously he hadn't been killed, but he had gone through a deathlike experience. The memory of that experience was so fresh that he described it in the perfect tense, an event that took place in the past but whose effect was still present. It was out of this living death that he cried out to God and *"He heard my voice from His temple"* (v. 7). This passage demonstrates clearly that David was a man who knew God and who had profound confidence in both God's compassion and God's power to change things. In our church's midweek service we often have time for individuals to express what they're thankful for. I've noticed that often it is those individuals who have gone through difficult experiences in their lives and found God adequate who are most articulate in their praise.

The poem continues with a description of God's response to his cry for help (vv. 8–16). It is a theophany that is reminiscent of God's coming at Sinai (Ex. 19) and uses some of the imagery that John would later use in his vision of God (Rev. 1). The dominant picture is that of power: shaking the earth, moving heaven's foundations, smoking nostrils, a fire-breathing mouth, bending the heavens, riding the winds, and splitting the heavens with arrows, lightning, and thunder. This was not the "still small voice" that Elijah heard. It was emphatically a vision of power.

The question of God's power is always relevant. I heard a missionary from Kenya respond to the question of what it was that was drawing so many people to Christ. He replied that the number-one question that was asked of the missionary was about the power of God, what God was able to do. Then he told of several incidents where whole communities were made aware of God's power through some very concrete experiences and how the result was hundreds of individuals turning to God. In the midst of God's love and grace we must not lose sight of His power, the same power that raised Jesus Christ up from the grave.

In the midst of the description of God's power David said, *"He made darkness canopies around Him"* (v. 12). To think of God wrapping himself in darkness seems in conflict with the other images, but it reflects David's awareness that there is always in God an element of mystery, a hiddenness, things we don't know or understand. Sometimes in our eagerness to understand God we try to capture all of Him in our definitions, our doctrines, and our creeds. We reduce the Cross to our theories of atonement, the hope of His Second Coming to our pet interpretations, and what it means to become a Christian to certain fixed steps. We need always to remember that we will never exhaust the mystery of God with our understanding.

This poem brings together the themes of deliverance and power in the next section (vv. 17–25). In the first verses David looks at his deliverance as a jeweler would look at the different facets of a diamond—from above, out of waters, and from strong enemies (vv. 17–18). A casual reading of the closing verses of this section would leave the impression that David thought God's goodness had come as a result of his own righteousness (vv. 20b–25). Rather than calling upon God to forgive his sins David calls upon God to note his obedience. Is this the same man who wrote Psalm 51, a psalm of repentance?

This section needs to be seen in terms of the covenant between God and Israel, however, and not in terms of claiming sinlessness. David's affirmation before God is that Israel has taken seriously the covenant she made with God at Sinai (Ex. 19:1–8). That was a covenant of grace which both parties entered into and which David claims as the basis of God's goodness to Israel. It is the same as a person coming before God in prayer, aware of his sinfulness, yet coming with boldness because of a relationship entered into through Christ.

This poem elaborates on the nature of God's dealings with people (vv. 26–30). More than anything else this stanza celebrates the character of God as it reflects itself in all His dealings. This is important since all moral and ethical actions flow from our understanding of God's nature. The poet pictures God as acting with purpose, dealing justly with all persons, as keeping all His promises, and as giving light and help to those who call upon Him. It is a living, acting God whom David celebrates in this psalm.

The poem continues by noting the stability of God's word and the uniqueness of His being undergirding David's belief (vv. 31–35).

These verses lay the foundation for David's affirmation that it was God who gave military power to the worshiper (vv. 36–46). He thanks God for allowing him to defeat all his enemies, delivering the people in their problems, keeping him as king, and giving him honor among the foreigners. While David's view of God's involvement with war may be questioned in the light of Christ's teaching, his perspective is consistent with the perspective of the rest of Samuel—that all which David accomplished was possible because God was in it. While it is always dangerous to confuse our agenda with God's, it is also true that too often we fail to give God credit for His part in what we are able to do.

David's poem closes as it opens, with an assertion of confidence in God (vv. 47–51). It praises the God who acts on behalf of all who call upon Him. It is a witness to God's steadfast love. When people pause to look back over the experiences of their lives one of the most natural reflexes is to thank God for His goodness in their lives.

The next chapter begins with another poem called David's last words. Actually they are really more his legacy. The chapter also finishes out the list of David's mighty men and tells of two special groups—the three and the thirty.

## DAVID'S LAST WORDS

**23:1** Now these are the last words of David.
Thus says David the son of Jesse;
Thus says the man raised up on high,
The anointed of the God of Jacob,
And the sweet psalmist of Israel:
2 "The Spirit of the LORD spoke by me,
And His word was on my tongue.
3 The God of Israel said,
The Rock of Israel spoke to me:
'He who rules over men must be just,
Ruling in the fear of God.
4 And he shall be like the light of the morning when the sun rises,
A morning without clouds,
Like the tender grass springing out of the earth,
By clear shining after rain.'
5 "Although my house is not so with God,
Yet He has made with me an everlasting covenant,
Ordered in all things and secure.

For this is all my salvation and all my desire;
Will He not make it increase?

6   But the sons of rebellion shall all be as thorns thrust away,
Because they cannot be taken with hands.

7   But the man who touches them
Must be armed with iron and the shaft of a spear,
And they shall be utterly burned with fire in their place."

—2 Samuel 23:1–7

This chapter begins with a second poem commonly referred to as "David's Last Words," although it represents more his legacy to Israel and his descendants than his last words. Kingship reached its peak under David to such an extent that one aspect of the messianic expectation was that of an ideal king. The second part of the chapter completes the list of David's mighty men begun in chapter 21. An even fuller treatment of the list is given in 1 Chronicles 11:10–47.

This oracle is set out as if it were David's final message to his descendants. The idea of a significant person delivering a goodbye message as he came to the end of his life is a familiar one in the Old Testament. Before his death Jacob gathered his sons around him and shared his last words with them and blessed them (Gen. 49). Moses did a similar thing as he spoke to the children of Israel before his death and pronounced God's blessing upon them (Deut. 33). One of the most moving incidents in the New Testament is Paul's final words to the elders of the church at Ephesus (Acts 20:17–38). Everyone who has ever found himself turning loose of a job he's done for a long time, or telling someone goodbye for the last time, knows the desire to speak with seriousness about the things that really matter. These verses are such a speech.

The first verse describes David in parallel expressions that stress his status. His roots are from the family of Jesse, his exaltation comes from God, his position is that of anointed prince, and he was a singer of psalms. The whole story of his life is told in that one verse: humble beginnings as a shepherd lad, the purpose of God for which he was set aside, made prince of Israel by divine appointment, and the organizer and leader of temple worship. This is the context in which this oracle was heard.

The second verse indicates that David's insight was not natural but came from God: *"His word was on my tongue"* (v. 2). Here the theme of David as God's spokesman is developed. He was a source of the revelation of God's will and purpose for Israel. His pride in how he had lived with the responsibility was revealed in his psalm of praise (2 Sam. 22:21–25). Everyone who teaches or preaches knows the awesome responsibility of having people look to them for a word from God that can guide them in making decisions about their lives.

The third verse tells of the basis of David's leadership, an upholder of justice. In contrast to the kings in the countries that surrounded Israel and with the kings who preceded and followed him, David had exemplified high standards of government. All the people were treated with fairness and justice. Thousands of years after David we still live in a world where there is more justice for some than for others and where there are leaders who pervert justice and oppress the people. Such a leader as David would be to a country as an extra blessing (v. 4), and the dynasty would be protected from its enemies (vv. 5–7).

## DAVID'S MIGHTY MEN

8 These are the names of the mighty men whom David had: Josheb-Basshebeth the Tachmonite, chief among the captains. He was called Adino the Eznite, because he had killed eight hundred men at one time. 9 And after him was Eleazar the son of Dodo, the Ahohite, one of the three mighty men with David when they defied the Philistines who were gathered there for battle, and the men of Israel had retreated. 10 He arose and attacked the Philistines until his hand was weary, and his hand stuck to the sword. The LORD brought about a great victory that day; and the people returned after him only to plunder. 11 And after him was Shammah the son of Agee the Hararite. The Philistines had gathered together into a troop where there was a piece of ground full of lentils. So the people fled from the Philistines. 12 But he stationed himself in the middle of the field, defended it, and killed the Philistines. So the LORD brought about a great victory.

13 Then three of the thirty chief men went down at harvest time and came to David at the cave of Adullam. And the troop of Philistines encamped in the Valley of Rephaim. 14 David was then in the stronghold, and the garrison of the Philistines was then in Bethlehem. 15 And David said with longing, "Oh, that someone would give me a drink of the

water from the well of Bethlehem, which is by the gate!"
<sup>16</sup> So the three mighty men broke through the camp of the Philistines, drew water from the well of Bethlehem that was by the gate, and took it and brought it to David. Nevertheless he would not drink it, but poured it out to the LORD. <sup>17</sup> And he said, "Far be it from me, O LORD, that I should do this! Is this not the blood of the men who went in jeopardy of their lives?" Therefore he would not drink it.

These things were done by the three mighty men.

<sup>18</sup> Now Abishai the brother of Joab, the son of Zeruiah, was chief of another three. He lifted his spear against three hundred men, killed them, and won a name among these three. <sup>19</sup> Was he not the most honored of three? Therefore he became their captain. However, he did not attain to the first three.

<sup>20</sup> Benaiah was the son of Jehoiada, the son of a valiant man from Kabzeel, who had done many deeds. He had killed two lion-like heroes of Moab. He also had gone down and killed a lion in the midst of a pit on a snowy day. <sup>21</sup> And he killed an Egyptian, a spectacular man. The Egyptian had a spear in his hand; so he went down to him with a staff, wrested the spear out of the Egyptian's hand, and killed him with his own spear. <sup>22</sup> These things Benaiah the son of Jehoiada did, and won a name among three mighty men. <sup>23</sup> He was more honored than the thirty, but he did not attain to the first three. And David appointed him over his guard.

<sup>24</sup> Asahel the brother of Joab was one of the thirty; Elhanan the son of Dodo of Bethlehem, <sup>25</sup> Shammah the Harodite, Elika the Harodite, <sup>26</sup> Helez the Paltite, Ira the son of Ikkesh the Tekoite, <sup>27</sup> Abiezer the Anathothite, Mebunnai the Hushathite, <sup>28</sup> Zalmon the Ahohite, Maharai the Netophathite, <sup>29</sup> Heleb the son of Baanah (the Netophathite), Ittai the son of Ribai from Gibeah of the children of Benjamin, <sup>30</sup> Benaiah a Pirathonite, Hiddai from the brooks of Gaash, <sup>31</sup> Abi-Albon the Arbathite, Azmaveth the Barhumite, <sup>32</sup> Eliahba the Shaalbonite (of the sons of Jashen), Jonathan, <sup>33</sup> Shammah the Hararite, Ahiam the son of Sharar the Hararite, <sup>34</sup> Eliphelet the son of Ahasbai, the son of the Maachathite, Eliam the son of Ahithophel the Gilonite, <sup>35</sup> Hezrai the Carmelite, Paarai the Arbite, <sup>36</sup> Igal the son of Nathan of Zobah, Bani the Gadite, <sup>37</sup> Zelek the Ammonite, Naharai the Beerothite (armorbearer of Joab the

son of Zeruiah), [38] Ira the Ithrite, Gareb the Ithrite, [39] and
Uriah the Hittite: thirty-seven in all.

*—2 Samuel 23:8–39*

David seemed to have what some have called two orders of
knighthood: the three and the thirty. These were his mighty men.
Josheb-Basshebeth, Eleazar, and Shammah were his chief warriors,
and the first verses tell of their exploits (vv. 8–12). In the border
skirmishes that continued to take place with the Philistines each
of them had distinguished himself in some memorable way. Of
that group of warriors who distinguished themselves by their
courage and loyalty these three had risen to the top. These verses
are a reminder to us all that those individuals who serve a cause
well should be remembered.

Dropped into this list of David's mighty men is a story that continues to capture the imagination of all who read it (vv. 13–17).
While chronologically it fits just before the events recorded in 2
Samuel 5:17–21, it is placed here because it tells of the exploits of
three warriors who were a part of the thirty. Although their names
are not given, their deed is remembered almost three thousand years
later.

David's fortunes were at a low ebb: Perils threatened his life, the
Philistines occupied his hometown, he was suffering from exposure
and privation, and he was hidden in a cave with his men. As he
brooded over his condition and thought of better days he said more
to himself than to anyone else, *"Oh, that someone would give me a
drink of the water from the well of Bethlehem"* (v. 15). Beneath the statement of his "want" was a much larger "need." David's longing was
for so much more than a drink of water. He wanted to taste again the
vigor of his youth. He needed to feel again the freedom to come and
go. He desired to go back to a less complicated life. He needed to be
reassured about God's blessings on his life. All these were wrapped
up in the sighing out of his desire.

This story is retold here to give readers insight into the caliber
of men with whom David surrounded himself. They treated his
wish almost as a command and risked their lives fighting their
way through the Philistine garrison in order to bring their leader
a drink from the well (v. 16). Although their names are not given,
they have modeled for succeeding generations a kind of enthusiastic, loving self-forgetfulness in relationship with others.

I first read this account while at a retreat for college students. The
inspirational speaker retold the story of the loyalty and bravery of

the three warriors and suggested that this is the kind of thinking that Christ needs from each of His children, that His slightest wish would be considered by us to be a command that we would joyfully do whatever the cost. I was moved by the pointedness of the appeal.

How David responded to their bravery gives us a further clue as to what had created the solidarity between David and his men. He was so moved by the risk they had taken to fulfill his whim that he refused to drink the water and instead poured it out as an act of worship (v. 16). His act is a reminder that the cost that is paid can make a thing sacred. He felt that there were some things that were too precious to be used only for one's self. It's good, as we use the things that have been made available to us in life, to remember what they have cost those who give them and to treat them as special.

Besides the three who are named and the unnamed three who brought the water to David, this section calls special attention to two other warriors who had gained distinction although they never became a part of the three. These are familiar names: Abishai, Joab's brother, and Benaiah, who was captain over David's personal guard (vv. 18–23). The list that follows begins with Asahel and ends with Uriah the Hittite and merely identifies them (vv. 24–39). Both Asahel and Uriah were already dead as David came to the end of his reign, indicating that the list came from an earlier time and had not been edited before its inclusion by the historian.

While the names on the list mean little to today's readers it should serve as a reminder that every movement, whether it is the building of a nation or a church, is dependent upon a host of loyal, faithful people who give themselves unselfishly. Often history lifts up the names of the leaders and tends to forget the faithful followers. Like the historian, we should preserve the names of God's mighty men and women.

The final chapter of 2 Samuel begins with an act of David that displeased God and the story of God's judgment. It concludes with a beautiful account of David's building an altar to God on a threshing floor that he had purchased. The book began with a lament for the death of Saul and Jonathan and ends with David interceding with God on behalf of the people Israel.

# CHAPTER EIGHTEEN—THE CENSUS AND THE SACRIFICE

## 2 SAMUEL 24:1–25

*Scripture Outline*

David's Census of Israel and Judah (24:1–9)

The Judgment on David's Sin (24:10–17)

The Altar on the Threshing Floor (24:18–25)

This chapter is closely linked with chapter 21. Both interpret natural disasters as divine judgment for human sin. The story of the taking of the census and the punishment that followed is also reported in 1 Chronicles 21:1–14 with a few significant differences. While many have tried to locate the census story at an earlier time, it probably occurred late in David's reign since it prepares the way for the purchase of the site for the temple that Solomon would later build. The one big problem that the interpreter must deal with is the fact that God seems to be the One who moved David to sin in taking the census (v. 1). The reader might logically expect to come to the end of the book and read of David's peacefully dying in his bed or of some great victory for Israel, instead there is the story of new trouble for David and the people as a result of David's sin against God. Yet at the end of the chapter David has bought the site for the temple and has made peace with God in an act of worship.

## DAVID'S CENSUS OF ISRAEL AND JUDAH

**24:1** Again the anger of the LORD was aroused against Israel, and He moved David against them to say, "Go, number Israel and Judah."

² So the king said to Joab the commander of the army who was with him, "Now go throughout all the tribes of

Israel, from Dan to Beersheba, and count the people, that I may know the number of the people."

³ And Joab said to the king, "Now may the LORD your God add to the people a hundred times more than there are, and may the eyes of my lord the king see it. But why does my lord the king desire this thing?" ⁴ Nevertheless the king's word prevailed against Joab and against the captains of the army. Therefore Joab and the captains of the army went out from the presence of the king to count the people of Israel.

⁵ And they crossed over the Jordan and camped in Aroer, on the right side of the town which is in the midst of the ravine of Gad, and toward Jazer. ⁶ Then they came to Gilead and to the land of Tahtim Hodshi; they came to Dan Jaan and around to Sidon; ⁷ and they came to the stronghold of Tyre and to all the cities of the Hivites and the Canaanites. Then they went out to South Judah as far as Beersheba. ⁸ So when they had gone through all the land, they came to Jerusalem at the end of nine months and twenty days. ⁹ Then Joab gave the sum of the number of the people to the king. And there were in Israel eight hundred thousand valiant men who drew the sword, and the men of Judah were five hundred thousand men.

*—2 Samuel 24:1–9*

If the text did not include verse 1 the rest of the story would be easier to interpret. It would tell of David's ordering the census over the objection of his commander Joab, of the sending of the epidemic in punishment for David's sin, of the sparing of Jerusalem, and of the purchase of the temple site. The problem created for the reader by verse 1 is that it says that David was motivated to do what he did by God: *"He moved David against them to say, 'Go, number Israel and Judah'"* (v. 1). The contemporary Christian finds it hard to think of God as telling David to do something for which he would then be punished. The Old Testament writers, however, did not hesitate to ascribe evil to God since they ascribed all human activity to God's control. That is why the account of Saul's effort to kill David with his spear was described as being caused by a "distressing spirit from the LORD" (1 Sam. 19:9). The other account of this event attributed the impulse to take the census to Satan: "Now Satan stood up against Israel, and moved David to number Israel" (1 Chr. 21:1). While this only moves the motivation one step away from God, it does make it more a matter of testing for David.

The passage gives no indication as to why the taking of the census was wrong. This is one of the few times in their relationship where Joab appears to be right and David wrong, although there is agreement that Joab's reluctance to take the census was more likely political rather than theological. He knew the resources that the task would consume and the potential for friction that it had. Most writers feel that the possible wrong in the taking of the census was the trust in military power that the census could have implied. Throughout David's life it had been demonstrated that God did not achieve victory through superior numbers but by His power. When he was overruled, Joab organized and conducted the census and did a thorough job of it (vv. 4–9). The account gives the reader a good sense of the boundaries at the time and the relative strength of the country in terms of available men in case of national emergency.

## THE JUDGMENT ON DAVID'S SIN

10 And David's heart condemned him after he had numbered the people. So David said to the LORD, "I have sinned greatly in what I have done; but now, I pray, O LORD, take away the iniquity of Your servant, for I have done very foolishly."

11 Now when David arose in the morning, the word of the LORD came to the prophet Gad, David's seer, saying, 12 "Go and tell David, 'Thus says the LORD: "I offer you three things; choose one of them for yourself, that I may do it to you."'"13 So Gad came to David and told him; and he said to him, "Shall seven years of famine come to you in your land? Or shall you flee three months before your enemies, while they pursue you? Or shall there be three days' plague in your land? Now consider and see what answer I should take back to Him who sent me."

14 And David said to Gad, "I am in great distress. Please let us fall into the hand of the LORD, for His mercies are great; but do not let me fall into the hand of man."

15 So the LORD sent a plague upon Israel from the morning till the appointed time. From Dan to Beersheba seventy thousand men of the people died. 16 And when the angel stretched out His hand over Jerusalem to destroy it, the LORD relented from the destruction, and said to the angel who was destroying the people, "It is enough; now restrain your hand." And the angel of the LORD was by the threshing floor of Araunah the Jebusite. 17 Then David spoke to the LORD when he saw the angel who was striking the

people, and said, "Surely I have sinned, and I have done wickedly; but these sheep, what have they done? Let Your hand, I pray, be against me and against my father's house."

—*2 Samuel 24:10–17*

The text reports that *"David's heart condemned him after he had numbered the people"* (v. 10). We are not told when or how he had come to believe he had sinned. There is the possibility that the prophet Gad was instrumental since he is the one who speaks the word of God to David about the punishment. Although David confessed his sin and asked God to *"take away the iniquity"* (v. 10), there was no response from God that is recorded. What is recorded is the offer for David to choose which of three punishments he wants (vv. 12–13). Some manuscripts list the seven years of famine as three years. This would make the choices three years, three months, or three days. While each of the three involved a different length of time, the idea seems to be that they were equal in the punishment that they rendered. The text does not record David's having made a choice, but the Septuagint—which is the Greek translation of the Old Testament—records that David chose the three days of plague.

David's response to what was about to befall Israel was in keeping with past action. He threw himself upon the mercies of God with the cry, *"Please let us fall into the hand of the LORD, for His mercies are great"* (v. 14). The plague spread quickly over the land, killing seventy thousand people (v. 15). It was said to have been the work of an angel sent from God that David saw as it spread out its hand to send the plague upon Jerusalem (v. 17). While it seems so unfair that innocent people should die because of the sins of their leader this still happens today. People still pay for the bad decisions made by their leaders. The plague stopped short of Jerusalem, however, stopping before it reached the threshing floor of Araunah the Jebusite (v. 16). Through it all David continued to confess his sin and plead with God not to punish the people for the sins that he had committed (v. 17). Since no mention is made of the connection between David's repentance and confession and the stopping of the plague, it must be assumed that it was halted before reaching Jerusalem because of God's grace and by God's plans for the place where it stopped.

## THE ALTAR ON THE THRESHING FLOOR

18 And Gad came that day to David and said to him, "Go up, erect an altar to the LORD on the threshing floor of Araunah the Jebusite."

¹⁹ So David, according to the word of Gad, went up as the LORD commanded.

²⁰ Now Araunah looked, and saw the king and his servants coming toward him. So Araunah went out and bowed before the king with his face to the ground.

²¹ Then Araunah said, "Why has my lord the king come to his servant?" And David said, "To buy the threshing floor from you, to build an altar to the LORD, that the plague may be withdrawn from the people." ²² Now Araunah said to David, "Let my lord the king take and offer up whatever seems good to him. Look, here are oxen for burnt sacrifice, and threshing implements and the yokes of the oxen for wood.

²³ "All these, O king, Araunah has given to the king." And Araunah said to the king, "May the LORD your God accept you."

²⁴ Then the king said to Araunah, "No, but I will surely buy it from you for a price; nor will I offer burnt offerings to the LORD my God with that which costs me nothing." So David bought the threshing floor and the oxen for fifty shekels of silver.

²⁵ And David built there an altar to the LORD and offered burnt offerings and peace offerings. So the LORD heeded the prayers for the land, and the plague was withdrawn from Israel.

*—2 Samuel 24:18–25*

This book closes with a beautiful story of the purchase of a threshing floor to be used as a place of worship. David went to the place under the instructions of Gad the prophet (vv. 18–19). When David announced the purpose of his coming, Araunah offered to give him the land and the oxen and all that was needed to make the sacrifice to God. Students of ancient culture remind us that this was a typical oriental way of beginning negotiations on the price of the property. His offer, though, was met with a statement by David that has captured the imagination of Christians through the ages: *"Nor will I offer burnt offerings to the LORD my God with that which costs me nothing"* (v. 24). When I was a seminarian I heard the great Andrew Blackwood preach on this text. He challenged us in whatever we did for God, whether it was a sermon preached or a ministry performed, to let it be a sacrificial offering of ourselves to God.

This book closes with David's building an altar to God on the future site of the temple and God withdrawing the plague from Israel (v. 25). Things are now ready for his successor to take the throne and build the temple. When later the people came back from captivity, they read the accounts of the beginning of the monarchy and of the building of the house of David and found in them encouragement. It created in them again the belief that the promises of God to His people are firm and can be relied upon. Today's readers can glean great insight into the nature of the God who revealed Himself fully in Jesus Christ from these stories of God's dealings with David and with Israel.

# BIBLIOGRAPHY

Ackroyd, Peter R. *The First Book of Samuel*. The Cambridge Bible Commentary. Cambridge: Cambridge University Press, 1971.

_____. *The Second Book of Samuel*. The Cambridge Bible Commentary. Cambridge: Cambridge University Press, 1977.

Albright, William F. *Samuel and the Beginnings of the Prophetic Movement*. The Goldenson Lectures. Cincinnati: Hebrew Union College Press, 1961.

Anderson, Arnold A. *2 Samuel*. Word Biblical Commentary, vol. 11. Dallas: Word Books, 1988.

Baldwin, Joyce. *1 and 2 Samuel*. Tyndale Old Testament Commentaries. Leicester, England: InterVarsity Press, 1988.

Blackwood, Andrew W. *Preaching from Samuel*. Reprint ed. Grand Rapids: Baker Book House, 1946.

Blaikie, William C. *The First and Second Books of Samuel*. The Expositor's Bible. New York: A. C. Armstrong and Son, 1888.

Boogaart, Thomas A. "History and Drama in the Story of David and Goliath." *Reformed Review* 38 (1985): 204–14.

_____. "Narrative Theology in the Story of the Capture of the Ark." *Reformed Review* 41(1988): 139–46.

Bowes, Paula J. *First Samuel, Second Samuel*. Collegeville Bible Commentary, Old Testament Series, no. 8. Collegeville, Minn.: Liturgical Press, 1985.

Bright, John. "1 and 2 Samuel." *Interpretation* 5 (1951): 450–61.

Brueggemann, Walter. "David and His Theologian." *Catholic Biblical Quarterly* 30 (1968): 156–81.

_____. "On Trust and Freedom." *Interpretation* 26 (1972): 3–19.

_____. "The Kerygma of the Deuteronomic Historian." *Interpretation* 22 (1968): 387–402.

Caird, George B., Ganse Little, and John C. Schroder. *The First and Second Books of Samuel*. The Interpreter's Bible, vol. 2. Nashville: Abingdon Press, 1953.

Carlson, R. A. *David the Chosen King*. Translated by Eric C. Sharpe. Stockholm: Almqvist and Wiksell, 1964.

Conroy, Charles. *Absalom, Absalom*. Analecta Biblica, no. 81. Rome: Biblical Institute Press, 1978.

Crockett, William Day. *A Harmony of the Books of Samuel, Kings, and Chronicles*. New York: Fleming H. Revell, 1887.

Culpepper, R. Alan. "Narrative Criticism as a Tool for Proclamation: I Samuel 13." *Review and Expositor* 84 (1987): 23–32.

Dhorme, P. Paul. *Les Livres de Samuel*. Etudes Bibliques. Paris: Librairie Victor LeCoffre, 1910.

Driver, Samuel R. *Notes on the Hebrew Text and the Topography of the Books of Samuel*. 2d ed. Oxford: Clarendon Press, 1913.

Eslinger, Lyle. *Kingship of God in Crisis*. Bible and Literature Series, no. 10. Sheffield, England: Almond Press, 1985.

Fokkelman, J. P. *Narrative Art and Poetry in the Books of Samuel*. 2 vols. Assen, The Netherlands: Van Gorcum, 1981, 1986.

Fretheim, Terence E. *Deuteronomic History*. Interpreting Biblical Texts. Nashville: Abingdon Press, 1983.

Gordon, R. P. *1 & 2 Samuel*. Old Testament Guides. Sheffield, England: JSOT Press, 1980.

Gunn, David M. "David and the Gift of the Kingdom." *Semeia* 3 (1975): 14–45.

_____. *The Fate of King Saul*. Journal for the Study of the Old Testament Supplement Series, no. 14. Sheffield, England: JSOT Press, 1980.

_____. *The Story of King David*. Journal for the Study of the Old Testament Supplement Series, no. 6. Sheffield, England: JSOT Press, 1980.

Hertzberg, Hans Wilhelm. *I and II Samuel*. Trans. J. S. Bowden. Old Testament Library. Philadelphia: Westminster Press, 1964.

Humphries, W. Lee. "The Tragedy of King Saul: A Study of the Structure of I Samuel 9—31." *Journal for the Study of the Old Testament* 6 (1978): 11–28.

James, Fleming. *Personalities of the Old Testament*. New York: Charles Scribner's Sons, 1939.

Jobling, David. "Jonathan: A Structural Study of 1 Samuel." *The Sense of Biblical Narrative*. Journal for the Study of the Old Testament Supplement Series, no. 7. Sheffield, England: JSOT Press, 1978.

Keil, Karl F. *Biblical Commentary on the Books of Samuel*. 2d ed. Edinburgh: T. & T. Clark, 1875.

Kirkpatrick, Alexander F. *The First and Second Books of Samuel*. 2d ed. Cambridge Bible. Cambridge: Cambridge University Press, 1930.

Klein, Ralph W. *1 Samuel*. Word Biblical Commentary, vol. 10. Waco, Tex.: Word Books, 1983.

_____. "The Song of Hannah." *Concordia* 41 (1970): 674–87.

Levenson, Jon D. "I Samuel 25 as Literature and History." *Catholic Biblical Quarterly* 40 (1978): 11–28.

Lewis, Joe O. *1 & 2 Samuel, 1 Chronicles*. Layman's Bible Book Commentary. Nashville: Broadman Press, 1980.

Lys, David. "Who Is Our President? (From Text to Sermon on I Samuel 12:12)." *Interpretation* 26 (1972): 401–20.

Martin, John A. "The Theology of Samuel." *Bibliotheca Sacra* 141 (1983): 303–14.

Mauchline, John. *1 and 2 Samuel*. London: Oliphants, 1971.

McCarter, P. Kyle. *I Samuel*. Anchor Bible, vol. 8. Garden City, N.Y.: Doubleday and Co., 1980.

_____. *II Samuel*. Anchor Bible, vol. 9. Garden City, N.Y.: Doubleday and Co., 1980.

McCarthy, Dennis J. "The Inauguration of Monarchy in Israel." *Interpretation* 27 (1973): 401–12.

McKane, William. *I and II Samuel*. Torch Bible Commentaries. London: SCM Press, 1963.

Meyer, Frederick B. *David, Shepherd, Psalmist, King*. New York: Fleming H. Revell, 1895.

Miscall, Peter D. *I Samuel: A Literary Reading*. Bloomington: Indiana University Press, 1986.

Newsome, James D. *1 Samuel, 2 Samuel*. Knox Preaching Guides. Atlanta: John Knox Press, 1982.

Petersen, David L. "Portraits of David: Canonical and Otherwise." *Iliff Review* 42 (1985): 3–21.

Pfeiffer, Charles F. *The United Kingdom*. Grand Rapids: Baker Book House, 1970.

Polzin, Robert. *Samuel and the Deuteronomist*. San Francisco: Harper & Row, 1989.

Rast, Walter E. *Joshua, Judges, Samuel, Kings*. Proclamation Commentaries. Philadelphia: Fortress Press, 1978.

Rigg, William H. *The First Book of Samuel*. The Devotional Commentary. London: Religious Tract Society, 1922.

_____. *The Second Book of Samuel*. The Devotional Commentary. London: Religious Tract Society, 1922.

Robinson, Gordon. *Historians of Israel (1)*. Bible Guides, no. 5. London: Lutherworth Press, 1962.

Rost, Leonard. *The Succession to the Throne of David*. Reprint ed. Translated by Michael D. Rutter. Historic Texts and Interpreters in Biblical Scholarship, no. 1. Sheffield, England: Almond Press, 1982.

Saxe, Grace. *Studies in I and II Samuel*. Chicago: Moody Press, 1968.

Skinner, John. *The Book of Samuel*. Books of the Old Testament in Colloquial Speech. London: National Adult School Union, 1927.

Smith, Henry Preserved. *A Critical and Exegetical Commentary on the Books of Samuel*. International Critical Commentaries. Edinburgh: T. &. T. Clark, 1898.

Smothers, Thomas C. "Historical Criticism as a Tool for Proclamation: I Samuel 13." *Review and Expositor* 84 (1987): 23–32.

Sternberg, Meir. "The Bible's Art of Persuasion: Ideology, Rhetoric, and Poetics in Saul's Fall." *Hebrew Union College Annual* 54 (1983): 45–82.

Vos, Howard F. *1, 2 Samuel*. Bible Study Commentary. Grand Rapids: Zondervan, 1983.

Welch, Adam C. *Kings and Prophets of Israel*. Edited by Norman W. Porteous. London: Lutherworth Press, 1952.

Whybray, Roger N. *The Succession Narrative*. Studies in Biblical Theology. 2d ser. No. 9. Naperville, Ill.: Alec R. Allenson, 1968.

Whyte, Alexander. *Bible Characters*. Vol. 1. Grand Rapids: Zondervan, 1952.

Wolff, Hans W. "The Kerygma of the Deuteronomic Historical Work." *The Vitality of Old Testament Traditions*. 2d ed. Edited by Walter Brueggemann and Hans W. Wolff. Atlanta: John Knox Press, 1982.

Yonick, Stephan. *Rejection of Saul as King of Israel*. Jerusalem: Franciscan Printing Press, 1970.

Young, Fred E. "I and II Samuel." *The Wycliffe Bible Commentary*. Edited by Everett F. Harrison and Charles Pfeiffer. Chicago: Moody Press, 1962.